Mississippian Beginnings

Florida Museum of Natural History: Ripley P. Bullen Series

Mississippian Beginnings

Edited by Gregory D. Wilson

UNIVERSITY OF FLORIDA PRESS
Gainesville

Copyright 2017 by Gregory D. Wilson
All rights reserved
Published in the United States of America

This book may be available in an electronic edition.

First cloth printing, 2017
First paperback printing, 2019

24 23 22 21 20 19   6 5 4 3 2 1

Library of Congress Control Number: 2017938936
ISBN 978-1-68340-010-3 (cloth)
ISBN 978-1-68340-139-1 (pbk.)

University of Florida Press
2046 NE Waldo Road
Suite 2100
Gainesville, FL 32609
http://upress.ufl.edu

Contents

List of Figures   vii
List of Tables   x

1. Mississippian Origins: From Emergence to Beginnings   1
   Gregory D. Wilson and Lynne P. Sullivan
2. Maize and Mississippian Beginnings   29
   Amber M. VanDerwarker, Dana N. Bardolph, and C. Margaret Scarry
3. Cahokia's Beginnings: Mobility, Urbanization, and the Cahokian Political Landscape   71
   Alleen Betzenhauser
4. The Mississippianization of the Illinois and Apple River Valleys   97
   Gregory D. Wilson, Colleen M. Delaney, and Phillip G. Millhouse
5. Mississippian Processes and Histories: The Evolution of Fort Ancient Culture in the Miami Valleys   130
   Robert A. Cook
6. The Relationship between Becoming Caddo and Becoming Mississippian in the Middle Red River Drainage   178
   Amanda Regnier
7. Early Mississippian in the North Carolina Piedmont   203
   Edmond A. Boudreaux III
8. The Hollywood Site (9RI1) and the Foundations of Mississippian in the Middle Savannah River Valley   234
   Adam King, Christopher L. Thornock, and Keith Stephenson
9. Fort Walton Mississippian Beginnings in the Apalachicola–Lower Chattahoochee River Valley of Northwest Florida, Southwest Georgia, and Southeast Alabama   260
   Jeffrey P. Du Vernay and Nancy Marie White
10. Mississippian Beginnings: Multiple Perspectives on Migration, Monumentality, and Religion in the Prehistoric Eastern United States   293
    David G. Anderson

List of Contributors   323
Index   327

Figures

1.1. Regional map of the Mississippian world showing the location of selected archaeological sites 3
3.1. Late Terminal Late Woodland and Early Mississippian site distribution in the American Bottom 76
3.2. Range site 82
3.3. Regional distribution of materials in the Lohmann phase 84
4.1. Selected sites in the Lower Illinois River Valley 101
4.2. Excavation map from the Audrey site in the Lower Illinois River Valley 102
4.3. Selected sites in the Central Illinois River Valley 103
4.4. Excavation map from the Eveland site in the Central Illinois River Valley 105
4.5. Selected sites in the Apple River Valley 107
4.6. Service-to-utility ware ratios for Lohmann horizon sites 115
4.7. Service-to-utility ware ratios for early Stirling horizon sites 115
4.8. Ramey Incised jar rim frequencies from early Stirling horizon sites 116
5.1. Map of the Fort Ancient and Middle Mississippian culture regions 131
5.2. Comparison of a common variant of the Middle Mississippian Ramey pottery design and the Fort Ancient guilloche pottery design and map of study region 133
5.3. Select Mississippian trade items in the study region 135
5.4. Select artifacts with a wide geographic distribution in the Early to Middle Fort Ancient Period 136
5.5. Key pottery styles associated with earlier and later Fort Ancient sites in the study region 139
5.6. Comparison of Fort Ancient and Mississippian villages and small mound centers 140
5.7. Artistic rendering of the lower Great Miami River illustrating the broad floodplains, oxbows, and wetlands 145
5.8. Changing drought conditions in the study area and adjacent regions 147
5.9. Summary ranges for radiocarbon dates from the study sites 149

5.10. Selection of Woodland and Fort Ancient house, projectile point, and pottery forms   150
5.11. Relationship between wall-trench houses, maize, shell-tempered pottery, and nonlocal individuals   153
5.12. Strontium ratios for burials from study sites for first molars   155
5.13. Biodistance results from a comparison of key Early (Guard, Turpin), Middle (Anderson, SunWatch), and Late (Madisonville) Fort Ancient sites   157
5.14. Solstice alignments between the Kern effigy sites and the Fort Ancient site   161
5.15. Biodistance dendrograms showing relationship of SunWatch burial with whelk shell pendant to rest of male burials at the site   162
5.16. Drawing of a Middle Mississippian gorget from the Hixon site   165
5.17. Venn diagram showing key aspects of Mississippian and Late Woodland cultures   167
6.1. Physiographic/vegetation zones along the middle Red River drainage   179
6.2. Locations of sites in this chapter   180
6.3. Digitized version of incomplete map of the Bud Wright site on file at the Museum of the Red River, Idabel, Oklahoma   184
6.4. Sherds from the Bud Wright site assemblage   185
6.5. Map of 1941 WPA excavations at the Clement site, showing locations of Mound A and concentration of Formative Caddo sherds   186
6.6. Selected Formative Caddo sherds from the 1941 WPA excavations at the Clement site   186
6.7. Locations of major centers in the Caddo area with respect to middle Red Formative Caddo sites   191
7.1. Regional map with sites discussed in text   204
7.2. Select architectural elements at Town Creek with areas and structures   209
7.3. Probable Early Mississippian houses from the Town Creek site   211
7.4. Structure 5a, an Early Mississippian domestic structure at the Town Creek site   212
7.5. Early Mississippian public buildings located along the west end of the plaza at the Town Creek site   217
8.1. Mississippian mound sites in the middle Savannah River valley   235
8.2. Map of the Hollywood site   240
8.3. Idealized profile of Hollywood's Mound B   241

8.4. Plan map of the lower burial deposit in Mound B, the Hollywood site   241
8.5. Tripod-form bottle, lower burial deposit, Mound B, Hollywood   242
8.6. Anthropomorphic soapstone pipe, lower burial deposit, Mound B, Hollywood   243
8.7. Engraved ceramic cup, lower burial deposit, Mound B, Hollywood   244
8.8. Plain and negative painted bottle, lower burial deposit, Mound B, Hollywood   245
8.9. Frontal-facing feline copper plate, lower burial deposit, Mound B, Hollywood   245
8.10. Plan map of the upper burial deposit in Mound B, Hollywood   246
9.1. The Fort Walton region, with the Apalachicola-lower Chattahoochee and Tallahassee Red Hills areas highlighted   261
9.2. Fort Walton and Woodland sites   263
9.3. Sample of some of the ceramic types discussed   270
9.4. Contour and digital elevation maps   276

Tables

3.1. Total Site Occupations, Surveyed Areas, and Site Densities by Sub-Region 79
4.1. Minimum Number of Vessels Data for Lohmann Horizon Sites in the American Bottom, Lower Illinois River Valley, Central Illinois River Valley, and Apple River Valley 112
4.2. Minimum Number of Vessels Data For Early Stirling Horizon Sites in the American Bottom, Lower Illinois River Valley, Central Illinois River Valley, and Apple River Valley 113
5.1. Radiocarbon Dates For Non-Local individuals, People Buried with Mississippian Artifacts, and Wall Trench Houses 151
6.1. Presence and Absence of Pottery Types at Selected Sites in the Red River Valley 188
7.1. Dates for Mississippian Phases of the North Carolina Piedmont 206
7.2. Early Mississippian Period Radiocarbon Dates from the North Carolina Piedmont 207
7.3. Attributes of Domestic Structures from Selected Late Prehistoric and Contact Period Sites 214
8.1. Middle Savannah River Valley Ceramic Phase Chronology 237
8.2. The Radiocarbon Dates from the Hollywood Site 248
9.1. Radiometric Data 264
9.2. Late Weeden Island and Fort Walton Site Ceramic Tabulations 266
9.3. Fort Walton Ceramic Chronology 268

1

Mississippian Origins

From Emergence to Beginnings

GREGORY D. WILSON AND LYNNE P. SULLIVAN

Nearly a quarter century has passed since Smith's (1990) seminal volume *The Mississippian Emergence* was published. That volume, through a set of collected works, was the first to attempt a region-wide synthesis of what was known and thought about Mississippian origins. Smith's volume was published in the wake of several, very large cultural resource management projects, including the FAI-270 (I-255) highway project in the American Bottom (Kelly 1990a, 1990b), the Tennessee–Tombigbee Waterway project in western Alabama and eastern Mississippi (Welch 1990), and the Tellico Dam project in eastern Tennessee (Schroedl 2009; Schroedl et al. 1990). Collectively, these projects rivaled New Deal era projects in the sheer volume of investigated archaeological deposits, and they produced large, well-dated collections relevant to Mississippian beginnings—a first for American archaeology. These projects also had the advantage of modern recovery techniques and radiocarbon dating. During the same time frame, work at key sites such as Zebree (Morse and Morse 1990a), Powell Canal (House 1990), and Toltec Mounds (Rolingson 1990) (along with other Plum Bayou phase sites) in Arkansas pushed Mississippian origins south of Cahokia further back in time than had been previously thought (Morse and Morse 1990b). Continued work and new dates for sites in the Florida panhandle also confirmed earlier beginnings for Mississippian lifestyles in the Fort Walton culture area (Scarry 1990).

Research postdating Smith's volume has not been oriented to large-scale excavations as much as it has been a reconsideration of existing collections, supplemented by smaller-scale excavations targeted to address specific problems. What has been large in scale is the paradigmatic shift in Mississippian studies, from a focus on generalizing models to nuanced histories of specific areas (typically aided by more precise dating technology) to a resurgence of interest in population movements and other far-flung interactions as factors in the spread of Mississippian cultural practices (Blitz 2010; Blitz and Lorenz 2002, 2006; Cobb and Butler 2002; Pauketat et al. 2015). What is becoming eminently clear, as documented by the chapters in this volume, is that there was no single process of Mississippianization. Another fact that has become clear is that "Mississippian" did not "emerge" from a Woodland base. For the most part, Mississippianization consisted of new traditions and cosmologies that were generated through the cultural entanglements among diverse groups of people. Such entanglements were mediated by a variety of processes, including migration, missionization, pilgrimage, and long-distance exchange and circulation of materials. These new threads became the beginnings of a tapestry of Mississippian lifestyles that covered southeastern and midcontinental North America.

What has not changed since the publication of the *Emergence* volume is the steadfast curiosity of archaeologists to learn about and understand how and why the Mississippian phenomenon began. Smith (1990:3) likened the study of Mississippian developments to regional sets of nested black boxes, connected by human interactions and filled with smaller-scale geographic areas and communities. He noted that some of these boxes had been opened to varying degrees, while others remained closed. Most authors contributing to this volume continue to open more of Smith's black boxes, some by sorting through already opened regional boxes and searching more thoroughly through the smaller nested boxes enclosed within (Figure 1.1). Amber VanDerwarker, Dana Bardolph, and C. Margaret Scarry (chapter 2) investigate the correlation of maize intensification with Mississippian beginnings in a variety of regions. Alleen Betzenhauser (chapter 3) digs deeper into the box for Cahokia, which was opened in Smith's volume, by investigating regional settlement patterns that correlate with Mississippian beginnings. Greg Wilson, Colleen Delaney, and Phil Milhouse (chapter 4), Robert Cook (chapter 5), and Amanda Regnier (chapter 6) add fresh perspectives from northern and western margins of the Mississippian area, including the Illinois River Valley, the Apple River Valley, the Mississippian/Fort Ancient interface in southern Ohio, and the Mississippian-related Caddo culture of southeastern Oklahoma. Moreover, Edmund Boudreaux opens up the boxes of the North Carolina Piedmont (chapter 7); and Adam King, Keith Stephenson, Chris Thornock, and Alex Corsi (chapter 8) dust off and crack open long-shut boxes for the middle Savannah River (Hollywood site). Finally, Jeff Du Vernay and Nancy White make significant adjustments to dated models for the Mississippianization of Late Woodland groups in the Apalachicola–lower Chattahoochee River valley.

This introductory chapter contextualizes the work of the contributing au-

Figure 1.1. Regional map of the Mississippian world showing the location of selected archaeological sites.

thors in several ways. We begin by defining some key terms used throughout the chapters and volume, and then we examine the history of grand theory and paradigmatic shifts in the study of Mississippian origins to illuminate the routes that led to today's thinking. This section includes an assessment of the current status of social theory in Mississippian studies. Special emphasis is placed on a discussion of cultural entanglements, a topic common to most of the contributions and that addresses the ways in which the various regional traditions that archaeologists recognize as Mississippian were negotiated. The final section considers the broad sweep of Mississippianization and its impacts on later developments across the Eastern Woodlands.

The Scope of the Volume

Mississippian culture was centered in contiguous portions of the Midwest and Midsouth from around AD 1000 to AD 1500 but also involved groups located in adjacent portions of the interior Southeast, Plains, and northern Midwest. Mississippian groups shared aspects of an emergent ethnic identity that transcended many other cultural differences as well as environmental and linguistic boundaries. This volume seeks to document and explore the origins and spread of this phenomenon throughout different portions of pre-Columbian eastern North America. The term *beginnings* was chosen to highlight remarkable historical and regional variation in the processes of Mississippianization. Indeed, the chapters in this volume clearly illustrate that this process unfolded in different ways at different times in different regional locations. Thus, Mississippian was not a monothetic cultural adaptation; rather, there were numerous and unique instances of Mississippian beginnings that were negotiated by distinct groups with different histories and cultural traditions.

The History of Scholarship on Mississippian Origins

Mississippian was first recognized as a complex of stylistically related shell-tempered pottery found in the Middle Mississippi Valley (Holmes 1903). Culture historians later documented spatial and temporal correlations between the distribution of shell-tempered pottery assemblages and other material traits, such as triangular projectile points, rectangular architecture, and earthen platform mounds (Cole and Deuel 1937; Deuel 1935; Griffin 1943). Much of this work was fueled by the large-scale excavations conducted by New Deal era workers primarily under the supervision of archaeology graduate students, predominantly trained by University of Chicago field schools run by Fay-Cooper Cole (Dye 2016; Fagette 1996; Lyon 1996; Means 2013). These excavations for the first time showed the construction of Mississippian platform mounds as "domiciliary," as opposed to burial mounds, and also exposed large tracts of village deposits that revealed a variety of architectural styles, plazas, and palisades, among other new revelations about the organization of Mississippian communities (e.g., Kelly 2010; Lewis and Kneberg 1946; Lewis et al. 1995; Wilson 2008). However, these traits and their co-occurrence were seldom explained in terms of organization or process. Rather, it was often assumed that Mississippian peoples, objects, and ideas diffused from the Central Mississippi Valley, converting or displacing groups along the way that were less adaptively competitive (Caldwell 1958; Ford and Willey 1941:350; Krieger 1951; Lewis and Kneberg 1946; Willey 1953).

Dissatisfied with the focus on culture history, processual archaeologists reconceptualized Mississippian as a maize-based adaptive strategy to floodplain environments that included a hereditary form of social ranking (Muller 1997:42; Muller and Stephens 1991; Smith 1978). This ecological approach emphasized the causal primacy of local environmental conditions, while downplaying a host of external factors such as migration, exchange, and warfare (Peebles 1978; Smith 1978, 1984). This paradigm led many to the conclusion that local eco-demographic stress was the principal cause of Mississippian origins in many regions (Scarry 1990; Schroedl et al. 1990; but see Scarry 1993) and was a widely held interpretation at the time Smith's (1990) *The Mississippian Emergence* was published.

The data sets on which the chapters in the *Emergence* volume were based were instrumental in fueling critics of the ecological approach who contended that the focus on floodplain environments arbitrarily excluded many otherwise Mississippian-like archaeological complexes located in upland or bluff edge environments (King and Myers 2002; Pauketat 2007:82–83). Subsequent analyses of archaeobotanical data also revealed that maize cultivation was not an important part of the subsistence economies of a number of Mississippian-related archaeological complexes (Fritz and Kidder 1993; Scarry 1993; Jefferies et al. 1996). Perhaps the greatest shortcoming of the ecological approach has been the abundance of new (and old) evidence indicating the fundamental and pervasive role of population movements and other forms of far-flung interactions in Mississippian origins throughout eastern North America. Indeed, culture contact scenarios involving emergent cultural pluralism and hybridity (discussed below) are documented by most contributors to this volume.

The debates surrounding the ecological approach were supplanted as political economic perspectives gained traction in the North American Midcontinent and the Southeast (Anderson 1994; Brown et al. 1990 Cobb 1989, 1993; Pauketat 1994; Peebles and Kus 1977; Steponaitis 1978, 1981; Welch 1991). The focus on environmental adaptation was replaced by a concern with chiefly control melded with (then widely accepted) neoevolutionary schemes to form general models of how Mississippian societies originated and operated. Consequently, Mississippian societies became synonymous with a modified version of Service's (1971, 1975) chiefdom model of political development. This Mississippian chiefdom model emphasized the articulation between a centralized political structure and a tributary economy. Mississippian leaders were conceived of as aggrandizers who came to power and perpetuated their chiefly authority through the production and control of food and certain elaborately crafted prestige goods and exotic materials.

Ultimately, the Prestige Goods Economy model (Frankenstein and Rowlands 1978; Friedman and Rowlands 1977) came to provide an important analytical lens by which many Mississippian political economists explained the establishment of hierarchical regional political orders in different portions of the southeast and Midwest (Anderson 1994; Brown et al. 1990; Pauketat 1992, 1994, 1997; Peebles and Kus 1977; Steponaitis 1981; Welch 1986, 1991). In its original formulation, the prestige-goods economy model posited that political power was achieved by those who could control access to exotic wealth items needed for a variety of different local social transactions. This model has been notably revised multiple times in its application to the Moundville and Cahokia polities as new information has been acquired about the distribution and quantity of both exotic and locally crafted items, in addition to the actual uses and meanings of such items (Brown et al. 1991; Marcoux 2007; Pauketat 1992, 1997; Peebles and Kus 1977; Steponaitis 1981, 2016).

This vertical control perspective of Mississippian chiefdoms was further characterized by a notable degree of social inequality manifested archaeologically in the presence of regional settlement hierarchies, differential investments in domestic architecture and mortuary ceremonialism, and large-scale labor projects, such as earthen monument construction, that transcended the basic household group (Anderson 1994:12–113; Peebles and Kus 1977:431–433). The Cahokia region's multitiered settlement pattern, large earthen mounds, and uneven distribution of crafting debris conformed nicely to the political economic expectations of the Mississippian chiefdom model (Pauketat 1994). Research at Moundville in the Black Warrior Valley in the 1970s and 1980s also generated a picture of a complex Mississippian polity with a tributary economy supporting an elite class and a variety of attached craft specialists (Peebles and Kus 1977; Scarry 1986, Steponaitis 1978; Welch 1991).

This apparent multipolity confirmation bolstered confidence in the widespread relevance of the chiefdom model to the Mississippian area (Knight 1990). One consequence was the blackboxing of the model itself such that when one or more components of the model were identified, it was sometimes implicitly assumed that the others were as well, even in the absence of direct archaeological evidence (see Marcoux and Wilson 2010 for critique). This problem fostered the belief that different Mississippian polities were more organizationally similar than they really were (see Sullivan and Mainfort 2010:6–7; Wilson et al. 2006). Another consequence was that the chiefdom model proved to be inherently biased toward interpretations of male leadership roles while downplaying or even masking the leadership roles of women (Sullivan 2009, 2014), even though strong evidence for gender duality and the kin-based nature of women's leadership roles could be identified in Southern Appalachian and other Mississippian communities (Cobb 2003; Rodning 1999, 2001; Rodning and Moore 2010; Sullivan 2001, 2006; Sullivan and Rodning 2001, 2011).

Critics of the political economy approach also argue that it has obscured the processes by which Woodland era leveling mechanisms and egalitarian social relations were circumvented to generate Mississippian political hierarchies. Indeed, Mississippian political hierarchies and elite identities too often have been explained by referencing the strategies that perpetuated inequalities and leadership positions rather than elucidating their origins (see Pauketat 2000, 2007). In the absence of managerial necessity, institutionalized leadership positions had to be created and legitimized. These were political projects that required consensus building and perhaps entailed varying degrees of resistance. Would-be leaders were not all-knowing and all-powerful. They may have possessed special talents and understandings, but their ability to influence political outcomes was otherwise enabled and constrained by their position in a network of social relationships.

Modeling Mississippian Origins

By the late 1990s the problems with *modeling* Mississippian origins had become apparent. Some scholars responded to this crisis by generating or applying new models such as dual processualism and other related constructs to southeastern and midwestern Mississippian groups (Beck 2006; Blanton et al. 1996; King 2001, 2003; Payne 2006). Such efforts succeeded in drawing attention to spatial and temporal variation among different Mississippian societies but were less successful in explaining how such societies originated and changed over time (see Marcoux and Wilson 2010; Pauketat 2007; Wilson et al. 2006).

The ritual economy model developed by Mesoamerican and southwestern archaeologists also gained traction within some Mississippian research circles over the last decade (see Kelly 2006; Knight 2010; Thompson 2011). Ritual economists contend that much of the ceremonial sphere has been overly conceptualized in terms of hierarchy and elite control (Mills 2004; Spielmann 2002; Wells 2006). Feasts, funerals, and other public festivals provided opportunities for aggrandizement, but they also facilitated a wide variety of communal transactions that helped to define group membership and horizontally integrate different social segments. Most ritual economy constructs posit that craft production, food production, and ritual practices principally reproduced nonhierarchical rather than hierarchical social formations. Accordingly, such approaches serve primarily as critical appraisals of the excesses of the political economy approach while doing little to explain the origins of ancient Mississippian political hierarchies when and where they existed. Indeed, the challenge for those developing a nuanced approach to Mississippian origins is to explore the many ways that Native American groups negotiated different kinds of social and political relationships through ritual practices and productive activities without analytically imposing hierarchies where they did not exist, or theoretically backsliding into a form of Durkheimian (1893) functionalism that artificially separates religion and politics, thus negating power and social inequality more generally.

Historicizing Mississippian Origins

The late 1990s and early 2000s were also a time when a number of scholars changed course from the task of model building and application toward developing theoretical approaches that emphasized the historical contingency of particular regional political and cultural developments (Cobb 1993; Cobb and Garrow 1996; Pauketat 2000). Since that time, a number of productive new approaches have resulted from rethinking the mind-set of intentionality often attributed to aggrandizers and usurpers in Mississippian origin explanations. For example, Pauketat (2000, 2010) has hypothesized that the institutionalization of hereditary leadership in the Cahokia region could have been the unintentional outcome of traditional forms of communal interaction such as mound construction, feasting, and mortuary rites staged on an exaggerated scale. These traditional forms of collective action served to negotiate corporate group identities and establish other socioeconomic boundaries in the pre-Mississippian world. Perhaps inspired by a dynamic religious revitalization movement, these events began to be organized on a massive scale at early Cahokia (Pauketat 2008, 2009; Pauketat et al. 2002). Such mega-events may have placed important politico-religious decision-making responsibilities in the hands of certain individuals at central locations, altering the social and physical landscape in ways that unintentionally promoted new hierarchical social formations. Pauketat argues that these large, public, and often theatrical forms of collective action served to institutionalize Cahokian leadership positions.

Likewise, Cobb and King (2005) argue that the development of the Etowah polity can be better understood through a consideration of its complicated history of abandonment and reoccupation that contrasts sharply with many other Mississippian regional polities where scholars have emphasized a smoother, longer-term trajectory of development and decline. The contradictions and conflicts of Etowah's tumultuous history were negotiated by Mississippian groups who selectively emphasized or deemphasized ties with ancestors and supernatural heroes, and broadly shared themes of renewal and the fertility of the earth.

Wilson (2010) employed a similar historical perspective to investigate the establishment and long-term occupation of the Moundville political center in west-central Alabama. Moundville had a complicated history of place-based identity politics in which different social groups made various claims on social and economic resources. Moundville's historical trajectory differed considerably from that of Etowah's (King 2001); however, the political and ideological changes at both centers were negotiated through the construction and leveling of earthen mounds, plazas, domestic buildings, council houses, and cemeteries.

Culture Contact and Entanglement

These historical ways of thinking about cultural and political change have also rekindled interests in the role of culture contact in the spread of Mississippian lifeways throughout the North American Midwest and Southeast. The Central Mississippi Valley, specifically Cahokia and the American Bottom, are once again being interpreted as the stage for the beginnings of Mississippian traditions. Over the last 15 years, archaeologists have documented a large influx of immigrants into the greater Cahokia area corresponding with the polity's regional political consolidation (Alt 2006, 2010; Pauketat 2003; Slater et al. 2014). Many of these newcomers settled in agricultural villages in the eastern uplands of the American Bottom. Some came to reside at the Cahokia site, while others established homes elsewhere throughout the region.

Concurrent with these events was the establishment of the multi-mound Emerald site complex in the uplands, which has recently been interpreted as a religious shrine that was sporadically visited by groups of foreign pilgrims (Pauketat and Alt 2015; Skousen 2015). The outcome of these events was not simply a mixture of American Bottom and nonlocal traditions but the development of a new *Mississippian* religion and regional political order that propelled waves of cultural influence throughout the Midwest and Midsouth and farther into the Plains. As detailed in several chapters in this volume, Cahokia's supralocal influence was often facilitated by the establishment of small intrusive outposts or by the arrival of small numbers of influential Cahokians in distant settlements (see Cook, chapter 5; Wilson et al., chapter 4).

It is becoming more difficult to ignore the accumulating evidence that migrations and other far-flung interactions played an important role in Mississippian origins throughout the Southeast and Midwest (Alt 2006; Blitz 2010; Blitz and Lorenz 2002; Cobb and Butler 2006; Pauketat et al. 2015). However, these different regional culture contact scenarios varied considerably in terms of scale, duration, and the motivations of local and nonlocal groups. For example, the Fort Walton Mississippian tradition in the Apalachicola–lower Chattahoochee River valley represents a different kind of Mississippian origins scenario than the Cahokia example. Around AD 1100 Rood phase Mississippian groups migrated into the Chattahoochee River Valley and established a fortified town in a sparsely occupied buffer zone between two non-Mississippian cultural groups (Blitz and Lorenz 2002, 2006). These two local groups negotiated this intrusion in dramatically different ways. Wakulla groups to the south were culturally resistant to this Mississippian intrusion, a strategy that may have factored directly into their apparent exodus from the region by AD 1300. However, Averett groups to the north were open to the cultural influences of intrusive Rood phase Mississippians and perhaps also to interactions with Mississippian Pensacola groups to the west (see Du Vernay and White, chapter 9). Although the actual mechanisms of interaction among Averett and neighboring Mississippian groups remain unclear, these exchanges ultimately resulted in the development of the Mississippian Fort Walton tradition in the Apalachicola–lower Chattahoochee River valley (see Du Vernay and White, chapter 9).

The fourteenth-century Central Illinois River Valley in west-central Illinois represents yet another kind of Mississippianization than those summarized above. Around AD 1300 the Bold Counselor Oneota migrated from the northern Midwest into the Central Illinois River Valley, a region defined by fortified towns engaged in chronic hostilities (Esarey and Santure 1990; Milner 1999). Some archaeologists have interpreted the arrival of the Oneota as a hostile intrusion by a culturally distinct group (Hollinger 2005). However, a close examination of the archaeological evidence from this era indicates that the Oneota and local Mississippian groups negotiated a political alliance that ultimately led to their cohabitation and cultural entanglement (Esarey and Conrad 1998; Esarey and Santure 1990). Elevated frequencies of serving ware from contemporaneous Mississippian and Oneota sites in the region suggest that this alliance was negotiated in part through commensal politics (Wilson 2010). Ultimately, both groups were shaped by their mutual interactions. The Bold Counselor Oneota, however, were the most visibly transformed of the two groups, as they came to renegotiate important aspects of their identities, ceremonialism, and everyday practices through the selective incorporation of a number of Mississippian traditions, religious symbols, and forms of material culture (Esarey and Conrad 1998; Lieto and O'Gorman 2014).

The regional examples of Mississippian beginnings summarized above come from different times and locations. They represent different kinds of culture contact scenarios that generated historically divergent examples of Mississippian culture. Many of the authors in this volume also highlight the role of culture contact in their regional case studies. Most agree that Mississippianization was not a process by which Mississippian outsiders completely replaced local Woodland peoples. Moreover, there is a near consensus that these earlier peoples took nonlocal characteristics, whatever their source, and melded them into their own traditions.

Processes of culture contact and change have long been the subject of anthropological inquiry. Among American archaeologists, it is an important focus for scholars of historic period colonialism (e.g., Deagan 1973, 1998; Lightfoot and Martinez 1995; Marcoux 2010; Silliman 2015; Voss 2005). The topic has only recently been brought to the fore by Alt (2006) as a focus of inquiry for scholars of the Mississippian period, although the idea that such processes relate to culture change during the Mississippian period dates back at least to the 1940s, when Lewis and Kneberg (1946:10) suggested that "the Dallas people merged with the earlier Hiwassee Island people and that the Dallas Component [at Hiwassee Island] actually represents an amalgamated community."

As demonstrated by several chapters in this volume, important work is under way to better theorize the social changes initiated by the different culture contact scenarios that played such an important part in Mississippianization. Interactions among local and nonlocal groups can generate situations in which the traditions of disparate groups are creatively reassembled. Concepts like creolization, syncretism, and hybridity have been criticized for their portrayal of this process as a simple combination of existing traditions. Bhabha's (1985, 1994) use of the hybridity concept, however, provides an important alternative perspective that has been embraced for its emphasis on the innovations that culture contact scenarios often generate (see Alt 2006). Alt has employed this notion of hybridity to explore the cultural changes resulting from the arrival of immigrants from northern Arkansas and southeastern Missouri to the eleventh-century American Bottom. She convincingly argues that the interactions among these immigrants and local groups "engendered new senses of space and place that themselves helped to create Mississippian culture as we know it" (Alt 2005:300).

The hybridity concept, however, is not without its critics. Recently a number of scholars have argued that the multiplicity of social, biological, and linguistic definitions for the term detract from its clarity of meaning and application. Still others point out inherent problems with the concept itself. Indeed, if applied uncritically, the term does tend to promote the idea that pure forms of culture exist in the world prior to some form of intergroup contact being initiated (Langlin-Hooper 2013:99). As no social entity exists in isolation, are all groups hybrid (see Pappa 2013:35)? Furthermore, it is not always made clear whether the term applies to objects, people, or practices, and if and when one of these entities eventually stops being hybrid (Silliman 2015:8–9). There is also concern that the term has been disproportionately applied to less politically or economically dominant groups in culture contact scenarios (Young 1995:23). Admittedly, many of these critiques are not new to culture contact research and cannot be easily resolved by the simple introduction of a new term.

Recent research using an entanglement perspective has made some headway in grappling with these issues. The term entanglement provides an interesting metaphor through which the disparate groups in *contact* can begin to be complementarily assessed (King et al. this volume; Langin-Hooper 2013; Stockhammer 2012). The complementarity of the metaphor derives from the difficulty of conceptualizing just one group as entangled without also considering other interacting groups as being likewise caught up and altered by the same process. A *theory* of entanglement, however, must move beyond this simple metaphor to conceptually anticipate the different scales, agents, and generative capacities involved in particular historical examples of culture contact. To fulfill this need a number of scholars are turning to relational perspectives on the ancient past (Fowler 2004; Gosden 2005; Hodder 2012; Marcoux and Wilson 2010; Meskell 2004; Pauketat 2013; Watts 2013; Whitridge 2004).

Relational perspectives vary in scope and detail but share a basic conceptualization of human meaning and agency as referential, distributed, or networked. Thus, what counts as an agent or a person is not unitary but ultimately divisible into a weblike network of entangled entities. Such networks are always emergent and in motion, and can be composed of both humans and objects in the material world (Ingold 2007, 2011). Ideas and values are also relational in that they are generated through citational practices (see Butler 1993). Many relational archaeological perspectives have been fundamentally influenced by actor–network theory, a dynamic corpus of ideas that can be traced back to the sociology of scientific knowledge (Callon 1986; Latour 1991, 1992, 1994, 1999, 2005; Law 1992, 1999). The crux of this approach is that the capacity for agency and meaning derives from the networked association of different people, places, and things. Places and things have agency to the extent that their physical dimensions shape the ideas and interests of the people who experience them (Latour 1994). These networks are not simple amalgamations of different entities. People's interests, understandings, and agentic capacities are enabled, constrained, and otherwise mediated through their networked associations (Callon 1986; Latour 1994).

Accordingly, interactions among disparate groups can be mediated through their experiences with new or exotic people, places, and things. For example, disparate Woodland groups from the Midsouth and Midwest appear to have renegotiated previous ideas about each other, themselves, and their collective place in the cosmos through their participation in large-scale purification and renewal ceremonies at Cahokia (Pauketat et al. 2002). The physical dimensions of the activities composing these events (i.e., mound construction, pipe smoking, feasting, and gaming) would have helped mediate the interactions among these groups and the broader field of relationships in which they came to assign meaning to their experiences (Emerson and Pauketat 2008; Pauketat 2013; Pauketat and Alt 2015). These different activities occurred on different scales and entailed the networked association of different combinations of people, places, and things. The Mississippianization of Cahokia's northern hinterland involved the transferal of these networks to new locations (Bardolph 2014; Wilson et al., chapter 4). The difficult work of recontextualizing these networks in hinterland locations involved modified associations, meanings, and practices, a process resulting in the different Mississippian cultural manifestations documented throughout the Midwest and Midsouth.

Indeed, the chapters in this volume demonstrate considerable variability in the ways different Mississippian societies began as much as they showcase the different ways Mississippian archaeologists are conceptualizing these beginnings. VanDerwarker, Bardolph, and Scarry (chapter 2) examine archaeobotanical evidence from the American Bottom, the Illinois River Valley, the Central Mississippi River Valley, the Lower Mississippi River Valley, the Black Warrior River Valley, and northern Georgia to consider the highly variable role of maize cultivation in the origins of Mississippian culture. They conclude that regional histories of maize use varied dramatically throughout the

Mississippian world, with adoption and intensification correlating with many different developmental factors. The myriad ways in which early Mississippian peoples produced and used plants (including maize) indicate complex relationships among people, plants, power, status, economy, ritual, tradition making, and community formation that is best understood within a region's particular sociopolitical history.

Betzenhauser (chapter 3) argues that the combined movements of local and foreign groups in the Terminal Late Woodland American Bottom redefined landscapes of identity and power relations, a dynamic that generated Cahokia as an urban space and the center of a regionally integrated polity. The next two chapters showcase research on Cahokia's northern and northeastern hinterland regions where local groups were engaged in various kinds of interactions with American Bottom Mississippians.

Moving northward, Wilson, Delaney, and Millhouse (chapter 4) argue that concurrent with Cahokia's eleventh-century regional consolidation, Mississippians groups from the American Bottom established small outposts in west-central and northwestern Illinois. The initial entanglements generated by these outposts were small in scale. Nevertheless, they spurred multiple regional-scale emulations of Cahokian lifeways during the early twelfth-century occupations of the Illinois and Apple River valleys. To the east, in southwestern Ohio, Cook (chapter 5) considers the long-known but little-understood entanglements of Mississippian and Fort Ancient cultures. He tackles this issue with an arsenal of biological and archaeological data. His analytical results indicate that a small number of migrating Mississippians from different geographic areas factored heavily into Fort Ancient cultural beginnings.

The development of a distinct ritual tradition in the Caddo region of southeastern Oklahoma is the subject of research by Regnier (chapter 6). By comparing her data to a generalized Mississippian model suited for Coles Creek culture in the Lower Mississippi Valley, she defines a set of distinctively Caddoan traditions that exhibit complex historical entanglements with the larger Mississippian world. Her exposition of these differences illustrates the local variation and history that has become the focus of much contemporary research on Mississippian groups. In fact, the differences she points out for the Caddo are similar in scale and scope to those of other local Mississippian traditions that have been freed from the generalizing chiefdom model.

The next three chapters showcase research on Mississippian beginnings in the southeastern United States. To the southeast, Mississippian traditions appeared late in the North Carolina Piedmont in the form of the locally defined Pee Dee culture. Boudreaux (chapter 7) places the beginnings of Pee Dee culture in the late twelfth century. The large Town Creek site had its beginnings at this time. Boudreaux posits that this Pee Dee culture transformation was generated in part by outside influences on local populations. His interpretation contrasts sharply with that of his predecessor Coe (1952), who envisioned Pee Dee as a short-term, intrusive Mississippian phenomenon.

King, Thornock, and Stephenson (chapter 8) employ an entanglement perspective to explore how Woodland groups in the middle Savannah River valley redefined important dimensions of their identities and cosmological understandings through mound construction and mortuary ritual mediated by the bundling of elaborate ceremonial objects from different parts of the Mississippian world. These mortuary bundles literally entangled different peoples, places, and things as well as the past and the present through their careful interment with ancestors. These events contributed to the development of "a new way of organizing society . . . a unique, local version of Mississippian ritual and political culture" (King et al., chapter 8).

Du Vernay and White (chapter 9) discuss an in situ amalgamation process in the Apalachicola–lower Chattahoochee River valley. They cite a large sample of investigated Fort Walton sites and describe a transition from resident late Weeden Island groups. Woodland ceramic traditions continued, but potters began to incorporate Mississippian forms. Platform mounds also began to be constructed, and maize agriculture was adopted at inland sites. This process likely began in response to sustained direct interaction with intrusive Rood phase peoples living along the lower Chattahoochee River (Blitz and Lorenz 2002). Du Vernay and White's analysis builds upon and reworks previous research by Blitz and Lorenz (2002, 2006), Brose (1975, 1984), Scarry (1990), and White (1982).

The concluding chapter by David Anderson offers a critical retrospective on Mississippian research while further summarizing and evaluating the individual chapters. His chapter also serves to highlight productive avenues of future research potential.

The Southern Cult Revitalized and Reformed

The chapters in this volume quite clearly show not only that the processes of Mississippianization were diverse, but that the results produced an amazing variety of cultural expressions. Coming to terms with cultural diversity has been a protracted process among scholars of the Mississippian phenomenon, in part because the search for the big picture created monochromatic renderings of a polychromatic landscape. For example, iconography and belief systems as well as societal and political organization were seen as basically similar throughout the region. An initial recognition that there were certain recurring themes in iconography prompted Antonio Waring and Preston Holder (1945) to publish their landmark article "A Prehistoric Ceremonial Complex in the Southeastern United States." Intensive study of this Southeastern Ceremonial Complex (SECC), as it came to be called, defined stylistic regions (Brown 2002; Muller 1966), refined chronologies (e.g., Brown and Rogers 1999; Muller 1989; Sullivan 2007), and began to unravel the meanings of related symbols (Knight et al. 2001; Lankford et al. 2011; Reilly and Garber 2007). As a result, new realizations that there are distinctive and unique characteristics of iconography, including its execution, meanings, and uses in Mississippian subregions (which also are not confined to the Southeast), and which documented diversity—not uniformity—led Knight (2006:1) 60 years later to bid the SECC farewell, because the concept had "become an impediment to understanding." In a similar fashion, 30 years after Peebles and Kus's (1977) pivotal study of mortuary practices at Moundville set scholars scurrying to overlay elites, chiefs, and all of the trappings of Polynesian-style chiefdom societies onto data from Mississippian sites, Pauketat (2007) proclaimed the once revered and uniformly embraced chiefdom model as a delusion and an obstacle to the study of historical processes that led to the Mississippian phenomena.

These hard-won understandings that Mississippian societies are not all alike, that they have unique histories, and that the processes of Mississippianization were not uniform, should not be a surprise. Indeed, what is most interesting to ponder is what led to the interactions of these diverse people that created cultural entanglements across a vast geographic area. If the earliest Mississippian beginnings were indeed at Cahokia (although building on a base of cultural trappings from farther south such as the construction of platform mounds), some sort of religious movement or phenomenon that required otherworldly intervention is as good a guess as any for the reason of the initial draw to Cahokia, as Pauketat (2013) suggests. The interaction of people from the south and other adjacent regions at Cahokia may have produced a sort of hybrid vigor for culture making (Alt 2006).

Whatever the cause for the gathering at Cahokia, the experiment must have been successful, because the site and population grew and became increasingly influential. Mississippianization had begun. New centers, such as Moundville and Etowah, arose, with each settlement interpreting the shared wisdoms in its own ways and in turn influencing others in their regions as cultural interactions and transmissions developed over time and space. Elements of what may have started as a cult at Cahokia became mainstream and then likely diversified into sects. Some of these held onto traditions more tightly than others. Great leaders arose in some areas, but not in others. Yet, after half a millennium, there was enough left of shared beginnings to provide a gloss of unity across the region. Whatever was being doled out at Cahokia was powerful stuff, but it was diluted by local preparations that created reformulations. Mississippian traditions may have begun at Cahokia, but the transformations did not end there. The chapters in this volume also do not represent the last words on Mississippian beginnings, but as did the cultures they discuss, the authors provide reformulations and insights into changes that influenced the broad sweep of North America's past. Each localized story unpacks yet another of Smith's (1990) black boxes and brings to light a new perspective and appreciation of the beginnings of the cultural phenomenon archaeologists have come to call Mississippian.

References Cited

Alt, Susan M.
    2006   The Power of Diversity: The Roles of Migration and Hybridity in Culture Change. In *Leadership and Polity in Mississippian Society*, edited by Brian M. Butler and Paul D. Welch, pp. 289–308. Center for Archaeological Investigations, Occasional Paper 33. Southern Illinois University, Carbondale.
    2010   Complexity in Action(s): Retelling the Cahokia Story. In *Ancient Complexities: New Perspectives in Pre-Columbian North America*, edited by Susan Alt, pp. 119–137. Foundations of Archaeological Inquiry Series. University of Utah Press, Salt Lake City.

Anderson, David G.
    1994   *The Savannah River Chiefdoms: Political Change in the Late Prehistoric Southeast*. University of Alabama Press, Tuscaloosa.

Bardolph, Dana N.
    2014   Evaluating Cahokian Contact and Mississippian Identity Politics in the Late Prehistoric Central Illinois River Valley. *American Antiquity* 79(1):69–89.

Beck, Robin A. Jr.
    2006   Persuasive Politics and Domination at Cahokia and Moundville. In *Leadership and Polity in Mississippian Society*, edited by Brian M. Butler and Paul D. Welch, pp. 19–42. Center for Archaeological Investigations, Occasional Paper No. 33. Southern Illinois University, Carbondale.

Bhabha, Homi K.
    1985   Signs Taken for Wonders: Questions of Ambivalence and Authority under a Tree outside Delhi, May 1817. *Critical Inquiry* 12:144–165.
    1994   *The Location of Culture*. Routledge, London.

Blanton, Richard E., Gary M. Feinman, Stephen A. Kowalewski, and Peter N. Peregrine
    1996   A Dual Processual Theory for the Evolution of Mesoamerican Civilization. *Current Anthropology* 37:1–14.

Blitz, John H.
 2009   New Perspectives in Mississippian Archaeology. *Journal of Archaeological Research* 18(1):1–39.

Blitz, John H., and Karl G. Lorenz
 2002   The Early Mississippian Frontier in the Lower Chattahoochee–Apalachicola River Valley. *Southeastern Archaeology* 21(2):117–135.
 2006   *The Chattahoochee Chiefdoms*. University of Alabama Press, Tuscaloosa.

Brose, David
 1975   Case Western Reserve University Contributions to the Archaeological Investigation of Two Early Fort Walton Sites in the Apalachicola River Valley, Northwest Florida: 1973. Manuscript on file, Department of Anthropology, Case Western Reserve University, Cleveland.
 1984   Mississippian Period Cultures in Northwest Florida. In *Perspectives on Gulf Coast Prehistory*, edited by David Davis, pp. 165–197. University Press of Florida, Gainesville.

Brown, James A.
 2002   Forty Years of the Southeastern Ceremonial Complex. In *Histories of Southeastern Archaeology*, edited by Shannon Tushingham, Jane Hill, and Charles H. McNutt, pp. 26–34. University of Alabama Press, Tuscaloosa.
 2007   Sequencing the Braden Style within Mississippian Period Art and Iconography. In *Ancient Objects and Sacred Realms: Interpretations of Mississippian Iconography*, edited by F. Kent Reilly III and James F. Garber, pp. 213–245. University of Texas Press, Austin.

Brown, James A., Richard A. Kerber, and Howard D. Winters
 1990   Trade and the Evolution of Exchange Relations at the Beginning of the Mississippian Period. In *The Mississippian Emergence*, edited by Bruce D. Smith, pp. 251–280. Smithsonian Institution Press, Washington, D.C.

Brown, James A., and J. Daniel Rogers
 1999   AMS Dates on Artifacts of the Southeastern Ceremonial Complex from Spiro. *Southeastern Archaeology* 18(2):134–141.

Butler, Judith
 1993   *Bodies That Matter: On the Discursive Limits of "Sex."* Routledge, New York.

Caldwell, Joseph R.
 1958   Trend and Tradition in the Prehistory of the Eastern United States. *Memoir* No. 88. American Anthropological Association, Menasha.

Callon, Michelle
 1986   Some Elements of a Sociology of Translation: Domestication of the Scallops and the Fishermen of Saint Brieuc Bay. In *Power, Action, and Belief: A New Sociology of Knowledge*, edited by John Law, pp. 196–233. Routledge and Kegan Paul, London.

Cobb, Charles R.
 1989   An Appraisal of the Role of Mill Creek Hoes in Mississippian Exchange Systems. *Southeastern Archaeology* 8:79–92.
 1993   Archaeological Approaches to the Political Economy of Nonstratified Societies. In *Archaeological Method and Theory*, edited by M. B. Schiffer, 5:43–99. University of Arizona Press, Tucson.
 2003   Mississippian Chiefdoms: How Complex? *Annual Review of Anthropology* 32:63–84.

Cobb, Charles R., and Brian M. Butler
 2002 The Vacant Quarter Revisited: Late Mississippian Abandonment of the Lower Ohio Valley. *American Antiquity* 67:625–641.

Cobb, Charles R., and Patrick H. Garrow
 1996 Woodstock Culture and the Question of Mississippian Emergence. *American Antiquity* 61:21–37.

Cobb, Charles R., and Adam King
 2005 Re-inventing Mississippian Tradition at Etowah, Georgia. *Journal of Archaeological Method and Theory* 12:167–192.

Coe, Joffre L.
 1952 The Cultural Sequence of the Carolina Piedmont. In *Archaeology of Eastern United States*, edited by James B. Griffin, pp. 301–311. University of Chicago Press, Chicago.

Cole, Faye-Cooper, and Thorne Deuel
 1937 *Rediscovering Illinois: Archaeological Explorations in and around Fulton County.* University of Chicago Press, Chicago.

Crumley, Carole L.
 1995 Heterarchy and the Analysis of Complex Societies. *Archeological Papers of the American Anthropological Association* 6(1):1–5.

Deagan, Kathleen A.
 1973 Mestizaje in Colonial St. Augustine. *Ethnohistory* 20(1):55–65.
 1998 Transculturation and Spanish American Ethnogenesis: The Archaeological Legacy of the Quincentenary. *Studies in Culture Contact: Interaction, Culture Change, and Archaeology*, edited by James G. Cusick, pp. 23–43. Center for Archaeological Investigations, Occasional Paper No. 25. Southern Illinois University, Carbondale.

Deuel, Thorne
 1935 Basic Cultures of the Mississippi Valley. *American Anthropologist* 37:429–445.

Durkheim, Emile
 1893 *The Division of Labor in Society.* Translated by Lewis A. Coser, 1997. Free Press, New York.

Dye, David H., editor
 2016 *New Deal Archaeology in Tennessee: Intellectual, Methodological, and Theoretical Contributions.* University of Alabama Press, Tuscaloosa.

Emerson, Thomas E., Timothy R. Pauketat, and Susan Alt
 2008 Locating American Indian Religion at Cahokia and Beyond. In *Religion, Archaeology, and the Material World*, edited by Lars Fogelin, pp. 216–236. Center for Archaeological Investigations, Occasional Paper No. 36. Southern Illinois University, Carbondale.

Esarey, Duane E., and Lawrence A. Conrad
 1998 The Bold Counselor Phase of the Central Illinois River Valley: Oneota's Middle Mississippian Margin. *Wisconsin Archaeologist* 79(2):38–61.

Esarey, Duane E., and Sharron K. Santure
 1990 Archaeological Investigations at the Morton Village and Norris Farms 36 Cemetery. Reports of Investigations No. 45. Illinois State Museum, Springfield.

Fagette, Paul
 1996 *Digging for Dollars: American Archaeology and the New Deal.* University of New Mexico Press, Albuquerque.

Ford, James A., and Gordon R. Willey
　1941　An Interpretation of the Prehistory of the Eastern United States. *American Anthropologist* 43(3):325–363.

Frankenstein, Susan, and Michael J. Rowlands
　1978　The Internal Structure and Regional Context of Early Iron Age Society in Southwest Germany. *University of London Institute of Archaeology Bulletin* 15:73–112.

Friedman, Jonathan, and Michael J. Rowlands
　1977　Notes toward an Epigenetic Model of Civilization. In *The Evolution of Social Systems*, edited by Jonathan Friedman and Michael J. Rowlands, pp. 201–276. Duckworth, London.

Fritz, Gayle J., and Tristram R. Kidder
　1993　Recent Investigations into Prehistoric Agriculture in the Lower Mississippi Valley. *Southeastern Archaeology* 12(1):1–14.

Gosden, Chris
　2005　What Do Objects Want? *Journal of Archaeological Method and Theory* 12:193–211.

Griffin, James B.
　1943　*The Fort Ancient Aspect, Its Cultural and Chronological Position in Mississippi Valley Archaeology.* Museum of Anthropology, Anthropological Papers No. 28. University of Michigan, Ann Arbor.

Hodder, Ian
　2012　*Entangled: An Archaeology of the Relationships between Humans and Things.* Wiley-Blackwell, Malden.

Hollinger, Eric R.
　2005　Conflict and Culture Change in the Late Prehistoric and Early Historic American Midcontinent. Unpublished Ph.D. dissertation, University of Illinois, Urbana.

Holmes, William H.
　1903　*Aboriginal Pottery of the Eastern United States.* Twentieth Annual Report, Bureau of American Ethnology, United States Government Printing Office, Washington, D.C.

House, John
　1990　Powell Canal: Baytown Period Adaptation on Bayou Macon, Southeast Arkansas. In *The Mississippian Emergence*, edited by Bruce D. Smith, pp. 9–26. Smithsonian Institution Press, Washington, D.C.

Ingold, Timothy
　2007　*Lines: A Brief History.* Routledge, London.
　2011　*Being Alive: Essays on Movement, Knowledge, and Description.* Routledge, London.

Jefferies, Richard W., Emanuel Breitburg, Jennifer Flood, and C. Margaret Scarry
　1996　Mississippian Adaptation on the Northern Periphery: Settlement, Subsistence and Interaction in the Cumberland Valley of Southeastern Kentucky. *Southeastern Archaeology* 15(1):1–28.

Kelly, Arthur, and edited by Gretchen Eggiman, Randy Heath, Richard Moss, Chris Webster, and Dylan Woodliff
　2010　*WPA Archaeological Excavations at the Macon North Plateau.* LAMAR Institute Publication 150. LAMAR Institute, Savannah.

Kelly, John E.
　1990a　Range Site Community Patterns and the Mississippian Emergence. In *The Mississip-*

pian Emergence, edited by Bruce D. Smith, pp. 67–112. Smithsonian Institution Press, Washington, D.C.

1990b The Emergence of Mississippian Culture in the American Bottom Region. In *The Mississippian Emergence*, edited by Bruce D. Smith, pp. 113–152. Smithsonian Institution Press, Washington, D.C.

2006 The Ritualization of Cahokia: The Structure and Organization of Early Cahokia Crafts. In *Leadership and Polity in Mississippian Society*, edited by Brian M. Butler and Paul D. Welch, pp. 236–263. Center for Archaeological Investigations, Occasional Paper No. 33. Southern Illinois University, Carbondale.

King, Adam

2001 Long-Term Histories of Mississippian Centers: The Developmental Sequence of Etowah and Its Comparison to Moundville and Cahokia. *Southeastern Archaeology* 20:1–17.

2003 *Etowah: The Political History of a Chiefdom Capital*. University of Alabama Press, Tuscaloosa.

King, Adam (editor)

2007 *Southeastern Ceremonial Complex: Chronology, Content, Context*. University of Alabama Press, Tuscaloosa.

King, Adam, and Maureen S. Myers

2002 Exploring the Edges of the Mississippian World. *Southeastern Archaeology* 21:113–116.

Knight, Vernon James Jr.

1990 Social Organization and the Evolution of Hierarchy in Southeastern Chiefdoms. *Journal of Anthropological Research* 46(1):1–23.

2006 Farewell to the Southeastern Ceremonial Complex. *Southeastern Archaeology* 25(1):1–5.

2010 *Mound Excavations at Moundville: Architecture, Elites and Social Order*. University of Alabama Press, Tuscaloosa.

Knight, Vernon James Jr., James A. Brown, and George E. Lankford

2001 On the Subject Matter of Southeastern Ceremonial Complex Art. *Southeastern Archaeology* 20(2):129–141.

Kraidy, Marwan

2005 *Hybridity, or the Cultural Logic of Globalization*. Temple University Press, Philadelphia.

Krieger, Alex D.

1951 A Radiocarbon Date on the Davis Site in East Texas. *American Antiquity* 17(2):144–145.

Langlin-Hooper, Stephanie M.

2013 Problematizing Typology and Discarding the Colonialist Legacy: Approaches to Hybridity in the Terracotta Figurines of Hellenistic Babylonia. *Archaeological Review from Cambridge* 28:95–113.

Lankford, George E., F. Kent Reilly III, and James Garber (editors)

2011 *Visualizing the Sacred: Cosmic Visions, Regionalism, and the Art of the Mississippian World*. University of Texas Press, Austin.

Latour, Bruno

1991 Technology Is Society Made Durable. In *A Sociology of Monsters: Essays on Power, Technology and Domination*, edited by John Law, pp. 103–131. Routledge, London.

1992 Where Are the Missing Masses? The Sociology of a Few Mundane Artifacts. In *Shaping Technology, Building Society: Studies in Sociotechnical Change*, edited by Wiebe Bijker and John Law, pp. 225–258. MIT Press, Cambridge.

1994   On Technical Mediation—Philosophy, Sociology, Genealogy. *Common Knowledge* 3(2):29–64.

Law, John
1992   *Notes on the Theory of the Actor–Network: Ordering, Strategy and Heterogeneity.* Centre for Science Studies, Lancaster University. Electronic document, http://www.lancaster.ac.uk/fass/resources/sociology-online-papers/papers/law-notes-on-ant.pdf.
1997   *Traduction/Trahison: Notes on ANT.* Centre for Science Studies, Lancaster University. Electronic document, http://www.comp.lancs.ac.uk/sociology/papers/Law-Traduction-Trahison.pdf.
1999   On Recalling ANT. In *Actor Network Theory and After*, edited by John Law and John Hassard, pp. 15–25. Blackwell and the Sociological Review, Oxford.
2005   *Reassembling the Social: An Introduction to Actor–Network Theory.* Oxford University Press, Oxford.

Lewis, Thomas M. N., and Madeline D. Kneberg
1946   *Hiwassee Island: An Archaeological Account of Four Tennessee Indian Peoples.* University of Tennessee Press, Knoxville.

Lewis, Thomas M. N., Madeline Kneberg Lewis, and Lynne P. Sullivan
1995   *The Prehistory of the Chickamauga Basin in Tennessee.* 2 vols. University of Tennessee Press, Knoxville.

Lieto, Joshua, and Jodie O'Gorman
2014   A Preliminary Analysis of Oneota and Mississippian Serving Vessels at the Morton Village Site. *North American Archaeologist* 35(3):243–255.

Lightfoot, Kent G., and Antoinette Martinez
1995   Frontiers and Boundaries in Archaeological Perspective. *Annual Review of Anthropology* 24:471–492.

Linton, Ralph
1936   *The Study of Man.* D. Appleton-Century, New York.

Lyon, Edwin A.
1996   *New Deal Archaeology in the Southeast.* University of Alabama Press, Tuscaloosa.

Maran, Joseph, and Philipp W. Stockhammer (editors)
2012   *Materiality and Social Practice: Transformative Capacities of Intercultural Encounters.* Papers of the Conference, Heidelberg, March 25–27, 2010. Oxbow, Oxford.

Marcoux, Jon B.
2007   On Reconsidering Display Goods Production and Circulation in the Moundville Chiefdom. *Southeastern Archaeology* 26(2):232–245.
2010   *Pox, Empire, Shackles, and Hides: The Townsend Site, 1670–1715.* University of Alabama Press, Tuscaloosa.

Marcoux, Jon B., and Gregory D. Wilson
2010   Categories of Complexity and the Preclusion of Practice. In *Ancient Complexities: New Perspectives in Pre-Columbian North America*, edited by Susan Alt, University of Utah Press.

Means, Bernard K.
2013   *Shovel Ready: Archaeology and Roosevelt's New Deal for America.* University of Alabama Press, Tuscaloosa.

Meskell, Lynn
2004   *Object Worlds in Ancient Egypt.* Berg, Oxford.

Mills, Barbara J.
   2004   The Establishment and Defeat of Hierarchy: Inalienable Possessions and the History of Collective Prestige Structures in the Pueblo Southwest. *American Anthropologist* 106(2):238–251.

Milner, George
   1999   Warfare in Prehistoric and Early Historic Eastern North America. *Journal of Archaeological Research* 7(2):105–151.

Morse, Daniel F. Jr., and Phyllis A. Morse
   1990a   The Zebree Site: An Emerged Early Mississippian Expression in Northeast Arkansas. In *The Mississippian Emergence*, edited by Bruce D. Smith, pp. 51–66. Smithsonian Institution Press, Washington, D.C.
   1990b   Emergent Mississippian in the Central Mississippi Valley. In *The Mississippian Emergence*, edited by Bruce D. Smith, pp. 153–173. Smithsonian Institution Press, Washington, D.C.

Muller, Jon
   1966   An Experimental Theory of Style. Unpublished Ph.D. dissertation. Department of Anthropology, Harvard University, Cambridge.
   1997   *Mississippian Political Economy*. Plenum Press, New York.
   1989   The Southern Cult. In *The Southeastern Ceremonial Complex, Artifacts and Analysis: The Cottonlandia Conference*, edited by Patricia Galloway, pp. 11–26. University of Nebraska Press, Lincoln.

Muller, Jon, and Jeanette E. Stephens
   1991   Mississippian Sociocultural Adaptation. In *Cahokia and the Hinterlands: Middle Mississippian Cultures of the Midwest*, edited by Thomas E. Emerson and R. Barry Lewis, pp. 297–310. University of Illinois Press, Urbana.

Pauketat, Timothy R.
   1992   The Reign and Ruin of the Cahokia Lords: A Dialectic of Dominance. In *Lords of the Southeast: Social Inequality and the Native Elites of Southeastern North America*, edited by Alex W. Barker and Timothy R. Pauketat, pp. 31–51. Archaeological Papers of the American Anthropological Association 3. Washington, D.C.
   1994   *The Ascent of Chiefs: Cahokia and Mississippian Politics in Native North America*. University of Alabama Press, Tuscaloosa.
   1997   Cahokian Political Economy. In *Cahokia: Domination and Ideology in the Mississippian World*, edited by Timothy R. Pauketat and Thomas E. Emerson, pp. 30–51. University of Nebraska Press, Lincoln.
   2000   The Tragedy of the Commoners. In *Agency in Archaeology*, edited by Marcia-Anne A. Dobres and John Robb, pp. 113–129. Routledge, London.
   2003   Resettled Farmers and the Making of a Mississippian Polity. *American Antiquity* 68(1):39–66.
   2007   *Chiefdoms and Other Archaeological Delusions*. AltaMira Press, Walnut Creek.
   2009   *Cahokia: Ancient America's Great City on the Mississippi*. Viking-Penguin, New York.
   2010   Of Leaders and Legacies in Native North America. In *The Evolution of Leadership and Complexity*, edited by John Kantner, Kevin Vaughn, and Jelmer Eerkins, pp. 169–192. School for Advanced Research Press, Santa Fe.
   2013   *An Archaeology of the Cosmos: Rethinking Agency and Religion in Ancient America*. Routledge, New York.

Pauketat, Timothy R., Robert Boszhardt, and Danielle Benden
   2015   Trempealeau Entanglements: An Ancient Colony's Cause and Effects. *American Antiquity* 80:260–289.

Pauketat, Timothy R., and Susan Alt
   2015   The Elements of Cahokian Shrine Complexes and the Basis of Mississippian Religion. In *Religion and Politics in the Ancient Americas*, edited by Sarah Barber and Arthur Joyce. University of Colorado Press, Boulder.

Pauketat, Timothy R., Lucretia Kelly, Gail Fritz, Neal Lopinot, Scott Elias, and Eve Hargrave
   2002   The Residues of Feasting and Public Ritual at Early Cahokia. *American Antiquity* 67(2):257–279.

Pappa, Eleftheria
   2013   Postcolonial Baggage at the End of the Road: How to Put the Genie Back into Its Bottle and Where to Go from There. *Archaeological Review from Cambridge* 28:29–50.

Payne, Claudine
   2006   The Foundations of Leadership in Mississippian Chiefdoms: Perspectives from Lake Jackson and Upper Nodena. In *Leadership and Polity in Mississippian Society*, edited by Brian M. Butler and Paul D. Welch, pp. 91–111. Center for Archaeological Investigations, Occasional Papers No. 33. Southern Illinois University, Carbondale.

Peebles, Christopher S.
   1978   Determinants of Settlement Size and Location in the Moundville Phase. *Mississippian Settlement Patterns*, edited by Bruce D. Smith, pp. 369–416. Academic Press, New York.

Peebles, Christopher S., and Susan M. Kus
   1977   Some Archaeological Correlates of Ranked Societies. *American Antiquity* 42(3):421–448.

Phillips, Philip, James A. Ford, and James B. Griffin
   1951   *Archaeological Survey in the Lower Mississippi Alluvial Valley 1940–1947*. Papers of the Peabody Museum of American Archaeology and Ethnology Vol. 25. Harvard University, Cambridge.

Reilly, F. Kent III, and James F. Garber (editors)
   2007   *Ancient Objects and Sacred Realms: Interpretations of Mississippian Iconography*. University of Texas Press, Austin.

Rodning, Christopher B.
   1999   Archaeological Perspectives on Gender and Women in Traditional Cherokee Society. *Journal of Cherokee Studies* 20:3–27.
   2001   Mortuary Ritual and Gender Ideology in Protohistoric Southwestern North Carolina. In *Gender in the Archaeology of the Mid-South*, edited by Jane M. Eastman and Christopher B. Rodning, pp. 77–100. University Press of Florida, Gainesville.

Rodning, Christopher B., and David G. Moore
   2010   South Appalachian Mississippian and Protohistoric Mortuary Practices in Southwestern North Carolina. *Southeastern Archaeology* 29(1):80–100.

Rolingson, Martha A.
   1990   The Toltec Mounds Site: A Ceremonial Center in the Arkansas River Lowland. In *The Mississippian Emergence*, edited by Bruce D. Smith, pp. 27–49. Smithsonian Institution Press, Washington, D.C.

Scarry, C. Margaret
  1986   Change in Plant Procurement and Production during the Emergence of the Moundville Chiefdom. Unpublished Ph.D. dissertation, Department of Anthropology, University of Michigan, Ann Arbor.

Scarry, John F.
  1990   Mississippian Emergence in the Fort Walton Area: The Evolution of the Cayson and Lake Jackson Phases. *The Mississippian Emergence*, edited by Bruce D. Smith, pp. 227–250. Smithsonian Institution Press, Washington, D.C.

Schroedl, Gerald F.
  2009   The Tellico Archaeological Project. In *TVA Archaeology: Seventy-Five Years of Prehistoric Site Research*, edited by Erin E. Pritchard with Todd M. Ahlman, pp. 62–110. University of Tennessee Press, Knoxville.

Schroedl, Gerald F., C. Clifford Boyd Jr., and R. P. Stephen Davis Jr.
  1990   Explaining Mississippian Origins in East Tennessee. *The Mississippian Emergence*, edited by Bruce D. Smith, pp. 175–196. Smithsonian Institution Press, Washington, D.C.

Service, Elman R.
  1971   *Primitive Social Organization: An Evolutionary Perspective*. Random House, New York.
  1975   *Origins of the State and Civilization*. Norton, New York.

Silliman, Stephen W.
  2015   A Requiem for Hybridity? The Problem with Frankensteins, Purees, and Mules. *Journal of Social Archaeology* 15(3):277–298.

Skousen, Jacob
  2015   Moonbeams, Water, and Smoke: Tracing Other*worldly* Relationships at the Emerald Site. In *Tracing the Relational: The Archaeology of Worlds, Spirits, and Temporalities*, edited by Meghan Buchanan and Jacob Skousen, pp. 40–55. University of Utah Press, Salt Lake City.

Slater, Phillip A., Kristin M. Hedman, and Thomas E. Emerson
  2014   Immigrants at the Mississippian Polity of Cahokia: Strontium Isotope Evidence for Population Movement. *Journal of Archaeological Science* 44:117–127.

Smith, Bruce D.
  1984   Mississippian Expansion: Tracing the Historical Development of an Explanatory Model. *Southeastern Archaeology* 3(1):13–32.

Smith, Bruce D. (editor)
  1978   *Mississippian Settlement Patterns*. Academic Press, New York.
  1990   *The Mississippian Emergence*. Smithsonian Institution Press, Washington, D.C.

Spielmann, Katherine A.
  2002   Feasting, Craft Specialization, and the Ritual Mode of Production in Small-Scale Societies. *American Anthropologist* 104(1):195–207.

Steponaitis, Vincas P.
  1978   Location Theory and Complex Chiefdoms: A Mississippian Example. In *Mississippian Settlement Patterns*, edited by Bruce D. Smith, pp. 417–453. Academic Press, New York.
  1981   Chronology and Community Patterns at Moundville. *Southeastern Archaeological Conference Bulletin* 24:99–104.
  2016   Moundville Palettes—Prestige Goods or Inalienable Possessions? In *Rethinking*

Moundville and Its Hinterland, edited by Vincas P. Steponaitis and C. Margaret Scarry, pp. 121–133. University Press of Florida, Gainesville.

Stewart, Charles
2007 *Creolization: History, Ethnography, Theory*. Left Coast Press, Walnut Creek.

Stockhammer, Philipp W.
2013 From Hybridity to Entanglement, from Essentialism to Practice. In *Archaeology and Cultural Mixture*, edited by W. Paul Van Pelt. *Archaeological Review from Cambridge* 28:11–28. Cambridge.

Sullivan, Lynne P.
2001 Those Men in the Mounds: Gender, Politics, and Mortuary Practices in Late Prehistoric Eastern Tennessee. In *Gender in the Archaeology of the Mid-South*, edited by J. M. Eastman and Christopher B. Rodning, pp. 101–126. University Press of Florida, Gainesville.
2006 Gendered Contexts of Mississippian Leadership in Southern Appalachia. In *Leadership and Polity in Mississippian Society*, edited by Brian M. Butler and Paul D. Welch, pp. 264–285. Southern Illinois University Press, Carbondale.
2007 Dating the Southeastern Ceremonial Complex in Eastern Tennessee. In *Southeastern Ceremonial Complex: Chronology, Content, and Context*, edited by Adam King, pp. 88–106. University of Alabama Press, Tuscaloosa.
2009 Deposing the Chiefdom Model "Monster-God." *Native South*, 2:88–97. (Invited Book Review Forum for *Chiefdoms and Other Archaeological Delusions*, by Thomas R. Pauketat; forum edited by David G. Anderson and R. Ethridge).
2014 What I Believe: Taking Up the Serpents of Social Theory in Southeastern Archaeology. In thematic section "Taking Stock of Social Theory in Southeastern Archaeology," edited by Vernon J. Knight. *Southeastern Archaeology* 33(2):238–245.

Sullivan, Lynne P., and Robert C. Mainfort Jr.
2010 Mississippian Mortuary Practices: The Quest for Interpretations. In *Mississippian Mortuary Practices: Beyond Hierarchy and the Representationist Perspective*, edited by Lynne P. Sullivan and Robert C. Mainfort Jr., pp. 1–13. University Press of Florida, Gainesville.

Sullivan, Lynne P., and Christopher B. Rodning
2001 Gender, Tradition, and Social Negotiation in Southern Appalachian Chiefdoms. In *The Archaeology of Historical Processes: Agency and Tradition before and after Columbus*, edited by Thomas R. Pauketat, pp. 107–120. University Press of Florida, Gainesville.
2011 Residential Burial, Gender Roles, and Political Development in Late Prehistoric and Early Cherokee Cultures of the Southern Appalachians. In *Residential Burial: A Multi-Regional Exploration*, edited by Ron Adams and Stacie King, pp. 79–97. AP3A Series. American Anthropological Association, Washington, D.C.

Stockhammer, Philipp W.
2012 Conceptualizing Cultural Hybridization in Archaeology. In *Conceptualizing Cultural Hybridization: A Transdisciplinary Approach*, edited by Philipp W. Stockhammer, pp. 43–58. New Springer, New York.

Thompson, Claire Elizabeth
2011 Ritual and Power: Examining the Economy of Moundville's Residential Population. Ph.D. dissertation, Department of Anthropology, University of Alabama, Tuscaloosa.

Van Pelt, W. Paul (editor)
2013   *Archaeology and Cultural Mixture.* Archaeological Review from Cambridge Vol. 28. University of Cambridge, Cambridge.

VanValkenburgh, Parker
2013   Hybridity, Creolization, Mestizaje: A Comment. In *Archaeology and Cultural Mixture*, edited by W. Paul Van Pelt, pp. 301–322. Archaeological Review from Cambridge Vol. 28, No. 1. University of Cambridge, Cambridge.

Voss, Barbara L.
2005   From Casta to California: Social Identity and the Archaeology of Culture Contact. *American Anthropologist* 107(3):461–474.

Waring, Antonio J., and Preston Holder
1945   A Prehistoric Ceremonial Complex in the Southeastern United States. *American Anthropologist* 47(1):1–34.

Watts, Christopher
2013   Relational Archaeologies: Roots and Routes. In *Relational Archaeologies: Humans, Animals, Things*, edited by Christopher Watts, pp. 1–20. Routledge, London.

Welch, Paul D.
1986   Models of Chiefdom Economy: Prehistoric Moundville as a Case Study. Ph.D. dissertation, Department of Anthropology, University of Michigan, Ann Arbor.
1990   Mississippian Emergence in West-Central Alabama. *The Mississippian Emergence*, edited by Bruce D. Smith, pp. 1977–225. Smithsonian Institution Press, Washington, D.C.
1991   *Moundville's Economy.* University of Alabama Press, Tuscaloosa.

Wells, E. Christian
2006   Recent Trends in Theorizing Prehispanic Mesoamerican Economies. *Journal of Archaeological Research* 14(4):265–312.

White, Nancy Marie
1982   The Curlee Site (8Ja7) and Fort Walton Development in the Upper Apalachicola-Lower Chattahoochee River Valley, Florida Georgia, Alabama. Unpublished Ph.D. dissertation, Department of Anthropology, Case Western Reserve University, Cleveland.

Whitridge, Peter
2004   Whales, Harpoons, and Other Actors: Actor–Network Theory and Hunter-Gatherer Archaeology. In *Hunters and Gatherers in Theory and Archaeology*, edited by G. M. Crothers, pp. 445–474. Center for Archaeological Investigations, Occasional Paper No. 31. Southern Illinois University, Carbondale.

Willey, Gordon R.
1953   A Pattern of Diffusion-Acculturation. *Southwestern Journal of Anthropology* 9(4):369–384.

Wilson, Gregory
2008   *The Archaeology of Everyday Life at Early Moundville.* University of Alabama Press, Tuscaloosa.
2010   Community, Identity, and Social Memory at Moundville. *American Antiquity* 75(1):3–18
2016   Mounds, Buildings, and Bodies: Long-Term Trends in the Making and Materialization of Mississippian Social Groups at Moundville. In *Rethinking Moundville and Its Hinterland*, edited by Vincas P. Steponaitis and C. Margaret Scarry. University Press of Florida, Gainesville.

Wilson, Gregory D., Jon Bernard Marcoux, and Brad Koldehoff
 2006 Square Pegs in Round Holes: Organizational Diversity between Early Moundville and Cahokia. In *Leadership and Polity in Mississippian Society*, edited by Brian M. Butler and Paul D. Welch, pp. 43–72. Occasional Paper No. 33. Center for Archaeological Investigations, Southern Illinois University, Carbondale.

Wilson, Gregory D., Vincas P. Steponaitis, and Keith P. Jacobi
 2010 Social and Spatial Dimensions of Moundville Mortuary Practices. In *Mississippian Mortuary Practices: Beyond Hierarchy and the Representationist Perspective*, edited by Lynne P. Sullivan and Robert C. Mainfort Jr., pp. 74–89. University Press of Florida, Gainesville.

Young, Robert J. C.
 1995 *Colonial Desire: Hybridity in Theory, Culture, and Race.* Routledge, London.

2

Maize and Mississippian Beginnings

AMBER M. VANDERWARKER, DANA N. BARDOLPH,
AND C. MARGARET SCARRY

The adoption and intensification of maize (*Zea mays*) farming has long been a topic of interest in Mississippian archaeology. At various times throughout the development and definition of "Mississippian" as a cultural tradition, maize has been cast as a central feature of Mississippian adaptation, alongside a suite of other traits that include long-distance exchange, platform mound building, and the development of ranked social systems (see Wilson and Sullivan, this volume). In (re)considering the topic of Mississippian beginnings, we continue to interrogate the nature of the relationship between maize farming and Mississippian origins. An archaeological review of regional patterns of plant production (archaeobotanical results) and plant consumption (isotopic results) reveals that Mississippians throughout southeastern and midwestern North America produced and consumed maize but varied significantly in their levels of production and consumption (see also Scarry 1993a). Nearly 40 years of research on maize adoption and intensification in the Greater Southeast/Midwest has revealed a significant amount of variability with regard to the timing of maize adoption and intensification, the level of maize reliance (in terms of maize abundance and ubiquity, and also in relation to other significant plant foods), the varieties of maize grown, and the cultivation strategies employed in any given region. Moreover, archaeologists have increasingly realized that maize cultivation practices are best understood within the context of broader plant-food production strategies, including the cultivation of indigenous starchy seed crops (e.g., Fritz and Lopinot 2003; Johannessen 1984, 1993; Lopinot 1992; Scarry 2008).

In this chapter we synthesize the extensive archaeobotanical and isotopic research in the Eastern Woodlands in order to consider the numerous ways in which diverse early Mississippian groups used plant foods (including maize) to negotiate their social, political, and economic relationships, in a time of heightened long-distance interactions between disparate peoples, intensified ritual practices, and the creation of new communities, social identities, and leadership positions. Our goal is to explore how plant use may have fueled interactions across various regions in the Eastern Woodlands during the Mississippian emergence; thus, we present both general and regional findings. More than 20 years have passed since Scarry (1993a) explored regional variability in the timing of both maize intensification and the development of early Mississippian sociopolitical complexity. Regional archaeologies have been fleshed out in greater detail since then, and we now have archaeobotanical data from some regions about which we could only speculate at the time of Scarry's original analysis. Ultimately in this review, we highlight a great deal of variability in plant food production and procurement strategies across the early Mississippian Southeast and Midwest. We draw attention to the importance of situating local processes and sociopolitical histories when considering the role of maize in Mississippian beginnings.

Theorizing Intensive Food Production

An updated picture emerges from the past few decades of archaeobotanical and isotopic research when considering the role(s) of plants in the development of Mississippian societies. Plant cultivation, including intensive maize cultivation, played variable roles in early Mississippian societies, some of which were not necessarily related to hierarchy or aggrandizement. Certainly, evidence from several Mississippian regions has revealed a correlation between the presence of a hierarchical regional polity and evidence for maize intensification at some point during the polity's developmental history (Kidder and Fritz 1993; Lopinot 1992, 1994, 1997; Raymer and Bonhage-Freund 2000; Scarry 1993a, 1993b). Some of the explanations explored for maize intensification include the development of a tributary economy, competitive feasting by aspiring elites, population pressure, and labor trade-offs related to harvesting maize versus starchy seeds (Fritz 2000; Holt et al. 2010; Jackson et al. 2016; Lopinot 1992, 1994; Nassaney 1987; Scarry 1986, 1993a, 1993b; Smith and Cowan 2003; VanDerwarker et al. 2013; Welch and Scarry 1995). Most models for the development of sociopolitical hierarchies in early Mississippian polities rely on emerging elites' ability to control and distribute agricultural surplus (e.g., Welch 1991). However, in the cases of the three largest Mississippian polities that we discuss in this chapter (Cahokia, Moundville, Etowah), intensive plant food production (whether maize or indigenous grains) preceded the formation of regional hierarchies. In certain cases, plant food production appears to have been intensified around the same time as the establishment of local and regional political hierarchies (which varied in scale, e.g., the Central Illinois River Valley and the Central Mississippi Valley), and in other cases, political complexity emerged in the context of wild food procurement (e.g., the Lower Mississippi Valley). That these various scenarios could occur throughout the Eastern Woodlands within the same general time frame indicates that complex forms of social organization are not prerequisites for the intensification of food production (*sensu* Ford 1985a:14; see also Buikstra and Milner 1991; Gremillion 2003).

As noted by Scarry (1993a:88; see also Johannessen 1993; Lopinot 1992), rather than having a causal role in the emergence of social hierarchies, changes in plant food cultivation likely were embedded in the changing social relations that eventually led to the development of those hierarchies. In situations where the intensification of plant food production preceded regional political consolidation, aspiring groups appear to have been able to leverage surplus food for political gain, investing in ceremonial feasts and crafting (e.g., at Moundville, see Scarry 1993a:88). However, it is important to emphasize the role of preexisting local kinship systems in relation to subsistence labor and resource allocation, which would have put a ceiling on the ability of any group to mobilize a surplus for purely political purposes (see Cobb 1993:47). At large centers like Cahokia, Moundville, and Etowah, plant food intensification may not have been orchestrated by those aspiring to *create* political hierarchies; rather, it likely occurred in the contexts of larger social/religious negotiations. The political dimensions of intensified food production that occurred in the Early Mississippian period were probably pursued alongside traditionally acceptable parameters (including ritual events) but ultimately reached an exaggerated scale, resulting in unintended consequences for the participants involved (see Pauketat 2000a, 2000b).

Food surpluses (made possible through intensive cultivation) are often used to support larger social and ritual events, in addition to funding large building/monument constructions and feeding larger, more sedentary populations. Many scholars emphasize the political and economic roles of prominent types of ritual negotiation—feasts—in creating and reinforcing power and status differences (e.g., Blitz 1993; Dietler 2001; Phillips and Sebastian 2004; Pollock 2003; VanDerwarker 1999; Wiessner and Schiefenhövel 1998; Welch and Scarry 1995). While some early Mississippian peoples certainly engaged in hierarchical negotiations involving foodways (including large-scale feasting events) to emphasize power or status differences, others likely participated in commensal events that reinforced shared group identities and traditions (see Maxham 2000, 2004; Pollock 2012; Potter 2000; Potter and Ortman 2004; Scarry et al. 2016; Wilson et al., this volume). Neither scenario is mutually exclusive; attempts at increasing solidarity within communities and emphasizing differences among their members through commensal activities likely happened simultaneously in the formation of early Mississippian societies (see VanDerwarker et al. 2016 for recent review of plant foods and commensal politics in the paleoethnobotanical literature).

The myriad ways in which people produced and used plants (including maize) during the early Mississippian period indicate a complex relationship among people, plants, power, status, economy, ritual, tradition making, and community formation that is best understood within a region's particular sociopolitical history. There are several key details that should be examined with respect to understanding the diverse roles of plant cultivation in Mississippian beginnings. Thus, in the remainder of this chapter, we consider several issues, including: the timing of adoption and intensification of maize in the greater Southeast and Midwest; how regional patterns of adoption and intensification have been interpreted; variability in the abundance and ubiquity of maize (both within and between regions); and cultivation strategies. Following this overview, we present a region-by-region discussion that places the role of plant cultivation within the region's broader sociopolitical context. While we would like to consider all of the regions included as case studies in this volume, we are necessarily limited to those regions that have produced a good record of archaeobotanical and/or isotopic data. In addition, due to constraints on space, we have not incorporated a review of the Mississippian polities that emerged in Florida (e.g., Fort Walton) or the Tennessee/Kentucky Cumberland region into our broader discussion. Nor do we address similar developments in the Caddo or Fort Ancient regions, although these areas share broad similarities with contemporaneous Mississippian societies and are presented as cases in this volume (see Cook and Price 2015; Cook, this volume; Du Vernay and White, this volume; Reigner, this volume).

It is important to keep in mind that while Mississippian groups all grew maize to some extent, maize itself is not a necessary and sufficient criterion for identifying Mississippian as a cultural category. Maize production and consumption in southeastern and midwestern North America were not restricted to Mississippian societies, as there is clear evidence of adjacent culture groups (e.g., Caddo, Fort Ancient) adopting and intensifying maize alongside their Mississippian neighbors, along with more distant peoples (e.g., Puebloan, Algonquian) throughout the continental United States. Moreover, wild plant foraging and hunting continued to remain important subsistence strategies alongside plant cultivation throughout the Southeast and Midwest. However, the introduction and intensification of maize in combination with other native cultigens had profound implications for early Mississippian groups, resulting in major changes in labor and scheduling (largely tied to the growing season), ties to/organization of the landscape, gender roles, and more (Scarry 2008; Simon 2014).

Situating Maize in the Eastern Woodlands

Recent microbotanical research has documented the presence of maize phytoliths in New York State as early as 300 BC, and even earlier in Michigan, between 400–350 BC (Hart et al. 2012; Raviele 2010).[1] Recent findings from Quebec have returned similar dates (circa 400–200 BC) for maize phytoliths (St-Pierre and Thompson 2015). Until recently, the earliest directly dated *macro* maize remains (170 BC.–AD. 60) were thought to come from the Middle Woodland Holding site in the American Bottom region of western Illinois (Riley et al. 1994). However, this purported maize kernel recovered from Holding has recently been stripped of its taxonomic status as maize; recent carbon isotope analysis has returned a $\delta^{13}C$ value inconsistent with typical maize values (Simon 2017, personal communication). Given the new status on the Holding "maize" specimen, the earliest macro maize remains now appear to come from several sites in Tennessee (Jernigan II, Ewell III, and Icehouse Bottom), dating between 200 BC and AD 200 (Crites 1978; Chapman and Crites 1987; see also Riley et al. 1990). There is a general consensus that maize was imported into the Eastern Woodlands from the American Southwest (Ford 1981, 1985a, 1985b; Fritz 2000; Hart 1999; but see Riley 1987 and Riley et al. 1990 for a contrasting view), making its way across the Plains and into the Midwest via native exchange networks (Ford 1981, 1985b). This process of maize introduction must have occurred many times (Ford 1981; Hart 1999; see also Lusteck 2006). A small handful of seeds from a single southwestern maize population would not contain a representative sample of the founding population's genetic diversity, resulting in a founder effect in the introduced sample (Hart 1999: 149–150). According to Hart (1999:152–153), this phenomenon, coupled with new environmental/growing conditions, would have resulted in a high rate of failure among founding maize populations because of inbreeding depression, which leads to significant decreases in yields. Based on this population genetics perspective, Hart (1999) argues that maize would have had to have been introduced repeatedly to overcome bottlenecks that limited the range of genetic diversity with each introduction (see also Simon 2014). Thus, it should be expected that maize would be represented across the Eastern Woodlands by multiple lineages and varieties (Hart 1999). Indeed, a recent pilot study by Lusteck (2006) of maize phytoliths sampled from artifacts recovered throughout the Southeast has identified a minimum of two different maize lineages, with the implication that more will likely be recognized once a larger sample is analyzed. There is also abundant macrobotanical evidence of at least two different varieties grown during the Mississippian period (see below).

Most researchers argue that maize was added as a dietary supplement to existing subsistence regimes (e.g., Parker and Scott 2003; Reber and Evershed 2004), a conclusion supported by the significant lag between maize's introduction into the Eastern Woodlands (circa 400 BC to AD 200) and its elevation to staple status (post–AD 900 [see Fritz 1992]). A variety of explanations have been offered to account for why native southeastern groups initially adopted maize, and for why there was a 600–700-year period following its introduction during which it remained relatively marginal in the diet. Ford (1981, 1985a) originally proposed that maize entered the broader region as simply another garden crop added to the existing starchy seed complex that served as additional insurance against the failure of seasonal nut mast and periodic hunts. Fritz (2000:231) reiterates this perspective by characterizing maize's adoption as part of a risk reduction strategy that included food production as a means to increase contributions to seasonal food storage.

However, a recent study by Mary Simon (2014) involving direct dating of maize remains from pre-Mississippian contexts throughout the American Bottom and the Illinois Valley has revealed that, with very few exceptions, these macro maize fragments are much more recent than originally presumed, postdating AD 900. These findings strongly suggest that maize use prior to AD 900 was minimal, confined to less than a handful of sites in the broader Midwest and Southeast, and was not "part of any Late Woodland subsistence economies in [the Midwestern] region" (Simon 2014:119; see also Smith 1989). One of the outcomes of Simon's study is the finding that maize was not gradually incorporated into the diet over a long period of time; rather, it was rapidly adopted into early midwestern Mississippian economies, where it quickly became a dietary staple.

The lag between maize's initial introduction (based on the phytolith data) and its intensification is less well understood. Fritz (1992:29) argues that maize would have required a gradual period of adaptation to local growing conditions before producing sufficient yields to warrant intensification, and that it is this period of adjustment that accounts for the lag between when maize was initially adopted and when it was later intensified. Hart's (1999) discussion of repeated introductions of maize to overcome genetic bottlenecks (see above) dovetails well with Fritz's argument. Another interpretation for this lag has been offered by Scarry (1993a:90), who suggests that early maize was a sacred food, and thus its limited spread and abundance in some archaeological contexts for hundreds of years may reflect the intentional restriction of its usage (but see Lopinot 1997). Scarry (1993a:90) argues that most Eastern Woodlands contexts in which early maize remains are found are associated with exotic/ritual objects or in areas of ceremonial importance, such as mounds or plazas (see also Johannessen 1993). There is no reason to think that these two explanations (time needed for maize to reach a productive threshold in a given environment and maize as ritually significant) are incompatible. Certainly there were biological and environmental constraints related to early maize production, and undoubtedly maize also acquired complex and varied cultural meanings within the regions into which it was adopted. Simon (2014) suggests that it may be problematic to attribute ritual significance to maize until well after it became a major dietary staple, at least in the lower Midwest; she argues that "Late Woodland people, without a long tradition of growing and relying on [maize], would not have viewed maize as the 'corn-mother,' unless that concept arrived with the plant" (Simon 2014:121). Nevertheless, it is possible that maize's very *newness* may have contributed to its early ritual status.

Regardless of the timing of *initial maize adoption*, it is clear that maize started to become a *significant component* of regional subsistence economies in the lower Midwest and the Southeast sometime after AD 900, corresponding with the development of Mississippian societies. As discussed above, the growing body of research focused on maize and Mississippian societies has made it increasingly clear that explanations for the presence and intensification of maize in areas of political development cannot be generalized for all cases and instead must be evaluated on a region-by-region basis. In addition to the timing of adoption and intensification, other factors relating to maize production (e.g., varieties grown and cultivation strategies) also varied by region. Scarry and Scarry's (2005; see also Scarry 1993b) review of southeastern ethnohistory as it pertains to native farming reveals that most groups grew at least three different varieties of maize with different maturation rates (Fritz 1990, 1992; Scarry 1994)—farmers grew both flour and flint varieties, which were used for different purposes (e.g., eaten green, dried and stored, ground into flour, processed into hominy). Cultivation strategies also varied by village and region in terms of scale/organization of production. Ethnohistoric evidence (Hann 1986; Hudson 1976; Swanton 1946) and biomechanical skeletal markers of (possible) hoeing and pounding (Bridges 1991) indicate that women were the primary food producers, in terms of both farming and food preparation (see Scarry and Scarry 2005 for summary). At contact, southeastern farmers practiced poly-cultivation of maize, beans, and squash using an extensive shifting field strategy that varied in scale, including some rather expansive farming systems (Scarry 2008:396; Scarry and Scarry 2005:206). Native cultigens (e.g., starchy and oily seeds) were most likely planted in dense, pure stands or in discrete zones within fields or gardens, depending on the scale of production (Scarry 2008:398). Farmers practiced a dual strategy of production/storage for both the household and the community, but the implementation of this strategy varied from group to group; for example, some groups might have cultivated family fields and communal fields while others may have simply cultivated a single set of fields and set aside a portion of the produce for storage in community larders (Scarry 2008:396; Scarry and Scarry 2005:263–264).

Although ethnohistoric documents provide interpretive richness not available to us archaeologically, it is important to remember that the observations recorded therein were made hundreds of years after maize became a primary staple in the diets of native southeastern groups. We must be cautious not to simply ascribe contact period production strategies to early Mississippians. Archaeologically, we can document regional variation in the abundance and ubiquity of maize (using standard density and ubiquity measures) as well as the overall dietary importance (using stable carbon isotopes and comparative ratios of maize relative to other plants). Although we are limited to these particular lines of reconstruction during the late prehistoric period, the ethnohistoric evidence reminds us that these archaeological signatures reflect broader cultural and economic patterns regarding the organization of production in both fields and villages. With these issues in mind, we shift our focus to the regional level, beginning with the Mississippi Valley, then moving south and east. Our goal is to explore regional variation in maize production in order to identify commonalities and dissimilarities that allow us to better understand connections between the intensification of food production and the shifts to sociopolitical complexity documented throughout the early Mississippian world.

Regional Patterns of Maize Adoption and Intensification

In synthesizing current information on regional patterns of maize use from the Eastern Woodlands, we focus primarily on archaeobotanical and isotopic data, as well as on the interpretations researchers have drawn from these data. Besides highlighting variation between regions of the greater Midwest and Southeast (see Figure 1.1), we call attention to the significant intraregional variation that has been observed by scholars. We document current understanding for: (1) when maize was adopted; (2) if and when maize was intensified; and (3) the overall contribution of maize to the diet, situating maize use within each region's specific social, economic, environmental and/or political circumstances. It is important to keep in mind that some regions have been investigated more thoroughly than others, resulting in a patchy coverage of these issues in some cases.

The American Bottom

We begin our survey in the American Bottom region of southwestern Illinois, the area with the earliest manifestations of Mississippian culture and agricultural intensification. The American Bottom is also home to Cahokia, the largest and most complex Mississippian polity in terms of population size, areal coverage, and sociopolitical organization, whose ritualism, religion, and sociopolitical milieu had a deep impact on surrounding groups. The American Bottom witnessed periods of rapid social transformation in the two and a half centuries between AD 800 and AD 1050, as small-scale and relatively mobile horticultural groups transitioned to life in sedentary villages committed to plant cultivation (Kelly 1990a, 1990b). An influx of locals and nonlocal immigrants from villages and hamlets into mound centers during the ninth and tenth centuries, combined with a greater investment in plant cultivation, appears to have contributed to a regional population increase (Pauketat 1998, 2004:58–59). Indeed, recent strontium isotope analyses confirm the presence of a large number of immigrants from multiple locations who moved into the greater Cahokian area (Slater et al. 2014). By the latter half of the Terminal Late Woodland period (AD 800–1050), a few villages had as many as 200 residents living in groups of small, flexed-pole structures arranged around courtyards (Kelly 1990a, 1990b). The Mississippian political order that emerged in the greater Cahokian area during the eleventh century entailed a number of sweeping organizational changes (Pauketat 1994:171–74). Social life, political organization, and religious beliefs were radically transformed as Terminal Late Woodland villages were abandoned throughout the region and large population centers were founded during the Lohmann phase (AD 1050–1100) (Pauketat 1997:31–32). These centers were home to chiefly leaders and ritual specialists who wielded considerable decision-making authority in the new regional hierarchy. Conservative estimates suggest a more than sevenfold population increase at Cahokia during the Terminal Late Woodland to the Early Mississippian transition, from nearly 1,500 to more than 10,000 people (Pauketat and Lopinot 1997:118). Considering the many other multi-mound and single-mound sites, besides villages and farmsteads occupied at this time, the total early Mississippian population size must have been staggering.

This region has been subject to a significant amount of archaeological research, including archaeobotanical and isotopic analyses, making it one of the best-documented Mississippian societies in the Eastern Woodlands. Indeed, Simon and Parker (2006) published a synthesis of archaeobotanical evidence from the American Bottom that includes data from more than 100 sites, a sample size that far outstrips any other region in the broader Mississippian world. As mentioned above, Simon's (2017) recent direct dating of early maize has demonstrated that most purported early specimens actually postdate AD 900. Even more recently, isotopic analysis of the earliest purported macro maize kernel in the region, from the Middle Woodland Holding site, has revealed that this specimen is not actually maize (Simon 2016, personal communication). Previously, researchers used the Holding "maize" kernel to suggest maize's introduction into the region between 179 cal BC and 62 cal AD (Riley et al. 1994; Stuiver and Reimer 1993;see also Fritz and Lopinot 2003; Simon 2000). Prior to Simon's (2014) dating study, the scholarly consensus was that the region witnessed a significant increase in maize abundance and ubiquity during the end of the Late Woodland period (AD 750–900) (Fritz 2000; Fritz and Lopinot 2003; Johannessen 1993; Lopinot 1994; Myers 2006; Simon and Parker 2006). Maize was thought to be a common element in the Late Woodland diet, although scholars argued that maize did not replace or eclipse the existing pattern of starchy seed consumption—rather, it was thought to have been adopted, grown and eaten alongside native starchy and oily seeds (Fritz and Lopinot 2003; Johannessen 1993; Lopinot 1994; Parker and Scott 2003; Reber and Evershed 2004; Scarry 1993a; Simon and Parker 2006).

Based on Simon's (2014) meticulous analysis and dating of presumably Late Woodland maize, we now know that maize did not become a common dietary element until the Terminal Late Woodland period (AD 900–1050), when regional farmers intensified agricultural production of starchy seeds and added maize as a significant staple crop (see also Parker and Scott 2003; Simon and Parker 2006). Macrobotanical data suggest that starchy seeds were more important to the diet than was maize, at least initially (Galloy et al. 2000; Johannessen 1993; Lopinot 1992). Indeed, the importance of nut mast declined significantly as the cultivation of starchy seeds increased toward the end of the Late Woodland period (Galloy et al. 2000; Holt et al. 2011; Lopinot 1994:135; Scarry 2003c; but see Parker and Scott 2003). Nevertheless, stable isotope data do indicate a significant shift toward maize consumption during this time (Buikstra and Milner 1991). It bears noting that maize use appears to have changed very little during the Mississippian transition in this region (Buikstra and Milner 1991; Simon and Parker 2006), suggesting that the intensification of maize preceded the development of the Cahokia polity (see also Lopinot 1992; Johannessen 1993; Scarry 1993a). Farmers, however, continued to intensify their production of starchy seeds during the emergence and consolidation of the Cahokia polity around AD 1050, which is particularly apparent at the site of Cahokia proper (Lopinot 1992, 1994).

American Bottom farmers likely produced several crops per year in a staggered fashion, a practice referred to as multi-cropping (see Lopinot 1994:135). The starchy seed complex includes species that have both spring (maygrass [*Phalaris caroliniana*] and little barley [*Hordeum pusillum*]) and fall harvests (chenopod or goosefoot [*Chenopodium berlandieri* ssp. *jonesianum*] and erect knotweed [*Polygonum erectum*]). In addition to starchy seeds, farmers were growing two or more varieties of maize (Fritz 1992; Simon and Parker 2006), which probably had different rates of maturation, resulting in both summer and fall harvests. Lopinot (1994:135) argues convincingly for intensive field cultivation of starchy seeds, on par with the scale of maize cultivation observed at contact. The average abundance of starchy seeds at early Mississippian Lohmann phase (AD 1050–1100) sites is approximately 75 percent of the recovered macro-seeds (see Simon and Parker 2006: Table 12). Given that starchy seeds compose three-quarters of the typical plant assemblage, it is unlikely that they were grown in small house gardens. Indeed, a consideration of the plants' growing requirements, modern methods of cultivation, and the archaeological data suggests that starchy seeds were broadcast by hand in dense stands (Scarry 2008:397). The American Bottom case differs significantly from the other regional cases in terms of the scale and diversity of its agricultural regime. Although there are regions in which farmers cultivated native grains alongside maize (Lower Illinois Valley, Lower Mississippi Valley, and northwestern Georgia), it is only in the American Bottom that farmers emphasized starchy seeds over maize. Given the population estimates for the Cahokia site and the broader American Bottom region (see Pauketat and Lopinot 1997), the number and size of agricultural fields under cultivation during an annual growing season must have been impressive.

The predominance of starchy seeds in typical early Mississippian assemblages has led Fritz and Lopinot (2003:91; see also Lopinot 1997) to question what they refer to as a "zeacentric bias" within studies of early Mississippian agriculture. Indeed, the first wave of agricultural intensification in the American Bottom was based on increases in starchy seed production, which occurred prior to regional political consolidation. If agricultural surplus was the basis for underwriting Cahokia's emergent economy, then it was a surplus of *starchy seeds,* not maize, that was the source of funds. When maize was intensified, it was after Cahokia had become a regional polity, and it was intensified alongside the native crops (Fritz and Lopinot 2003). It was not until that point in the polity's history that cultivation strategies would have changed, resulting in adjustments in labor and scheduling as planting strategies shifted from broadcast sowing to hilling, and the timing of planting and harvesting changed (Scarry 2008:397). Cooking strategies would have changed with intensification of maize as well, as maize was most likely roasted or boiled for hominy production (Briggs 2016; King 1987; Myers 2006:514). Indeed, it has been observed that macro-maize assemblages from the broader Mississippian region are often composed of a substantial proportion of complete kernels lacking their germs, which is indicative of hominy production (Dezendorf 2013; Goette et al. 1994; King 1987, 1994).

Maize does not appear to have been imbued with ritual or ceremonial significance as some scholars have speculated (e.g., Scarry 1993a), at least not in the American Bottom. Evidence from sub-Mound 51 at the Cahokia site, which has been convincingly argued to represent the remains of feasting (see Pauketat et al. 2002), indicates that starchy seeds and fleshy fruits were more integral to elite-sponsored ritual events than was maize (Fritz and Lopinot 2003:105). Moreover, stable isotope data from the American Bottom and neighboring regions indicate that maize was less important at Cahokia than in the Illinois River Valley during the period immediately preceding Cahokia's Lohmann phase consolidation (Bender et al. 1981; Buikstra and Milner 1991). In addition, at the site of Cahokia proper, a comparison of elite and non-elite individuals from the Mound 72 burial population dating to the Lohmann phase (AD 1050–1100) revealed that elites consumed less maize than non-elites (Ambrose et al. 2003). Together, these lines of evidence strongly suggest that maize was not held in particular esteem as a high-status or ritually important food in the greater American Bottom region.

Thus, while maize-based agriculture is often considered a hallmark of Mississippian societies, we can question the role of maize in Mississippian *beginnings*— maize does not appear to have been a significant resource in the American Bottom until after the period of political consolidation. Ultimately, maize was incorporated into a longer history of social and religious negotiations involving plant foods (including fleshy fruits and starchy seeds) in which surplus production aided in the support of craftspeople and the fueling of community events that simultaneously reinforced status differences and community cohesion.

Illinois River Valley

We now turn to the Illinois River Valley, a fairly broad region that includes several areas of occupation inhabited by distinct cultural groups, including the Central Illinois River Valley (CIRV) and the Lower Illinois River Valley (LIRV). The Central and Lower Illinois valleys are contiguous and extend from the northern limits of the American Bottom northward to present-day Hennepin, Illinois (see Figure 1.1). The modern town of Meredosia marks the boundary between the Lower Valley to the south and the Central Valley to the north. Political development occurred on a much smaller scale in the Illinois Valley than in the American Bottom; there were no regionally consolidated polities, and different settlement areas appear to have been politically autonomous, perhaps organized as several small, competing polities (see Conrad 1991).

In the Central Illinois River Valley, in the Terminal Late Woodland period, most people lived in small, dispersed settlements in portions of the valley and western uplands (Esarey 2000:398; Green and Nolan 2000:362). However, the presence of village-sized settlements on natural levees and floodplain ridges indicates an emerging focus on the valley's riverine environment (Esarey 2000:392). Mississippian groups from the American Bottom began interacting with Terminal Late Woodland groups in the CIRV around AD 1050 (Conrad 1989, 1991; Harn 1991; McConaughy et al. 1993). Recent research in the Illinois Valley has demonstrated that small groups of Cahokians made contact with Late Woodland (AD 1000–1100) and Early Mississippian (AD 1100–1150) groups, bringing with them the trappings of Cahokia-inspired ritual practices, including Mississippian ceremonial buildings, mounds, and mortuary practices, as well as finely crafted Cahokia-style artifacts, including Ramey Incised pots and copper ornaments (Bardolph 2014; Conrad 1989, 1991; Harn 1991; Wilson et al., this volume). The purpose and extent of this contact is still unclear, but the result was the rapid Mississippianization of local Late Woodland groups during the subsequent Early Mississippian period (AD 1100–1200). Early Mississippian settlement patterns consist of dispersed villages and small nodal ceremonial sites (Conrad 1989:100, 1991:131; Harn 1991:141). Based on the uneven distribution of elaborate artifacts interred with early Mississippian burials, Conrad (1991:130) has argued for the development of hierarchical social organization at this time. Social ranking appears not to have resulted in regional political consolidation, but rather in the emergence of two or more localized settlement hierarchies.

In the Lower Illinois River Valley, Terminal Late Woodland settlements were located along the Illinois River floodplains and its tributaries, with some small occupations in the uplands (Cross and Bittinger 1996; Studenmund 2000; Studenmund et al. 1995). The Mississippian transition is marked by a shift toward larger villages, of which two have been identified (Audrey and Whiteside), paired with cemeteries (Delaney-Rivera 2000, 2004; see also Wilson et al., this volume). In addition to these two villages were more than 30 smaller farmsteads. Although we lack a clear understanding of sociopolitical organization in the LIRV, it is clear that the population size and scale of complexity were much reduced here in comparison to the neighboring American Bottom. Indeed, any emerging political hierarchies likely did not surpass the village level.

Late Woodland residents of both the CIRV and LIRV were engaged in the cultivation of starchy seeds prior to the introduction of maize, but at very difference scales. Whereas starchy-seed densities at Late Woodland CIRV sites are low to moderate (Simon 2000; VanDerwarker et al. 2013), data from the LIRV are more comparable to the American Bottom (Simon 2000). Indeed, Late Woodland residents of the LIRV may have practiced intensive starchy seed cultivation, an inference suggested by the several large seed masses recovered from sites in this region—some of which have seeds numbering in the thousands to tens of thousands from individual features (Asch and Asch 1978; Simon 2000). Thus, maize was added to two very different food production/procurement strategies, an existing system of intensive cultivation in the LIRV versus a more mixed system of foraging/gardening in the CIRV.

Prior to Simon's (2014) intensive program of direct-dating early maize, Illinois Valley scholars had documented the presence of maize in various Late Woodland contexts dating between AD 300 and 800.[2] The results of Simon's (2014) research have revealed that only two sites in west-central Illinois (Elledge and Edward Hoerner) with purported Late Woodland maize actually returned dates of that age (pre–AD 900); all other maize fragments from Late Woodland sites returned more recent dates (post–AD 900) (Simon 2014: 111). As in the American Bottom, it appears that maize use in the Illinois Valley was spotty and rare during the Late Woodland period, becoming more widespread after AD 900 during the end of the period (see also Esarey et al. 2000; Green 1987; McConaughy et al. 1993; Schroeder 2000). Thus, our understanding of maize's entry into this region has changed significantly.

Our evidence for Early Mississippian maize in the Illinois Valley is much more limited than what we have for the American Bottom. Data from the LIRV suggest that a program of intensive maize cultivation was already under way by AD 1000, with maize added to an existing system of intensive production, similar to that of the American Bottom (Asch and Asch 1985:183, 187; King

1993; see also Simon 2000). In the CIRV, maize was fairly unimportant until around AD 1050, when maize densities increased dramatically, signaling a shift toward intensive production. Unlike in the American Bottom and the LIRV, however, this increase in maize *occurred at the expense* of starchy seeds (VanDerwarker et al. 2013; see also Kuehn and Blewitt 2013). Indeed, it is difficult to be certain whether people in the Early Mississippian CIRV cultivated starchy seeds or simply managed wild stands. The most abundant starchy seed species are chenopods and knotweeds, but none of the knotweeds are consistent with domesticated erect knotweed, and the few chenopods that retained their seed coats do not exhibit the truncated margins consistent with domesticated varieties (VanDerwarker et al. 2013). And while the presence of maygrass and little barley alongside the knotweed and chenopod seeds suggests the possibility that these seeds were cultivated, this inference is by no means certain. Despite the apparent decrease in starchy seeds, the only statistical changes in the archaeobotanical record of the CIRV between the Late Woodland and Early Mississippian periods are an increase in maize and a corresponding decrease in nuts (VanDerwarker et al. 2013). Thus, the intensification of maize in the CIRV occurred *during* the Early Mississippian period, in contrast to the American Bottom and LIRV where it occurred earlier, during the preceding Terminal Late Woodland period. Similar to the American Bottom, however, is a significant decline in nuts.

The available stable isotope data from the Illinois Valley lend support to the inferences drawn from the archaeobotanical data. Based on skeletal data from Dickson Mounds, Buikstra and Milner (1991) demonstrate an increase in maize consumption from Late Woodland to Early Mississippian times. Combined, the archaeobotanical and isotopic data indicate that maize was a significant component of the diets of Mississippians living in the Illinois Valley. Indeed, Illinois Valley farmers may have produced and consumed as much as or more maize than their American Bottom neighbors to the south (Bardolph 2012; Buikstra and Milner 1991). Regardless of whether or not Illinois Valley groups grew and ate more maize than farmers residing in the American Bottom, it is clear that American Bottom farmers (and possibly LIRV farmers) had a more complicated production system than groups living in the Central Illinois Valley, as evidenced by the many different starchy crops they grew (maize, chenopod, erect knotweed, maygrass, little barley).

While explanations for maize intensification occurring in the Illinois Valley are still being developed, it is clear that maize was intensified in the absence of a well-developed political hierarchy or a regionally consolidated polity (VanDerwarker et al. 2013; see also Emerson et al. 2005). In addition, regional population levels remained fairly low throughout the Mississippian period, hindering arguments that might invoke population pressure. Maize intensification appears to have occurred earlier in the Lower Valley than in the Central Valley, which Simon (2000:54) attributes to its proximity to the American Bottom. If proximity to the American Bottom is indeed a factor in explaining the timing of maize intensification in the LIRV, then it is interesting that maize was intensified in the CIRV at the same time that Cahokians entered this region. Indeed, it is plausible that maize cultivation intensified as a result of Cahokian contact, perhaps within the context of competitive generosity (VanDerwarker et al. 2013). The fact that intensification of maize in the Illinois Valley occurred in the context of cultural exchange with the American Bottom (where it had already been intensified) suggests that intensive maize production may have been incorporated into societies involved in Mississippian culture contact as part of a complete Mississippian "package"—a suite of objects, ideas, and ideologies that had been previously negotiated at Cahokia and in the American Bottom as part of the process of Mississippianization that was later spread throughout the Southeast and Midwest. Ongoing research programs in the Illinois Valley will further refine our understanding of Mississippian development in this Cahokian hinterland.

Central Mississippi Valley

The Central Mississippi Valley is the region situated to the immediate south and west of the American Bottom that includes the Mississippi River alluvial valley and the eastern Ozarks of southern Missouri and Northern Arkansas (see Figure 1.1). This region has been conceptualized as the "heartland" of Mississippian emergence (Pauketat 2000b:21; see Smith 1984); however, the tempo and extent of social change during the Late Woodland/Mississippian transition is still debated. As with the Illinois Valley, the Central Mississippi Valley encompasses several subregions, and research within and among these areas has been patchy (O'Brien and Wood 1998; see also McNutt 1996). In general, the transition from the Late Woodland to the Early Mississippian period was marked by settlement shifts from small, dispersed seasonal household occupations to larger, nucleated, permanent settlements, as diverse, small-scale communities were forged into larger unified political communities (Dunnell and Feathers 1991; Morse and Morse 1983; O'Brien and Wood 1998:277–278; Pauketat 2000b). After AD 900, more than a dozen large villages were settled throughout southeastern Missouri, some with palisades and mounds (O'Brien and Wood 1998:288). Many of these large sites were likely political centers administering a series of connected villages and farmsteads (O'Brien and Wood 1998:288).

Archaeobotanical data from the Late Woodland Central Mississippi Valley have been summarized by Simon (2000). Data from southern Missouri and northern Arkansas indicate a Late Woodland adaptation of a mixed farming and foraging economy—the entire spectrum of starchy seeds appears to be present at most sites, in addition to fruits and nuts, the latter forming a significant component of the regional diet (Simon 2000; see also Lopinot 1995; Voigt 1989). Maize was absent from the region's cultivation repertoire until Mississippian times, although it has been identified at a site in central Missouri (23Co156) whose radiocarbon dates indicate an occupation dating as early as cal AD 441–603 (Hoard 2000). However, this site also has later occupations, and the maize remains were not directly dated, making it possible that these maize remains date as late as AD 1200 (see also Simon 2014). Other more tightly dated sites indicate the possible presence of maize by AD 700 in the Maramec Springs area (Reeder 2000:196–199) and after AD 900 in northeastern Missouri (Herndon et al. 2014:61). While maize could have been introduced to the region sometime within the AD 400–700 range, without directly dated specimens it seems better to err on the side of caution as advised by Simon (2014). Regardless of when it was introduced, maize does not appear to have been a significant component of the diet before AD 1000 (Martin and Parks 1994). After this time (AD 1050–1200), subsistence appears to have focused on maize and nuts, at least in the lower Missouri River Valley (Wright 2007), similar to the CIRV pattern during the Early Mississippian period.

The importance of starchy seeds during the Early Mississippian, however, seems to vary within the broader Central Mississippi Valley region. In the lower Missouri River Valley along the western periphery of the region, starchy seeds were relatively unimportant in the diet, and their representation declines throughout the occupational sequence (Martin and Parks 1994). Similar to Wright's (2007) observations, starchy seed representation seems to be rather sparse at sites in southeastern Missouri; squash and beans were also generally lacking, suggesting a farming strategy focused primarily around maize cultivation (Martin and Parks 1994). In contrast, Fritz's (1994) analysis of desiccated plant remains from several rockshelters in the Ozarks of southwestern Missouri and northwestern Arkansas reveals a greater emphasis on starchy seeds than documented by Wright (2007) or Martin and Parks (1994). In addition to documenting the persistence of starchy seeds in the diet until AD 1200, she also identified other crop plants, including domesticated sunflower, sumpweed, pale-seeded amaranth, and mixta squash (Fritz 1994). The evidence for domesticated amaranth is especially significant, as amaranth seeds are rarely cited as more than a source of wild weedy greens in the southeastern and midwestern literature (Fritz 1994, 2007b). Fritz (1994:123) argues that starchy-seed cultivation was important as a means of offsetting the risk associated with years of low nut mast, thus highlighting a trade-off between starchy seeds and nuts. The notion of starchy seeds and acorn nuts as cognates for nutritional sources of carbohydrates is relatively common in the literature (see Scarry 2003c). Indeed, in areas where starchy seeds became a significant component of the diet, acorn nuts tend to decline in abundance (e.g., American Bottom); alternately, in areas where starchy seeds are of minimal importance, acorn nuts are identified in great abundance (e.g., Central Illinois River Valley).

Isotopic analysis of human skeletons dating between 3200 BC and AD 1880 reveals that the region's inhabitants consumed virtually no maize prior to AD 1000; if maize was present in the diet prior to this time, then its consumption was limited (Lynott et al. 1986:61). After AD 1000, there was a rapid shift toward maize consumption and, by extension, production (Lynott et al. 1986:61). The reasons for this sudden and significant increase in maize use after AD 1000 have not been fully explored. Lynott and colleagues (1986:62) correlate this shift to maize reliance with regional changes in settlement patterns from dispersed hamlets and small villages to civic-ceremonial centers tied to villages and farmsteads. The implication is that maize was intensified around the same time as the establishment of local and regional political hierarchies, a pattern that differs from the American Bottom region to the northeast. Thus, it is possible in some areas of the Central Mississippi Valley that maize intensification occurred either just prior to regional political development, perhaps in the context of competitive generosity (e.g., King 1985, 1988; Nassaney 1987; Scarry 1993a) or in relation to large-scale community events involving intensified ceremonialism and feasting that would have served to reinforce new shared Mississippian affiliations and identities (e.g., at the Toltec site, where maize was recovered among the feasting debris encountered at the bases of platform mounds [Fritz 2000:238; Rolingson 1998]). Even members of dispersed farmsteads were integrated into commensal events during the process of Mississippianization—Smith (1995:243) observes that members of outlying communities "participated in various village-centered ceremonies, feasts, and other scheduled activities of social integration throughout the annual cycle." Villagers likely continued this level of community participation as they transitioned toward acceptance of a "collective order" (Pauketat 2000b:24), with events presumably articulated by large Mississippian centers. These possibilities, however, require testing with additional data.

Lower Mississippi Valley

The Lower Mississippi Valley (LMV) encompasses southern Arkansas, eastern Louisiana, and western Mississippi (see Figure 1.1; Rees and Livingood 2007). Subregions within the LMV include the Tensas and Yazoo basins, the Natchez Bluffs, and the lower Ouachita and Red River valleys (Rees and Livingood 2007:1). The general trajectory includes a cultural tradition called Coles Creek (AD 750–1200) that spans the Late Woodland and Early Mississippian periods. Plaquemine, the regional variant of Mississippian culture, follows on the heels of Coles Creek and begins later than observed in the American Bottom and adjacent regions to the north, around AD 1200. It was during the latter part of the Coles Creek period that some local groups began adding Mississippian elements (e.g., shell-tempered pottery) to their material culture, although there is a great deal of regional variation regarding the timing of the adoption of Mississippian traits or the intrusion of Mississippian groups. Settlement changes occurred during this time, with a shift toward population aggregation, leading to fewer and larger mound sites by the end of the Coles Creek period (Kidder 1992; Rees and Livingood 2007). It was at this time that scholars argue for the emergence of hereditary social ranking and political centralization in some of the region's emerging polities (Rees and Livingood 2007:14; see also Barker 1999; Kidder 1992, 2002; Steponaitis 1986).

In comparison to the aforementioned regions, the LMV presents a unique pattern of maize adoption and intensification with respect to the timing of Mississippian beginnings. Maize remains are present but exceptionally rare in Early Coles Creek contexts (AD 750–900) in Arkansas (Fritz 1990; Fritz and Kidder 1993; Kidder 1992; see also Scarry 1993a); in the southern portion of the LMV (in Louisiana and Mississippi), maize has not been documented until after AD 900/1000, during the late Coles Creek (AD 1000–1200) at the Bird's Creek, Jolly, Osceola, St. Gabriel, and Rock Levee sites (Fritz 1990, 2007a; Kidder 1992:22; 1993; Lee et al. 1997; Scarry 1995; Woodiel 1993:53–54). In both areas, maize did not achieve dietary importance until after AD 1100/1200, during the Coles Creek/Mississippian transition, well after the expansion of platform mound-building activities, and likely also postdating the initial development of chiefly hierarchies (Fritz 1992, 2007a; Fritz and Kidder 1993; Kidder 1992; Kidder and Fritz 1993; Listi 2011, 2013; Rose et al. 1991; see also Scarry 1993a).

Archaeobotanical evidence indicates that maize was introduced into a subsistence system that was based on the intensive management of wild plants (especially acorns and hickory) and the cultivation of native seed crops, although the scale of starchy-seed cultivation was minimal in comparison to that documented in the American Bottom region to the north (Fritz 2007a; Kassabaum 2014; Kidder and Fritz 1993; Williams 2008). Rose et al. (1991) hypothesize that early uses of maize were restricted to ceremonial and high-status contexts (e.g., Scarry 1993a), arguing that low population levels coupled with high local plant density made widespread cultivation of maize largely unnecessary. Maize grown for religious ceremonies and social events may have been eaten only by certain designated individuals (Rose et al. 1991:20) and perhaps only in some portions of the Lower Valley, whereas the majority of LMV residents were actively engaged in tree management of oak, hickory, pecan, and persimmon trees (Fritz 2007a). Evidence for small-scale cultivation of starchy seeds to complement the reliance on tree resources comes from the Coles Creek mound site at Feltus in the Natchez Bluffs, where domesticated forms of chenopod are found alongside a rich assemblage of wild plant foods (Kassabaum 2014). It is possible that wild plant foods, made more abundant through direct human management, provided a solid economic base for funding community projects such as mound construction (Kassabaum 2014; Williams 2008). Indeed, it was not until after the Coles Creek period, hundreds of years after the appearance of communal mound centers, that maize cultivation became a significant subsistence activity (Fritz 1992, 2007a; Kidder 1992; Kidder and Fritz 1993).

Bioarchaeological evidence provides additional support to the inferences drawn from the archaeobotanical data (Listi 2011, 2013; Rose et al. 1991). Changes in dental health reveal a shift toward a slightly greater consumption of starchy foods with the shift to Coles Creek after AD 750, which Listi (2011:37–38; see also Rose et al. 1991) argues to reflect greater use of starchy seeds in the diet. This interpretation is supported by stable isotope analysis, which indicates a clear lack of maize in the Coles Creek diet, as seen at the Lake George site in the Yazoo Basin of western Mississippi (Listi 2013:120–121). Despite the lack of a C_4 signature, the Lake George skeletal population revealed clear dental evidence for a diet high in starchy foods (Listi 2013:121), likely represented by the consumption of acorns or plants from the native starchy seed complex. This inference is also supported by paleopathology studies of Coles Creek skeletons that found very limited evidence for porotic hyperostosis, a condition commonly associated with maize-dependent diets (Rose et al. 1991:14–15).

While the timing of the adoption and intensification of maize has been fairly well documented in the Lower Mississippi Valley, our understanding of the social and political contexts of these dietary shifts is less developed than in other regions. The shift to maize dependence has been characterized by Fritz (2007a:205) as accompanying "the opening up of previously inward-looking societies, more interactions than before with increasingly powerful Mississippian polities to the east, and a radical shift in settlement patterning with larger Plaquemine mound centers surrounded by smaller farmsteads." This statement suggests that the shift to maize dependence was correlated with the ramping up of incipient political complexity in the region, possibly stimulated by extraregional interaction with other Mississippian groups (e.g., Moundville in west-central Alabama). Yet others (Rose et al. 1991:20) argue that the shift to maize dependence resulted from regional population pressure, in which Coles Creek groups expanded beyond the limits of the wild food resource base; this argument, however, is difficult to evaluate, as we have virtually no data from non-mound contexts at Coles Creek sites. Ongoing and future archaeological projects in this region will allow us to more critically assess these different causal interpretations for maize intensification in the Lower Mississippi River Valley.

Black Warrior Valley

This region includes Moundville and its broader hinterland in west-central Alabama, but we also refer to data from the Bottle Creek site, located in southern Alabama along the Mobile Delta (see Figure 1.1). The Moundville polity emerged from a Terminal Late Woodland period occupation known as the West Jefferson phase (AD 1020–1120). The West Jefferson settlement system consisted of small villages ranging from .2 to .5 ha in size scattered along the floodplain terraces and adjacent uplands of the Black Warrior River Valley (Bozeman 1982; Welch 1990:211). There is little evidence of social inequality at this time; however, a significant increase in the manufacture of marine shell beads has been interpreted as evidence of factional competition among kin-based residential groups through the production and exchange of exotic wealth items (Knight and Steponaitis 1998:11; Pope 1989).

The early Moundville I phase (AD 1120–1200) marks the emergence of Mississippian culture in the Black Warrior River Valley. In the first decades of the twelfth century AD, a suite of highly visible and sudden changes in settlement patterns, community organization, and material culture occurred. Small-scale village life in the region was abandoned for a settlement system consisting primarily of dispersed farmsteads and small ceremonial centers with earthen platform mounds (Ensor 1993; Knight and Steponaitis 1998:12–13; Michals 1998; Mistovich 1988). Several autonomous hierarchical political groups may have existed in the region at this time.

The late Moundville I phase (AD 1200–1260) marks the establishment of

Moundville as a regionally consolidated Mississippian polity (Knight and Steponaitis 1998:14–17). The dynamics of regional consolidation transformed socioeconomic relationships throughout the Black Warrior River Valley. A regional administrative center was established at the Moundville site, where an estimated 1,050–1,680 residents settled to form a nucleated community (Steponaitis 1998:42; Wilson 2008). The Moundville ceremonial precinct was constructed during this era, which involved the erection of at least 29 mounds arranged around a rectangular plaza (Knight 1992, 1998).

Maize was adopted into a Late Woodland subsistence system based primarily on the collection of nuts and other wild plants—starchy-seed cultivation was relatively unimportant in this region, likely limited to small garden plots (Scarry 1986, 1993a, 1993b). Scarry's analysis of plant remains from Moundville and surrounding sites has revealed that the initial intensification of maize occurred prior to the establishment of the Moundville polity, during the transition from the early to late West Jefferson phase (AD 900–1050) [Scarry 1986, 1993a, 1993b]. After its initial increase during the Late West Jefferson phase, maize production remained fairly stable during the Moundville I phase (AD 1050–1250), a time marked by both significant mound construction at the site of Moundville and regional political consolidation (Scarry 1993a, 1993b). Although the Moundville I phase did not witness an increase in maize *cultivation*, people may have changed the way they prepared maize for consumption, shifting toward hominy production (Briggs 2016).

Although maize production stabilized after its initial intensification during the Late West Jefferson phase, abundances of both hickory and acorn shells decreased statistically during the Moundville I phase (Scarry 1993b:166–167). Scarry and Steponaitis (1997; see also Jackson et al. 2016) interpret this pattern as reflecting the possible provisioning of Moundville's residential population with shelled nutmeats. These nuts may have been processed by residents of rural hamlets, after which they were transported to Moundville; another possibility is that Moundville's residents had cut down their local nut groves to clear fields for maize cultivation, requiring them to travel further for nut collection and conduct initial shelling at collection sites in order to reduce transport costs (Jackson et al. 2016).

Stable isotope evidence reveals that a second wave of maize intensification occurred between the Moundville I and II phases, during a time when the political system had already become entrenched (Schoeninger and Schurr 1998). It is during this time (circa AD 1250) that the site of Bottle Creek was settled in southern Alabama; a small Middle Mississippian multi-mound site, Bottle Creek shares features with Moundville to the north and Fort Walton to the southeast. Comparison of the Moundville and Bottle Creek plant assemblages reveals little difference between these sites; as with Moundville, maize is ubiquitous and abundant at Bottle Creek, while starchy and oily seeds are present but not abundant (Scarry 2003a, 2003b).

Archaeobotanical research in the Black Warrior Valley has clearly demonstrated that initial maize intensification occurred *prior* to regional political development (Scarry 1986, 1993b). Scarry (1993a:88) interprets this pattern to reflect the "prestige-building activities" of competing social groups. She envisions kin groups as increasing production to create surpluses that could then be invested into ceremonial feasts and the support of craftspeople; ultimately, the wealthiest group boasting the most indebted followers emerged as Moundville's leadership at the beginning of the Moundville I phase. Welch and Scarry's (1995) regional comparison of plant remains from Moundville I phase contexts (primary center [Moundville], secondary center [Hog Pen], and farmsteads [Big Sandy and Oliver]) reveals elevated levels of maize processing at sites outlying the Moundville capital. The addition of data from more recent excavations confirm this spatial pattern of differential levels of plant processing debris at different levels of the regional site hierarchy (Jackson et al. 2016). Jackson, Scarry, and Scott (2016:207) argue that this pattern reflects the mobilization of maize along kinship or lineage lines between "hinterland farmers and their kinfolk living in neighborhoods at Moundville as well as their clan leaders residing atop newly constructed mounds" (see also Welch and Scarry 1995). Thus, the Black Warrior Valley presents a situation in which maize was intensified by competing kin groups who were able to command a portion of the food produced by lineage members living at a distance from the capital.

Northern Georgia

This region covers northern Georgia, as it abuts North Carolina at its northern boundary and Tennessee at its western boundary (see Figure 1.1). Specifically, we discuss two subregions, the Etowah and Brasstown River valleys; the Brasstown Valley is situated north of the Etowah Valley along the border with North Carolina. The Late Woodland to Mississippian transition in northern Georgia is similar to that described for other southeastern and midwestern areas. The latter portion of the Late Woodland period (AD 800–1000, referred to as the Woodstock phase) was marked by the appearance of large, permanent settlements located along major rivers and their tributaries (Cobb and Garrow 1996; King 2003; Markin 2007). Settlements from this period span a range of sizes, but evidence of regional settlement hierarchies is lacking (Hally and Rudolph 1986; Markin 2007). The subsequent Early Mississippian period (AD 1000–1250, referred to as the early Etowah phase) witnessed the erection of platform mounds at major settlements such as the Etowah site, which itself is a multi-mound center. In addition to platform mound building, this period is also argued to mark increasing political centralization, the appearance of social ranking, and the establishment of a regional settlement hierarchy (Hally and Langford 1988; King 2003).

We consider the Brasstown Valley (in addition to the Etowah Valley) because it has produced much more archaeobotanical data as a result of targeted CRM projects, which provide a more solid picture of changing plant subsistence from the Late Woodland to Mississippian periods than is available from the Etowah settlement system. To better understand subsistence shifts related to plant cultivation, we begin with patterns documented in the Brasstown Valley during the Middle Woodland Cartersville phase (AD 1–600). At this time, approximately 60 percent of Brasstown plant assemblages were composed of starchy seeds, including maygrass, chenopod, and erect knotweed (Raymer and Bonhage-Freund 2000). Not only are the chenopod seeds clearly domesticated, but the maygrass seeds occur in deposits 60 miles north of the plant's natural range, which indicates that people were intentionally sowing these seeds (Raymer and Bonhage-Freund 2000). By the Late Woodland period (AD 600–900), starchy seeds composed 75 percent of the seeds in the Brasstown assemblages (Raymer and Bonhage-Freund 2000). While this pattern of starchy-seed reliance seems comparable to the contemporaneous American Bottom assemblages and suggests that pre-Mississippian groups in northern Georgia may have been involved in intensive cultivation of native starchy grains, the absolute numbers of starchy seeds in the Brasstown assemblages do not come close to approaching those reported for the American Bottom. Nevertheless, this pattern of increasing proportions of starchy seeds prior to the Mississippian transition suggests that locals were putting more effort into cultivation. During the same period (AD 600–900), maize remains are relatively sparse, but occur in higher ubiquities than in previous periods (Raymer and Bonhage-Freund 2000). Data from the corresponding period at the Woodstock site in the Etowah Valley demonstrate a similar increase in starchy seeds just prior to the Mississippian period (Markin 2007; Tickner 2007). Moreover, Markin (2007) argues that even though maize was not a staple food in Woodstock-phase diets, it was nevertheless a consistent dietary element.

It was not until the beginning of the Mississippian period, during the early Etowah phase (AD 1000–1200), that maize became a significant staple in the

Brasstown Valley diet (Raymer and Bonhage-Freund 2000). Raymer and Bonhage-Freund's (2000) synthesis of archaeobotanical data from this valley documents a consistent increase in maize abundance and ubiquity during this time. At the Woodstock site in the Etowah Valley, this transition to the Etowah phase was marked by a decline in nuts (Markin 2007), a pattern we have noted for other regions as well (e.g., CIRV).

These archaeobotanical patterns are supported by isotopic data obtained from human skeletal remains in this region, which indicate that people consumed negligible amounts of maize prior to AD 1000 at both inland and coastal locations (Hutchinson et al. 1998). These same data demonstrate a trend of increasing maize consumption between AD 1000 and 1600 (Hutchinson et al. 1998). Similar to the Central Illinois River Valley, the elevation of maize to staple status occurred simultaneously with the transition to the Mississippian period in northern Georgia. However, the Georgia case differs in that its Mississippian manifestation included the development of a regional hierarchy and the establishment of a political center at the site of Etowah. It is premature to speculate regarding the causal relationship between incipient political complexity and maize reliance as seen at Etowah. The Etowah phase is represented by a 300-year block of time; the lack of a tight chronological framework with corresponding macrobotanical samples makes it difficult to assess the timing of maize increases relative to sociopolitical developments at the site. Moreover, very little archaeobotanical analysis has been conducted thus far at the site of Etowah, and no maize remains have been directly dated. Thus, it is difficult to pin down whether maize intensification occurred during the early, middle, or latter part of the Etowah phase, or whether maize intensification occurred as one or more waves of production increase. Determining the timing of maize intensification in this region is key to understanding how maize use was tied to sociopolitical developments—was maize incorporated into existing hierarchical negotiations involving foodways (including feasts) whose antecedents involved starchy seeds? Was surplus maize produced in the context of competitive generosities? Did maize form the basis of newly emerging political economies in the Etowah region? This region is clearly ripe for a targeted study combining archaeobotanical analysis with a program of direct dating.

Summary and Conclusion

What can we say about maize and Mississippian beginnings? In this chapter we have synthesized the most up-to-date picture of maize use throughout the broader Southeast and Midwest, exploring how the timing of its adoption and intensification corresponds to Mississippian developments on a regional basis. We have been able to add new regions to our synthesis of Early Mississippian maize (Central Illinois River Valley, northern Georgia) and incorporate new data and interpretations. Mary Simon's (2014) recent program of AMS dating of purportedly early maize in the American Bottom and Illinois Valley represents perhaps the most dramatic revision of how we understand maize's entry into midwestern subsistence economies. We now know that the vast majority of Late Woodland groups living in the lower Midwest did not adopt maize until after AD 900, and that maize was elevated to a primary food resource much more quickly than originally hypothesized (Simon 2014). This AD 900 horizon that marks the widespread adoption of maize corresponds to the appearance of emerging Mississippian elements in some areas of the Midwest and Southeast; in other areas, it predates the adoption of Mississippian practices.

The synthesis we have presented in this paper supports Scarry's (1993a) original findings that the relationship between maize adoption/intensification and Mississippian development is highly variable from region to region. Maize had many different meanings in early Mississippian societies, in areas that evinced varying levels of sociopolitical hierarchy and attempts of aggrandizement by emerging leaders. Our review in this chapter reveals that maize use was tied to each region's unique social and political history—thus, while we can document a lot of variation in the relative importance of and intensification of maize in a particular polity's history, we can also consider how maize may have been related to the actual processes of Mississippianization in a particular region. These processes included hierarchies negotiated through competitive generosities (and the creation of new political economies underwritten by surplus foods); participation in large-scale ritual events that drew on antecedent traditions (simultaneously reinforcing new Mississippian identities while drawing attention to emerging status differences); as well as possible adoptions of a Mississippian "package" that included intensive maize production as a result of culture contact and interaction.

At Moundville, intensive maize production appears to have underwritten the polity's formation, perhaps within the context of competitive generosity. As Scarry's (1993b; Jackson et al. 2016) primary research has demonstrated, maize intensification in the Black Warrior Valley preceded political consolidation, which strongly suggests that aspiring groups were able to leverage surplus food for political gain. In the American Bottom and particularly at Cahokia, Mississippianization was the result of complex negotiations of statuses, hierarchies, identities, rituals, gender roles, etc., as people came together from diverse regions and quickly witnessed dramatic social change. Maize intensification did not occur until well after Cahokia's political consolidation and may represent a production increase aimed at securing surplus tribute (Lopinot 1994). However, while *maize* intensification happened late in Cahokia's political development, the region's inhabitants had nevertheless intensified agricultural production both before and during political consolidation, in the form of *starchy seed* cultivation. In considering Cahokia, as well as Moundville (which represent the two largest Mississippian polities in the broader Southeast), it is clear that plant cultivation was intensified (probably for the purpose of surplus production) in both cases prior to the florescence of hierarchical sociopolitical institutions and relationships. At Cahokia maize was incorporated into an existing regime of starchy seed cultivation, which appears to have intensified within traditionally accepted parameters of preexisting kin networks. In addition to surplus production that funded monumental construction, plant foods also fueled community events, including feasting rituals—given the evidence that starchy seeds were deeply embedded within the region's ritual economy. Morevoer, the correspondence between starchy-seed intensification and Cahokia's regional consolidation lends support to recent ideas regarding the religious nature of Cahokia's political development (see Fritz 2014; Pauketat 2000a, 2000b). Eventually, maize appears to have been folded into a longer history of commensal activities (that had already included starchy seeds and fleshy fruits) that solidified community identities through ritual negotiations.

In some respects, the archaeobotanical data relevant to the Etowah complex are similar to findings in the American Bottom. Starchy-seed cultivation was emphasized in the periods immediately preceding Etowah's political consolidation (Raymer and Bonhage-Freund 2000). Corresponding to the period of regional consolidation, starchy seed abundance dropped, and maize production increased substantially (Hutchinson et al. 1998; Raymer and Bonhage-Freund 2000). However, the lack of a tight chronological framework with corresponding macrobotanical data makes it difficult to assess the timing of maize increases relative to relevant sociopolitical developments in the region.

In the Central Illinois Valley to the east of Cahokia, maize was intensified early in the Mississippian period, but this episode of increased production occurred in an area in which political development was relatively weak and lacked regional coherence during the Mississippian period. Rather, the establishment of political hierarchies and accompanying systems of social ranking appears to have been highly localized and restricted to the site level in the CIRV. From these findings, it is clear that political complexity at a regional level is not a necessary factor in maize intensification (see also Bush 2004; Gremillion 2003; Wagner 1983, 1986). In the broader Illinois Valley, an area that was impacted by

Cahokian contact (whether direct or indirect, see Wilson et al., this volume), intensified maize cultivation may have arrived as part of the Mississippian "package"—that is, the practices of producing and consuming large amounts of maize may have been accepted along with Mississippian-style ceramics, lithics, architecture, and other religious items that were adopted and negotiated as a result of culture contact and interaction between Cahokians and local Late Woodland groups. In this case, maize does not appear to have been directly correlated with the establishment of political hierarchies. Evidence from the Lower Mississippi Valley demonstrates that agricultural intensification is not a necessary causal factor in spurring political development either (Fritz and Kidder 1993; Kassabaum 2014; Kidder and Fritz 1993). Here, public works projects like mound building were funded by surplus food *collection*, not *production*, indicating that early social complexity emerged in the context of wild-food procurement. Maize clearly had a different meaning for Lower Mississippi Valley residents when it was later adopted, and similar to the CIRV case, it was not necessarily tied to hierarchy and aggrandizement.

It is clear from this broader regional comparison that maize intensification cannot be directly linked to political development in any of the cases, excepting Moundville. However, if we consider the role of intensive cultivation more generally, a clear pattern emerges. At Cahokia, Moundville, and Etowah—the three largest Mississippian polities—there was a clear increase in plant-food production prior to the consolidation of a regional political hierarchy. While the Lower Mississippi Valley case demonstrates that agriculture was not necessary to spur increasing social complexity, we speculate that systems of agricultural production likely played a role in the development of larger political institutions in the Mississippian world. Larger food surpluses (made possible through intensive cultivation) can support larger social and ritual events, in addition to funding larger buildings and monument constructions.

We began this chapter with the intention of synthesizing patterns of early Mississippian plant use in the broader Midwest and Southeast in order to better understand the relationship between maize and Mississippian beginnings. Our review of the literature, however, leads us to reframe the issue. By focusing on maize, we can highlight a great deal of variability and draw attention to local process. By widening our lens beyond maize to encompass plant cultivation writ large and its intensification, we are able to highlight a common trend shared by the three largest Mississippian polities—an increase in food production followed by regional political development. Clearly, food production increases are not sufficient causes in and of themselves to account for the emergence of regional political institutions (the CIRV is a case in point).

Surplus production does not determine political complexity, but it certainly appears to be an element that when combined with other variables (e.g., ambitious kin groups, community religious/ritual events, and other antecedent traditions that defined group identities and solidarities), can potentially transform the social and political history of a region.

Acknowledgments

We thank Greg Wilson for inviting us to contribute to this volume. Mary Simon and Gayle Fritz kindly provided us with preprints of their forthcoming publications. We acknowledge Megan Kassabaum and Patrick Livingood for looking over our section on the Lower Mississippi Valley. We are also grateful to Kandace Hollenbach, Nancy White, Adam King, Leslie Raymer, Robert Lusteck, Mark Schurr, and Matt Biwer for sharing their thoughts, answering questions, and in some cases assisting us in tracking down reports and publications. Finally, we acknowledge our anonymous reviewers for their helpful comments and suggestions.

Notes

1. Radiocarbon dates throughout this chapter are reported as they are represented by the researchers cited; no attempt has been made at calibration or standardization.

2. Sites at which maize was identified include the Rench site (McConaughy 1991; McConaughy et al. 1993) and the Elledge site (Schroeder 1994; Stafford 1994) in the CIRV, and the Edward Hoerner site (Schroeder and Studenmund 1998) in the LIRV (see also Asch and Asch 1985; Rose 2008).

References Cited

Ambrose, Stanley H., Jane Buikstra, and Harold W. Krueger
   2003   Status and Gender Differences in Diet at Mound 72, Cahokia, Revealed by Isotopic Analysis of Bone. *Journal of Anthropological Archaeology* 22(3): 217–226.

Asch, David L., and Asch, Nancy B.
   1985   Prehistoric Plant Cultivation in West-Central Illinois. In *Prehistoric Food Production in North America*, edited by Richard I. Ford, pp. 149–203. Anthropological Papers 75. University of Michigan, Museum of Anthropology, Ann Arbor.

Asch, Nancy B., and David L. Asch
   1978   The Economic Potential of *Iva annua* and Its Prehistoric Importance in the Lower Illinois Valley. In *The Nature and Status of Ethnobotany*, edited by Richard I. Ford, pp. 301–341. Anthropological Papers No. 67. Museum of Anthropology, University of Michigan, Ann Arbor.

Bardolph, Dana N.
 2012   Community, Cuisine, and Cahokian Contact: Changes in Mississippian Plant Foodways in the Central Illinois River Valley. Paper presented at the 35th Annual Meeting of the Society of Ethnobiology, Denver.
 2014   Evaluating Cahokian Contact and Mississippian Identity Politics in the Late Prehistoric Central Illinois River Valley. *American Antiquity* 79(1):69–89.

Barker, Alex W.
 1999   Chiefdoms and the Economics of Perversity. Unpublished Ph.D. dissertation, Department of Anthropology, University of Michigan, Ann Arbor.

Bender, Margaret M., David A. Baerreis, and Raymond L. Steventon
 1981   Further Light on Carbon Isotopes and Hopewell Agriculture. *American Antiquity* 46(2):346–353.

Blitz, John
 1993   Big Pots for Big Shots: Feasting and Storage in a Mississippian Community. *American Antiquity* 58(1):80–96.

Bozeman, Tandy Key
 1982   Moundville Phase Communities in the Black Warrior River Valley, Alabama. Unpublished Ph.D. dissertation, Department of Anthropology, University of California, Santa Barbara.

Bridges, Patricia S.
 1991   Degenerative Joint Disease in Hunter-Gatherers and Agriculturalists from the Southeastern United States. *American Journal of Physical Anthropology* 85(4):379–391.

Briggs, Rachel V.
 2016   The Civil Cooking Pot: Hominy and the Mississippian Standard Jar in the Black Warrior Valley, Alabama. *American Antiquity* 81(2):316–332.

Buikstra, Jane E., and George R. Milner
 1991   Isotopic and Archaeological Interpretations of Diet in the Central Mississippi Valley. *Journal of Archaeological Science* 18(3):319–329.

Bush, Leslie L.
 2004   *Boundary Conditions: Macrobotanical Remains and the Oliver Phase of Central Indiana, A.D. 1200–1450*. University of Alabama Press, Tuscaloosa.

Chapman, Jefferson, and Gary D. Crites
 1987   Evidence for Early Maize (*Zea mays*) from the Icehouse Bottom Site, Tennessee. *American Antiquity* 52(2):352–354.

Cobb, Charles R.
 1993   Archaeological Approaches to the Political Economy of Nonstratified Societies. In *Archaeological Method and Theory*, Volume 5, edited by M. B. Schiffer, pp. 43–100. University of Arizona Press, Tucson.

Cobb, Charles R., and Patrick H. Garrow
 1996   Woodstock Culture and the Question of Mississippian Emergence. *American Antiquity* 61(1):21–37.

Conrad, Lawrence A.
 1989   The Southeastern Ceremonial Complex on the Northern Middle Mississippian Frontier: Late Prehistoric Politico-Religious Systems in the Central Illinois River Valley.

In *The Southeastern Ceremonial Complex: Artifacts and Analysis*, edited by Patricia Galloway, pp. 93–113. University of Nebraska Press, Lincoln.
1991 The Middle Mississippian Cultures of the Central Illinois Valley. In *Cahokia and the Hinterlands: Middle Mississippian Cultures of the Midwest*, edited by Thomas E. Emerson and R. Barry Lewis, pp. 119–63. University of Illinois Press, Urbana.

Cook, Robert A., and T. Douglas Price
2015 Maize, Mounds, and the Movement of People: Isotope Analysis of a Mississippian/Fort Ancient Region. *Journal of Archaeological Science* 61:112–128.

Crites, Gary D.
1978 Paleoethnobotany of the Normandy Reservoir in the Upper Duck River Valley, Tennessee. Unpublished master's thesis, University of Tennessee, Knoxville.

Cross, Paula, and Melissa Bittinger
1996 "The Old Road." Phase I Historic Properties Investigations for the FAP 310 Project. Report of Investigations No. 224B. Contract Archaeology Program, Center for American Archaeology, Kampsville, Illinois.

Delaney-Rivera, Colleen
2000 Mississippian and Late Woodland Cultural Interaction and Regional Dynamics: A View from the Lower Illinois River Valley. Unpublished Ph.D. dissertation, Department of Anthropology, University of California, Los Angeles.
2004 From Edge to Frontier: Early Mississippian Occupation of the Lower Illinois River Valley. *Southeastern Archaeology* 23(1):41–56.

Dezendorf, Caroline
2013 The Effects of Food Processing on the Archaeological Visibility of Maize: An Experimental Study of Carbonization of Lime-Treated Maize Kernels. *Ethnobiology Letters* 4:12–20.

Dietler, Michael
2001 Theorizing the Feast: Rituals of Consumption, Commensal Politics, and Power in African Contexts. In *Feasts: Archaeological and Ethnographic Perspectives on Food, Politics, and Power*, edited by Michael Dietler and Brian Hayden, pp. 65–114. Smithsonian Series in Archaeological Inquiry, Washington, D.C.

Dunnell, Robert C., and James K. Feathers
1991 Late Woodland Manifestations of the Malden Plain, Southeast Missouri. In *Stability, Transformation, and Variation: The Late Woodland Southeast*, edited by Michael S. Nassaney and Charles R. Cobb, pp. 21–45. Plenum, New York.

Emerson, Thomas E., Kristen M. Hedman, and Mary L. Simon
2005 Marginal Horticulturalists or Maize Agriculturalists? Archaeobotanical, Paleopathological, and Isotopic Evidence Relating to Langford Tradition Maize Consumption. *Midcontinental Journal of Archaeology* 30(1):67–118.

Ensor, H. Blaine
1993 Big Sandy Farms: A Prehistoric Agricultural Community near Moundville, Black Warrior River Floodplain, Tuscaloosa County, Alabama. Report of Investigations 68. Division of Archaeology, Alabama Museum of Natural History, University of Alabama, Tuscaloosa.

Esarey, Duane
2000 The Late Woodland Maples Mills and the Mossville Phase Sequence in the Central Illinois River Valley. In *Late Woodland Societies: Tradition and Transformation across*

the Midcontinent, edited by Thomas E. Emerson, Dale L. McElrath, and Andrew C. Fortier, pp. 387–412. University of Nebraska Press, Lincoln.

Esarey, Duane, Michael D. Wiant, Dawn Ellen Harn, Terrance J. Martin, Marjorie B. Schroeder, and Robert E. Warren
- 2000 The Liverpool Lake Site: A Late Woodland Village on the Chautauqua Unit of the Illinois River National Wildlife Refuges, Mason County, Illinois. Illinois State Museum, Quaternary Studies Program, Technical Report No. 00-767-5.

Ford, Richard I.
- 1981 Gardening and Farming before AD 1000: Patterns of Prehistoric Cultivation North of Mexico. *Journal of Ethnobiology* 1(1):6–27.
- 1985a The Processes of Plant Food Production in Prehistoric North America. In *Prehistoric Food Production in North America*, edited by Richard I. Ford, pp. 1–18. Anthropological Papers 75. University of Michigan, Museum of Anthropology, Ann Arbor.
- 1985b Patterns of Prehistoric Food Production in North America. In *Prehistoric Food Production in North America*, edited by Richard I. Ford, pp. 341–364. Anthropological Papers 75. University of Michigan, Museum of Anthropology, Ann Arbor

Fritz, Gayle J.
- 1990 Multiple Pathways to Farming in Precontact Eastern North America. *Journal of World Prehistory* 4(4):387–435.
- 1992 Newer, "Better" Maize and the Mississippian Emergence: A Critique of Prime Mover Explanations. In *Late Prehistoric Agriculture: Observations from the Midwest*, edited by William I. Woods, pp. 19–43. Illinois Historic Preservation Agency, Springfield.
- 1994 In Color and in Time: Prehistoric Ozark Agriculture. *Agricultural Origins and Development in the Midcontinent*, edited by William Green, pp. 105–126. Office of the State Archaeologist Report 19. University of Iowa, Iowa City.
- 2000 Native Farming Systems and Ecosystems in the Mississippi River Valley. In *Imperfect Balance: Landscape Transformations in the Pre-Columbian Americas*, edited by David Lentz, pp. 225–250. Columbia University Press, New York.
- 2007a Keepers of Louisiana's Levees: Early Mound Builders and Forest Managers. In *Rethinking Agriculture: Archaeological and Ethnoarchaeological Perspectives*, edited by Timothy Denham, José Iriarte, and Luc Vrydaghs, pp. 189–209. Left Coast Press, Walnut Creek.
- 2007b Pigweeds for the Ancestors: Cultural Identities and Archaeobotanical Identification Methods. In *The Archaeology of Food and Identity*, edited by Katheryn Twiss, pp. 288–307. Center for Archaeological Investigations, Occasional Paper No. 34. Southern Illinois University, Carbondale.
- 2014 Maygrass (*Phalaris caroliniana* Walt.): Its Role and Significance in Native Eastern North American Agriculture. In *New Lives for Ancient and Extinct Crops*, edited by Paul E. Minnis, pp. 13–43. University of Arizona Press, Tucson.

Fritz, Gayle J., and Tristram R. Kidder
- 1993 Recent Investigations into Prehistoric Agriculture in the Lower Mississippi Valley. *Southeastern Archaeology* 12(1):1–14.

Fritz, Gayle J., and Neal H. Lopinot
- 2003 Native Crops at Early Cahokia: Comparing Domestic and Ceremonial Contexts. In *People, Plants, and Animals: Archaeological Studies of Human–Environment Interactions in the Midcontinent*, edited by Robert Warren. *Illinois Archaeology* 15/16:90–111.

Galloy, Joseph M., Kathryn E. Parker, and Nathan J. Babcook
  2000 The Bivouac Site (11MS1665): An Emergent Mississippian Camp in the American Bottom Uplands. *Illinois Archaeology* 12:218–243.
Goette, Susan, Michelle Williams, Sissel Johannessen, and Christine A. Hastorf
  1994 Towards Reconstructing Ancient Maize: Experiments in Processing and Charring. *Journal of Ethnobiology* 14(1):1–21.
Green, William
  1987 Between Hopewell and Mississippian: Late Woodland in the Prairie Peninsula as viewed from the Western Illinois Uplands. Unpublished Ph.D. dissertation, Department of Anthropology, University of Wisconsin, Madison.
Green, William, and David J. Nolan
  2000 Late Woodland Peoples in West-Central Illinois. In *Late Woodland Societies: Tradition and Transformation across the Midcontinent*, edited by Thomas E. Emerson, Dale L. McElrath, and Andrew C. Fortier, pp. 345–386. University of Nebraska Press, Lincoln.
Gremillion, Kristen
  2003 Eastern Woodlands Overview. In *People and Plants in Eastern North America*, edited by Paul Minnis, pp. 17–49. Smithsonian Institution Press, Washington, D.C.
Hally, David, and James B. Langford Jr.
  1988 *Mississippi Period Archaeology of the Georgia Valley and Ridge Province*. Laboratory of Archaeology Series, Report No. 25. University of Georgia, Athens.
Hally, David, and James Rudolph
  1986 *Mississippi Period Archaeology of the Georgia Piedmont*. Laboratory of Archaeology Series, Report No. 24. University of Georgia, Athens.
Hann, John H.
  1986 Translation of Alonso de Leturiondo's Memorial to the King of Spain. *Florida Archaeology* 2:165–225.
Harn, Alan D.
  1991 The Eveland Site: Inroad to Spoon River Mississippian Society. In *New Perspectives on Cahokia: Views from the Periphery*, edited by James B. Stoltman, pp. 129–53. Prehistory Press, Madison.
Hart, John P.
  1999 Maize Agriculture Evolution in the Eastern Woodlands of North America: A Darwinian Perspective. *Journal of Archaeological Method and Theory* 6(2):137–180.
Hart, John P., William A. Lovis, Robert J. Jeske, and John D. Richards
  2012 The Potential of Bulk $\delta^{13}C$ on Encrusted Cooking Residues as Independent Evidence for Regional Maize Histories. *American Antiquity* 77(2):315–325.
Herndon, Richard L., Andrew P. Bradbury, Neal H. Lopinot, Brian G. DelCastello, and Gina S. Powell
  2014 The Artesian Branch Site: Late Woodland Occupations in the Mississippi Floodplain of Northeastern Missouri. *Illinois Archaeology* 26:56–84.
Hoard, Robert J.
  2000 Late Woodland in Central Missouri, the Boone Phase. In *Late Woodland Societies: Tradition and Transformation across the Midcontinent*, edited by Thomas E. Emerson, Dale L. McElrath, Andrew C. Fortier, pp. 211–239. University of Nebraska Press, Lincoln.

Holt, Julie Zimmerman, Toshia Evans, Marge Schroeder, Shannon L. Moore, and Cassandra Buskohl
- 2010 Late Woodland–Emergent Mississippian Occupation and Plant Use at the AE Harmon Site (11MS136). *Midcontinental Journal of Archaeology* 35(1):57–90.

Holt, Julie Zimmerman, Miranda Yancey, and Erin Marks Guntren
- 2011 Anthropogenic Change at the D. Hitchens Site (11MSS1124). *Illinois Archaeology* 23:173–205.

Hudson, Charles
- 1976 *The Southeastern Indians.* University of Tennessee Press, Knoxville.

Hutchinson, Dale L., Clark S. Larsen, Margaret J. Schoeninger, and Lynette Norr
- 1998 Regional Variation in the Pattern of Maize Adoption and Use in Florida and Georgia. *American Antiquity* 63(3):397–416.

Jackson, H. Edwin, C. Margaret Scarry, and Susan Scott
- 2016 Domestic and Ritual Meals in the Moundville Chiefdom. In *Rethinking Moundville and Its Hinterland*, edited by Vincas P. Steponaitis and C. Margaret Scarry, pp. 187–233. University Press of Florida, Gainesville.

Johannessen, Sissel
- 1984 Paleoethnobotany. In *American Bottom Archaeology*, edited by Charles J. Bareis and James W. Porter, pp. 197–214. University of Illinois Press, Urbana.
- 1993 Farmers of the Late Woodland. In *Foraging and Farming in the Eastern Woodlands*, edited by C. Margaret Scarry, pp. 57–77. University Press of Florida, Gainesville.

Kassabaum, Megan C.
- 2014 Communal Feasting, Ritual Activity, and Mound Building at the Feltus Site, Jefferson County, Mississippi. Unpublished Ph.D. dissertation, Department of Anthropology, University of North Carolina, Chapel Hill.

Kelly, John E.
- 1990a The Emergence of Mississippian Culture in the American Bottom Region. In *The Mississippian Emergence*, edited by Bruce D. Smith, pp. 113–52. Smithsonian Institution Press, Washington, D.C.
- 1990b Range Site Community Patterns and the Mississippian Emergence. In *The Mississippian Emergence*, edited by Bruce D. Smith, pp. 67–112. Smithsonian Institution Press, Washington, D.C.

Kidder, Tristram R.
- 1992 Timing and Consequences of the Introduction of Maize Agriculture in the Lower Mississippi Valley. *North American Archaeologist* 13(1):15–41.
- 1993 *1992 Archaeological Test Excavations in Tensas Parish, Louisiana.* Center for Archaeology, Archaeological Report 3. Tulane University, New Orleans.
- 2002 Woodland Period Archaeology of the Lower Mississippi Valley. In *The Woodland Southeast*, edited by David G. Anderson and Robert C. Mainfort Jr., pp. 66–90. University of Alabama Press, Tuscaloosa.

Kidder, Tristram R., and Gayle J. Fritz
- 1993 Subsistence and Social Change in the Lower Mississippi Valley: The Reno Brake and Osceola Sites, Louisiana. *Journal of Field Archaeology* 20(3):281–297.

King, Adam
- 2003 *Etowah: The Political History of a Chiefdom Capital.* University of Alabama Press, Tuscaloosa.

King, Frances B.
1985   Presettlement Vegetation and Plant Remains. In *The Alexander Site, Conway County, Arkansas*, edited by E. Thomas Hemmings and John House, pp. 47–57. Research Series 24. Arkansas Archeological Survey, Fayetteville.
1987   Prehistoric Maize in Eastern North America: An Evolutionary Evaluation. Unpublished Ph.D. dissertation, Department of Agronomy, University of Illinois, Urbana.
1988   Presettlement Vegetation and Plant Remains. In *Results of Final Testing for Significance at the Ink Bayou Site (3PU252), Pulaski County, Arkansas*, by David Waddell, John. House, Frances King, M. L. Colburn, and M. K. Marks, pp. 235–249. Report to the Sponsored Research Program, Arkansas Archeological Survey, to the Arkansas Highway and Transportation Department.
1993   Floral Remains. In *Rench: A Stratified Site in the Central Illinois River Valley*, edited by Mark A. McConaughy, pp. 121–124. Reports of Investigations No. 49. Illinois State Museum, Springfield.
1994   Variability in Cob and Kernel Characteristics of North American Maize Cultivars. In *Corn and Culture in the Prehistoric New World*, edited by Sissel Johannessen and Christine A. Hastorf, pp. 35–54. Westview, Boulder.

Knight, Vernon J., Jr.
1992   Preliminary Report on Excavations at Mound Q, Moundville. Paper presented at the 49th Annual Southeastern Archaeological Conference, Little Rock, Arkansas.
1998   Moundville as a Diagrammatic Ceremonial Center. In *Archaeology of the Moundville Chiefdom*, edited by Vernon J. Knight Jr. and Vincas P. Steponaitis, pp. 44–62. Smithsonian Institution Press, Washington, D.C.

Knight, Vernon J., Jr., and Vincas P. Steponaitis
1998   A New History of Moundville. In *Archaeology of the Moundville Chiefdom*, edited by Vernon J. Knight Jr. and Vincas P. Steponaitis, pp. 1–25. Smithsonian Institution Press, Washington, D.C.

Kuehn, Steven R., and Rosemarie Blewitt
2013   Mississippian Faunal and Botanical Remains from the Tree Row (11F53) and Baker-Preston (11F20) Sites, Fulton County, Illinois. *Illinois Archaeology* 25:27–62.

Lee, Aubra L., Rhonda L. Smith, Jill-Karen Yakubik, Tristram R. Kidder, Ruben Saenz II, Benjamin Maygarden, Gayle J. Fritz, and Roger T. Saucier
1997   *Archaeological Data Recovery at the Birds Creek Site (16CT416), Catahoula Parish, Louisiana*. Earth Search, New Orleans.

Listi, Ginessa A.
2011   Bioarchaeological Analysis of Diet during the Coles Creek Period in the Southern Lower Mississippi Valley. *American Journal of Physical Anthropology* 144(1):30–40.
2013   Bioarchaeological Analysis of Subsistence and Health at the Lake George Site, Mississippi (22YZ557). *Southeastern Archaeology* 32(1):111–128.

Lopinot, Neal H.
1992   Spatial and Temporal Variability in Mississippian Subsistence: The Archaeobotanical Record. In *Late Prehistoric Agriculture: Observations from the Midwest*, edited by William I. Woods, pp. 44–94. Illinois Historic Preservation Agency, Springfield.
1994   A New Crop of Data on the Cahokian Polity. *Agricultural Origins and Development in the Midcontinent*, edited by William Green, pp. 127–153. Office of the State Archaeologist Report 19. University of Iowa, Iowa City.

1995   Archaeobotanical Remains. In *Woodland and Mississippian Occupations at the Hayti Bypass Site (23PM572), Pemiscot County, Missouri*, edited by Michael D. Conner, pp. 221–262. Special Publication No. 1. Center for Archaeological Research, Southwest Missouri State University, Springfield.

1997   Cahokian Food Production Reconsidered. In *Cahokia: Domination and Ideology in the Mississippian World*, edited by Timothy R. Pauketat and Thomas E. Emerson, pp. 52–68. University of Nebraska Press, Lincoln.

Lusteck, Robert

2006   The Migrations of Maize into the Southeastern United States. In *The Histories of Maize: Multidisciplinary Approaches to the Prehistory, Linguistics, Biogeography, Domestication, and Evolution of Maize*, edited by John Staller, Robert Tykot, and Bruce Benz, pp. 521–528. Academic, Burlington.

Lynott, Mark J., Thomas W. Boutton, James E. Price, and Dwight E. Nelson

1986   Stable Carbon Isotopic Evidence for Maize Agriculture in Southeast Missouri and Northeast Arkansas. *American Antiquity* 51(1):51–65.

Markin, Julie G.

2007   Woodstock: The Rise of Political Complexity in North Georgia. Unpublished Ph.D. dissertation, Department of Anthropology, University of Georgia, Athens.

Martin, William W., and LuElla M. Parks

1994   Early Middle Mississippian-Period Land-Use and Settlement-Subsistence Practices, Site 23S0132, Stoddard County, Missouri. *Missouri Archaeologist* 55:47–76.

Maxham, Mintcy D.

2000   Rural Communities in the Black Warrior Valley, Alabama: The Role of Commoners in the Creation of the Moundville I Landscape. *American Antiquity* 65(2):337–354.

2004   Native Constructions of Landscapes in the Black Warrior Valley, Alabama, AD 1020–1520. Unpublished Ph.D. dissertation, Department of Anthropology, University of North Carolina, Chapel Hill.

McConaughy, Mark A.

1991   The Rench Site Late Woodland/Mississippian Farming Hamlet from the Central Illinois River Valley: Food for Thought. In *New Perspectives on Cahokia: Views from the Periphery*, edited by James B. Stoltman, pp. 101–128. Monographs in World Archaeology 2. Prehistory Press, Madison.

McConaughy, Mark A., Terrance J. Martin, and Frances B. King

1993   Late Woodland/Mississippian Period Component. In *Rench: A Stratified Site in the Central Illinois River Valley*, edited by Mark A. McConaughy, pp. 76–128. Reports of Investigations No. 49. Illinois State Museum, Springfield.

McNutt, Charles H.

1996   The Central Mississippi Valley: A Summary. In *Prehistory of the Central Mississippi Valley*, edited by Charles H. McNutt, pp. 187–257. University of Alabama Press, Tuscaloosa.

Michals, Lauren M.

1998   The Oliver Site and Early Moundville I Phase Economic Organization. In *Archaeology of the Moundville Chiefdom*, edited by Vernon J. Knight Jr. and Vincas P. Steponaitis, pp. 167–182. Smithsonian Institution Press, Washington, D.C.

Mistovich, Tim S.

1988   Early Mississippian in the Black Warrior River Valley: The Pace of Transition. *Southeastern Archaeology* 7(1):21–38.

Morse, Dan F., and Phyllis A. Morse
   1983   *Archaeology of the Central Mississippi Valley*. Academic, San Diego.
Myers, Thomas P.
   2006   Hominy Technology and the Emergence of Mississippian Societies. In *The Histories of Maize: Multidisciplinary Approaches to the Prehistory, Linguistics, Biogeography, Domestication, and Evolution of Maize*, edited by John Staller, Robert Tykot, and Bruce Benz, pp. 511–520. Academic, Burlington.
Nassaney, Michael S.
   1987   On the Causes and Consequences of Subsistence Intensification in the Mississippi Alluvial Valley. In *Emergent Horticultural Economies of the Eastern Woodlands*, edited by William F. Keegan, pp. 129–151. Center for Archaeological Investigations, Occasional Paper 7. Southern Illinois University, Carbondale.
O'Brien, Michael J., and W. Raymond Wood
   1998   *The Prehistory of Missouri*. University of Missouri Press, Columbia.
Parker, Kathryn E., and Elizabeth M. Scott
   2003   Prehistoric Plant and Animal Use in the Interior Uplands of Silver Creek, Southwestern Illinois. *Illinois Archaeology* 15/16:58–89.
Pauketat, Timothy R.
   1994   *The Ascent of Chiefs: Cahokia and Mississippian Politics in Native North America*. University of Alabama Press, Tuscaloosa.
   1997   Cahokian Political Economy. In *Cahokia: Domination and Ideology in the Mississippian World*, edited by Timothy R. Pauketat and Thomas E. Emerson, pp. 30–51. University of Nebraska Press, Lincoln.
   1998   *The Archaeology of Downtown Cahokia: The Tract-15A and Dunham Tract Excavations*. Studies in Archaeology No. 1. Illinois Transportation Archaeological Research Program, University of Illinois, Urbana-Champaign.
   2000a The Tragedy of the Commoners. In *Agency in Archaeology*, edited by Marcia-Anne Dobres and John E. Robb, pp. 113–129. Routledge, London.
   2000b Politicization and Community in the Pre-Columbian Mississippi Valley. In *The Archaeology of Communities: A New World Perspective*, edited by Marcello-Andrea Canuto and Jason Yaeger, pp. 16–43. Routledge, London.
   2004   *Ancient Cahokia and the Mississippians*. Cambridge University Press, Cambridge.
Pauketat, Timothy R., Lucretia S. Kelly, Gayle J. Fritz, Neal H. Lopinot, Scott Elias, and Eve Hargrave
   2002   The Residues of Feasting and Public Ritual at Early Cahokia. *American Antiquity* 67(2):257–279.
Pauketat, Timothy R., and Neal H. Lopinot
   1997   Cahokian Population Dynamics. In *Cahokia: Domination and Ideology in the Mississippian World*, edited by Timothy R. Pauketat and Thomas E. Emerson, pp. 103–123. University of Nebraska Press, Lincoln.
Phillips, David A. Jr., and Lynne Sebastian
   2004   Large-scale Feasting and Politics: An Essay on Power in Precontact Southwestern Societies. In *Identity, Feasting, and the Archaeology of the Greater Southwest*, edited by Barbara J. Mills, pp. 233–260. University of Colorado Press, Boulder.
Pollock, Susan
   2003   Feasts, Funerals, and Fast Food in Early Mesopotamian States. *The Archaeology and*

Politics of Food and Feasting in Early States and Empires, edited by Tamara L. Bray, pp. 17–38. Springer, New York.

2012 Towards an Archaeology of Commensal Spaces: An Introduction. *eTopoi Journal for Ancient Studies* special vol. 2:1–20.

Pope, Melody K.
 1989 Microtools from the Black Warrior Valley: Technology, Use, and Context. Unpublished Master's thesis, Department of Anthropology, State University of New York, Binghamton.

Potter, James M.
 2000 Pots, Parties, and Politics: Communal Feasting in the American Southwest. *American Antiquity* 65(3):471–492.

Potter, James M., and Scott G. Ortman
 2004 Community and Cuisine in the Prehispanic American Southwest. In *Identity, Feasting, and the Archaeology of the Greater Southwest*, edited by Barbara J. Mills, pp. 173–191. University of Colorado Press, Boulder.

Raviele, Maria E.
 2010 Assessing Carbonized Archaeological Cooking Residues: Evaluation of Maize Phytolith Taxonomy and Density through Experimental Residue Analysis. Unpublished Ph.D. dissertation, Department of Anthropology, Michigan State University, East Lansing.

Raymer, Leslie R., and Mary T. Bonhage-Freund
 2000 Archaeobotanical Analysis. *Early Georgia* 28(2):74–91.

Reber, Eleanora A., and Richard P. Evershed
 2004 How Did Mississippians Prepare Maize? The Application of Compound-Specific Carbon Isotope Analysis to Absorbed Pottery Residues from Several Mississippi Valley Sites. *Archaeometry* 46(1):19–33.

Reeder, Robert L.
 2000 The Meramec Spring Phase. In *Late Woodland Societies: Tradition and Transformation across the Midcontinent*, edited by Thomas E. Emerson, Dale L. McElrath, and Andrew C. Fortier, pp. 187–210. University of Nebraska Press, Lincoln.

Rees, Mark A., and Patrick C. Livingood
 2007 Introduction and Historical Overview. In *Plaquemine Archaeology*, edited by Mark A. Rees and Patrick C. Livingood, pp. 1–19. University of Alabama Press, Tuscaloosa.

Riley, Thomas J.
 1987 Ridged-Field Agriculture and the Mississippian Economic Pattern. *Emergent Horticultural Economies of the Eastern Woodlands*, 295–304. Center for Archaeological Investigations, Occasional Paper 7. Southern Illinois University, Carbondale.

Riley, Thomas J., Richard Edging, and Jack Rossen
 1990 Cultigens in Prehistoric Eastern North America: Changing Paradigms. *Current Anthropology* 31(5):525–541.

Riley, Thomas J., Gregory R. Walz, Charles J. Bareis, Andrew C. Fortier, and Kathryn E. Parker
 1994 Accelerator Mass Spectrometry (AMS) Dates Confirm Early *Zea mays* in the Mississippi River Valley. *American Antiquity* 59(3):490–498.

Rolingson, Martha A.
 1998 *Toltec Mounds and Plum Bayou Culture: Mound D Excavations*. Research Series No. 54. Arkansas Archaeological Survey, Fayetteville.

Rose, Fionnuala
  2008   Intra-Community Variation in Diet during the Adoption of a New Staple Crop in the Eastern Woodlands. *American Antiquity* 73(3):413–439.

Rose, Jerome C., Murray K. Marks, and Larry L. Tieszen
  1991   Bioarchaeology and Subsistence in the Central and Lower Portions of the Mississippi Valley. In *What Mean These Bones? Studies in Southeastern Bioarchaeology*, edited by Mary Lucas Powell, Patricia S. Bridges, Ann Marie W. Mires, pp. 7–21. University of Alabama Press, Tuscaloosa.

Scarry, C. Margaret
  1986   Change in Plant Procurement and Production during the Emergence of the Moundville Chiefdom. Unpublished Ph.D. dissertation, Department of Anthropology, University of Michigan, Ann Arbor.
  1993a   Variability in Mississippian Crop Production Strategies. In *Foraging and Farming in the Eastern Woodlands*, edited by C. Margaret Scarry, pp. 78–90. University Press of Florida, Gainesville.
  1993b   Agricultural Risk and the Development of the Moundville Chiefdom. In *Foraging and Farming in the Eastern Woodlands*, edited by C. Margaret Scarry, pp. 157–181. University Press of Florida, Gainesville.
  1994   Variability in Late Prehistoric Corn from the Lower Southeast. In *Corn and Culture in the Prehistoric New World*, edited by Sissel Johannessen and C. A. Hastorf, pp. 347–367. Westview, Boulder.
  1995   Plant Remains. In *The Rock Levee Site: Late Marksville through Late Mississippi Settlement, Bolivar County, Mississippi*, edited by Richard Weinstein, Richard Fuller, Susan Scott, C. Margaret Scarry, and Sylvia Duay, pp. 263–286. The Beulah Levee Project: Archaeology and History, Vol. 3. Coastal Environments, Baton Rouge.
  2003a   Food Plant Remains from Excavations in Mounds A, B, C, D, and L at Bottle Creek. In *Bottle Creek: A Pensacola Culture Site in South Alabama*, edited by Ian W. Brown, pp. 103–113. University of Alabama Press, Tuscaloosa.
  2003b   Use of Plants in Mound-Related Activities at Bottle Creek and Moundville. In *Bottle Creek: A Pensacola Culture Site in South Alabama*, edited by Ian W. Brown, pp. 114–129. University of Alabama Press, Tuscaloosa.
  2003c   Patterns of Wild Plant Utilization in the Prehistoric Eastern Woodlands. In *People and Plants in Ancient Eastern North America*, edited by Paul E. Minnis, pp. 50–104. Smithsonian Books, Washington, D.C.
  2008   Crop Husbandry Practices in North America's Eastern Woodlands. In *Case Studies in Environmental Archaeology*, 2nd ed., edited by Elizabeth Reitz, C. Margaret Scarry, and Sylvia J. Scudder, pp. 391–404. Springer, New York.

Scarry, C. Margaret, and John F. Scarry
  2005   Native American 'Garden Agriculture' in Southeastern North America. *World Archaeology* 37(2):259–274.

Scarry, C. Margaret, and Vincas P. Steponaitis
  1997   Between Farmstead and Center: The Natural and Social Landscape of Moundville. In *People, Plants, and Landscapes: Studies in Paleoethnobotany*, edited by Kristen Gremillion, pp. 107–122. University of Alabama Press, Tuscaloosa.

Scarry, John F., H. Edwin Jackson, and Mintcy D. Maxham
  2016   Late Prehistoric Social Practice in the Rural Black Warrior River Valley. In *Rethinking Moundville and Its Hinterland,* edited by Vincas P. Steponaitis and C. Margaret Scarry, pp. 162–186. University Press of Florida, Gainesville.

Schoeninger, Margaret J., and Mark R. Schurr
  1998   Human Subsistence at Moundville: The Stable-Isotope Data. In *Archaeology of the Moundville Chiefdom,* edited by Vernon J. Knight Jr. and Vincas P. Steponaitis, pp. 120–132. Smithsonian Institution Press, Washington, D.C.

Schroeder, Marjorie B.
  1994   Archaeobotany. In *Central Illinois Expressway Archeology: Upland Occupations of the Illinois Valley Crossing,* edited by B. Stafford, pp. 105–120. Kampsville Archeological Center, Technical Report, Volume 5. Center for American Archeology, Kampsville.
  2000   Archaeobotanical Sampling. In *Ancient Life on the Illinois River: Excavations at the Liverpool Landing Site (11F2713), West Central Illinois.* Technical Report No. 97-1076-2. Quaternary Studies Program, Illinois State Museum, Springfield.

Schroeder, Marjorie B., and Sarah J. Studenmund
  1998   *Archaeobotanical Analysis of Select Bluff-Component Sites in the Lower Illinois River Valley.* Manuscript on file, Center for American Archaeology, Kampsville.

Simon, Mary L.
  2000   Regional Variations in Plant Use Strategies in the Midwest during the Late Woodland. In *Late Woodland Societies: Tradition and Transformation across the Midcontinent,* edited by Thomas E. Emerson, Dale L. McElrath, and Andrew C. Fortier, pp. 37–76. University of Nebraska Press, Lincoln.
  2014   Re-evaluating the Introduction of Maize into the American Bottom and Western Illinois. *Midcontinental Journal of Archaeology Occasional Papers* 1, edited by Maria E. Raviele and William A. Lovis, pp. 97–134. Illinois State Archaeological Survey, Urbana.
  2017   Reevaluating the Evidence for Middle Woodland Maize from the Holding Site. *American Antiquity* 82(1):140–150.

Simon, Mary L., and Kathryn E. Parker
  2006   Prehistoric Plant Use in the American Bottom: New Thoughts and Interpretations. *Southeastern Archaeology* 25(2):212–257.

Slater, Philip A., Kristin M. Hedman, and Thomas E. Emerson
  2014   Immigrants at the Mississippian Polity of Cahokia: Strontium Isotope Evidence for Population Movement. *Journal of Archaeological Science* 44(1):117–127.

Smith, Bruce D.
  1984   Mississippian Expansion: Tracing the Historical Development of an Explanatory Model. *Southeastern Archaeology* 3:13–32.
  1989   Origins of Agriculture in Eastern North America. *Science* 246(4397):1566–1571.
  1995   The Analysis of Single-Household Mississippian Sites. In *Mississippian Communities and Households,* edited by J. Daniel Rogers and Bruce D. Smith, pp. 224–49. University of Tuscaloosa Press, Alabama.

Smith, Bruce D., and Cowan, C. Wesley
  2003   Domesticated Crop Plants and the Evolution of Food Production Economies in Eastern North America. In *People and Plants in Ancient Eastern North America,* edited by Paul E. Minnis, pp. 105–125. Smithsonian Books, Washington, D.C.

St-Pierre, Christian Gates, and Robert G. Thompson
    2015   Phytolith Evidence for the Early Presence of Maize in Southern Quebec. *American Antiquity* 80(2):408–415.
Stafford, Barbara
    1994   *Central Illinois Expressway Archaeology: Upland Occupations of the Illinois Valley Crossing.* Technical Report 5. Center for American Archaeology, Kampsville.
Steponaitis, Vincas P.
    1986   Prehistoric Archaeology in the Southeastern United States, 1970–1985. *Annual Review of Anthropology* 15:363–404.
    1998   Population Trends at Moundville. In *Archaeology of the Moundville Chiefdom*, edited by Vernon J. Knight Jr. and Vincas P. Steponaitis, pp. 26–43. Smithsonian Institution Press, Washington, D.C.
Studenmund, Sarah J.
    2000   Late Woodland Occupations in the Lower Illinois Valley: Research Questions and Data Sets. In *Late Woodland Societies: Tradition and Transformation across the Midcontinent*, edited by Thomas E. Emerson, Dale L. McElrath, and Andrew C. Fortier, pp. 301–344. University of Nebraska Press, Lincoln.
Studenmund, Sarah J., Marjorie B. Schroeder, and Karli White
    1995   Late Woodland Settlement Patterns at the Confluence of the Illinois and Mississippi Rivers: A Comparison of Upland and Lowland Sites. *Illinois Archaeology* 7:148–201.
Stuiver, Minze, and Paula J. Reimer
    1993   Extended ^{14}C Data Base and Revised CALIB 3.0 ^{14}C Age Calibration Program. *Radiocarbon* 35(1):215–230.
Swanton, John R.
    1946   *The Indians of the Southeastern United States.* Bulletin 137, Bureau of American Ethnology, Washington, D.C.
Tickner, Amanda
    2007   Appendix B: Botanical Report for 9MU103 and 9CK9. In Woodstock: The Rise of Political Complexity in North Georgia, by Julie Markin, pp. 266–279. Unpublished Ph.D. dissertation, Department of Anthropology, University of Georgia, Athens.
VanDerwarker, Amber M.
    1999   Feasting and Status at the Toqua site. *Southeastern Archaeology* 18(1):24–34.
VanDerwarker, Amber M., Gregory D. Wilson, and Dana N. Bardolph
    2013   Maize Adoption and Intensification in the Central Illinois River Valley: An Analysis of Archaeobotanical Data from the Late Woodland through Early Mississippian Periods (AD 600–1200). *Southeastern Archaeology* 32(2):147–168.
VanDerwarker, Amber M., Dana N. Bardolph, Kristin M. Hoppa, Heather B. Thakar, Lana S. Martin, Allison L. Jaqua, Matthew E. Biwer, and Kristina M. Gill
    2016   New World Paleoethnobotany in the New Millennium (2000–2013). *Journal of Archaeological Research* 24(2):125–177.
Voigt, Eric E.
    1989   Late Woodland and Emergent Mississippian Plant Use. In *New World Paleoethnobotany*, edited by Eric E. Voigt and Deborah M. Pearsall. *Missouri Archaeologist* 47:197–232.
Wagner, Gail E.
    1983   Fort Ancient Subsistence: The Botanical Record. *West Virginia Archaeologist* 35:27–39.

1986   The Corn and Cultivated Beans of the Fort Ancient Indians. *Missouri Archaeologist* 47:107–135.

Welch, Paul D.
1990   Mississippian Emergence in West Central Alabama. In *The Mississippian Emergence*, edited by Bruce D. Smith, pp. 197–225. Smithsonian Institution Press, Washington, D.C.
1991   *Moundville's Economy.* University of Alabama Press, Tuscaloosa.

Welch, Paul D., and C. Margaret Scarry
1995   Status-Related Variation in Foodways in the Moundville Chiefdom. *American Antiquity* 60(3):397–419.

Wiessner, Pauline W., and Wulf Schiefenhövel (editors)
1998   *Food and the Status Quest: An Interdisciplinary Perspective.* Berghahn Books, New York.

Williams, Leah
2008   *The Paleoethnobotany of the Feltus Mounds Site.* Senior honor's thesis, Department of Anthropology, University of North Carolina, Chapel Hill.

Wilson, Gregory D.
2008   *The Archaeology of Everyday Life at Early Moundville.* University of Alabama Press, Tuscaloosa.

Woodiel, Deborah Kay
1993   The St. Gabriel Site: Prehistoric Life on the Mississippi. *Louisiana Archaeology* 20:1–136.

Wright, Patty J.
2007   Early Mississippian Plant Use along the Lower Missouri River. *Missouri Archaeologist* 68:119–133.

3

Cahokia's Beginnings

Mobility, Urbanization, and the Cahokian Political Landscape

ALLEEN BETZENHAUSER

The combined movements of local and foreign people from pre-Mississippian villages and hamlets into mound centers and out to isolated farmsteads resulted in the creation of Cahokia as an urbanized space and the center of a regionally integrated polity. Through these movements landscapes were redefined, and identities and power relations among local and foreign groups were negotiated. It is asserted that such movements interfered with local sources of power at the same time a sense of shared identity was fostered through participation in communal events. In this chapter the historical effects of these movements are traced through analyses of site location, layout, occupational history, and the distribution of material culture throughout the American Bottom.

Mississippian Beginnings in the American Bottom

Early thoughts concerning the development of Mississippian society in the American Bottom predominantly concerned the wholesale transportation of Mississippian culture from a heartland, possibly by traders who then interacted with local Late Woodland populations (Freimuth 1974; O'Brien 1972; Porter 1974). While this may be the case in other areas of the Southeast and Midwest, it does not appear to hold true for the American Bottom. Although there is general agreement today that Mississippian culture derived from local Late Woodland populations in the American Bottom, researchers continue to disagree about the impetus and rate of change (for ideas concerning rates of change outside the American Bottom, see Bandy 2004 and Beck et al. 2007). Several researchers view the rise of Cahokia and the development of Mississippian society in the American Bottom as a gradual evolutionary process that slowly unfolded over the course of a few hundred years (Kelly 1980, 1990a,

1990b, 2002; Milner 1990, 1991, 1996, 2006; Milner and Schroeder 1999; Muller and Stephens 1991; Schroeder 1997; Smith 2007), while others view it as much more rapid, occurring over a large space over the course of a generation or two (Alt 2006a; Emerson 1997a, 2002; Fortier et al. 2006; Fortier and McElrath 2002; Pauketat 1994, 1998a, 2003, 2004; Pauketat and Emerson 1999, 2008).

Those who favor a gradual development or evolution of Mississippian society in the American Bottom tend to privilege economic or environmental factors as causes of or motivations for sociopolitical change. Within this framework, the groups that occupied the American Bottom during the period immediately preceding the Mississippian period (i.e., Terminal Late Woodland) must have been organized as simple chiefdoms, because Cahokia, considered a complex chiefdom, had to develop or emerge from such earlier sociopolitical organizations (see Milner 2006; Smith 2007). This process would necessarily take a long time, because it depends on a combination of a gradual increase in population due to decreased birth spacing associated with sedentism and agricultural production, competition over access to or control of resources, and a decrease in perceived violence (Kelly 1990a:143–146). Mississippian settlement patterns, in particular the dispersed farmsteads located on floodplain ridges, have been interpreted as an agriculturally based adaptation to floodplain and riverine environments (Mehrer 1995; Milner 2006; Muller and Stephens 1991). Similarly, environmental factors are invoked to explain why certain sites experienced the greatest longevity or grew to a larger size (Schroeder 1997, 2004).

Those who view the Mississippian transition in the Cahokia area as a gradual evolutionary process cite population increase, a decrease in violence, changes in the distribution of power, differential control of resources, or all of the above as the impetus for sociopolitical change. These researchers also tend to view contemporaneous Mississippian mound centers as seats of independent chiefdoms whose elites would occasionally interact and exchange resources (Kelly 2002; Milner 2006). For example, Kelly (1990a, 1991) suggested Cahokia became the center of American Bottom Mississippian society because of its strategic location near the confluence of the Mississippi, Missouri, and Illinois rivers, and hence Cahokians' ability to control trade routes. Other mound centers presumably were located near particular resources and on or near important rivers and streams that could have been used to transport goods and other resources throughout the region (Kelly 1990a, 1991).

Rarely do these researchers identify the agency of past people and their relationships with one another as causal factors for sociopolitical change, which ultimately denies these past people an active role in culture construction and their own history. Since the 1980s, new data from excavations outside Cahokia, analyses of collections from large-scale excavations at Cahokia during the 1960s and 1970s, and theoretical shifts have led some researchers to question the gradual, evolutionary explanations for the development of Mississippian society (see Emerson 1997a; Fortier and McElrath 2002; Pauketat 1994, 1998a, b; Pauketat and Emerson 1999). Instead, they viewed the Mississippian transition as a historical process rather than evolutionary response. This historical perspective places people, both local and nonlocal, at the forefront of the creation of Cahokia as a sociopolitical and religious center within the region.

Pauketat has been the most vocal proponent of a historical perspective and the rapid transformation associated with the beginning of the Mississippian period (Pauketat 1994, 1997, 1998a, 2002, 2003, 2004). Through the analysis of large-scale excavations at Cahokia and investigations in the Richland Complex in the uplands, Pauketat and his colleagues have documented changes in material culture, architecture styles, and scale of mound and plaza construction at Cahokia and at rural villages that indicate a more rapid transition at the onset of the Mississippian period (Alt 2001, 2002a, 2006a; Emerson and Pauketat 2002; Fortier and McElrath 2002; Fortier et al. 2006; Pauketat 1994, 1997, 2000a, 2002, 2003, 2004; Pauketat and Emerson 1997, 2008).

These well-documented changes include a significant increase in regional population, new architectural construction techniques and forms, the intensification of monumental construction, the reorganization of site layout, changes in pottery production, greater quantities of exotic chert and mineral resources, new tool types and forms, large-scale feasting events, and the abandonment or establishment of entire sites (Barrier and Horsley 2014; Collins 1990; Dalan et al. 2003; Emerson 1997a; Fowler 1978; Holley 1989; Milner 1986; Pauketat 1998a, 1998b, 2003; Pauketat and Lopinot 1997; Pauketat et al. 1998). The fact that these changes occurred over a wide expanse of the northern American Bottom floodplain and uplands at nearly the same time points to a change in community and identity at the local level as well as the regional level. These changes are presumably associated with the founding of a sociopolitical and religious center at Cahokia (Emerson 1997a, b; Milner 2006; Pauketat 2003, 2004, 2013).

Mobility, Landscapes, and Complexity

In order to fully investigate the timing and extent of the Mississippian transition, it is necessary to approach the topic from multiple perspectives and scales. In this analysis I employ a spatial perspective with a focus on mobility, because lived space is relatively easy to access archaeologically through mapping and excavation. Also, changes in lived space and movement within the landscape, especially on a regional scale, are entangled with changes in society, including community identities, political organization, social relations, and ideology.

Movements of people and objects as well as the physical construction of urbanized spaces, including plazas, avenues, and monuments, also involve the reconstruction of landscapes. As Tilley (2004) notes, landscapes are a medium for action and hence are valued and political. Similarly, Adam Smith (2003) views landscapes as relational spaces constructed through social practices and relations among people and objects. He notes that landscapes reflexively constrain and enable practices. Therefore, changes in landscapes can also alter daily practices and movements. If we view landscapes as constructed through social relations, then we might consider that alterations to landscapes can result in changes to sociopolitical formations.

The movements of people and objects have tangible historical effects, not only for social life but also for effecting sociopolitical change and cultural construction (Alt 2006b; Bradley 2002; Cobb and Butler 2006; Lekson 1999; Pauketat 2003; Wallis 2008). Through analyses of the distribution of settlements, site layout, occupational histories, and material culture, I trace localized movements that occurred in the American Bottom region at the beginning of the Mississippian period. These localized movements combined with an influx of foreign individuals (see Ambrose et al. 2003; Emerson and Hedman 2016; Pauketat 2003; Slater et al. 2014) and families from as far away as present-day Wisconsin and Louisiana altered the landscape physically and conceptually and were critical to the creation of a regionally integrated polity centered at Cahokia.

Movements, ranging from the permanent relocation of households to cyclical movements, including those with religious or economic motivations, necessitate the renegotiation of social, political, and economic relations, because people are extracted, voluntarily or otherwise, from the places and people with which they most closely identify (Alt 2006b; Bender 2001; Nanoglou 2008; Pauketat 2003, 2007). Movements of foreigners and local groups into centralized locations, often combined with large-scale construction projects, result in the concentration of population and potentially the creation of urban areas (M. Smith 2003). Urbanization is dependent upon such movements of people, often on a grand scale. As centers of dense population, these urban spaces are places where relationships are renegotiated on a daily basis through interactions between groups, often with differing interests and goals based on kinship, ethnicity, and status among other asserted identities (M. Smith 2003; Yaeger 2003).

Processes of urbanization also alter nonurban areas. This can include movements out into uninhabited or less densely populated areas in order to produce foodstuffs and extract resources for use locally and to supply urban residents. In some cases, political allies, either drawn from rural populations or sent out from the center, occupy positions of power within the countryside and serve to monitor, administer, and integrate isolated rural families (Alt 2006a; Emerson 1997a, b; Yaeger 2003). This can be achieved through localized communal activities and the distribution of items associated with the center and higher-status groups. Often, symbols and items drawn from local and foreign groups in both urban and rural areas are combined into novel ways (M. Smith 2003; Yaeger 2003).

One way that rural residents can assert a shared identity and connection with the sociopolitical center is by emulating the styles of urban residents (Yaeger 2003). The inclusion of rural and urban residents in periodic festivities such as feasting, gaming, and religious celebrations can instill a feeling of camaraderie among disparate groups by virtue of shared experiences.[1] Participation in monumental construction can also foster a shared identity by making the participants a physical part of the new landscape (Bender 2001; Joyce 2003; Pauketat 2000a; Pauketat and Alt 2003; Tilley 2004). In these ways, both permanent and repeated temporary movements of people and goods are implicated in the creation of regionally integrated polities.

Methodology

In this analysis I employ multiple lines of evidence at various scales within the American Bottom to identify past movements of people and objects and to access changes in space that occurred during the Mississippian transition (AD 975–1100). These lines of evidence include the identification of architectural styles and construction methods, the reorganization of space visible in site layout and occupation history, and the distribution of ceramic and lithic materials. Through this research it is possible to identify the historical effects of movement and urbanization on the American Bottom political landscape (*sensu* A. Smith 2003) and ultimately how Cahokia came to be a sociopolitical center through the severing of local ties and construction of a large-scale community.

I first compiled a list of sites recorded in the Illinois Archaeological Survey site files.[2] I included only sites located within three Illinois counties (Madison, St. Clair, and Monroe) with evidence (from surface collection or excavation) indicating they were occupied during the late Terminal Late Woodland and/or Early Mississippian period.[3] I also recorded the subregions within which they are located, in order to delineate differences or similarities between sites

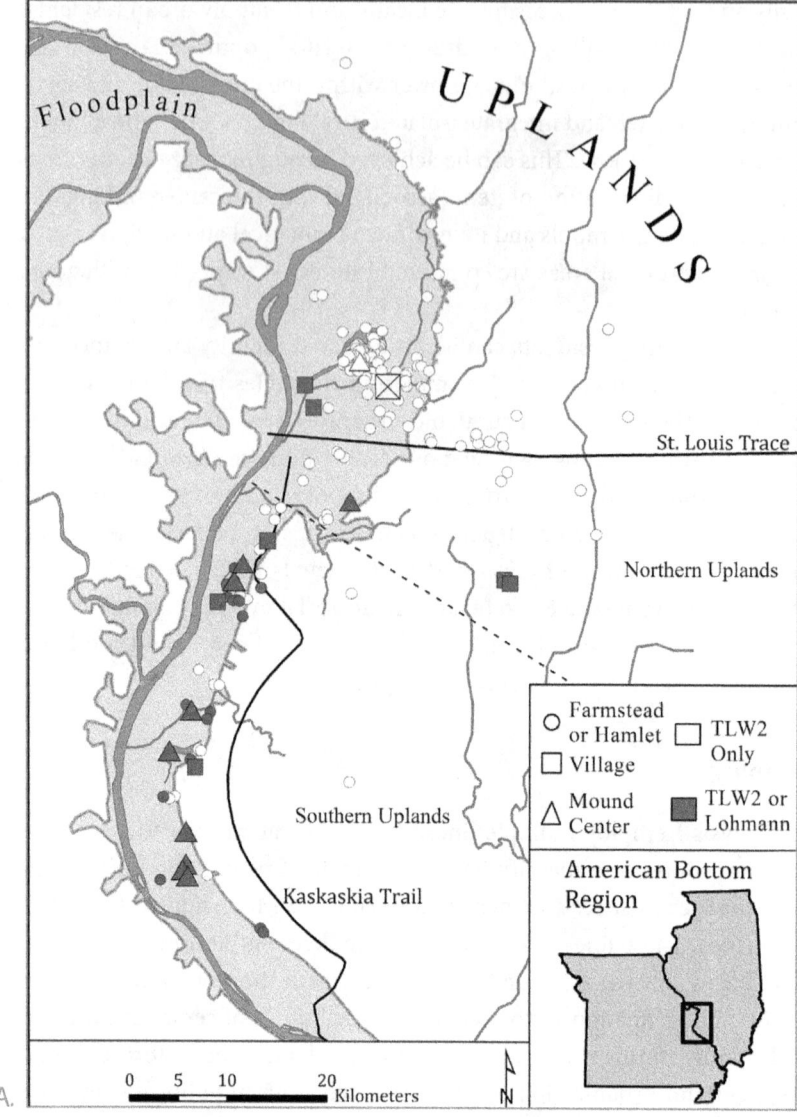

Figure 3.1. Late Terminal Late Woodland (*a, above*) and Early Mississippian (*b, opposite*) site distribution in the American Bottom.

located in different areas. The four subregions (northern floodplain, northern uplands, southern floodplain, and southern uplands) were defined based on physiographic features of the natural landscape, namely, the bluff edge and the Prairie du Pont Creek (see Figure 3.1). The division between the northern and southern uplands is an arbitrary extension of the division created by Prairie du Pont Creek, since there is no obvious natural division.

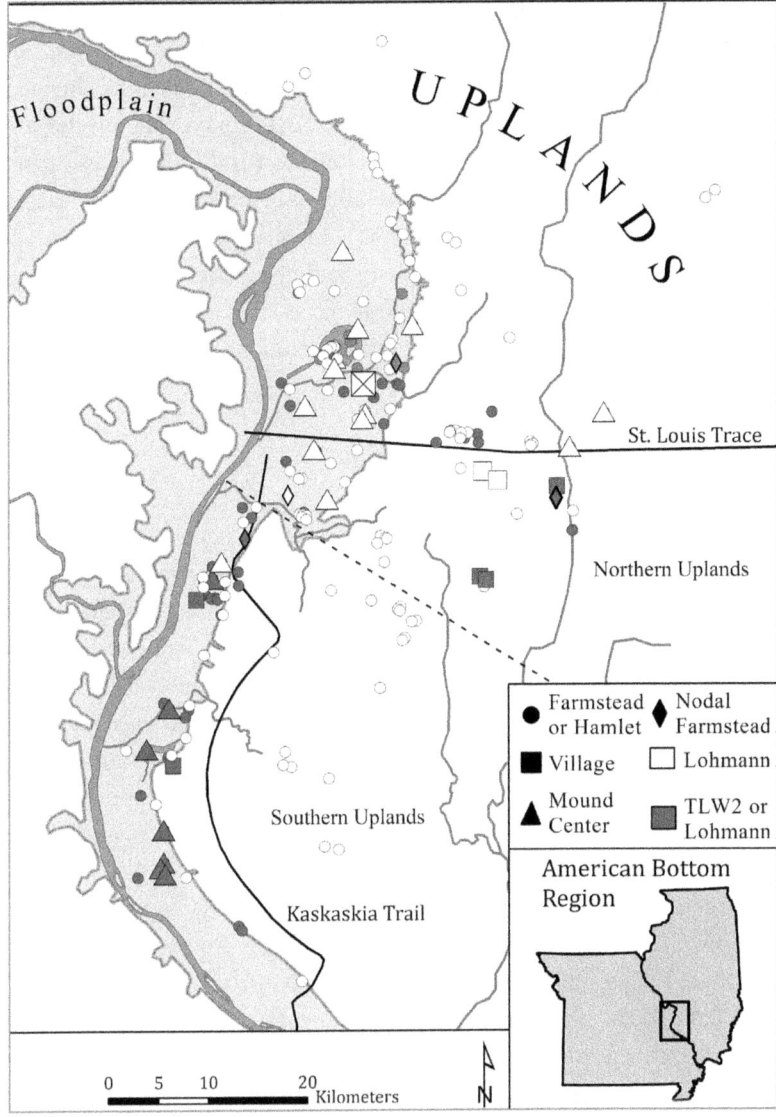

Sites that were completely excavated were classified based on the number of structures. Following terminology established by Holley and colleagues (2001), sites with fewer than 20 structures are referred to as hamlets, while those with more than 20 structures are referred to as villages. Sites with one or more mounds are classified as mound centers, while sites with fewer than four domestic structures are considered farmsteads. This classification of site types serves as a proxy for population size. Larger sites with more structures presumably were home to larger numbers of people. I digitized plan maps of 10 excavated sites in order to identify whether and how site layouts changed during this transitional period. Finally, I compiled data concerning the density and distribution of material remains at Cahokia and rural farmsteads during the Lohmann phase to investigate the possibility of centralized production or control of goods and rural production possibly intended as tribute.[4] This data set illustrates the movement of local residents and objects *within* the region as evidenced by population changes; abandonment, establishment, or reorganization of sites; changes in types of sites; and integration of residents through participation in communal events and exchanges.

Site Location

In total, 635 sites were identified with either surface (i.e., diagnostic pottery) or excavation data (i.e., architecture, diagnostic pottery) indicating occupations dating to the late Terminal Late Woodland and/or Early Mississippian period (Table 3.1).[5] Of these, nearly one-third (32 percent) might date to either period or both. Included in this subset are several unexcavated mound centers located in the southern American Bottom. Twenty-nine percent of the sites appear to have been abandoned, because they exhibit evidence for occupation during the late Terminal Late Woodland period but not the Early Mississippian. Most late Terminal Late Woodland sites are located within the floodplain and on or near the bluff edge. Sites are predominantly small hamlets, although a few large villages composed of a few hundred to a few thousand people were present, including Cahokia, Range, East St. Louis, and likely Pulcher (Fortier and McElrath 2002; Kelly 1990b; Kelly et al. 2007). The Morrison site, located near Horseshoe Lake, is the only site with evidence suggesting the construction of mounds during this period, although it is possible that mound construction commenced at Cahokia and Pulcher as well (Betzenhauser 2011; Betzenhauser et al. 2015; Lopinot et al. 1998; Pauketat et al. 1998). There is no evidence for mound construction or large villages in the uplands during the late Terminal Late Woodland.

The subsequent early Mississippian period occupation of the American Bottom region exhibits a wide range of site sizes and types, an increased number of sites in the uplands, and a dramatic increase in monumental construction. Of the 451 sites in the sample with evidence for occupation during the Lohmann phase, more than half (55 percent) were newly established in areas not occupied during the late Terminal Late Woodland period. Mound construction

Table 3.1. Total Site Occupations, Surveyed Areas, and Site Densities by Sub-Region

Sub-Region	Abandoned		Established		Reorganized		Total	
	Ct.	Row %	Ct.	Row %	Ct.	Row %	Ct.	Column %
Northern Floodplain	104	32.1	95	29.3	125	38.6	324	51.0
Northern Uplands	60	26.8	120	53.6	44	19.6	224	35.3
Southern Floodplain	18	28.6	17	27.0	28	44.4	63	9.9
Southern Uplands	2	8.3	18	75.0	4	16.7	24	3.8
Total	184	29.0	250	39.4	201	31.7	635	100.0

Sub-Region	Total Area (km²)	Area Surveyed (km²)	%	Site Density (Ct./km²)
Northern Floodplain	476	148	31.1	2.19
Northern Uplands	2,507	428	17.1	0.52
Southern Floodplain	320	35	10.9	1.80
Southern Uplands	1,393	93	6.7	0.26
Total	4,696	704	15.0	0.90

Note: Abandoned sites were occupied in the late TLW but not in the Lohmann phase; established sites were not occupied in the late TLW but were occupied during the Lohmann phase; reorganized sites were possibly occupied in both the late TLW and Lohmann phase. Each site is counted only once even if there were multiple occupations. The sample includes both excavated sites and unexcavated sites with surface data.

during this period is evident at several sites in the floodplain north and south of Cahokia and appears for the first time in the uplands to the east. Mounds were built in previously unoccupied areas as well as in the same locales as late Terminal Late Woodland settlements, including small hamlets and larger villages. The construction of mounds at previously occupied sites might suggest that individuals or families that occupied positions of power allied themselves with particular places and possibly ancestors. Farmsteads were widely dispersed throughout the floodplain and uplands. Some farmsteads, referred to as nodal, exhibit evidence for suprahousehold activities, including feasting, communal storage, or ceremonies, suggesting their role in the integration of rural populations (Emerson 1997a, 1997b; Mehrer 1995).

The difference in number of sites in each subregion may be related to the more limited survey coverage of the southern American Bottom region (see also Schroeder 2004). Less than 10 percent of the southern uplands and only 11 percent of the southern floodplain have been surveyed, in contrast to over

30 percent of the northern uplands and 17 percent of the northern floodplain. Site density, measured as the total number of sites per surveyed area (km^2) illustrates that late Terminal Late Woodland and Lohmann phase sites are most concentrated in the floodplain, particularly in the northern floodplain (2.19 sites/km^2). This suggests that there is a higher density of Mississippian transition sites located in the northern American Bottom region than in the south. The greatest increase in site density is in the northern and southern uplands, while the density of floodplain sites decreases slightly. The increase in small sites and villages in the uplands is suggestive of resettlement in order to take advantage of arable land for the production of maize. Although there are fewer early Mississippian sites in the floodplain, the sites tend to be much larger than those in the uplands, indicating a greater concentration of population. The largest sites (Cahokia and East St. Louis) are located in close proximity to each other in the northern floodplain (Betzenhauser and Plocher 2014; Pauketat and Lopinot 1997). Only the Pulcher site, located in the northern reaches of the southern floodplain, can come close to these sites in terms of size. Therefore, based on the distribution of sites and site sizes, there appears to be a significant increase in population in the northern floodplain and an expansion of inhabitation in the uplands in both the north and south. The site and population shifts in the southern floodplain appear to be minor in comparison. This pattern is partly related to the limited amount of excavation in the southern portion of the American Bottom and the difficulty in determining whether a site dates to the late Terminal Late Woodland or early Mississippian period based on surface data in this subregion.

Site Layout and Architecture

Late Terminal Late Woodland villages typically include one or more courtyards surrounded by several structures (for examples, see Benson and Betzenhauser 2012; Kelly et al. 2007; Pauketat 1998b, 2013b). Many courtyards contain central features such as communal storage pits or marker posts. Domiciles were typically built using single posts set in deep, rectangular basins. Many late Terminal Late Woodland sites were occupied during only one phase, suggesting that the residents were not tied to these locales for multiple generations. However, there are several sites that were occupied continuously for at least a century prior the Lohmann phase. These include large village sites such as Cahokia and Range, as well as hamlets, including the Divers and George Reeves sites (Betzenhauser 2011; Freimuth 2010; Kelly 1980; Kelly et al. 2007; McElrath and Finney 1987; Pauketat 1998b, 2013b).

In many cases, changes to site layout during the early Mississippian period are dramatic. At Tract 15A at Cahokia, multiple late Terminal Late Woodland courtyards were replaced by Lohmann phase wall trench structures, including new types of structures (T-shaped and circular) arranged around rectangular plazas (Pauketat 1998b). The ICT-II Tract was unoccupied during the late Terminal Late Woodland, but during the Lohmann phase, over 20 structures were built along the southwestern corner of a possible plaza, including T-shaped, circular, and storage structures (Collins 1997; Mehrer and Collins 1995). Most structures and plazas are oriented to the north or slightly east of north, an orientation shared by the Grand Plaza, the distribution of mounds in the central area of the site, and the Rattlesnake Causeway, suggesting the reorganization of space along a shared axis (Baires 2014; Collins 1997; Fowler 1969; Pauketat 1998b, 2013a). These data indicate the site underwent a rapid increase in population and a site-wide reorganization of space related to urbanization (Alt et al. 2010; Dalan et al. 2003; Fowler 1997; Pauketat 1998a).

Outside the mound centers, spatial organization varies, although there are some common elements that suggest direct connections between Cahokians and rural residents. For example, the presence of Cahokia-style pottery, structure orientations, and architecture such as T-shaped structures and storage facilities at the Grossmann site in the uplands are consistent with the creation of an administrative center that was established among the rural population (Alt 2006b). Similarly, many nodal farmsteads also exhibit Cahokia-style architecture, including circular structures, storage facilities, and marker posts (Betzenhauser 2006; Emerson 1997a).

Based on data derived from excavation (see Alt 2002b; Benson and Betzenhauser 2012; Betzenhauser 2011; Betzenhauser et al. 2009; Freimuth 2010; Kelly et al. 2007; Pauketat 1998b, 2013b), it appears that villages occupied during the late Terminal Late Woodland that were not abandoned were altered in one of only two ways. As previously discussed, some villages were transformed into large mound centers through large-scale construction projects. Others were significantly depopulated and supplanted by farmsteads, including nodal farmsteads. There are no sites documented in this sample that indicate a Terminal Late Woodland village site remained a village site during the Lohmann phase. They increased in size and became mound centers, decreased in population and became farmsteads, or were completely abandoned.

The Range site is an excellent example of a depopulated Terminal Late Woodland village (Hanenberger 2003; Kelly et al. 2007). The final Lindeman phase occupation at Range comprises 35 structures, four pits, and an arc of posts (Figure 3.2). Kelly (2007) suggested the structures were arranged to form

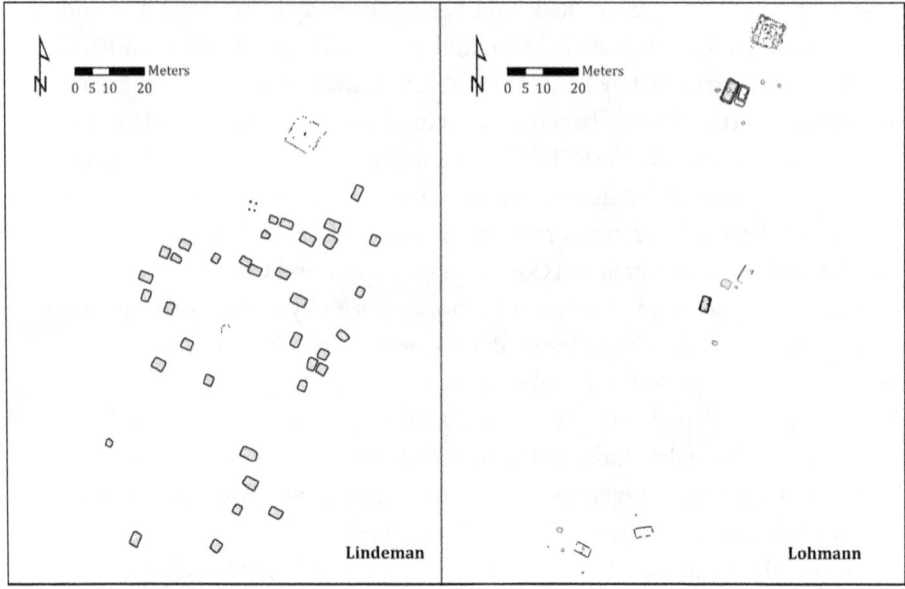

Figure 3.2. Range site (after Kelly 1990b, Figure 43; and Hanenberger 2003 Figures 5.4–5.7).

two courtyards, one with the arc of posts at its center and the other immediately to the south. In contrast, the earliest Mississippian settlements at the site are characterized by a series of four spatially separated farmsteads composed of two or three contemporaneous structures and a handful of pits. In total, only 10 structures date to the Lohmann phase, and all but one were built using wall trenches. Although the size of the occupation decreased drastically, there is evidence for suprahousehold activities, most notably in the form of a large single post structure located in the northern settlement, and a large refuse pit possibly associated with feasting located in the next settlement to the south. This depopulation is particularly significant given that the Range site was continuously occupied as a village site beginning during the Late Woodland Patrick phase (AD 650–900).

Direct evidence for the Terminal Late Woodland to Mississippian transition exists at the Divers site in the form of two Lindeman phase structures that were superimposed by Lohmann phase structures exhibiting the opposite orientation (Betzenhauser 2011; Freimuth 2010). This pattern has been noted at other contemporaneous sites in the region. The use of the same space suggests that the structures were occupied by the same people or family group. Alternatively, the change in orientation might indicate that the Lohmann phase residents appropriated local sources of power through referencing past inhabitants. Similarly, the presence of three burned Lindeman phase structures with intact floor assemblages may indicate intentional incineration, either by the Lindeman phase residents before leaving or by the Mississippian residents prior to the construction of the new buildings. If the Lohmann phase residents intentionally burned these structures, then it may indicate an attempt to remove reminders of the past occupants while tapping into established local sources of power (Bradley 2002; Joyce 2003; Van Dyke and Alcock 2003).

Material Remains

Material remains recovered from late Terminal Late Woodland sites in the American Bottom and uplands indicate the existence of localized pottery traditions, the use of local and nonlocal raw materials for expedient and formal stone tools, the cultivation of maize and Eastern Agricultural Complex cultigens, and very limited evidence for nonlocal immigrants. Tempering agents vary depending on the section of the region in which the pottery was produced (Kelly 1990a). Vessel forms are limited to jars, bowls, stumpware, and bottles (Kelly et al. 1984). A significant proportion of vessels exhibit red-slipped surfaces, particularly seed jars and bowls. Many lips on jars and bowls are embellished, some with effigy lugs. A certain degree of mobility and interaction within the region existed during the late Terminal Late Woodland period, as evidenced by the presence of a few pots produced in the northern American Bottom and uplands at sites in the southern American Bottom and vice versa (Emerson and Jackson 1984; Kelly et al. 2007; Milner 1984; Pauketat 1998b, 2013b). Although exotic pottery has been recovered from a few late Terminal Late Woodland occupations, the overall quantity is very low and limited to the largest sites (Fortier and McElrath 2002). Fortier and McElrath (2002) note that the distribution of certain materials and objects (e.g., discoidals) appears to indicate these items were held as community possessions.

Material assemblages recovered from Lohmann phase contexts at farmsteads, villages, and mound centers differ from late Terminal Late Woodland assemblages in several significant ways. There is greater standardization in terms of pottery temper, surface treatment, and form (Pauketat 1994). Most vessels are tempered with shell, surfaces are predominantly plain or burnished slip, and rolled rims are common (Milner et al. 1984). Nonlocal pottery from the northern Midwest, Plains, Lower Mississippi Valley, and Caddo and Yankeetown regions constitute a larger proportion of assemblages, and not only at larger sites (Alt 2006a; Bareis 1965; Harken et al. 2014; Holley 1989; Pauketat

1998b, 2003; Watts and Kruchten 2010). Nonlocal and special lithic materials are more common, including Mill Creek hoes, quartz crystal, hematite, galena, flint clay, and pipestone (Cobb 2000; Emerson et al. 2003; Koldehoff and Brennan 2011; Koldehoff and Wilson 2011; Milner et al. 1984).

The distributions of certain types of materials and artifacts provide evidence for rural production of foodstuffs and other items possibly intended as tribute. Pauketat (2003) noted a high concentration of Mill Creek hoes and flakes at upland villages, suggesting surplus production of maize. In a previous analysis (Betzenhauser 2006), I identified higher concentrations of points, ceramic spindle whorls, pigments, and storage structures at farmsteads located between 10 and 20 km from Cahokia (Figure 3.3). The points could have been used to procure meat for urban residents, as is suggested by the overrepresentation of

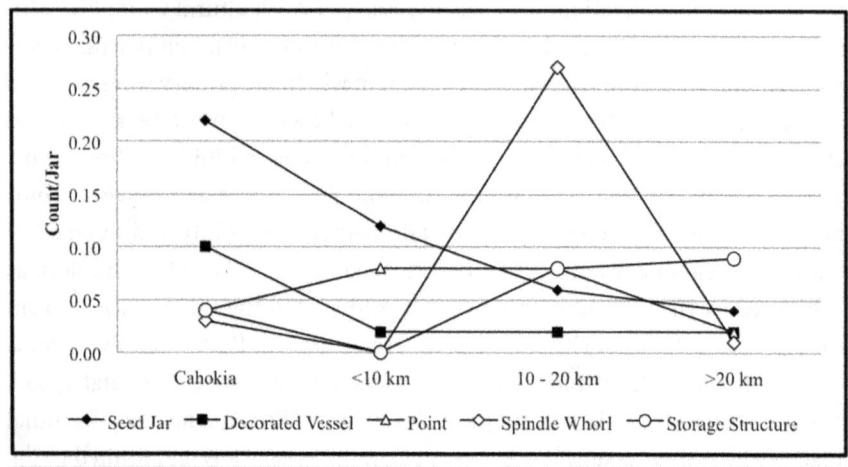

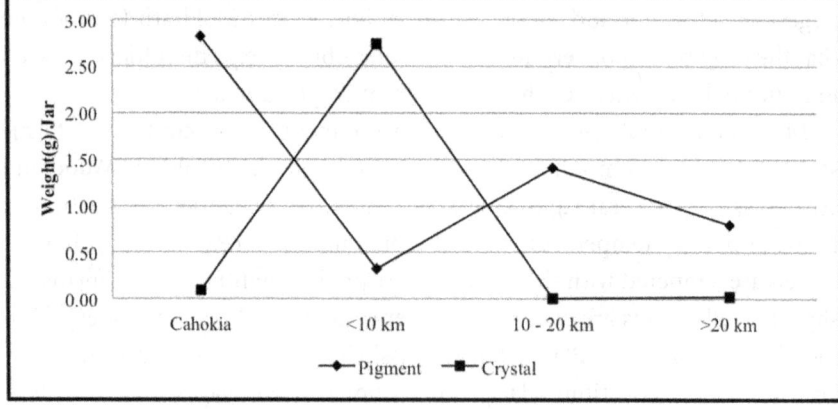

Figure 3.3. Regional distribution of materials in the Lohmann phase.

high-utility parts of deer at Cahokia (Kelly 1997). The high density of spindle whorls and pigments at sites in the uplands and floodplain may indicate the production of dyed cloth as tribute (Alt 1999), although pigments are most concentrated at Cahokia. The concentration of storage structures at nodal sites in the countryside may indicate that people living at nodal sites held stores of food and/or objects intended as tribute or for redistribution among rural residents. Other items and materials, including crystals, seed jars, and decorated vessels, are most concentrated at and near Cahokia, suggesting centralized control (Betzenhauser 2011; Pauketat 1994; Yerkes 1983).

Large-scale public events held at Cahokia included both urban and rural residents (Fowler et al. 1999; Pauketat et al. 2002). The Grand Plaza itself is suggestive of large-scale events and gaming, due its sheer size and ability to accommodate large groups of people. The submound 51 pit, located on the east side of the Grand Plaza, contained a high concentration of food remains and broken pots, suggesting large feasting events (Pauketat et al. 2002). Finally, isotopic analyses of human remains at Mound 72 reveal that both living and nonliving rural and high-status urban residents, as well as foreign and local groups, were participants in mortuary-related performances (Ambrose et al. 2003; Fowler et al. 1999; Slater et al. 2014).

Discussion

Although the Lohmann phase occupations exhibit greater variation than Terminal Late Woodland occupations in terms of types of sites and structures, there is a higher degree of standardization in domestic structure size and shape, pottery forms and surface treatments, and lithic raw materials (Betzenhauser 2011; Milner et al. 1984). Many items identified in Terminal Late Woodland assemblages are also associated with Mississippian contexts (e.g., celts, discoidals, and Mill Creek hoes). However, the production and use of pre-Mississippian pottery, tools, and architecture continued alongside new structure and tool forms. These earlier traditions did not maintain the same meanings and associations for Mississippian people throughout the region. Most were physically altered in some way or were associated with particular types of structures, items, raw materials, settlements, or groups of people (DeBoer 1993; Emerson 1997a; Pauketat 1994, 2001, 2000b).

These changes in the construction of space, community, and material culture are not limited to a few sites but are evident throughout the region at multiple scales, from the individual artifact to the regional landscape. The regional data gathered through this research indicate that some people were moving away from southern floodplain sites (as indicated by depopulation evident at some sites and the smaller site sizes compared to northern floodplain sites) at the same time people were moving to sites in the northern floodplain and uplands (as indicated by the increased site density and large site sizes). The fact that these movements occurred at the same time suggests that at least some of the southern American Bottom residents moved north, possibly to be closer to Cahokia. The traditions and daily practices of commoners, including architectural style, pottery production, foodways, and the treatment of the dead, were altered, invented, or suppressed in an effort to unite a diverse, even multi-ethnic population into the Cahokian community (Ambrose et al. 2003; Emerson and Hargrave 2000; Emerson and Hedman 2016; Pauketat 2000b, 2003; Slater et al. 2014). Commoners as well as elites throughout the region asserted connections with the Cahokian community through these practices and traditions as well as their use of items produced, procured, and redistributed through Cahokia (Alt 2002a, Pauketat 2000b, 2003; Wilson 1996). These connections were also mediated through nodal sites and villages that served as places of power in the countryside (Betzenhauser 2006; Emerson 1997a, b). New types of sites with distinctly Cahokia-style architecture were established among smaller villages and farmsteads and served as points of articulation where rural farmers and Cahokia-related political and religious figures interacted (Alt 2006a; Emerson et al. 2008).

People changed where they lived and how they interacted through the abandonment, establishment, and reorganization of sites at the beginning of the Mississippian period. The movement of entire households and the abandonment of some villages opened new spaces for the negotiation of power and identity. In some cases neighbors and family members that once lived in the same courtyard group were now living separately, as indicated by the decrease in population or abandonment of some sites and the establishment of dispersed farmsteads. In essence, this means a shift from local community-focused living on a day-to-day basis (within courtyards) to relative isolation, with periodic interaction at nodal sites and mound centers. Conversely, they could have moved to urbanized mound centers that would have necessitated interacting with even larger groups of people, including recently arrived immigrants from outside the region (Alt 2008).

The movement of people and objects into and within the American Bottom at the beginning of the Mississippian period resulted in the urbanization of Cahokia as well as the ruralization of the uplands and nonurban areas of the floodplain. Concurrent with the construction of Cahokia as an urban space (complete with monumental architecture) was the construction of the countryside with rural mound centers, villages, and farmsteads. Both local and foreign people settled in previously unoccupied areas in the uplands (Emerson 1997a, b; Pauketat 2003:54). It is reasonable to postulate that the farmers who established rural farmsteads moved from Terminal Late Woodland floodplain villages and hamlets as part of a region-wide reconstruction of the landscape (Emerson 1997a, b; Kelly 1990b; Pauketat 1997, 2003). New site types associated with the administration and integration of rural populations also appeared, indicating political, economic, and religious connections between urban and rural residents (Alt 2006a, Emerson 1997a, b).

The Cahokian community was a region-wide phenomenon composed of diverse groups of people in terms of wealth, ethnicity, and political clout. It included a complex sociopolitical structure with administrators, religious figures, rural farmers, and urban residents united through altered and invented traditions and styles in terms of material culture (e.g., pottery, stone tools, and raw materials) and architecture, exchanges of food and objects, and participation in community-constructing events. The maintenance of some pre-Mississippian traditions while participating in other aspects of the Cahokian community indicates that those who enacted these traditions held on to local community identities, in essence resisting the Cahokian community either actively or subconsciously (Alt 2002a, Emerson and Pauketat 2002; Hutson 2002; Pauketat 1998a, 2000b, 2001, 2003; Silliman 2001; Wilson 1998).

The data presented here indicate that the people who lived within the region were not separate or politically autonomous but were integral to the construction and maintenance of the Cahokian community and polity as well as the landscape. Cahokia became the center of a polity, not due to environmental factors but as a result of the actions and interactions of past agents at all socioeconomic levels and in all subregions. People throughout the region (e.g., urban and rural, local and nonlocal) were actively involved with creating Cahokia as a sociopolitical phenomenon through their movements, place making, interactions, and production (Alt 2010; Pauketat 2000b, 2003, 2013a; Pauketat and Alt 2005). The fact that rural residents were relatively isolated spatially does not mean they were independent or autonomous (Emerson 1997a, b; *contra* Muller and Stephens 1991). They lived with constant reminders of their membership in the larger constructed community, including the houses they lived in, the food they ate, and the pottery and stone tools they used.

The permanent relocations and repeated, temporary movements throughout the American Bottom region combined with economic, social, political, and religious interactions and events irreversibly altered the American Bottom political landscape. These changes were not identical and did not occur at the same exact time in all places throughout the region. They were negotiated differently depending on the people involved in such negotiations. It is now evident not only that labor was mobilized in constructing Cahokia, but that entire communities, shared memories, cosmologies, and the landscape itself were also critical to its creation.

Acknowledgments

I would like to thank Dr. Greg Wilson for inviting me to participate in the SEAC symposium and to contribute to this volume. Many of the data presented here are the result of research completed in partial fulfillment of the Ph.D. degree in the Department of Anthropology at the University of Illinois, Urbana-Champaign. Staff at the Illinois State Archaeological Survey provided me with ample assistance, particularly in locating site reports and grey literature. Many thanks to Dr. Greg Wilson and Dr. Timothy Pauketat, and two anonymous reviewers, for providing comments and critiques on an earlier draft. This chapter is largely based on a paper contributed to the Mobility, Temporality, and Social Memory: Locating Objects and Persons in the Southeast symposium organized by Melissa Baltus Zych and Sarah (Otten) Baires at the 67th Annual Southeastern Archaeology Conference, October 30, 2010—Lexington. Any errors or omissions are my own.

Notes

1. It is also worth noting that communal interaction can also reaffirm inequity through the juxtapositioning of high- and low-status groups, resulting in unintended consequences (Yaeger 2003).

2. As most researchers are aware, state site file data are not always complete or recorded in the same way. Variation in the site files data exists due to differences in project methodology, when the site was recorded, who recorded the site, if a revisit form was completed after more-recent fieldwork, etc. However, the breadth of data is incomparable. They include site type, size, geographical location, and survey coverage areas.

3. Although contemporaneous sites are recorded in Missouri directly across the Mississippi River from the American Bottom, the data are less complete and not directly comparable to those in Illinois. Therefore, sites in Missouri are excluded from this analysis.

4. Hamlets, villages, and mound centers other than Cahokia are excluded from the analysis of the distribution of materials. The original analysis was intended to investigate if and how interconnected the people living at the smallest Mississippian sites were with Cahokians. In the interest of space, the other site types were excluded. I assume that the inclusion of these other site types would reveal that they were connected with Cahokians as well.

5. I accessed the Illinois State site file data through the GIS created and maintained by the Illinois State Museum at http://geoserver.dnr.illinois.gov/archaeologyviewer/. For a complete list of sites included in the sample, see Betzenhauser 2011 appendices A and B.

References Cited

Alt, Susan M.
1999   Spindle Whorls and Fiber Production at Early Cahokian Settlements. *Southeastern Archaeology* 18:124–133.
2001   Cahokian Change and the Authority of Tradition. In *The Archaeology of Traditions: Agency and History before and after Columbus*, edited by Timothy R. Pauketat, pp. 141–156. University Press of Florida, Gainesville.
2002a Identities, Traditions, and Diversity in Cahokia's Uplands. *Midcontinental Journal of Archaeology* 27(2):217–235.
2002b The Knoebel Site: Tradition and Change in the Cahokian Suburbs. Unpublished master's thesis, Department of Anthropology, University of Illinois, Urbana.
2006a Cultural Pluralism and Complexity: Analyzing a Cahokian Ritual Outpost. Unpublished Ph.D. dissertation, Department of Anthropology, University of Illinois, Urbana.
2006b The Power of Diversity: The Roles of Migration and Hybridity in Culture Change. In *Leadership and Polity in Mississippian Society*, edited by Brian M. Butler and Paul D. Welch, pp. 289–308. Center for Archaeological Investigations, Occasional Paper No. 33. Southern Illinois University, Carbondale.
2008   Unwilling Immigrants: Culture, Change and the "Other." In *Invisible Citizens: Captives and Their Consequences*, edited by Catherine M. Cameron, pp. 205–222. Foundation of Archaeological Inquiry series. University of Utah Press, Salt Lake City.
2010   Complexity in Action(s): Retelling the Cahokia Story. In *Ancient Complexities: New Perspectives in Precolumbian North America*, edited by Susan M. Alt, pp. 119–137. University of Utah Press, Salt Lake City.

Alt, Susan M., Jeffery D. Kruchten, and Timothy R. Pauketat
2010   The Construction and Use of Cahokia's Grand Plaza. *Journal of Field Archaeology* 35(2):131–146.

Ambrose, Stanley H., Jane Buikstra, and Harold W. Krueger
2003   Status and Gender Differences in Diet at Mound 72, Cahokia, Revealed by Isotopic Analysis of Bone. *Journal of Anthropological Archaeology* 22:217–226.

Baires, Sarah
2014   Cahokia's Origins: Religions, Complexity, and Ridge-Top Mortuaries in the Mississippi River Valley. Unpublished Ph.D. dissertation, Department of Anthropology, University of Illinois, Urbana.

Bandy, Matthew S.
2004   Fissioning, Scalar Stress, and Social Evolution in Early Village Societies. *American Anthropologist* 106(2):322–333.

Barrier, Casey R., and Timothy J. Horsley
2014   Shifting Communities: Demographic Profiles of Early Village Population Growth and Decline in the Central American Bottom. *American Antiquity* 79(2):295–313.

Bareis, Charles J.
1965   Megascopic and Petrographic Analyses of a Foreign Pottery Vessel from the Cahokia Site. *American Antiquity* 31(1):95–101.

Beck, Robin A. Jr., Douglas J. Bolender, James A. Brown, and Timothy K. Earle
2007   Eventful Archaeology: The Place of Space in Structural Transformation. *Current Anthropology* 48(6):833–860.

Bender, Barbara
   2001   Landscapes On-the-Move. *Journal of Social Archaeology* 1(1):75–89.
Benson, Erin, and Alleen Betzenhauser
   2012   Terminal Beginnings at the East St. Louis Mound Complex. Paper presented at the 69th Annual Meeting of the Southeastern Archaeological Conference, Baton Rouge.
Betzenhauser, Alleen
   2006   Greater Cahokian Farmsteads: A Quantitative and Qualitative Analysis of Diversity. Unpublished master's paper, Department of Anthropology, University of Illinois, Urbana.
   2011   Creating the Cahokian Community: The Power of Place in Early Mississippian Sociopolitical Dynamics. Unpublished Ph.D. dissertation, Department of Anthropology, University of Illinois, Urbana.
Betzenhauser, Alleen, Loryl Breitenback, and Brad Koldehoff
   2009   The Terminal Late Woodland Occupation at the Fish Lake Site, Monroe County, Illinois. Paper presented at the Kincaid Field Conference, Metropolis.
Betzenhauser, Alleen, Timothy R. Pauketat, Elizabeth Watts Malouchos, Neal H. Lopinot, and Daniel Marovitch
   2015   The Morrison Site: Evidence for Terminal Late Woodland Mound Construction in the American Bottom. *Illinois Archaeology* 27:1–27.
Betzenhauser, Alleen, and Luke Plocher
   2014   Early Residents of East St. Louis: Architecture and Community Organization (A.D. 900–1100). Paper presented at the 60th Annual Meeting of the Midwest Archaeological Conference, Champaign.
Bradley, Richard
   2002   *An Archaeology of Natural Places*. Routledge, New York.
Cobb, Charles R.
   2000   *From Quarry to Cornfield: The Political Economy of Mississippian Hoe Production*. University of Alabama Press, Tuscaloosa.
Cobb, Charles R., and Brian M. Butler
   2006   Mississippian Migration and Emplacement in the Lower Ohio Valley. In *Leadership and Polity in Mississippian Society*, edited by Brian M. Butler and Paul D. Welch, pp. 328–347. Center for Archaeological Investigations, Southern Illinois University, Carbondale.
Collins, James M.
   1990   *The Archaeology of the Cahokia Mounds ICT-II: Site Structure*. Illinois Cultural Resources Study 10. Illinois Historic Preservation Agency, Springfield.
   1997   Cahokia Settlement and Social Structures as Viewed from the ICT-II. In *Cahokia: Domination and Ideology in the Mississippian World*, edited by Timothy R. Pauketat and Thomas E. Emerson, pp. 124–140. University of Nebraska Press, Lincoln.
Dalan, Rinita A., George R. Holley, William I. Woods, Harold W. Watters Jr., and John A. Koepke
   2003   *Envisioning Cahokia: A Landscape Perspective*. Northern Illinois University Press, DeKalb.
DeBoer, Warren R.
   1993   Like a Rolling Stone: The Chunkey Game and Political Organization in Eastern North America. *Southeastern Archaeology* 12:83–92.
Emerson, Thomas E.

1997a   *Cahokia and the Archaeology of Power.* University of Alabama Press, Tuscaloosa.

1997b   Reflections from the Countryside on Cahokian Hegemony. In *Domination and Ideology in the Mississippian World*, edited by Timothy R. Pauketat and Thomas E. Emerson, pp. 167–189. University of Nebraska Press, Lincoln.

2002   An Introduction to Cahokia 2002: Diversity, Complexity, and History. *Midcontinental Journal of Archaeology* 27(2): 127–148.

Emerson, Thomas E., Susan M. Alt, and Timothy R. Pauketat

2008   Locating American Indian Religion at Cahokia and Beyond. In *Religion, Archaeology, and the Material World*, edited by Lars Fogelin, pp. 216–236. Center for Archaeological Investigations, Occasional Paper No. 36. Southern Illinois University at Carbondale.

Emerson, Thomas E., and Eve Hargrave

2000   Strangers in Paradise: Recognizing Ethnic Mortuary Diversity on the Fringes of Cahokia. *Southeastern Archaeology* 19:1–23.

Emerson, Thomas E., and Kristin M. Hedman

2016   The Dangers of Diversity: The Consolidation and Dissolution of Cahokia, Native North America's First Urban Polity. In *Beyond Collapse: Archaeological Perspectives on Resilience, Revitalization, and Transformation in Complex Societies*, edited by Ronald K. Faulseit, pp. 147–175. Center for Archaeological Investigations, Occasional Paper No. 42. Southern Illinois University Press, Carbondale.

Emerson, Thomas E., Randall E. Hughes, Mary R. Hynes, and Sarah U. Wisseman

2003   The Sourcing and Interpretation of Cahokia-Style Figurines in the Trans-Mississippi South and Southeast. *American Antiquity* 68(2):287–314.

Emerson, Thomas E., and Douglas K. Jackson

1984   *The BBB Motor Site (11-MS-595).* American Bottom Archaeology, FAI-270 Site Reports 6. University of Illinois Press, Urbana.

Emerson, Thomas E., and Timothy R. Pauketat

2002   Embodying Power and Resistance at Cahokia. In *The Dynamics of Power*, edited by Maria O'Donovan, pp. 105–125. Center for Archaeological Investigations, Occasional Paper No. 30. Southern Illinois University at Carbondale.

Fortier, Andrew C., and Dale L. McElrath

2002   Deconstructing the Emergent Mississippian Concept: The Case for the Terminal Late Woodland in the American Bottom. *Midcontinental Journal of Archaeology* 27(2):171–215.

Fortier, Andrew C., Thomas E. Emerson, and Dale L. McElrath

2006   Calibrating and Reassessing American Bottom Culture History. *Southeastern Archaeology* 25(2):170–211.

Fowler, Melvin L.

1969   Middle Mississippian Agricultural Fields. *American Antiquity* 34(4):365–375.

1978   Cahokia and the American Bottom: Settlement Archaeology. In *Mississippian Settlement Patterns*, edited by Bruce D. Smith, pp. 455–478. Academic Press, New York.

1997   *The Cahokia Atlas: A Historical Atlas of Cahokia Archaeology (Revised).* University of Illinois at Urbana–Champaign Studies in Archaeology No. 2. Illinois Transportation Archaeological Research Program, University of Illinois, Urbana.

Fowler, Melvin L., Jerome Rose, Barbara VanderLeest, and Steven R. Ahler

1999   The Mound 72 Area: Dedicated and Sacred Space in Early Cahokia. Reports of Investigations No. 54. Illinois State Museum Society, Springfield.

Freimuth, Glen A.
1974   The Lunsford-Pulcher Site: An Examination of Selected Traits and Their Social Implications in American Bottom Prehistory. Unpublished master's thesis, Department of Anthropology, University of Illinois, Urbana.
2010   Segmented and Ascendant Chiefdom Polity as Viewed from the Divers Site. Unpublished Ph.D. dissertation, Department of Anthropology, University of Illinois, Urbana.

Hanenberger, Ned H.
2003   The Range Site 3: Mississippian and Oneota Occupations. Research Reports No. 17. Illinois Transportation Archaeological Research Program, University of Illinois, Urbana.

Harken, Sarah, Alleen Betzenhauser, Ross Brady, and Alexandra Freyer
2014   Chronological Implications and External Connections within East St. Louis Ceramics. Paper presented at the 60th Annual Meeting of the Midwest Archaeological Conference, Champaign.

Holley, George R.
1989   Archaeology of the Cahokia Mounds ICT-II: Ceramics. Illinois Cultural Resources Study No. 11. Illinois Historic Preservation Agency, Springfield.

Holley, George R., Mikels Skele, Harold W. Watters Jr., Kathryn E. Parker, Elizabeth M. Scott, Joyce A. Williams, Donald L. Booth, Julie N. Harper, Alan J. Brown, Christina L. Fulton, and Laura L. Harmon
2001   Introduction to the Prehistoric Archaeology of the Scott Joint-Use Archaeological Project. Contract Archaeology Series. Southern Illinois University, Edwardsville.

Hutson, Scott R.
2002   Built Space and Bad Subjects: Domination and Resistance at Monte Albán, Oaxaca, Mexico. Journal of Social Archaeology 2(1):53–80.

Joyce, Rosemary A.
2003   Concrete Memories: Fragments of the Past in the Classic Maya Present (500–1000 AD). In Archaeologies of Memory, edited by Ruth M. Van Dyke and Susan E. Alcock, pp. 104–125. Blackwell, Malden.

Kelly, John E.
1980   Formative Developments at Cahokia and the Adjacent American Bottom: A Merrell Tract Perspective. Unpublished Ph.D. dissertation, Department of Anthropology, University of Wisconsin, Madison.
1990a The Emergence of Mississippian Culture in the American Bottom Region. In The Mississippian Emergence, edited by Bruce D. Smith, pp. 113–152. University of Alabama Press, Tuscaloosa.
1990b Range Site Community Patterns and the Mississippian Emergence. In The Mississippian Emergence, edited by Bruce D. Smith, pp. 67–112. University of Alabama Press, Tuscaloosa.
1991   Cahokia and Its Role as a Gateway Center in Interregional Exchange. In Cahokia and the Hinterlands: Middle Mississippian Cultures of the Midwest, edited by Thomas E. Emerson and R. Barry Lewis, pp. 61–80. University of Illinois Press, Urbana.
2002   The Pulcher Tradition and the Ritualization of Cahokia: A Perspective from Cahokia's Southern Neighbor. Southeastern Archaeology 21(2):136–149.
2007   Lindeman Phase Features. In The Range Site 4: Emergent Mississippian George Reeves

and Lindeman Phase Occupations, by John E. Kelly, Steven J. Ozuk, and Joyce A. Williams, pp. 243–318. Research Reports No. 18. Illinois Transportation Archaeological Research Program, University of Illinois, Urbana.

Kelly, John E., Steven J. Ozuk, Douglas K. Jackson, Dale L. McElrath, Fred A. Finney, and Duane Esarey
  1984 Emergent Mississippian Period. In *American Bottom Archaeology: A Summary of the FAI-270 Project Contribution to the Culture History of the Mississippi River Valley*, edited by Charles J. Bareis and James W. Porter, pp. 128–157. University of Illinois Press, Champaign.

Kelly, John E., Steven J. Ozuk, and Joyce A. Williams
  2007 *The Range Site 4: Emergent Mississippian George Reeves and Lindeman Phase Occupations*. Research Reports No. 18. Illinois Transportation Archaeological Research Program, University of Illinois, Urbana.

Kelly, Lucretia
  1997 Patterns of Faunal Exploitation at Cahokia. In *Cahokia: Domination and Ideology in the Mississippian World*, edited by Timothy R. Pauketat and Thomas E. Emerson, pp. 69–88. University of Nebraska Press, Lincoln.

Koldehoff, Brad, and Tamira Brennan
  2011 Exploring Mississippian Polity Interaction and Craft Specialization with Ozark Chipped-Stone Resources. *Missouri Archaeology* 71:132–164.

Koldehoff, Brad, and Gregory D. Wilson
  2011 Mississippian Celt Production and Resource Extraction in the Upper Big River Valley of St. Francois County, Missouri. *Missouri Archaeology* 71:217–248.

Lekson, Stephen H.
  1999 *The Chaco Meridian: Centers of Political Power in the Ancient Southwest*. Altamira Press, Walnut Creek.

Lopinot, Neal H., Michael D. Conner, Jack H. Ray, and Jeffrey K. Yelton
  1998 *Prehistoric and Historic Properties on Mitigation Lands, Horseshoe Lake Peninsula, Madison County, Illinois*. St. Louis District Army Corps of Engineers, Historic Property Management Report 56. Center for Archaeological Research, Southwest Missouri State University, Springfield.

McElrath, Dale L., and Fred A. Finney
  1987 *The George Reeves Site*. American Bottom Archaeology, FAI-270 Site Reports Vol. 15. University of Illinois Press, Urbana.

Mehrer, Mark W.
  1995 *Cahokia's Countryside: Household Archaeology, Settlement Patterns, and Social Power*. Northern Illinois University Press, DeKalb.

Mehrer, Mark W., and James M. Collins
  1995 Household Archaeology at Cahokia and Its Hinterlands. In *Mississippian Communities and Households*, edited by J. Daniel Rogers and Bruce D. Smith, pp. 32–57. University of Alabama Press, Tuscaloosa.

Milner, George R.
  1984 *The Robinson's Lake Site*. American Bottom Archaeology, FAI-270 Site Reports Vol. 10. University of Illinois Press, Urbana.
  1986 Mississippi Period Population Density in a Segment of the Central Mississippi River Valley. *American Antiquity* 51(2):227–238.

1990   The Late Prehistoric Cahokia Cultural System of the Mississippi River Valley: Foundations, Florescence, and Fragmentation. *Journal of World Prehistory* 4(1):1–43.
1991   American Bottom Mississippian Culture: Internal Developments and External Relations. In *New Perspectives on Cahokia: Views from the Periphery*, edited by James B. Stoltman, pp. 29–47. Monographs in World Archaeology 2. Prehistory Press, Madison.
1996   Development and Dissolution of a Mississippian Society in the American Bottom, Illinois. In *Political Structure and Change in the Prehistoric Southeastern United States*, edited by John F. Scarry, pp. 27–52. University Press of Florida, Gainesville.
2006   *The Cahokia Chiefdom: The Archaeology of a Mississippian Society*. University Press of Florida, Gainesville.

Milner, George R., and Sissel Schroeder
1999   Mississippian Sociopolitical Systems. In *Great Towns and Regional Polities in the Prehistoric American Southwest and Southeast*, edited by Jill E. Neitzel, pp. 95–107. University of New Mexico Press, Albuquerque.

Milner, George, Thomas E. Emerson, Mark W. Mehrer, Joyce A. Williams, and Duane Esarey
1984   Mississippian and Oneota Period. In *American Bottom Archaeology: A Summary of the FAI-270 Project Contribution to the Culture History of the Mississippi River Valley*, edited by Charles J. Bareis and James W. Porter, pp. 158–186. University of Illinois Press, Urbana.

Muller, Jon, and Jeanette E. Stephens
1991   Mississippian Sociocultural Adaptation. In *Cahokia and the Hinterlands: Middle Mississippian Cultures of the Midwest*, edited by Thomas E. Emerson and R. Barry Lewis, pp. 297–310. University of Illinois Press, Urbana.

Nanoglou, Stratos
2008   Building Biographies and Households: Aspects of Community Life in Neolithic Northern Greece. *Journal of Social Archaeology* 8(1):139–160.

O'Brien, Patricia
1972   Urbanism, Cahokia, and Middle Mississippian. *Archaeology* 25(3):88–197.

Pauketat, Timothy R.
1994   *Ascent of Chiefs: Cahokia and Mississippian Politics in Native North America*. University of Alabama Press, Tuscaloosa.
1997   Cahokian Political Economy. In *Cahokia: Domination and Ideology in the Mississippian World*, edited by Timothy R. Pauketat and Thomas E. Emerson, pp. 30–51. University of Nebraska Press, Lincoln.
1998a Refiguring the Archaeology of Greater Cahokia. *Journal of Archaeological Research* 6(1):45–89.
1998b *The Archaeology of Downtown Cahokia: The Tract 15A and Dunham Tract Excavations*. Illinois Transportation Archaeological Research Program, Studies in Archaeology 1. University of Illinois, Urbana.
2000a The Tragedy of the Commoners. In *Agency in Archaeology*, edited by Marcia-Anne A. Dobres and John E. Robb, pp. 113–129. Routledge, London.
2000b Politicization and Community in the Pre-Columbian Mississippian Valley. In *The Archaeology of Communities: A New World Perspective*, edited by Marcello-Andrea Canuto and Jason Yaeger, pp. 16–43. Routledge, London.
2001   A New Tradition in Archaeology. In *The Archaeology of Traditions: Agency and History*

before and after Columbus, edited by Timothy R. Pauketat, pp. 1–16. University Press of Florida, Gainesville.
2002 A Fourth-Generation Synthesis of Cahokia and Mississippianization. *Midcontinental Journal of Archaeology* 27:149–170.
2003 Resettled Farmers and the Making of a Mississippian Polity. *American Antiquity* 68:39–66.
2004 *Ancient Cahokia and the Mississippians*. Cambridge University Press, Cambridge.
2007 *Chiefdoms and Other Archaeological Delusions*. AltaMira Press, Walnut Creek.
2013a *An Archaeology of the Cosmos: Rethinking Agency and Religion in Ancient America*. Routledge, New York.
2013b *The Archaeology of Downtown Cahokia II: The 1960 Excavations of Tract 15B*. Illinois State Archaeological Survey, Studies in Archaeology Vol. 8. University of Illinois at Urbana.

Pauketat, Timothy R., and Susan M. Alt
2003 Mounds, Memory, and Contested Mississippian History. In *Archaeologies of Memory*, edited by Ruth M. Van Dyke and Susan E. Alcock, pp. 151–179. Blackwell, Malden.
2005 Agency in a Postmold? Physicality and the Archaeology of Culture-Making. *Journal of Archaeological Method and Theory* 12(3):213–236.

Pauketat, Timothy R., and Thomas E. Emerson
1997 Introduction: Domination and Ideology in the Mississippian World. In *Cahokia: Domination and Ideology in the Mississippian World*, edited by Timothy R. Pauketat and Thomas E. Emerson, pp. 1–29. University of Nebraska Press, Lincoln.
1999 The Representation of Hegemony as Community at Cahokia. In *Material Symbols: Culture and Economy in Prehistory*, edited by John E. Robb, pp. 302–317. Center for Archaeological Investigations, Occasional Paper No. 26. Southern Illinois University, Carbondale.
2008 Star Performances and Cosmic Clutter. *Cambridge Archaeological Journal* 18(1):78–85.

Pauketat, Timothy R., Lucretia S. Kelly, Gayle J. Fritz, Neal H. Lopinot, Scott Elias, and Eve Hargrave
2002 The Residues of Feasting and Public Ritual at Early Cahokia. *American Antiquity* 67:257–279.

Pauketat, Timothy R., and Neal H. Lopinot
1997 Cahokia Population Dynamics. In *Cahokia: Domination and Ideology in the Mississippian World*, edited by Timothy R. Pauketat and Thomas E. Emerson, pp. 103–123. University of Nebraska Press, Lincoln.

Pauketat, Timothy R., Mark A. Rees, and Stephanie L. Pauketat
1998 *An Archaeological Survey of the Horseshoe Lake State Park, Madison County, Illinois*. Illinois State Museum Reports of Investigations No. 55. Illinois State Museum Society, Springfield.

Porter, James
1974 Cahokia Archaeology as Viewed from the Mitchell Site: A Satellite Community at A.D. 1150–1200. Unpublished Ph.D. dissertation, Department of Anthropology, University of Wisconsin, Madison.

Schroeder, Sissel
1997 Place, Productivity, and Politics: The Evolution of Cultural Complexity in the Cahokia

Area. Unpublished Ph.D. dissertation, Department of Anthropology, Pennsylvania State University, State College.

2004 Power and Place: Agency, Ecology, and History in the American Bottom, Illinois. *Antiquity* 78:812–827.

Silliman, Stephen

2001 Agency, Practical Politics and the Archaeology of Culture Contact. *Journal of Social Archaeology* 1(2):190–209.

Slater, Philip A., Kristin M. Hedman, and Thomas E. Emerson

2014 Immigrants at the Mississippian Polity of Cahokia: Strontium Isotope Evidence for Population Movement. *Journal of Archaeological Science* 44:117–127.

Smith, Adam T.

2003 *The Political Landscape: Constellations of Authority in Early Complex Polities*. University of California Press, Berkeley.

Smith, Bruce D.

2007 Preface to the New Edition. In *The Mississippian Emergence*, edited by Bruce D. Smith, pp. xix–xxxi. University of Alabama Press, Tuscaloosa.

Smith, Monica L.

2003 *The Social Construction of Ancient Cities*. Smithsonian Institution Press, Washington, D.C.

Tilley, Christopher

2004 From Body to Place to Landscape: A Phenomenological Perspective. In *The Materiality of Stone: Explorations in Landscape Phenomenology*, edited by Christopher Tilley, pp. 1–31. Berg, New York.

Van Dyke, Ruth M., and Susan E. Alcock

2003 Archaeologies of Memory: An Introduction. In *Archaeologies of Memory*, edited by Ruth M. Van Dyke and Susan E. Alcock, pp. 1–14. Blackwell, Malden.

Wallis, Neill J.

2008 Networks of History and Memory: Creating a Nexus of Social Identities in Woodland Period Mounds on the Lower St. Johns River, Florida. *Journal of Social Archaeology* 8(2):236–271.

Watts, Elizabeth L., and Jeffrey D. Kruchten

2010 Moving Objects, Moving People: Non-Local Pottery at East St. Louis. Paper presented at the 67th Annual Meeting of the Southeastern Archaeological Conference, Lexington.

Wilson, Gregory D.

1996 Insight through Icons. *Illinois Archaeology* 8(1, 2):23–37.

1998 A Case Study of Mississippian Resistance in the American Bottom. Unpublished master's thesis. University of Oklahoma, Norman.

Yaeger, Jason

2003 Untangling the Ties That Bind: The City, the Countryside, and the Nature of Maya Urbanism at Xunantunich, Belize. In *The Social Construction of Ancient Cities*, edited by Monica L. Smith, pp. 121–155. Smithsonian Institution Press, Washington, D.C.

Yerkes, Richard W.

1983 Microwear, Microdrills, and Mississippian Craft Specialization. *American Antiquity* 48(3):499–518.

4

The Mississippianization of the Illinois and Apple River Valleys

GREGORY D. WILSON, COLLEEN M. DELANEY,
AND PHILLIP G. MILLHOUSE

The Mississippianization of the upper Midwest provides one of the best-documented examples of culture contact in pre-Columbian North America (Conrad 1989, 1991; Emerson 1991, 1999; Finney and Stoltman 1991; Gibbon and Dobbes 1991; Goldstein and Richards 1991; Hall 1991; Tiffany 1991a). During the eleventh and twelfth centuries, a number of discontiguous regions occupied by Woodland era Native American groups witnessed a cultural transformation represented archaeologically in the appearance of Cahokian-style material culture. The nature of this transformation was highly variable, as the inhabitants of some regions came to embrace a more complete assortment of Cahokian traditions than others. This variability has complicated archaeological attempts at understanding the Mississippianization of Cahokia's northern hinterland. Were Cahokians present and directly engaged with locals in some regions and not others? If so, in what numbers and capacities were they present? Answering these questions is critical to understanding Mississippian beginnings in the upper Midwest, but it necessitates the archaeological ability to differentiate between the entangled processes of population movement and cultural emulation.

We begin by discussing a productive set of ideas and methods developed by southwestern archaeologists to identify and assess the scale of ancient population movements. Based on the effectiveness of these methods in the Southwest, we believe that they have analytical potential for investigating similar issues in the Mississippian region of eastern North America. Specifically, we employ these methods to evaluate archaeological evidence of eleventh- and twelfth-century culture contact among Cahokia Mississippian groups in the American

Bottom region and Woodland groups in the Lower Illinois River Valley (LIRV), the Central Illinois River Valley (CIRV), and the Apple River Valley (ARV). On the basis of our findings, we argue that the Mississippianization of the CIRV was an outcome of the arrival of small groups of Cahokians around AD 1050 followed by a regional process in which local Woodland groups broadly but selectively emulated aspects of a Cahokian way of life. Less extensive archaeological research in the LIRV and ARV constrains what can be said about the initial stages of Cahokia contact in these regions. However, the later stages of Mississippianization in both the LIRV and ARV entailed the broad-scale but selective emulation of a Cahokian way of life by local Woodland groups. We also discuss emerging ceramic evidence of pilgrimages or other sporadic journeys by northern groups to mound centers in the Cahokia area.

Jeffrey Clark's (2001) *Tracking Prehistoric Migrations: Pueblo Settlers among the Tonto Basin Hohokam* has been particularly influential among southwestern identity studies published within the last decade. His investigation employs a broad-ranging cross-cultural comparison to identify categories of material culture that are useful in tracking prehistoric migrations. The results of this comparison led Clark to conclude that material-culture attributes with low physical and contextual visibility, such as "domestic spatial organization, foodways, and the non-decorative production steps of ceramic vessel," are most useful in determining the origins of prehistoric immigrants. These attributes are useful as migration trackers specifically because they are seldom discursively intended to convey information about group identity, but instead are often the enculturative result of groups who share a settlement history and traditional ways of doing things. Drawing on earlier theoretical work by Christopher Carr (1995a, 1995b), Clark argues that highly visible forms of material culture such as decorative techniques, personal ornamentation, mortuary practices, and projectile points are less useful for tracking prehistoric migrations, as those were objects and attributes often subject to emulation by recent immigrants trying to *fit into* a new cultural milieu.

Using these analytical methods, Clark and other scholars (Lyons 2003; Neuzil 2008) conclude that beginning in the thirteenth century, Puebloan groups migrated from the northern Southwest southward into the Hohokam area. In most cases these migrations entailed the renegotiation of identities and social relationships. Despite these changes, many immigrant Pueblo groups maintained traditional ways of organizing domestic space, as well as low-visibility architectural construction and ceramic manufacturing techniques. They also continued manufacturing and using a variety of utilitarian pottery vessels with low physical and contextual visibility, including planters and base molds for pottery manufacture.

The southwestern literature has also been effective at demonstrating that the social impact and archaeological visibility of migrations vary on the basis of the size and composition of the migrating group and whether the population moved to an occupied or vacant region (Neuzil 2008:5–8). For example, community-level population movements tend to generate a more pervasive signature of nonlocal styles and attributes than the movement of individuals and/or households. Moreover, migrants moving into a previously occupied region must contend with social challenges to stylistically conform or stand out that are not present in unoccupied areas. Motivation is also important to consider, as invaders and other unwelcome intruders will have a different impact than the arrival of allies, emissaries, missionaries, or extended kin.

These concepts and analytical methods have great potential for assessing culture-contact scenarios in the Mississippian world. The mid-eleventh-century emergence of political complexity in the American Bottom had a profound influence on neighboring groups. In several cases this influence appears to have resulted in the northern movement of Cahokian objects, ideas, practices, and, in some cases, people into portions of the upper Midwest, including the Lower Illinois River Valley (Delaney-Rivera 2000; Farnsworth et al. 1991), the Central Illinois River Valley (Conrad 1989, 1991; Harn 1991), the Apple River Valley of northwestern Illinois (Emerson 1991; Millhouse 2012), the Trempealeau site in western Wisconsin (Pauketat et al. 2015), the Aztalan site in southeastern Wisconsin (Goldstein 1991), and the Red Wing area of Minnesota (Gibbon 1991; Rodell 1991). This dynamic is represented archaeologically in the early twelfth-century appearance of elaborate Mississippian ceremonial buildings, mound construction, and the proliferation of well-crafted Cahokian-style artifacts, including Ramey Incised and Powell Plain pots, tri-notched arrow points, and stone discoidals.

The role of Cahokian migration in the changes that took place in Cahokia's northern hinterland has been heavily debated. Some investigators have argued that the abrupt cultural changes in the region were principally orchestrated by a large influx of Cahokian migrants (Conrad 1991). However, the results of later biodistance studies in the Illinois Valley suggest that large-scale migrations into some of these areas from the American Bottom are improbable (Droessler 1981; Steadman 1998, 2001). These findings, however, do not preclude the northern movement of small groups of Cahokians into the Illinois Valley, or the movement of larger groups of Cahokians into other portions of the upper Midwest.

The historical ambiguities of these regional contact scenarios make them well suited for the kinds of identity and migration approaches that have been successfully employed in the southwestern United States. This study focuses on domestic ceramic assemblages, the analysis of which is directed toward evaluating the role of Cahokian immigration in the Mississippianization of the Lower Illinois River Valley, Central Illinois River Valley, and Apple River Valley. Although the Cahokian culture contact is apparent in other types of material culture, and population movements can be tracked directly from the analysis of human skeletal remains (DNA, isotope, biodistance), we target domestic ceramic data because potsherds are ubiquitous at pre-Columbian sites in the region and are imbued with important information about style, identity, and socioeconomic organization. Furthermore, ceramics can be recovered and analyzed in an inexpensive and nondestructive manner. The same cannot always be said for architecture and human skeletal remains. Moreover, it is not always possible to identify and excavate the mortuaries associated with particular residential sites, and destructive forms of bone chemistry may not always be acceptable to affiliated Native American groups.

Cahokia's Northern Hinterland

The eleventh-century political consolidation of the Cahokia polity in the American Bottom region of southwestern Illinois sent cultural shock waves throughout much of the Midsouth and Midwest and into the Plains (Pauketat 2004). Early Cahokia was a center of cultural entanglement, a dynamic that now appears to have entailed both an influx of nonlocal peoples and the centrifugal movement of Cahokians to hinterland locations (Pauketat 2003. Some of these newcomers appear to have permanently relocated to the greater Cahokia area in the context of village-scale migrations (Alt 2001, 2002, 2006). Others may have been pilgrims attending large-scale theatrical events at Cahokia and related sites (Pauketat 2013b; Pauketat et al. 2002; Pauketat et al. 2010; Skousen 2016). Although exchange goods and local emulations of Cahokian artifacts and architecture have been identified throughout much of the North American midcontinent, Cahokian politico-religious influence appears to have been most pervasive in regions north of the American Bottom (Conrad 1991; Emerson 1991; Kelly 1991; Stoltman et al. 2008), including the Lower Illinois River Valley, Central Illinois River Valley, and the Apple River Valley.

The Lower Illinois River Valley

The Lower Illinois River Valley (LIRV) begins at the confluence of the Illinois and Mississippi rivers just 30 km north of the northern limits of the American Bottom and extends northward to the present-day town of Meredosia, Illinois (see Figure 4.1). The Terminal Late Woodland occupation of the LIRV is referred to as the Jersey Bluff phase, the settlements of which can be found in the Illinois River Valley and its major tributaries. Large sites (> 2 ha) are located on alluvial fans at the mouths of entering tributary streams on both the eastern and western sides of the valley trench (Studenmund 2000:326). Currently the known distribution of Jersey Bluff sites is as far north as the Apple Creek drainage, west into the adjacent Mississippi Valley, and east up the Macoupin Valley (Farnsworth et al. 1991). Survey work has located small occupations in

Figure 4.1. Selected sites in the Lower Illinois River Valley.

the upland tributary valleys east and west of the Illinois River trench (Cross and Bittinger 1996; Studenmund et al. 1995), and in the northern quarter of the Lower Illinois Valley (Studenmund 2000). Most of the excavated sites are large bluff-base settlements located at either the main valley trench or the mouth of tributary valleys.

Jersey Bluff phase ceramic assemblages consist of grit-tempered and cord-marked vessels. Jars are the dominant vessel form and have flat-squared lips and undecorated rims, necks, and shoulders. Cord marking extends only up to the vessel shoulder; the neck and rim are smoothed or plain. Lugs, lip notching, castellations, and shell temper appear after AD 1000 (Farnsworth et al. 1991), although jar form remains unchanged. Bowls are scarce but can be found in large assemblages.

Two Early Mississippian villages have been identified in the LIRV, Audrey and Whiteside (Delaney-Rivera 2000, 2004; Perino 1973). The Early Mississippian occupation of the Audrey site village covers approximately 3 ha and is linked with a nearby mortuary complex known as the Moss Cemetery site (Goldstein 1980). Excavations at Audrey uncovered eight buildings arranged around the northern portion of a central plaza (Figure 4.2). Two sections of a

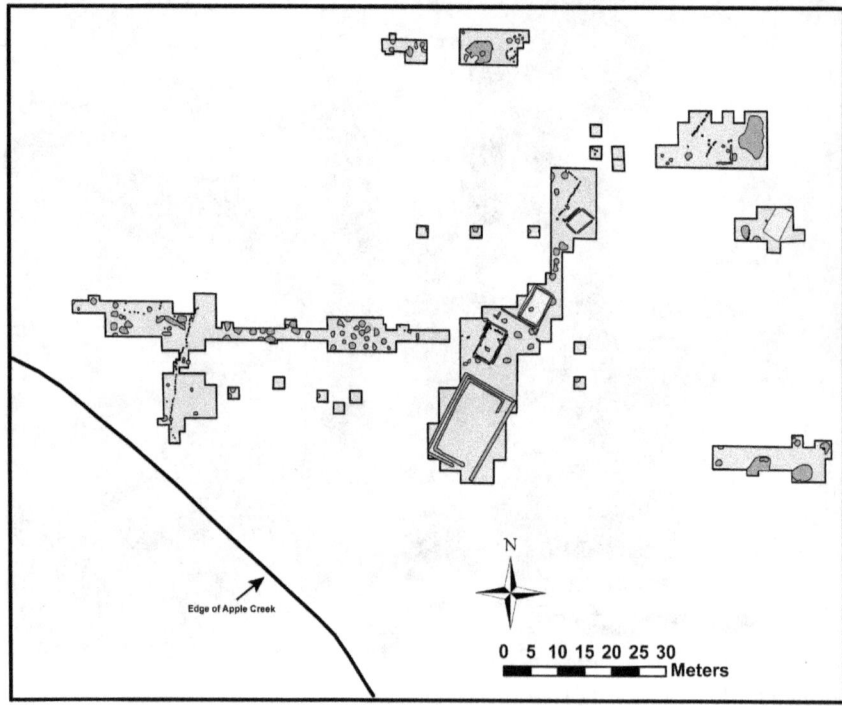

Figure 4.2. Excavation map from the Audrey site in the Lower Illinois River Valley.

palisade wall encircling the site were also uncovered by the excavations. Whiteside is a badly damaged and poorly understood single-mound and village site located 16 km to the south of Audrey and is paired with a mortuary site of 400+ burials known as the Schild cemetery (Droessler 1981; Goldstein 1980; Perino 1973:90). Both villages are located along the eastern side of the LIRV, along with 30 or more small Early Mississippian sites that likely represent farmsteads.

The Central Illinois River Valley

The Central Illinois River Valley represents a 210-km stretch of floodplain and bluff areas located between present-day Hennepin, Illinois, to the north and Meredosia, Illinois, to the south (Figure 4.3; Conrad 1991). There is archaeo-

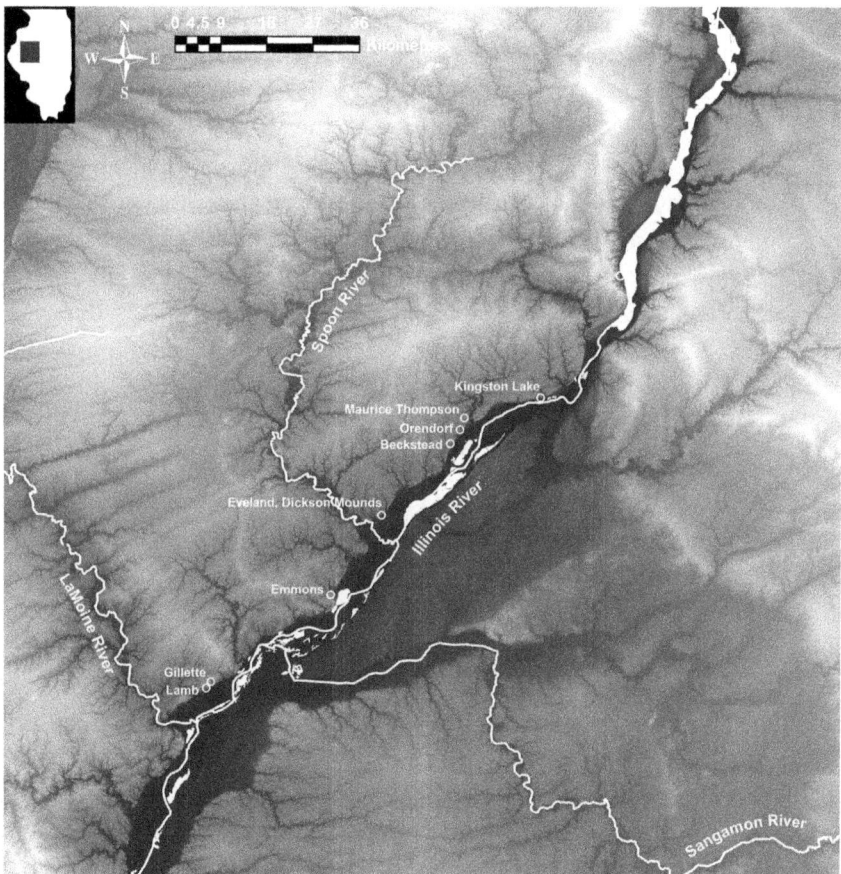

Figure 4.3. Selected sites in the Central Illinois River Valley.

logical evidence of two contemporaneous Late Woodland groups, represented by the Bauer Branch phase in the southern CIRV and the Maples Mills and subsequent Mossville phase in the northern portion of the CIRV. These two groups are represented primarily by small and dispersed settlements in portions of the valley and western uplands (Esarey 2000:398; Green and Nolan 2000:362). However, a number of villages have also been identified on natural levees and floodplain ridges along the Illinois River (Esarey 2000).

Bauer Branch phase pottery assemblages consist almost exclusively of grit-tempered and cord-marked jars. These vessels have pronounced shoulders and weakly squared-off orifices (Green and Nolan 2000:365). Jar shoulders and lip interiors are typically decorated with a horizontal band of individually applied punctates. Maples Mills phase jars exhibit broad morphological similarities with Bauer Branch phase jars but sometimes have necks that bear single pressed cord decorations (Esarey 2000). Sometimes these decorations are abstract geometric designs such as line-filled triangles but in other cases depict stylized quadrupeds, birds, and Birdman figures (Sampson 1988).

Mississippian material culture first appeared in the northern portion of the CIRV around AD 1050 in conjunction with Cahokia's Lohmann phase (AD 1050–1100) consolidation. Excavations at the Mossville phase Rench site uncovered two domestic buildings and a number of associated pit features (McConaughy 1993). One of the two structures was constructed using a combination of Mississippian (wall trench) and Late Woodland (single post) architectural construction techniques. Lohmann horizon Cahokian ceramics have also been recovered from three other sites in the northern CIRV: Clear Lake, Mossville, and Fandel. However, these materials were recovered from either surface collection or poorly documented excavations.

The subsequent early Eveland phase (AD 1100–1150) settlement pattern in the CIRV consisted of small farmstead-sized sites linked to a number of small ceremonial complexes (Conrad 1991; Harn 1991). The Eveland site is the best understood of these complexes and consists of an arrangement of four elaborate ceremonial buildings and two habitation structures located at the base of the western Illinois River bluff (Figure 4.4; Conrad 1989, 1991). The Dickson Mounds mortuary site is located on a bluff spur above Eveland and contained an estimated 250 early-twelfth-century burials (Conrad 1991; Harn 1980). Four additional early-twelfth-century bluff-top mortuary mounds have been identified in the region, along with several mounds that can only be generally dated to the twelfth century. Each of these mounds likely represents the mortuary facilities for one or more social groups and may have been paired with Eveland-like temple complexes that have not yet been identified, due to their small size

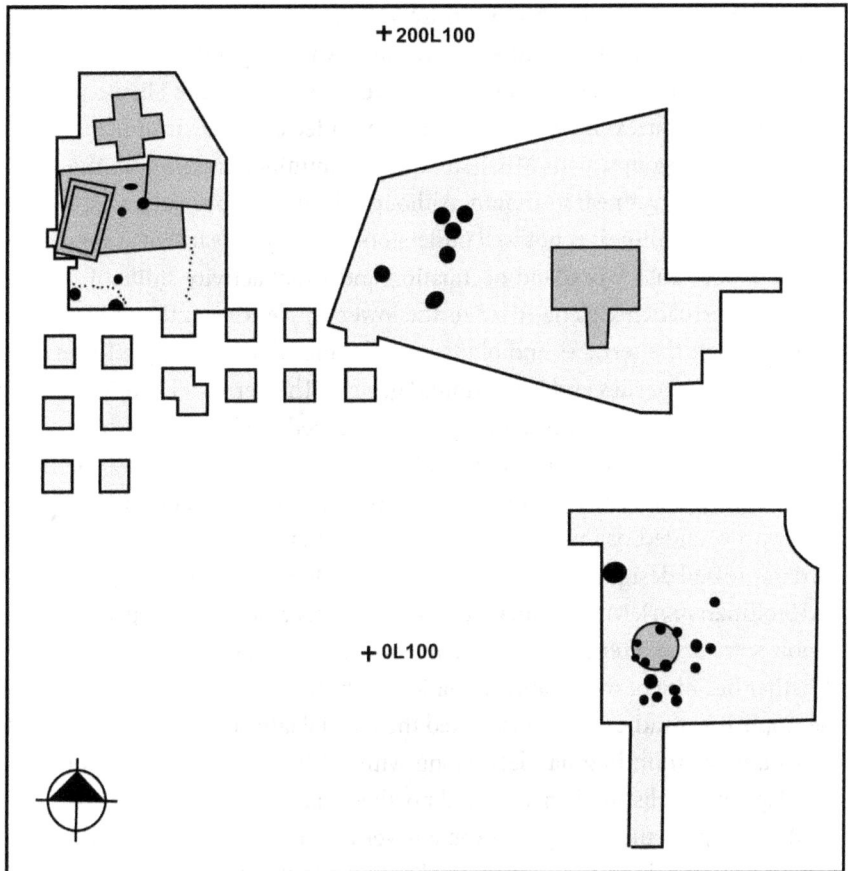

Figure 4.4. Excavation map from the Eveland site in the Central Illinois River Valley.

and a lack of systematic pedestrian survey in the area. Little is known about rural habitation sites dating to this period. However, excavations at the Garren site, a bluff base site located eight miles north of the Eveland site, uncovered a linear arrangement of several early Eveland phase wall trench buildings and associated pit features (Wray and MacNeish 1958). Moreover, excavations at Lamb, a small early-twelfth-century habitation site in the southern CIRV, uncovered two feature clusters consisting of earth ovens and storage and processing pits (Bardolph 2014).

The Apple River Valley

The Apple River rises in southern Wisconsin and flows southwest through the rugged Driftless Area of Jo Daviess County, Illinois, emptying into the Mississippi River just over the border in Carroll County (Figure 4.5). The river is approximately 90 km long and winds through a variety of deep canyons, wide floodplains, and backwater sloughs near its confluence with the Mississippi. The numerous tributaries and diverse ecotones provided a rich environment for Native American groups, with Mississippian communities clustered in the lower eight km of the river near its mouth. Although the indigenous cultural sequence in northwestern Illinois is not well understood, it does appear that at some time after AD 900, Late Woodland occupation and ritual activity shifted from the effigy-mound-laden Galena River to the lower Apple River valley. This settlement shift left the terraces and bluffs near the mouth of the Apple River peppered with village sites and large mound groups. The Terminal Late Woodland people living in the area produced ceramics labeled as Grant ware that consist of grit-tempered, single cord impressed castellated and collared vessels. These assemblages are dominated by jars with constricted necks and curved or flaring rims with rounded or thickened lips that are sometimes decorated with single cord impressed designs, collars, or castellations (Benn 1997; Finney 1993; Finney and Stoltman 1991). Mississippian forms of material culture first appeared in the region sometime after AD 1050 (Benn 1997; Brown 1982:108; Emerson 1991). Whether because of migration, emulation, or both, it is clear that the people of the Apple River radically reconstructed their social landscape to include temple towns and surrounding hamlets, along with a Mississippian-like ceramic assemblage with a distinctly hybrid and northern flavor.

Mississippian sites along the Apple River consist of two large villages with associated mounds surrounded by smaller hamlets. The two sites, Mills (11JD11) and John Chapman (11JD12), effectively bracket the southern and northern ends of the Mississippian occupation along the Apple River. The Mills site (11JD11) is situated within a horseshoe bend of the Apple River and consists of a central precinct with an embanked depression and paired conical and platform mounds surrounded by habitation areas. A long line of small conical mounds connects the village area with a Woodland mound group to the northwest. The Mills site is surrounded by seven smaller satellite communities, including the partially excavated Lundy (11JD140) site to the north (Bennett 1945; Emerson 1991; Emerson et al. 2007; Millhouse 2012; Nickerson 1913).

The John Chapman (11JD12) site is also situated on a terrace along the Apple River and contains a series of occupation areas with a plaza and plowed down mound at the northern end of the site (Bennett 1945; Emerson 1991; Hargrave 2005; Millhouse 2012). Attached to the Mississippian village are the Grace Chapman (11JD10) mounds, a large Woodland group consisting of conicals, linears, and a bear effigy. Testing of these mounds found large internal pit fea-

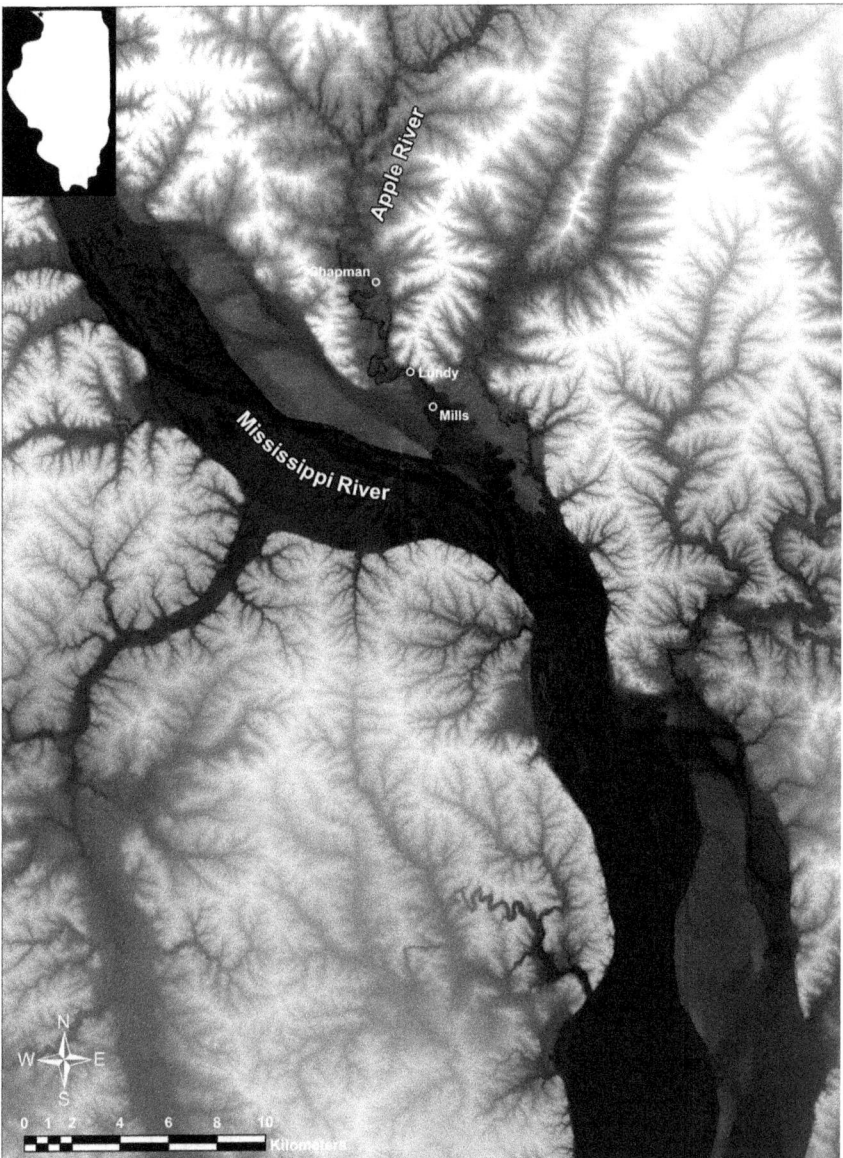

Figure 4.5. Selected sites in the Apple River Valley.

tures with feasting remains, charred maize, and Grant series ceramics (Bennett 1945; Lewis 1888). It is currently unclear whether these mounds were earlier constructions or part of a contemporary multi-ethnic occupation of the terrace. Excavations at John Chapman have uncovered single-post, semisubterranean houses surrounded by clusters of pit features. The plowed-down mound at the site may be a charnel mound of some kind, as collectors have picked up hundreds of shell beads from the surface, and additional coring and remote sensing indicate intact stratigraphy and possible subsurface structures (Hargrave 2005; Millhouse 2012; Schroeder and Millhouse 2009). As with Mills, a series of small satellite communities occupy the terraces and floodplain ridges south of the site (Millhouse 2012).

The people living in the Apple River likely had ties with contemporary villagers at the Fred Edwards (47GT377) site situated 60 km to the north on a terrace above the Grant River in Wisconsin (Emerson et al. 2007:179–180; Finney 1993; Finney and Stoltman 1991:231–233). Fred Edwards consisted of a series of rectangular houses organized around a plaza and protected by a palisade wall (Finney 1993:230–281; Finney and Stoltman 1991:234–240). The site's inhabitants had access to some Ramey Incised vessels but predominantly utilized Terminal Woodland cord impressed Grant series and Aztalan collared wares, along with a variety of hybrid vessels. In addition, there are ceramics that indicate close ties with people at the Hartley Fort site in northeast Iowa (Finney 1993:109–151; Finney and Stoltman 1991:240–247; Theler and Boszhardt 2006:457).

Ceramic Analysis

The ceramic data for this investigation derive from excavations at the Audrey site in the LIRV, the Rench, Eveland, and Lamb sites in the CIRV, and the Lundy and John Chapman sites in the ARV. The Rench site assemblage from the CIRV dates to the latter half of the eleventh century. A small number of possible late-eleventh-century rim sherds have also been identified at the Audrey site. However, the majority of ceramic materials from Audrey and the other sites considered in this study date to the early twelfth century. Distinguishing between the presence of actual Cahokians at these sites and the emulation of Mississippian material culture by local inhabitants (or some combination thereof) is a critical part of our analysis of these materials. To do so we consider not only the regional ceramic tradition in which pots were manufactured, but also the composition of vessel assemblages in terms of the relative percentages of storage, cooking, processing, and serving vessels.

A minimum number of vessels (MNV) approach is used to determine the relative frequency of different vessel shape classes in each assemblage. Rim sherds were selected for the purpose of identifying individual vessels, because they are easily sorted into discrete vessel classes and provide a suite of other important information about vessel function. Data on vessel size (orifice diameter), paste composition, use wear, and surface treatment were also gathered from the rim sherds in each assemblage. Due to interassemblage differences in data availability, certain analyses were focused exclusively on the CIRV data sets.

Lohmann Horizon (AD 1050–1100) Ceramic Data

A total of 63 percent of the northern CIRV Rench site ceramic assemblage consisted of sherds from grit-tempered, sandy paste vessels manufactured in the local late Woodland Mossville stylistic tradition (McConaughy 1991, 1993). A number of these vessels bear subtle indications that local Woodland potters were beginning to emulate the extruded lips and angled shoulders of Cahokia-made Powell Plain jars (Esarey 2000:396; McConaughy 1993:93–94, 125).

The remaining 37 percent of the Rench site assemblage consisted of sherds from shell-tempered vessels manufactured in a Mississippian style. The rims in this assemblage consisted of 16 jars, four bowls, and one seed jar (McConaughy 1993:93–94). There is little evidence of stylistic hybridity among these Mississippian vessels, and thin section analysis revealed that most were made from a distinctive grey, shell-tempered paste comparable to clays found in the American Bottom (McConaughy 1991:110; Stoltman 1991). In other words, the Mississippian vessels in this assemblage appear to have been made in the American Bottom by Lohmann phase Cahokians. There is no clear evidence of Cahokian contact in the Lohmann horizon Apple River Valley or Lower Illinois River Valley. However, additional research is required in both regions to fully evaluate this possibility.

Early Stirling Horizon (AD 1100–1150) Ceramic Data

The majority of the rims in early Stirling horizon pottery assemblages from the CIRV and ARV are stylistically Mississippian. However, the classification *Mississippian* as it is used here requires some qualification. Although a number of the vessels in these assemblages display strong stylistic similarities to Cahokian vessels from the American Bottom, others exhibit a blending of Woodland and Mississippian characteristics (Millhouse 2012:174–175). For example, some early Stirling horizon jars from northern hinterland sites have more rounded shoulders and elongated bases than contemporaneous vessels produced in the American Bottom. In terms of paste composition, some were are also tempered with grit or a mix of grit and shell, rather than purely mussel shell (which is the dominant tempering agent throughout most of the Mississippian world). Moreover, surface treatments vary from Cahokia-style black slipping and burnishing to more Woodland-like plain or smoothed-over cord marking. Thin section analyses conducted on stylistically Mississippian vessels from Eveland revealed that they were most likely manufactured from local clays (Harn 1991:142–143). Thus, some northern hinterland potters appear to have been skilled at emulating Cahokian vessels.

Stylistically Woodland rims that do not visibly exhibit Mississippian influence represent a minority of the vessels in each assemblage. Generally speaking, these vessels bear strong similarities to local ceramic traditions. Woodland jars from the Lamb and Eveland sites are similar to vessels from the Bauer Branch and Mossville phases, respectively, and those from the Lundy and John Chapman sites have an attenuated resemblance to the Grant series jars produced by earlier indigenous Late Woodland groups in the area (Esarey 2000; Green and Nolan 2000). It is noteworthy that the broken and discarded remains of Mississippian and Woodland vessels are widespread at the sites from all three regions, and not concentrated in particular features (Bardolph 2014; Emerson et al. 2007; Delaney-Rivera 2000; Millhouse 2012). Thus, it does not appear that one or the other pottery type was reserved for special occasions or manufactured and used by a spatially delimited subset of each site's inhabitants.

The Audrey site ceramic assemblage from the LIRV exhibits far less Woodland stylistic influence than either the ARV or CIRV assemblages. Indeed, the majority of this assemblage is stylistically similar to contemporaneous early Stirling phase assemblages from the northern American Bottom. However, thin section analyses conducted on Audrey site vessels revealed that they were most likely manufactured from local clays (Delaney-Rivera 2000).

Interassemblage Comparison

Based on the widespread distribution and mixture of Woodland and Mississippian pottery and the common occurrence of stylistically hybrid vessels, we argue that none of the Lohmann or early Stirling horizon sites from the three regions considered in this study were occupied exclusively by Cahokians but must have included local Woodland individuals, some of whom were mixing and matching Woodland and Mississippian ceramic production techniques, others of whom were still entrenched in Woodland traditions. It is also possible that these sites were exclusively occupied by Woodland groups who were variably emulating aspects of Cahokian ceramic traditions. Considering the equifinality of this pattern, an additional set of analyses is required to differentiate between these two possibilities for both the Lohmann and early Stirling horizons.

Extending the logic of the southwestern migration research mentioned earlier, we propose that the presence of Cahokian households or communities will not only be represented in the presence of pottery that is *stylistically* Cahokian. Because domestic foodways tend to be culturally conservative and slow to change (see Scarry and Reitz 2005:118; Simoons 1994), we also expect that the relative frequencies of different cooking, processing, storage, and serving vessels should be consistent with what was *organizationally* Cahokian. This entails a consideration of the period leading up to the polity's twelfth-century regional consolidation. A dramatic increase in the amount and variety of serving vessels relative to cooking and storage vessels differentiates Terminal Late Woodland and Early Mississippian assemblages from earlier Late Woodland assemblages in the greater Cahokia area. This pattern indicates that the development of social complexity in the region corresponded with an intensification in commensal politics and other food-related ceremonial practices. Indeed, archaeological research at the Cahokia site has documented the material remains of large, Early Mississippian feasting events that occurred near the site's grand plaza (Pauketat 2002). Despite these changes, certain vessel types, such as jars, bowls, bottles, seed jars, stumpware, and pans, had a deep history of use in the region that began in the early Terminal Late Woodland period (Johannessen 1993).

Tables 4.1 and 4.2 list minimum number of vessel (MNV) counts and percentages from Lohmann and early Stirling phase assemblages from the greater Cahokian area. MNV data are also provided from contemporaneous sites in the LIRV, CIRV, and ARV. The Lohmann phase assemblages consist of excavated materials from Tract-15A Cahokia (Pauketat 1998), the Lohmann site mound center (Esarey and Pauketat 1992), the Knoebel (Alt 1997) and Halliday site (Wilson 1998) villages, and the Range (Hanenberger 2003), and BBB motor (Emerson 1997), nodal farmsteads. The Stirling phase assemblages come from the Tract-15A and ICT-II excavations at the Cahokia site (Holley 1989; Pauketat 1998), the Lohmann site mound center (Esarey and Pauketat 1992), the Range site nodal farmstead (Hanenberger 2003), and the Miller's Farm site village (Wilson and Koldehoff 1998). These data provide compositional profiles for Lohmann and early Stirling phase vessel assemblages. Eight general functional-shape classes are present in these assemblages.

Jars used for cooking and storing are most frequent, followed by bowls used for serving and eating. Seed jars, beakers, and bottles are less common vessel forms found in Cahokian assemblages. Seed jars may have been used for the temporary storage, exchange, and presentation of foodstuffs. Recent residue analysis using laser-induced mass spectrometry has revealed that some

Table 4.1. Minimum Number of Vessels Data for Lohmann Horizon Sites in the American Bottom, LIRV, CIRV, and Apple River Valley

Site	Region		Jars	Bowls	Seed Jars	Beakers	Bottles	Funnels	Stumpware	Pans	Total	Serving %
Cahokia (Tract 15A L1)	AB	N	149	54	0	34	7	4	5	15	268	35%
		%	55.60%	20.15%	0%	12.69%	2.61%	1.49%	1.87%	5.60%	100%	35%
Lohmann	AB	N	272	83	0	33	6	7	8	4	413	30%
		%	65.86%	20.10%	0%	7.99%	1.45%	1.69%	1.94%	.97%	100%	30%
Halliday	AB	N	86	17.00	0	9	0	1	5	0	118.00	22%
		%	72.88%	14.41%	0%	7.63%	0%	.85%	4.24%	0%	100%	22%
Knoebel	AB	N	56	13	5	0	1	0	2	1	78	24%
		%	71.79%	16.67%	6.41%	0%	1.28%	0%	2.56%	1.28%	100%	24%
BBB Motor	AB	N	71	21	0	2	0	0	3	3	100	23%
		%	71.00%	21.00%	0%	2.00%	0%	0%	3.00%	3.00%	100%	23%
Range	AB	N	23	10	0	0	0	1	0	0	34	29%
		%	67.65%	29.41%	0%	0%	0%	2.94%	0%	0%	100%	29%
Rench	CIRV	N	16	4	0	1	0	0	0	0	21	24%
		%	76.19%	19.05%	0%	4.76%	0%	0%	0%	0%	100%	24%

Table 4.2. Minimum Number of Vessels Data for Early Stirling Horizon Sites in the American Bottom, LIRV, CIRV, and Apple River Valley

Site	Region		Jars	Bowls	Seed Jars	Beakers	Bottles	Funnels	Stumpware	Pans	Total	Serving %
Cahokia (ICT II)	AB	N	359	130	54	9	15	22	2	5	596	35%
		%	60.44%	21.89%	9.09%	1.52%	2.53%	3.70%	.34%	.84%	100%	35%
Cahokia (Tract 15A)	AB	N	42	12	5	9	4	2	1	0	75	40%
		%	56.00%	16.00%	6.67%	12.00%	5.33%	2.67%	1.33%	.00%	100%	40%
Lohmann	AB	N	95	39	12	3	5	1	1	0	155	38%
		%	61.00%	25.00%	8.00%	2.00%	3.00%	.70%	.70%	0%	100%	38%
Range	AB	N	70	30	5	0	3	1	5	4	118	32%
		%	59.32%	25.42%	4.24%	0%	2.54%	.85%	4.24%	3.39%	100%	32%
Miller Farm	AB	N	10	4	1	1	0	0	0	2	18	33%
		%	55.56%	22.22%	5.56%	5.56%	0%	0%	0%	11.11%	100%	33%
Eveland	CIRV	N	127	10	1	1	1	0	0	0	140	9%
		%	90.71%	7.14%	.71%	.71%	.71%	0%	0%	0%	100%	9%
Lamb	CIRV	N	17	0	1	1	0	0	0	0	19	11%
		%	89.47%	0%	5.26%	5.26%	0%	0%	0%	0%	100%	11%
Audrey	LIRV	N	114	13	5	4	5	0	0	1	142	19%
		%	80.28%	9.15%	3.52%	2.82%	3.52%	0%	0%	.70%	100%	19%
Lundy	ARV	N	116	17	2	0	0	0	0	0	135	14%
		%	85.93%	12.59%	1.48%	0%	0%	0%	0%	0%	100%	14%
John Chapman	ARV	N	133	17	0	0	0	0	0	0	150	11%
		%	88.67%	11.44%	0%	0%	0%	0%	0%	0%	100%	11%

Cahokian beakers were used for the ritual consumption of black drink, a highly caffeinated beverage brewed from the leaves of *Ilex vomitoria* (Crown et al. 2012). Water bottles and hooded water bottles were used for liquid storage and serving or perhaps for pourable solids like seeds. Pans are low-frequency vessels used for parching or baking tasks. Funnels and stumpware are also low-frequency vessel types thought to be used for funneling and straining activities. Also present in American Bottom assemblages are examples of distinctively Cahokian fineware vessels. These are exceptionally well-made bowls, beakers, and bottles with thin walls, compact pastes, and curvilinear incised and excised surface decorations (Wilson 1999).

Comparing these American Bottom data to those from the LIRV, CIRV, and ARV reveals a number of relevant spatial and diachronic patterns. We distill these trends into two bar graphs by calculating a serving-ware percentage consisting of the number of serving-ware vessels divided by the total number of vessels in each assemblage (see Figures 4.6 and 4.7). A comparison of Lohmann horizon sites is presented in Figure 4.6. This bar graph reveals that the relative proportion of serving-ware vessels in the Rench site assemblage from the northern CIRV is directly comparable to that of non-mound, Lohmann phase site assemblages from the American Bottom. This emphasis on serving/ceremonialism is a Cahokian pattern that departs notably from the previous late Woodland occupation of the region. Combined with thin section data indicating that the Mississippian vessels at Rench probably derived from the American Bottom, this serving-ware pattern strongly suggests that small but influential groups of Cahokians were present in the late-eleventh-century northern CIRV.

The early Stirling horizon interregional pattern contrasts sharply with that of the earlier Lohmann horizon just discussed. The mean serving-ware percentage for American Bottom assemblages (57 percent) is over twice that of the Audrey site assemblage (19 percent) in the LIRV. Moreover, it is over five times higher than the Lamb (9 percent) and Eveland sites (11 percent) assemblages in the CIRV. The two ARV assemblages are comparable to those from the CIRV. And while the Audrey site assemblage includes an elaborately decorated water bottle and beaker, such distinctive fineware vessels are notably missing from the CIRV and ARV site assemblages.

The early Stirling horizon focus on jars north of Cahokia, particularly in the CIRV and ARV, indicates that social interactions linked to foodways were organized in a fundamentally different way than in the contemporaneous American Bottom. Indeed, the scarcity of serving ware at hinterland sites is a pattern that is more similar to the Late Woodland period American Bottom, when

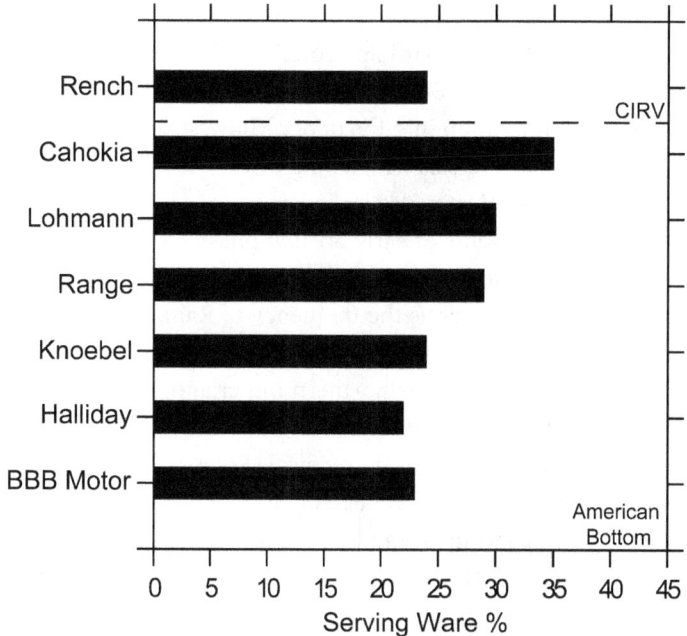

Figure 4.6. Service-to-utility ware ratios for Lohmann horizon sites.

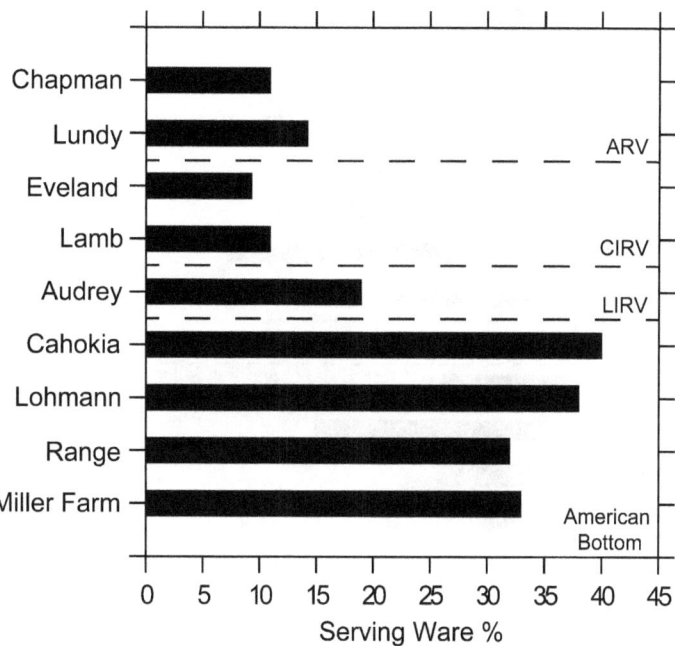

Figure 4.7. Service-to-utility ware ratios for early Stirling horizon sites.

foodways had not yet been reorganized to emphasize the ceremonial dimensions of commensal politics (see Bardolph 2014. The absence of stumpware and funnels north of the American Bottom also runs counter to our expectations for a major Cahokian migration into the upper Midwest, as these are low-visibility domestic processing vessels with a long history of use in the American Bottom. The CIRV and ARV sites also lacked pans.

But while some components of early Stirling phase Cahokian ceramic assemblages are underrepresented north of the American Bottom, others are overrepresented. Figure 4.8 graphs the frequency of Ramey Incised jars relative to other shell-tempered jars in various early-twelfth-century site assemblages from greater Cahokia and its northern hinterland. Ramey Incised jars are well-made, dark-slipped vessels that were embellished with cosmological symbolism related to fertility and world renewal (Emerson 1989; Pauketat and Emerson 1991). A striking pattern revealed by this comparison is the high frequency of Ramey Incised jars in assemblages north of the LIRV. Ramey incised jars constitute less than 13 percent of American Bottom jar assemblages with the exception of Tract 15A. The Tract 15A portion of the Cahokia site fell out of residential use during the early twelfth century and was the location of the Cahokian woodhenge, a large circular arrangement of wooden posts thought to have been used to ritually track the movement of celestial objects (Wittry 1969). Thus, the high frequency of Ramey Incised jars at Tract 15A may have

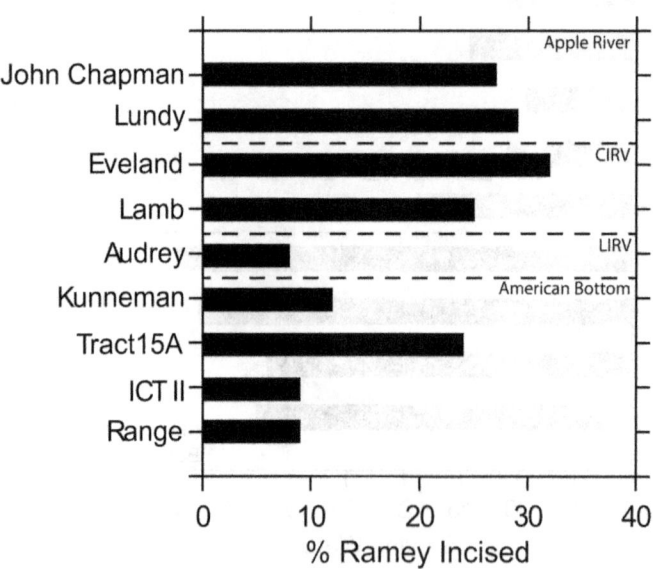

Figure 4.8. Ramey Incised jar rim frequencies from early Stirling horizon sites.

been related to the specialized use of this area. The overrepresentation of Ramey Incised jars north of the LIRV is important for several reasons. Thus far we have emphasized the persistence of Woodland organizational conventions north of Cahokia. But this pattern indicates that some Cahokian traditions were *exaggerated* during processes of Mississippianization, a trend that indicates the importance of the cosmological themes embodied by these vessels and perhaps the ritual exchanges in which they were mobilized.

Northern Pilgrims in the American Bottom

Recent and ongoing research has documented the presence of stylistically northern jars with exotic grit-tempered pastes in the Terminal Late Woodland and Early Mississippian American Bottom. These probable northern vessels are not present at every site and are exceedingly rare at the sites where they have been recovered. For example, a small number (< 1 percent of the total assemblage) of these vessels are present in assemblages from the Emerald and East St. Louis mound centers (Betzenhauser et al. 2017, Skousen 2016). However, they are apparently not present in assemblages from multiple extensively excavated portions of the Cahokia and Lohmann site mound centers (see Esarey and Pauketat 1992; Holley 1989; Kelly 1991; Pauketat 1998, 2013a). This uneven distribution and general scarcity suggests that certain settlements were the focus of interactions among Cahokians and small groups of northern visitors. Thus, while this study has primarily explored the variable roles of migration and emulation in the Mississippianization of the northern Midwest, it is important to note that sporadic pilgrimages to the American Bottom may have also played a role in this process (see Pauketat 2013b; Skousen 2016).

Discussion

The CIRV is the best understood of the three regional cases considered in this study. In the era of Cahokia's Lohmann phase (AD 1050–1100) consolidation, Woodland potters in the northern CIRV began emulating aspects of Cahokian ceramic manufacture. Some of these Woodland groups also acquired Mississippian vessels that appear to have been made in the American Bottom. These Cahokia-derived wares represent a minority of the vessels that were used by these Woodland groups. However, the relative abundance of serving bowls and bottles among these Mississippian pots is a distinctively Cahokian organizational pattern. We argue that this pattern indicates direct interactions among locals and small groups of intrusive Cahokians; however, some of these Mississippian vessels may have been transported by Woodland individuals returning from Cahokian pilgrimages.

Pauketat et al.'s (2015) recent research at the Trempealeau and Fisher mound site complexes in western Wisconsin have also documented the presence of Cahokian-made pottery, including red-slipped jars, bowls, and elaborate fineware serving containers that date to the Lohmann horizon. They also document the presence of wall-trench architecture, mound building, and American Bottom cherts. They conclude from this evidence that these settlements were established around AD 1050 by a group of Cahokians who brought along their Mississippian pots and stone tools from the American Bottom homeland. If and where such a Cahokia colony may have been located in the CIRV is uncertain, but the Mossville village site near Peoria, Illinois, is one possibility. Surface collections and small-scale excavations there have documented the presence of both Mossville, Late Woodland and Lohmann phase, Mississippian pottery, and the site appears to be considerably larger than a farmstead like Rench.

We currently lack definitive evidence of a Lohmann horizon Cahokian presence in the LIRV and ARV. However, it is important to emphasize how spatially circumscribed both the northern CIRV and Tempealeau/Fisher cases are. Such subtle archaeological traces of a Lohmann horizon Cahokian presence could be totally obscured in larger collections from multicomponent sites. Clearly, additional research in the LIRV and ARV are required to sort out the initial period of Cahokian culture contact in these regions.

The clearest and most abundant evidence for early Mississippian occupation in the LIRV, CIRV, and ARV dates to the early Stiring horizon. The composition of vessel assemblages from this period suggests that these hinterland settlements were not site-unit intrusions (see Stoltman et al. 2000; Willey et al. 1956) from the American Bottom. Why would discrete Cahokian immigrant groups alter their manufacture and use of pottery vessels to deemphasize broadly shared and deeply rooted ways of preparing and serving meals in the American Bottom homeland? Indeed, the migration and identity studies coming out of the Southwest indicate that material attributes associated with mundane aspect of foodways ought to be culturally conservative and embody the enculturative background of the immigrant group. The absence or scarcity of distinctively Cahokian cooking and processing vessels such as stumpware, pans, and funnels is particularly telling, as the presence of such low-visibility utilitarian wares was vital in tracking Hopi migrations in the Southwest (see Lyons 2003).

On the basis of both the stylistic and vessel compositional evidence, we argue that all of the early Stiring horizon hinterland sites discussed in this paper were primarily occupied by local groups who were variably emulating Cahokian potting traditions as well as other forms of material culture. The use of Mississippian pottery manufacturing and decorative techniques appears to have been combined with traditional Woodland ways of using pots. While the early-twelfth-century residents of the LIRV, CIRV, and ARV employed Cahokian stylistic traditions in manufacturing many of their pots, they perpetuated local Woodland era conventions in terms of the kinds of functional vessel classes they manufactured and the ways in which they prepared and served food.

While the upper Midwest assemblages discussed here contrast with those in the American Bottom, they also differ from one another. The Audrey site assemblage in the LIRV exhibits little evidence of Woodland stylistic influences and contains considerably more serving-ware containers than those from the CIRV and ARV. The Audrey assemblage also includes examples of fineware containers and pans, vessel types completely missing from the early Mississippian assemblages from the CIRV and ARV. Location likely played an important role in these differences. The Audrey site is located in the LIRV, which begins just 30 km past the northern limits of the American Bottom, while the Lamb and Eveland sites are located over 200 river km away from the Cahokia site. Thus, Audrey is perhaps best understood as part of a complex of Mississippianized Woodland groups on the immediate fringe of the Cahokia polity, while the CIRV and ARV sites are true hinterland settlements. Audrey may have also been home to a number of expatriates or marginal lineages from the American Bottom (see Emerson 1991).

That so few Cahokians could have had such a profound impact indicates that what they had to offer was viewed favorably by many of the region's Woodland inhabitants. However, the construction of a palisade wall at the Audrey site in the Lower Illinois River Valley dating to this era of culture contact indicates that these changes may not have been viewed favorably by all. The persistence of Woodland ceramic traditions in all three regions likewise indicates that the motivations and efforts to emulate Cahokia varied, even within individual communities. And while there is variation among the LIRV, CIRV, and ARV culture contact scenarios, each of these regions also differed from the way in which Cahokian and Woodland interactions played out in other portions of the Midwest and Midsouth.

Progress toward understanding Mississippian beginnings in Cahokia's northern hinterland will require looking beyond the spread of Cahokian objects to consider the composition and structure of material culture assemblages as they relate to the organization of daily and ceremonial practice, social organization, and identity politics. This needs to be done on a site-by-site and region-by-region basis with frequent interregional comparisons. There is much we still do not understand about the Mississippianization of the upper Midwest. However, we believe that distinguishing between the movement of people, ideas, and things is an important first step.

References Cited

Alt, Susan M.
  2001 Cahokian Change and the Authority of Tradition. In *The Archaeology of Traditions: Agency and History before and after Columbus*, edited by Timothy R. Pauketat, pp. 141–156. University Press of Florida, Gainesville.
  2002 Identities, Traditions, and Diversity in Cahokia's Uplands. *Midcontinental Journal of Archaeology* 27(2):217–235.
  2006 The Power of Diversity: The Roles of Migration and Hybridity in Culture Change. In *Leadership and Polity in Mississippian Society*, edited by Brian M. Butler and Paul D. Welch, pp. 289–308. Center for Archaeological Investigations, Occasional Paper No. 33. Southern Illinois University, Carbondale.

Bardolph, Dana N.
  2014 Evaluating Cahokian Contact and Mississippian Identity Politics in the Late Prehistoric Central Illinois River Valley. *American Antiquity* 79(1):69–89.

Benden, Daniel
  2004 The Fisher Mounds Site Complex: Early Middle Mississippian Exploration in the Upper Mississippi Valley. *Minnesota Archaeologist* 63:7–24.

Benn, David W.
  1995 Woodland People and the Roots of Oneota. In *Oneota Archaeology: Past, Present and Future*, edited by William Green, pp. 91–139. Report No. 20. Office of the State Archaeologist, University of Iowa, Iowa City.
  1997 Who Met the Mississippians at the Mouth of the Apple River? *Illinois Archaeology* 9(1–2):1–35.
  2007 Data Recovery Excavations at the Terminal Late Woodland Period Union Bench Site (13DB497), Dubuque County, Iowa. Report prepared for the Iowa Department of Transportation, Bear Creek Archaeology, Cresco.

Benn, David W., Jeffrey D. Anderson, Robert C. Vogel, Lawrence Conrad
  1989 *Archaeology, Geomorphology and Historic Surveys in Pools 13 and 14, Upper Mississippi River.* CAR-752, Center for Archaeological Research, Southwest Missouri State University, Springfield.

Benn, David W., and William Green
  2000 Late Woodland Cultures in Iowa. In *Late Woodland Societies: Tradition and Transformation across the Midcontinent*, edited by Thomas E. Emerson, Dale L. McElrath, and Andrew C. Fortier, pp. 429–496. University of Nebraska Press, Lincoln.

Bennett, John W.
  1945 *Archaeological Explorations in Jo Daviess County, Illinois.* University of Chicago Press, Chicago.

Betzenhauser, Alleen, Tamira Brennan, Michael Brent Lansdell, Sarah E. Harken, and Victoria E. Potter
    2017   Chronological Implications and External Connections in the East St. Louis Ceramic Assemblage. In Creating Greater Cahokia: Rediscovery and Large-Scale Excavation of the East St. Louis Precinct, edited by Thomas E. Emerson, Brad Koldehoff, and Tamira Brennan. Manuscript on file, Illinois State Archaeological Survey, Champaign.

Birmingham, Robert A.
    2010   *Spirits of Earth: The Effigy Mound Landscape of Madison and the Four Lakes*. University of Wisconsin Press, Madison.

Birmingham, Robert A., and Leslie E. Eisenberg
    2000   *Indian Mounds of Wisconsin*. University of Wisconsin Press, Madison.

Birmingham, Robert A., and Lynn G. Goldstein
    2005   *Aztalan: Mysteries of an Ancient Indian Town*. Wisconsin Historical Society Press, Madison.

Boszhardt, Robert F.
    2004   The Late Woodland and Middle Mississippian Component at the Iva Site, La Crosse County, Wisconsin in the Driftless Area of the Upper Mississippi River Valley. *Minnesota Archaeologist* 63:60–79.

Boszhardt, Robert F., and Natalie Goetz
    2000   An Apparent Late Woodland Boundary in Western Wisconsin. *Midcontinental Journal of Archaeology* 25(2):269–288.

Boszhardt, Robert F., Timothy R. Pauketat, and Danielle M. Benden
    2011   Assessing the Little Bluff Platform Mounds at Trempealeau. Poster presented at the 57th Annual Midwest Archaeological Conference, Lacrosse, Wisconsin.

Brown, James
    1982   What Kind of Economy Did the Oneota Have? In *Oneota Studies*, edited by Guy E. Gibbon, pp. 107–112. Publications in Anthropology No. 1. University of Minnesota, Minneapolis.

Brown, James, and John E. Kelly
    2000   Cahokia and the Southeast Ceremonial Complex. In *Mounds, Modoc, and Mesoamerica: Papers in Honor of Melvin L. Fowler*, edited by Steven R. Ahler, pp. 469–510. Illinois State Museum Scientific Papers 28. Illinois State Museum, Springfield.

Carr, Christopher
    1995a   Building a Unified Middle-Range Theory of Artifact Design. In *Style, Society, and Person: Archaeological and Ethnological Approaches*, edited by Christopher Carr and Jill E. Neitzel, pp. 151–258. Plenum Press, New York.
    1995b   A Unified Middle-Range Theory of Artifact Design. In *Style, Society, and Person: Archaeological and Ethnological Perspectives*, edited by Christopher Carr and Jill E. Neitzel, pp. 171–258. Plenum Press, New York.

Clark, Jeffrey
    2001   *Tracking Prehistoric Migrations: Pueblo Settlers among the Tonto Basin Hohokam*. Anthropological Papers No. 65. University of Arizona Press, Tucson.

Collins, James, Richard W. Slaughter, David L. Asch, K. Kris Hirst, and John L. Cordell
    1997   A Brief Evaluation of the Carroll Rock Shelter, Dubuque County, Iowa. *Journal of the Iowa Archaeological Society* 44:84–101.

Conrad, Lawrence A.
- 1989 The Southeastern Ceremonial Complex on the Northern Middle Mississippian Frontier: Late Prehistoric Politico-Religious Systems in the Central Illinois River Valley. In *The Southeastern Ceremonial Complex: Artifacts and Analysis*, edited by Patricia K. Galloway, pp. 93–113. University of Nebraska Press, Lincoln.
- 1991 The Middle Mississippian Cultures of the Central Illinois Valley. In *Cahokia and the Hinterlands: Middle Mississippian Cultures of the Midwest*, edited by Thomas E. Emerson and R. Barry Lewis, pp. 119–163. University of Illinois Press, Urbana.

Cross, Paula, and Melissa Bittinger
- 1996 The Old Road: Phase I Historic Properties Investigations for the FAP 310 Project. Submitted to Contract Archaeology Program. Report of Investigations 224B. Manuscript on file at the Center for American Archaeology, Kampsville.

Crown, Patricia L., Thomas E. Emerson, Jiyan Gu, Jeffrey W. Hurst, Timothy R. Pauketat, and Timothy Ward
- 2012 Ritual Black Drink Consumption at Cahokia. *Proceedings of the National Academy of Sciences* 109(35):13944–13949.

Delaney-Rivera, Colleen
- 2000 Mississippian and Late Woodland Cultural Interaction and Regional Dynamics: A View from the Lower Illinois River Valley. Ph.D. dissertation, Department of Anthropology, University of California, Los Angeles.
- 2004 From Edge to Frontier: Early Mississippian Occupation of the Lower Illinois River Valley. *Southeastern Archaeology* 23(1):41–56.

Diaz-Granados, Carol, and James R. Duncan
- 2000 *The Petroglyphs and Pictographs of Missouri*. University of Alabama Press, Tuscaloosa.

Douglas, John
- 1976 Collins: A Late Woodland Ceremonial Complex in the Woodfordian, Northeast. Unpublished Ph.D. dissertation, Department of Anthropology, University of Illinois at Urbana-Champaign. University Microfilms, Ann Arbor.

Droessler, Judith
- 1981 Craniometry and Biological Distance: Biocultural Continuity and Change in the Late Woodland–Mississippian Interface. Research Series 1. Center for American Archaeology at Northwestern University, Evanston.

Emerson, Thomas E.
- 1989 Water, Serpents, and the Underworld: An Exploration into Cahokia Symbolism. In *The Southeastern Ceremonial Complex: Artifacts and Analysis*, edited by Patricia K. Galloway, pp. 45–92. University of Nebraska Press, Lincoln.
- 1991 The Apple River Mississippian Culture of Northwestern Illinois. In *Cahokia and the Hinterlands: Middle Mississippian Cultures of the Midwest*, edited by Thomas E. Emerson and R. Barry Lewis, pp. 221–236. University of Illinois Press, Urbana.
- 1999 The Langford Tradition and the Process of Tribalization on the Middle Mississippian Borders. *Midcontinental Journal of Archaeology* 24(1):3–56.

Emerson, Thomas E., and R. Barry Lewis (editors)
- 1991 *Cahokia and the Hinterlands: Middle Mississippian Cultures of the Midwest*. University of Illinois Press, Urbana.

Emerson, Thomas E., Phillip G. Millhouse, and Marjorie B. Schroeder
 2007 The Lundy Site and the Bennett Phase in the Apple River Valley of Northwestern Illinois. *Wisconsin Archaeologist* 88(2):1–23.

Esarey, Duane
 2000 The Late Woodland Maples Mills and the Mossville Phase Sequence in the Central Illinois River Valley. In *Late Woodland Societies: Tradition and Transformation across the Midcontinent*, edited by Thomas E. Emerson, Dale L. McElrath, and Andrew C. Fortier, pp. 387–412. University of Nebraska Press, Lincoln.

Esarey, Duane, and Timothy R. Pauketat
 1992 *The Lohmann Site: An Early Mississippian Center in the American Bottom*. American Bottom Archaeology FAI-270 Site Report 25. University of Illinois Press, Urbana.

Farnsworth, Kenneth B., Thomas E. Emerson, and Rebecca Miller Glenn
 1991 Patterns of Late Woodland/Mississippian Interaction in the Lower Illinois Valley Drainage: A View from Starr Village. In *Cahokia and the Hinterlands: Middle Mississippian Cultures of the Midwest*, edited by Thomas E. Emerson and R. Barry Lewis, pp. 83–118. University of Illinois Press, Urbana.

Finney, Fred A.
 1993 Cahokia's Northern Hinterland as Viewed from the Fred Edwards Site in Southwest Wisconsin: Intrasite and Regional Evidence for Production, Consumption and Exchange. Unpublished Ph.D. dissertation, Department of Anthropology, University of Wisconsin, Madison.
 2000 Exchange and Risk Management in the Upper Mississippi Valley: A.D. 1000–1200. *Midcontinental Journal of Archaeology* 25(2):353–376.

Finney, Fred A., and James B. Stoltman
 1991 The Fred Edwards Site: A Case of Stirling Phase Culture Contact in Southwestern Wisconsin. In *New Perspectives on Cahokia: Views from the Periphery*, edited by James B. Stoltman, pp. 229–252. Monographs in World Archaeology 2. Prehistory Press, Madison.

Gibbon, Guy E.
 1979 *The Mississippian Occupation of the Red Wing Area*. Minnesota Prehistoric Archaeology Series No. 13. Minnesota Historical Society, St. Paul.
 1991 The Middle Mississippian Presence in Minnesota. In *New Perspectives on Cahokia: Views from the Periphery*, edited by James B. Stoltman, pp. 207–220. Monographs in World Archaeology 2. Prehistory Press, Madison.

Gibbon, Guy E., and Clark A. Dobbes
 1991 The Mississippian Presence in the Red Wing Area, Minnesota. In *New Perspectives on Cahokia: Views from the Periphery*, edited by James B. Stoltman, pp. 281–306. Monographs in World Archaeology 2. Prehistory Press, Madison.

Gilbert, William H.
 1928a Archaeology of the Rock River Valley. Field report prepared for the University of Chicago.
 1928b Preliminary Report on the Archaeological Survey in Northwestern Illinois during the Summer, 1928. Field report prepared for the University of Chicago.

Goldstein, Lynn G.
 1980 *Mississippian Mortuary Practices: A Case Study of Two Cemeteries in the Lower Illinois*

Valley. Northwestern Archaeological Program, Paper No. 4. Northwestern University Archaeological Program, Evanston, Illinois.

1991 The Implications of Aztalan's Location. In *New Perspectives on Cahokia: Views from the Periphery,* edited by James B. Stoltman, pp. 209–227. Monographs in World Archaeology, No. 2. Prehistory Press, Madison.

Goldstein, Lynn G., and John D. Richards

1991 Ancient Aztalan: The Cultural and Ecological Context of a Late Prehistoric Site in the Midwest. *Cahokia and the Hinterlands,* edited by Thomas E. Emerson and R. Barry Lewis, pp. 93–206. University of Illinois Press, Urbana.

Green, William, and David J. Nolan

2000 Late Woodland Peoples in West-Central Illinois. In *Late Woodland Societies: Tradition and Transformation across the Midcontinent,* edited by Thomas E. Emerson, Dale L. McElrath, and Andrew C. Fortier, pp. 345–386. University of Nebraska Press, Lincoln.

Green, William, and Roland L. Rodell

1994 The Mississippian Presence and Cahokia Interaction at Trempealeau, Wisconsin. *American Antiquity* 59(2):334–359.

Hall, Robert L.

1991 Cahokia Identity and Interaction Models of Cahokia Mississippian. In *Cahokia and the Hinterlands: Middle Mississippian Cultures of the Midwest,* edited by Thomas E. Emerson and R. Barry Lewis, pp. 3–34. University of Illinois Press, Urbana.

1993 Red Banks, Oneota, and the Winnebago: Views from a Distant Rock. *Wisconsin Archaeologist* 74(1–4):10–79.

1997 *Archaeology of the Soul: North American Belief and Ritual.* University of Illinois Press, Urbana.

Hanenberger, Ned H., George R. Milner, Stevan C. Pullins, Richard Paine, Lucretia S. Kelly, and Kathryn E. Parker

2003 *The Range Site 3: Mississippian and Oneota Occupations.* Research Reports No. 17. Illinois Transportation Archaeological Research Program, University of Illinois, Urbana.

Hargrave, Michael L.

2005 A Geophysical Investigation of the John Chapman Site (11JD12), Jo Daviess County, Illinois. Report submitted to Dr. Paul Gartner, the Archaeological Conservancy, Midwest Regional Office, Columbus, Ohio.

Harn, Alan D.

1980 *The Prehistory of Dickson Mounds: The Dickson Excavation.* Rev. ed. Reports of Investigations No. 35. Illinois State Museum, Springfield.

1991 The Eveland Site: Inroad to Spoon River Mississippian Society. In *New Perspectives on Cahokia: Views from the Periphery,* edited by James B. Stoltman, pp. 129–153. Prehistory Press, Madison.

Holley, George R.

1989 *The Archaeology of the Cahokia Mounds ICT-II: Ceramics.* Illinois Cultural Resources Study No. 11. Illinois Historic Preservation Agency, Springfield.

2007 The Red Wing Locality Prehistoric Ceramic Sequence. Manuscript on file, Department of Anthropology and Earth Science, Minnesota State University, Moorhead.

Johannessen, Sissel

1993 Food, Dishes, and Society in the Mississippi Valley. In *Foraging and Farming in the*

Kelly, John E.
    1991   Cahokia and Its Role as a Gateway Center in Interregional Exchange. *Cahokia and the Hinterlands*, edited by Thomas E. Emerson and R. Barry Lewis, pp. 61–80. University of Illinois Press, Urbana.

Lewis, Theodore H.
    1888   Effigy Mounds in Northern Illinois. *Science* 12(292):118–119.

Logan, Wilfred D.
    1976   *Woodland Complexes in Northeastern Iowa*. Publications in Archaeology 15. U.S. Department of the Interior, National Park Service. U.S. Government Printing Office, Washington, D.C.

Lyons, Patrick D.
    2003   *Ancestral Hopi Migrations*. Anthropological Papers of the University of Arizona No. 68. University of Arizona Press, Tucson.

McConaughy, Mark A.
    1991   The Rench Site Late Late Woodland/Mississippian Farming Hamlet from the Central Illinois River Valley: Food for Thought. In *New Perspectives on Cahokia: Views from the Periphery*, edited by James B. Stoltman, pp. 101–128. Monographs in World Archaeology 2. Prehistory Press, Madison.

McConaughy, Mark A., Terrance J. Martin, and Frances B. King
    1993   Late Late Woodland/Mississippian Period Component. In *Rench: A Stratified Site in the Central Illinois River Valley*, edited by Mark A. McConaughy, pp. 76–128. Reports of Investigations 49. Illinois State Museum, Springfield.

Millhouse, Phillip G.
    2012   The John Chapman Site and Creolization on the Northern Frontier of the Mississippian World. Ph.D. dissertation, Department of Anthropology, University of Illinois at Urbana-Champaign.

Neuzil, Anna
    2008   *In the Aftermath of Migration: Renegotiating Ancient Identity in Southeastern Arizona*. Anthropological Papers of the University of Arizona No. 73. University of Arizona Press, Tucson.

Nickerson, William B.
    1913   Archaeology of Jo Daviess County Illinois: 1895–1901. Report submitted to the Peabody Museum of American Archaeology, Harvard University, Cambridge.

Pauketat, Timothy R.
    1994   *The Ascent of Chiefs: Cahokia and Mississippian Politics in Native North America*. University of Alabama Press, Tuscaloosa.
    1998   *The Archaeology of Downtown Cahokia: The Tract 15A and Dunham Tract Excavations*. Studies in Archaeology 1. Illinois Transportation Archaeological Research Program, University of Illinois, Urbana.
    2003   Resettled Farmers and the Making of a Mississippian Polity. *American Antiquity* 68(1):39–66.
    2004   *Ancient Cahokia and the Mississippians*. Cambridge University Press, Cambridge.
    2008   Founders' Cults and the Archaeology of Wa-kan-da. In *Memory Work: The Archaeolo-*

    gies of Material Practice, edited by Barbara J. Mills and William H. Walker, pp. 61–79. School of American Research Press, Santa Fe.
 2010 The Missing Persons in Mississippian Mortuaries. In *Mississippian Mortuary Practices: Beyond Hierarchy and the Representationist Perspective*, edited by Lynne P. Sullivan and Robert C. Mainfort, pp. 14–29. University Press of Florida, Gainesville.
 2013a *The Archaeology of Downtown Cahokia II: The 1960 Excavation of Tract 15B*. Studies in Archaeology, No. 8. Illinois Archaeological Survey, Prairie Research Institute, University of Illinois, Urbana-Champaign.
 2013b *An Archaeology of the Cosmos: Rethinking Agency and Religion in Ancient America*. Routledge, Abingdon.

Pauketat, Timothy, Danielle M. Benden, and Robert F. Boszhardt
 2009 Early Mississippian Colonists in the Upper Mississippi Valley: 2009 Investigations at the Fisher Mounds Complex. Poster presented at the 55th Annual Midwestern Archaeological Conference, Iowa City.
 2010 New Evidence of the Cahokian Occupation of Trempealeau. Poster presented at the 56th Annual Midwest Archaeological Conference, Bloomington.
 2011 Cosmic Contact in the Upper Mississippi Valley. Paper presented at the 76th Society for American Archaeology Meeting, Sacramento.

Pauketat, Timothy R., Robert F. Boszhardt, and Danielle M. Benden
 2015 Trempealeau Entanglements: An Ancient Colony's Causes and Effects. *American Antiquity* 80(2):260–289.

Pauketat, Timothy R., and Thomas E. Emerson
 1991 The Ideology of Authority and the Power of the Pot. *American Anthropologist* 93:919–941.
 1997 Introduction. In *Cahokia: Domination and Ideology in the Mississippian World*, edited by Timothy R. Pauketat and Thomas E. Emerson, pp. 1–29. University of Nebraska Press, Lincoln.

Pauketat, Timothy R., Lucretia S. Kelly, Gayle J. Fritz, Neal H. Lopinot, Scott Elias, and Eve Hargrave
 2002 The Residues of Feasting and Public Ritual at Early Cahokia. *American Antiquity* 67(2):257–279.

Perino, Gregory
 1973 The Late Woodland Component and the Schild Sites, Greene County, Illinois. In *Late Woodland Site Archaeology in Illinois I: Investigations in South-Central Illinois*, pp. 90–140. Bulletin 9. Illinois Archaeological Survey, Urbana.

Phillips, Philip, and James A. Brown
 1984 *Pre-Columbian Shell Engravings from the Craig Mound at Spiro, Oklahoma*. Peabody Museum Press, Cambridge.

Radin, Paul
 1915 The Social Organization of the Winnebago Indians: An Interpretation. Bulletin No. 10. Anthropological Series No. 5. Canada Geologic Survey Museum, Ottawa.
 1948 *Winnebago Hero Cycles: A Study in Aboriginal Literature*. Indiana University Publications in Anthropology and Linguistics, Memoir 1. Waverly Press, Baltimore.

Richards, John D.
 1992 Ceramics and Culture at Aztalan: A Late Prehistoric Village in Southeast Wisconsin. Unpublished PhD. dissertation, University of Wisconsin–Milwaukee.

2003   Collars, Castellations, and Cahokia: A Regional Perspective on the Aztalan Ceramic Assemblage. *Wisconsin Archaeologist* 84:139–153.

Riley, Thomas J., and Gary A. Apfelstadt
1978   Prehistoric Missionaries in East Central Illinois. *Field Museum of Natural History Bulletin* 49(4):16–21.

Rodell, Roland L.
1991   Diamond Bluff Site Complex and Cahokia Influence in the Red Wing Locality. In *New Perspectives on Cahokia: Views from the Periphery*, edited by James B. Stoltman, pp. 229–252. Monographs in World Archaeology 2. Prehistory Press, Madison.
1997   The Diamond Bluff Site Complex: Time and Tradition in the Northern Mississippi Valley. Unpublished Ph.D. dissertation, Department of Anthropology, University of Wisconsin–Milwaukee.

Roseborough, Amy
2008   Jar-ing Conclusions: What We Think We Know about Effigy Mound Culture. Paper presented at the 54th Annual Midwest Archaeological Conference, Milwaukee.

Rudolph, Katie Z.
2009   A Taphonomic Analysis of Human Skeletal Material from Aztalan: Cannibalism, Hostility and Mortuary Variability. Unpublished master's thesis, University of Wisconsin–Milwaukee.

Salzer, Robert J., and Grace Rajnovich
2001   *The Gottschall Rock Shelter: An Archaeological Mystery*. Prairie Smoke Press, Saint Paul.

Sampson, Kelvin W.
1988   Conventionalized Figures on Late Woodland Ceramics. *Wisconsin Archaeologist* 69(3): 163–188.

Scarry, C. Margaret, and Elizabeth J. Reitz
2005   Changes in Foodways at the Parkin Site, Arkansas. *Southeastern Archaeology* 24(2): 107–120.

Schroeder, Marjorie, and Phillip G. Millhouse
2009   National Register of Historic Places Nomination for the John Chapman (11JD12) Site. Submitted to the Illinois Historic Preservation Agency and U.S. Department of the Interior, National Park Service.

Simoons, Frederick J.
1994   *Eat Not This Flesh: Food Avoidances from Prehistory to the Present*. University of Wisconsin Press, Madison.

Skousen, Jacob B.
2016   Pilgrimage and the Construction of Cahokia: A View from the Emerald Site. Ph.D. dissertation, Department of Anthropology, University of Illinois at Urbana-Champaign.

Steadman, Dawnie W.
1998   The Population Shuffle in the Central Illinois Valley: A Diachronic Model of Mississippian Biocultural Interactions. *World Archaeology* 30(2):306–326.
2001   Mississippians in Motion? A Population Genetic Analysis of Interregional Gene Flow in West-Central Illinois. *American Journal of Physical Anthropology* 114(1):61–73.

Stoltman, James B. (editor)
1991   *New Perspectives on Cahokia: Views from the Periphery*. Monographs in World Archaeology No. 2. Prehistory Press, Madison.

Stoltman, James B.
   2000 A Reconsideration of the Cultural Processes Linking Cahokia to Its Northern Hinterlands during the Period A.D. 1000–1200. In *Mounds, Modoc, and Mesoamerica: Papers in Honor of Melvin L. Fowler*, edited by Steven R. Ahler, pp. 439–467. Scientific Papers Vol. 28. Illinois State Museum, Springfield.

Stoltman, James B., Danielle M. Benden, and Robert F. Boszhardt
   2008 New Evidence in the Upper Mississippi Valley for Pre-Mississippian Cultural Interaction with the American Bottom. *American Antiquity* 73(2):317–336.

Stoltman James B., and George W. Christiansen
   2000 The Late Woodland Stage in the Driftless Area of the Upper Mississippi Valley. In *Late Woodland Societies: Tradition and Transformation Across the Midcontinent*, edited by Thomas E. Emerson, Dale L. McElrath, and Andrew C. Fortier, pp. 497–524. University of Nebraska Press, Lincoln.

Studenmund, Sarah J.
   2000 Late Woodland Occupations in the Lower Illinois Valley: Research Questions and Data Sets. In *Late Woodland Societies: Tradition and Transformation across the Midcontinent*, edited by Thomas E. Emerson, Dale L. McElrath, and Andrew C. Fortier, pp. 301–343. University of Nebraska Press, Lincoln.

Studenmund, Sarah J., Laura E. Johnson, Marjorie B. Schroeder, and Karli White
   1995 Late Woodland Settlement Patterns at the Confluence of the Illinois and Mississippi Rivers: A Comparison of Upland and Lowland Sites. *Illinois Archaeology* 7(1 and 2):148–201.

Theler, James L., and Robert F. Boszhardt
   2003 *Twelve Millennia: Archaeology of the Upper Mississippi River Valley*. University of Iowa Press, Iowa City.
   2006 Collapse of Crucial Resources and Cultural Change: A Model for the Woodland to Oneota Transformation in the Upper Midwest. *American Antiquity* 71(3):433–472.

Tiffany, Joseph
   1982 Hartley Fort Ceramics. *Proceedings of the Iowa Academy of Science* 89:133–150.
   1991a Models of Mississippian Culture History in the Western Prairie Peninsula: A Perspective from Iowa. In *Cahokia and the Hinterlands: Middle Mississippian Cultures of the Midwest*, edited by Thomas E. Emerson and R. Barry Lewis, pp. 183–192. University of Illinois Press, Urbana.
   1991b Modeling Mill Creek–Mississippian Interaction. In *New Perspectives on Cahokia: Views from the Periphery*, edited by James B. Stoltman, pp. 319–347. Monographs in World Archaeology 2. Prehistory Press, Madison.

Willey, Gordon R., Charles C. DiPeso, William A. Ritchie, Irving Rouse, John H. Rowe, and Donald W. Lathrap
   1956 An Archaeological Classification of Culture Contact Situations. In *Seminars in Archaeology: 1955*, edited by Robert Wauchope, pp. 1–30. Memoir No. 11. Society for American Archaeology, Salt Lake City.

Wilson, Gregory D.
   1999 The Production and Consumption of Mississippian Fineware in the American Bottom. *Southeastern Archaeology* 18(2):98–109.

Wilson, Gregory D., and Brad Koldehoff
- 1998 The Miller Farm Site: Early Mississippian Occupations on Turkey Hill. *Illinois Antiquity* 33(2):4–8.

Wray, Donald E., and Richard S. MacNeish
- 1958 The Weaver Site: Twenty Centuries of Illinois Prehistory. Manuscript on file, Dickson Mounds Museum, Lewistown.

Wittry, Warren L.
- 1969 The American Woodhenge. In *Explorations into Cahokia Archaeology*, edited by Melvin O. Fowler, pp. 43–48. Illinois Archaeological Survey Bulletin No. 7. University of Illinois, Urbana.

5

Mississippian Processes and Histories

The Evolution of Fort Ancient Culture in the Miami Valleys

ROBERT A. COOK

One of the perennial interests in the archaeology of the eastern United States is the origin and spread of Mississippian cultural traditions (e.g., Emerson and Lewis 1991; Griffin 1943; Holmes 1903; Pauketat 2004; Smith 1978, 1990; Wilson and Sullivan, this volume). This chapter addresses this topic in the Middle Ohio River Valley with a focus on the Fort Ancient culture (Griffin 1943; see also Cowan 1987; Drooker 1997; and Pollack and Henderson 1992, 2000a) (Figure 5.1). The Fort Ancient archaeological culture was initially defined in relation to Mississippians in the Midwestern Taxonomic System when it was essentially seen as being a periphery (Upper Mississippian) in relation to a core (Middle Mississippian) (e.g., Griffin 1943). However, the view of Fort Ancient as a form of being Mississippian has not remained steady since it was defined as such in the Culture History period of American archaeology. The intervening Processual period in American archaeology was a time when a strong linkage of Fort Ancient to Mississippians was rejected, with the focus being on Fort Ancient as an in situ development (e.g., Church 1987; Pollack and Henderson 1992). These two ends of the interpretive spectrum that have characterized much of Fort Ancient research are related to the more widely known theoretical camps of culture process and culture history, with the former being more focused on internal developments such as environmental adaptation, and the latter on external forces such as migration and exchange as sources of culture change. However, I view a choice between what are often perceived as alternative theoretical orientations as unnecessary; in contrast, interpretations of Fort Ancient origins benefit greatly through the inclusion of both process and history considerations. This approach adheres well with one that holds that external and internal

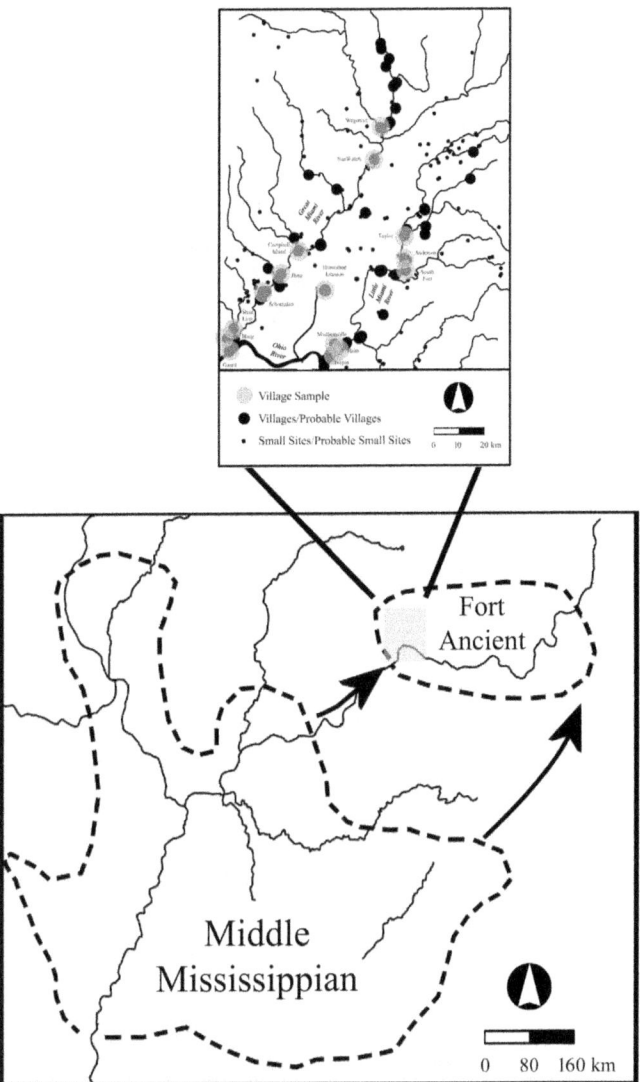

Figure 5.1. Map of the Fort Ancient and Middle Mississippian culture regions (after Griffin 1967: Figure 5) with an inset showing the study region (site locations based on the Ohio Archaeological Inventory).

constraints should be integrated as much as possible to form more complete archaeological interpretations (Trigger 1991).

I begin the chapter by briefly outlining the predominant interpretations of Fort Ancient origins. This is followed by my own theoretical orientation and results from recent investigations in a specific Fort Ancient subregion. The focus is on a relatively small geographic area, encompassed by the Great and Little Miami rivers of southwest Ohio and southeast Indiana. This area is also the locus of a particular style of pottery decoration (guilloche), which appears to this author to be a design similar to a common variant of the Mississippian Ramey design on incised pottery at Cahokia. The Ramey design style was a relatively early development in the Mississippian world. Ramey-style designs are a regular occurrence on pottery at several early sites in the study region, sites that also have high percentages of guilloche-style designs (Figure 5.2). Further research is needed to examine the strength of this connection, but I suggest that the development of a particular symbolic marker of identity such as this often occurs during times of intercultural interaction (Barth 1969). Furthermore, many of the villages in this region reveal a close similarity in site form and a close biological relationship among human populations (e.g., Cook and Aubry 2014).

My methodological approach includes equal parts physical and archaeological anthropology. The archaeological component of the project is focused on examining the occurrence and social contexts of Mississippian-style wall-trench houses and artifacts such as marine shell pendants, gorgets, shell-tempered pottery, and large chert knives. The goal of these efforts is to establish as much of a social context as possible in which to interpret human relationships. The physical part of the project is focused on biodistance and chemical analyses to examine inferred genetic, dietary, and geographic markers within burial populations (Cook and Aubry 2014; Cook and Price 2015; Cook and Schurr 2009). The goal of these efforts is to examine human relationships and movements into and within the study region during the origins of the Fort Ancient culture. A focus on chronology considerably assists with the project as a whole, effectively establishing both the timing of the processes and histories associated with the development of Fort Ancient culture vis-à-vis surrounding Mississippians.

Conclusions to the study find considerable evidence to combine processual and historical elements that were emphasized in isolation in most previous interpretations. The most important finding is that Mississippians directly factored into the beginnings of Fort Ancient culture at large sites, the key part of the historical interpretation. The arrival of Mississippians was coterminous with the onset of Fort Ancient culture, which was expressed in the first large villages and a rapid shift to wall-trench house construction, shell-tempered pottery, and intensive maize consumption. The large and early sites are also located in an optimal environmental niche type for intensive maize agriculture, a focus comfortable with a strictly processual orientation. While these types of

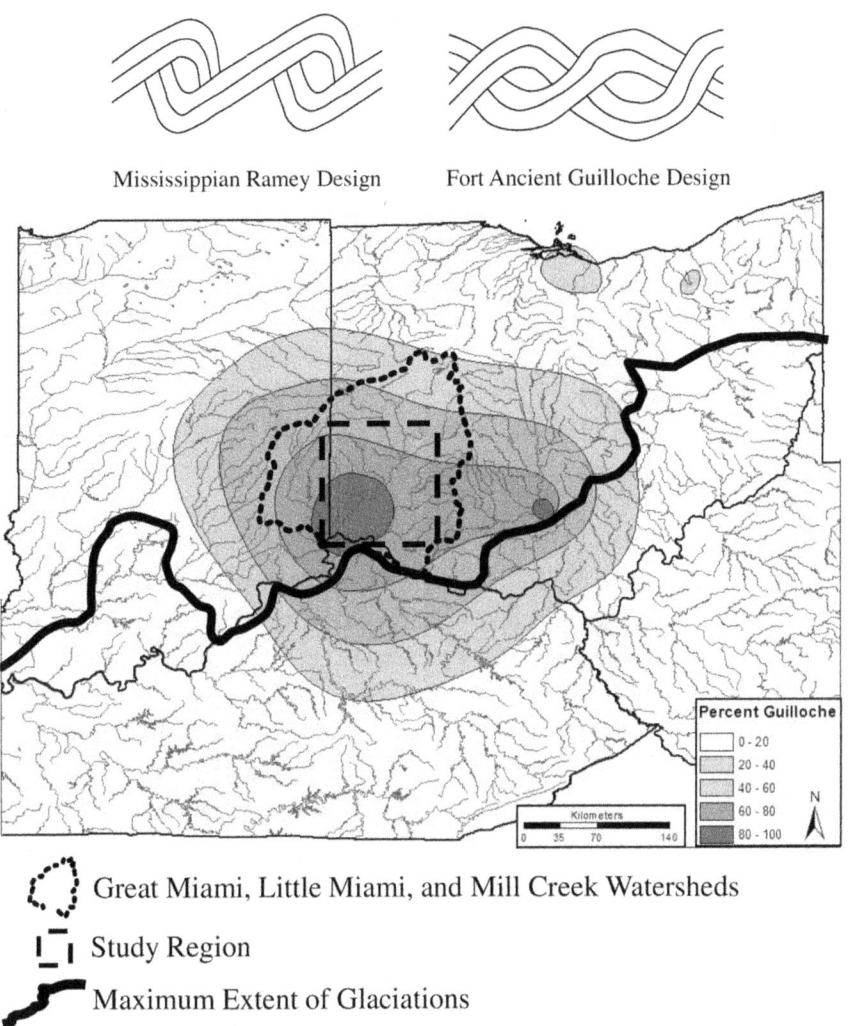

Figure 5.2. Comparison of a common variant of the Middle Mississippian Ramey pottery design and the Fort Ancient guilloche pottery design (*top*). Map of study region in relation to natural features and the concentration of the guilloche pottery design (*bottom*) (guilloche distribution map produced by Aaron Comstock).

historical and processual orientations are often seen as contradictory, they can be integrated to some degree. The key, however, lies in the stimulus of change. In our processual case, it would be the emphasis on local population growth leading to development of villages. In our historical case, it would be the emphasis on migrants directly influencing subsequent developments, including knowledge regarding village formation. However, I do not see these as opposing viewpoints and see ways for both to be correct, forming a more perfect explanation when married together with additional data sets, which will be accomplished herein and the larger study from which it is derived (Cook 2017).

After identifying that human movement occurred, the next step was to assess some of the potential push (e.g., drought, disease, war) and pull (e.g., leadership opportunities, better environment) factors that may have influenced Mississippians to make the effort to come into a new land. To this end, I will show how the Fort Ancient culture originated in a time of increasingly common droughts in some Mississippian regions but a time of optimal moisture conditions in the Fort Ancient region. The historical focus is that Mississippians were attracted to the region because it was not experiencing comparable conditions, and the climate in the Fort Ancient region remained excellent for intensive agriculture much longer than any of the geographic areas from which the Mississippian migrants came. The processual focus is that locations within the Fort Ancient region with the largest and earliest sites are indeed in the most optimal environments, which is consistent with processual expectations regarding habitat usage over time (i.e., initial settlements are in the most optimal environmental patches).

The bioarchaeological context of Mississippian objects illustrates both processual and historical particulars regarding the formation of individual villages. A variety of Mississippian objects are present in the study region, such as Ramey knives and pottery; painted pottery (negative and positive); whelk shell pendants, gorgets, and beads/discs; and human and animal effigy pipes (Figure 5.3), several of which have wide geographic distributions with regular connections to several Mississippian regions to the south and west of the Fort Ancient region (Figure 5.4). Additionally, a variety of Fort Ancient objects were locally made but imbued with various Mississippian and local characteristics. A general finding is that village authorities (as expressed by the interment with Mississippian status symbols) are closely related to only one other male and are otherwise biological outsiders to the local site population. However, their histories within the local populations can be distinct, as captured in the following scenarios that will be summarized in greater detail below: (1) burial of such a pair of males in a mound initially constructed by Middle Woodland peoples (ca. 100 BC–AD 400), followed by construction of the residential part of a village; (2) interment of a similarly defined group of male authorities during the main part of a village occupation and not interred in a mound. The first scenario is more consistent with a mythic origin to a village whose first acts were to inter Mississippian-style leaders

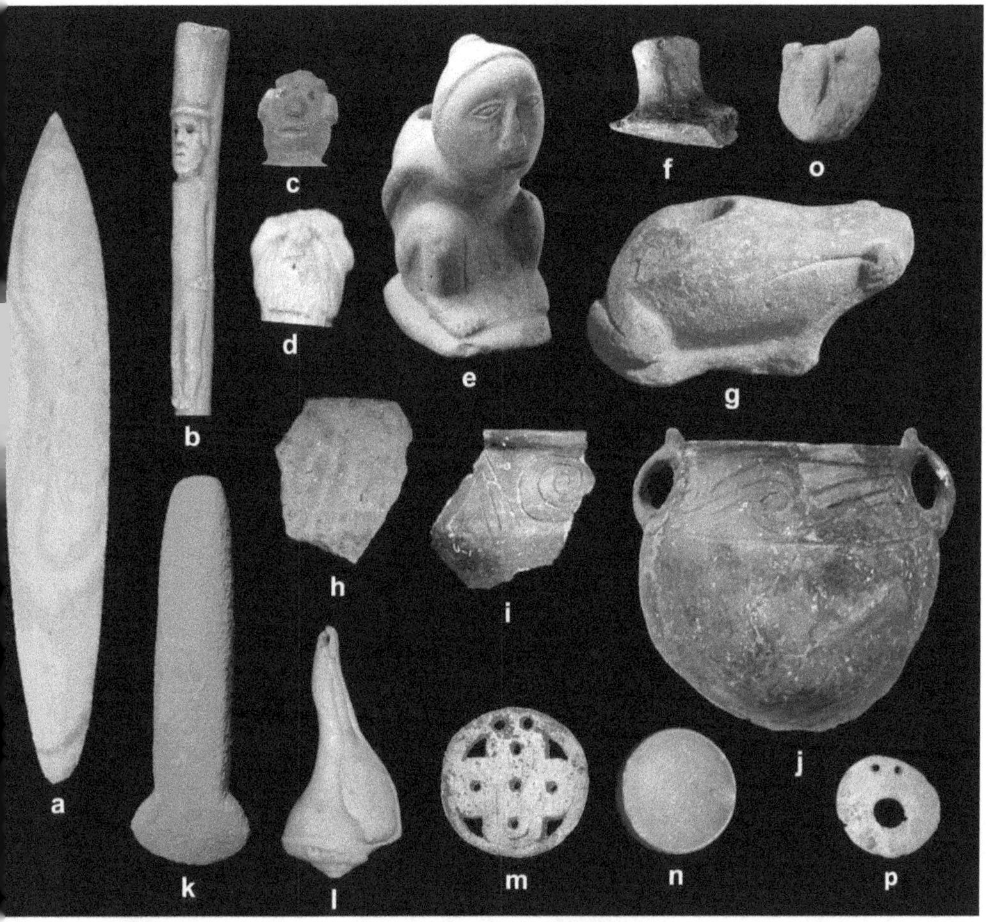

Figure 5.3. Select examples of eleventh–fourteenth-century Mississippian-style objects from the study sites (not to scale): *a*, Ramey knife [Guard]; *b*, human effigy pin [Turpin]; *c*, human effigy prisoner pipe [Turpin]; *d*, human effigy pin [Guard]; *e*, human effigy prisoner pipe [Turpin]; *f*, ceramic platform pipe [Turpin]; *g*, frog effigy pipe [Turpin]; *h*, negative painted pottery bowl rim [Turpin]; *i* and *j*, Ramey-like designs on pottery jars [Turpin]; *k*, spud [Guard]; *l*, whelk shell pendant [SunWatch]; *m*, cross-in-circle gorget [Anderson]; *n*, chunkey stone [Turpin]; *o*, effigy pipe [Taylor]; *p*, annular shell gorget [Madisonville]) (from Cook and Price 2015:Figure 4).

in an earlier mound, literally around which a village formed. The second scenario works well with a scalar threshold model whereby local population grew to the point where there was a managerial need for a village-level authority (Johnson 1982). These and other findings will be detailed herein to demonstrate the power of an approach that blends both processual and historical dimensions of human behavior.

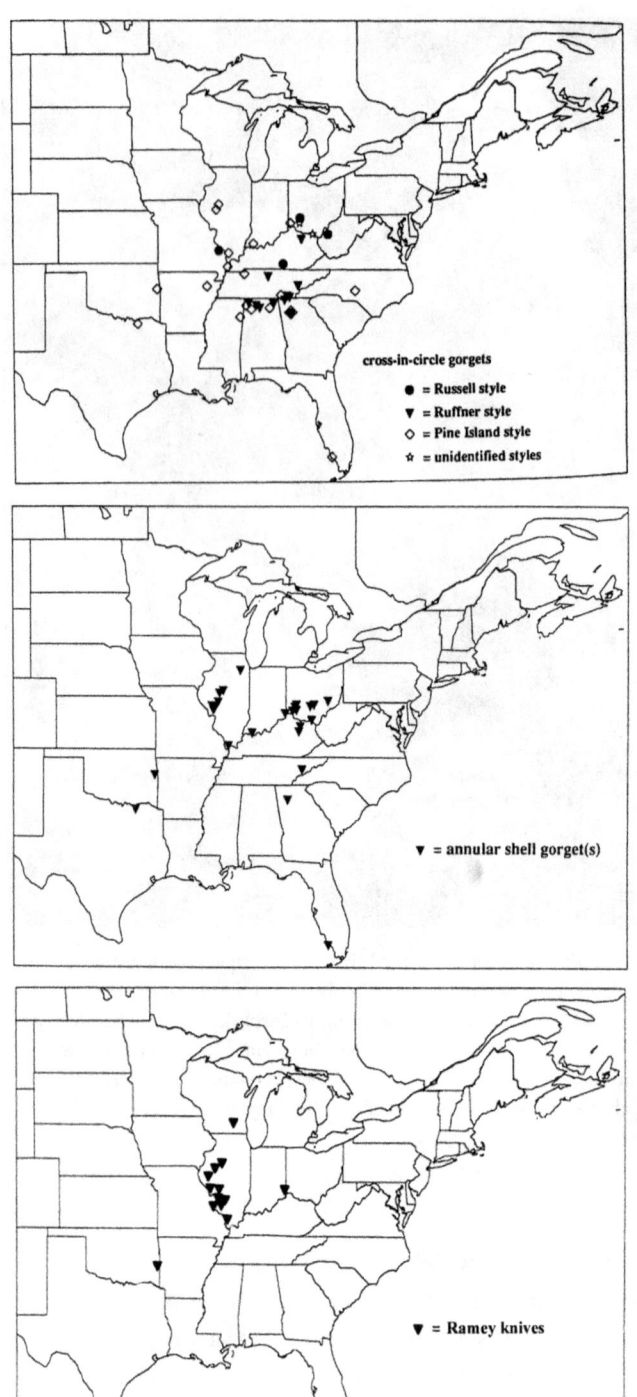

Figure 5.4. Select artifacts with a wide geographic distribution in the Early to Middle Fort Ancient Period (top two maps after Drooker 1997:Figures 8–20, 8–22; bottom map after Vermillion et al. 2003:Figure 6). (Note the connections to the south [cross-in-circle gorgets] and west [annular shell gorgets, Ramey knives].)

Theories of Fort Ancient Culture History and Process

Previous studies in the Fort Ancient region reflect general trends in the discipline where there have been oscillations between theories of culture history and culture process largely without more fully exploring the integration of the two aspects of culture change. As was common for the time, investigations in the Culture History period of American archaeology (1930–1960) explained all social change as resulting from diffusion and/or migration. All cultures were ultimately seen to have been the result of another "mother" culture splitting off and moving into the area and/or diffusion from external sources. Fort Ancient culture was viewed in this respect in relation to Mississippi groups. Griffin (1967) suggested that Fort Ancient was the result of migration and diffusion from two different Mississippian cultures, those from the lower portion of the Ohio Valley and those from Tennessee (see Figure 5.1). It was argued that Fort Ancient culture was less complex than its chiefly neighbors because the Middle Ohio Valley provided an environment less productive for agriculture than the larger river floodplains from whence the Fort Ancient settlers came, thus obfuscating the need for the more complex chiefdom form of organization. A brief summary of this scenario follows:

> The Fort Ancient Aspect appears to have been strongly influenced by Middle Mississippi, both by actual migration of peoples bearing a "Mississippi" culture into the southwestern part of the Fort Ancient territory and by diffusion of traits . . . Fort Ancient could hardly have appeared as a cultural entity until after the Middle Mississippi peoples had formed a strong group . . . their marginal relationship to what is thought of as "pure" Middle Mississippi. (Griffin 1943:257–258)

Prufer and Shane (1970:258–262) followed a similar approach but shifted the geographic focus from the southwest part of the Fort Ancient region to central Ohio as the point of origin for Mississippian migrants. While we will see that the Mississippian association to Fort Ancient has validity, the early timing and focus of Mississippians in the Fort Ancient region is more likely in southwest Ohio and southeast Indiana. However, there is some evidence in central Ohio of Fort Ancient villages with Mississippian characteristics (e.g., a sub-structure mound at Baum) that might be contemporaneous (see Brady-Rawlins 2007:Table 5.2 and Figures 5.4 and 5.5 for radiocarbon dates and relative occupation sequences within the region). There also appears to be a very close biological (see Robbins and Neumann 1972) and archaeological relationship (e.g., guilloche designs [see Figure 5.2]) between these regions.

During the Processual period in American archaeology (1960–2000), emphasis turned toward understanding actual people rather than using taxonomies of material traits in order to discern human behavior. Unfortunately, due to a strict focus on local systems, anything foreign to an area was dismissed as being unimportant to local developments (e.g., as discussed by Henderson 1998 and Pollack and Henderson 1992, 2000a). This is not to imply that processualists fail to recognize variability and the situational nature of leadership in Fort Ancient culture, which Drooker (1997:329) and Henderson (1998) nicely situate within heterarchy theory (Crumley 1979). A problem that arises in some applications of heterarchy theory to Fort Ancient is that only internal variation is considered to be a factor of culture change, when such an internal restriction was never specified in the original theory (Crumley 1979). Most processual-style studies have concluded that Mississippian involvement was minimal in the formation of Fort Ancient societies, focusing instead on continuity with Late Woodland predecessors (e.g., Church 1987; Greenlee 2002; Pollack and Henderson 1992, 2000a). In this perspective, Mississippian characteristics of Fort Ancient assemblages have been largely depicted as inconsequential to the development of Fort Ancient societies (Henderson 1998; Pollack and Henderson 1992, 2000a; but see Drooker 1997:89–95, 301–302, Figure 8–23). Significant interactions with Mississippians are noted only during the Late Fort Ancient period (Pollack et al. 2002; but see Drooker 1997:283–337; Drooker and Cowan 2001:96–98, 103–104).

Other research during the Processual period considered the development of Fort Ancient as stemming from local groups interacting with Mississippian societies, but not emphasizing direct human movements (Essenpreis 1978; Robertson 1980:77–78). Robertson (1980:77–78) specifically focused on the emergence of social institutions as a response to interaction with Mississippian groups, a process that created the need for social solidarity, particularly among male members. Essenpreis (1978) argued that distinctions in Fort Ancient assemblages and settlement systems reflect different levels of interaction between local groups and Mississippians. Groups located closer to Mississippians became more Mississippianized. Nass and Yerkes (1995) specifically compared Fort Ancient and Mississippian site structures, suggesting that they were similar, although parts of very different settlement systems.

Whether it was intended to or not, the following processual model has become deeply engrained throughout the entire Fort Ancient region and formed the basis of the much-needed testing in the present study. This dominant model contends that there was a relatively smooth progression from Late Woodland to Fort Ancient, with Early period (ca. AD 1000–1200) hamlets transitioning to Middle period (ca. AD 1200–1400) circular villages to larger Late Period

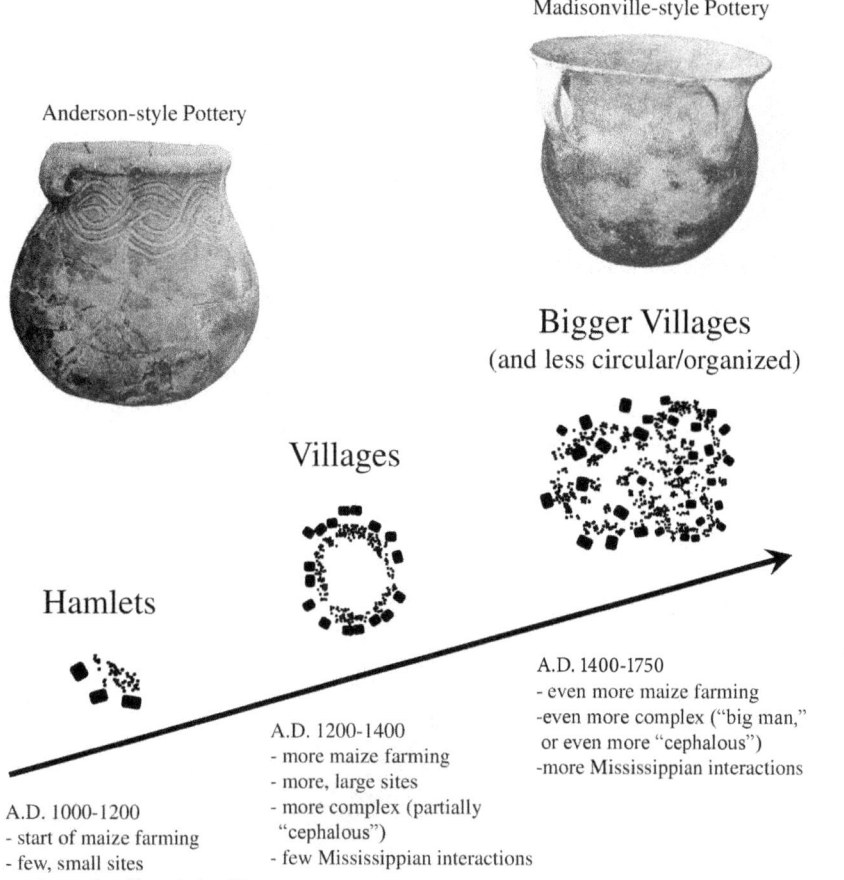

Figure 5.5. Key pottery styles associated with earlier (pre-AD 1400) and later (post-AD 1400) Fort Ancient sites in the study region (*top*) (modified from Griffin 1943:Plate XLIX.6, LXII.2). General model of Fort Ancient development that was found to not be applicable to the study region (*bottom*). In contrast, a few of the more notable findings are that village form in the study region was large throughout the Fort Ancient period, and maize consumption and Mississippian interactions were highest and most frequent at the onset of the tradition.

(ca. AD 1400–1750) sites, with a corresponding increase through time in social complexity, reliance on maize agriculture, and increased interactions outside of the region (Church and Nass 2002; Pollack and Henderson 1992, 2000a; see Drooker 1997:Figure 4–3 for more details on the chronological scheme) (Figure 5.5). The key parts of the model hold that there was an insular and linear progression from small to large sites, and less to more maize, and an increase in external interaction over time, with a pronounced change occurring at about

AD 1400 at the onset of what is referred to as the Madisonville horizon, a time of marked change across much of the Midwest and Southeast.

My Approach

My initial research efforts in the study region delineated what I termed a process of "periphery peer" interaction (Cook 2008). This approach expanded the Renfrew (1986) "peer polity" model for examining coevolutionary processes by considering the impact that peripheral or smaller sites in settlement systems had on neighboring groups. By utilizing this approach, I was able to examine why the structures of Fort Ancient and Mississippian villages were similar (Figure 5.6). In subsequent studies I have examined evidence for changes in pottery production, maize consumption, and residence patterning that resulted

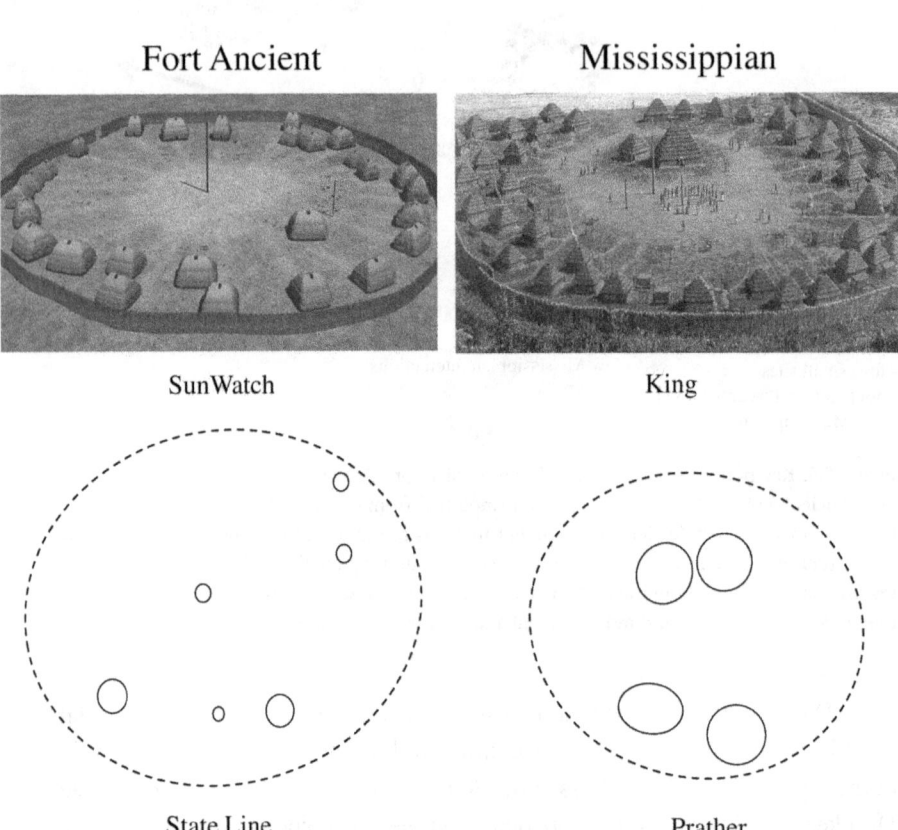

Figure 5.6. Comparison of Fort Ancient and Mississippian villages (*top*) and small mound centers (*bottom*) (top images modified from Cook 2008:Figure 7.2; note for bottom site plans, solid lines denote approximate limits of mounds and dashed lines denote approximate limits of site boundaries).

from long-distance interactions and movements between groups in Mississippian and Fort Ancient territory as indicated in pottery composition (Cook and Fargher 2007, 2008), human carbon isotopes (Cook and Schurr 2009), and variation in biodistance measurements (Cook and Aubry 2014). I have also investigated human conflict as reflected in interpersonal trauma among members of the mortuary population at SunWatch, concluding that there was a male-war-focused sodality that was intimately connected with a Mississippian component of the village (Cook 2012). The present study further examines how Fort Ancient developed by delving into the particular cultural patterns and human biology within sites and directly examining human movement. This has allowed for the painting of a much more complete picture.

The theoretical orientation developed for the present study grew out of my earlier studies and draws on a wide range of processual- and historical-style approaches. I support the call for a blend of such approaches (see also Hegmon 2003; Stark et al. 2008), to continue to search for the "wide theoretical middle ground between these polar opposites" (Smith 1990:2). Specifically, in this study I refer to my use of a macroevolutionary perspective to integrate generalizing aspects of culture change such as the rapid appearance of new organizational forms (*Bauplänes*) during times of rapid environmental change, and historical aspects of culture change that are conceived of as directed variation and agency (see Prentiss et al. 2009 and Zeder 2009 for further details on macroevolution). Within this overarching theoretical framework, I view human migration as a form of directed variation. Additionally, there are regularities associated with relationships between site size and optimal environmental zones and push/pull factors that influence human movement.

To further investigate historical dimensions, I examine how people in new regions produce a sense of place (emplacement) by focusing on the landscapes in which migrations occur (Cobb and Butler 2006; Gupta and Ferguson 1997). There are two dimensions to the investigation of the landscape, one that focuses on ecological processes and one that considers historical and experiential dimensions of how people interact with the land. These two characteristics of the environment can often affect each other (Cobb and Butler 2006; see also Ingold 1993 and Schroeder 2004). To illustrate the potential of considering landscape issues of human movement, I consider a brief example. Cobb and Butler (2006) have investigated the Mississippian Millstone Bluff polity in southern Illinois, suggesting that these people were once more hierarchically organized, but as they resettled they became less so. The small villages and associated burials lack any strong sense of social distinctions, but some elements of their past were incorporated into the new landscape. The migrants incorporated a prominent topographic feature into their overall settlement design, but without a hierarchy reflected in their mortuary patterning.

Memories are often anchored to the landscape in monumental constructions that can be used repeatedly, serving as persistent places (Schlanger 1992; see also Thompson and Pluckhahn 2012). Persistent places are locations on the landscape reused over extended durations of time and are usually imbued with unique environmental or economic characteristics (Schlanger 1992). A subset of this general pattern is "persistent monumental places," which are defined as "locations where the actions and process of monumentalization takes place incrementally over extended time frames relative to other sites in a given region ... where people continually return to alter, expand, and reinvent the built environment" (Thompson and Pluckhahn 2012: 50; see also Nelson 2007). In a study of Mesoamerican mound construction, mounds increasingly structured social developments over time as they became "physical marks of communal and individual memory" (Joyce 2004:21–22). These places formed an axis mundi as they created central points in areas where none had previously existed (Joyce 2004:25). "Places of memory anchor the past in the present and, alternatively, the present in the past" (Meskell 2003:36; also see Kuijt 2001:81). Archaeological remains shape subsequent behaviors (Barrett 1999:257; Gillespie 2008:135); and long-term human–land interactions during the process of domestication often involve reuse of significant places on the landscape (e.g., Erickson 2006; Dillehay 2007).

Monumentality and social memory have recently garnered attention in the southeastern United States (e.g., Thompson and Pluckhahn 2012; Wilson 2010), as well as the midwestern United States (Buikstra and Charles 1999; Pauketat and Alt 2003). It has been argued that earlier Woodland Coles Creek centers in the southeastern United States were invoked as memories in the construction of Mississippian centers such as Cahokia, and, in turn, Cahokia may have served as a memory for some subsequent Mississippian centers (Pauketat and Alt 2003). This observation may well be extended to apply to other times and places, including the study region, where there are many earthen monuments, often with long histories, and we know of many cases of Late Woodland burials intruding into Middle Woodland mounds (e.g., Mann 2005; Seeman 1992). In a few cases, Late Prehistoric villages are located near Middle Woodland (ca. 100 BC–AD 400) mounds in the Fort Ancient region (e.g., Burks and Cook 2011). However, whether these cases are coincidental or intentional remains to be demonstrated. Furthermore, the cases of intrusive burials have not been examined with respect to human movement. Who was reusing these monuments, where were they from, when did it happen, and why did they do it? Here I focus on movement in relation to monumentality, as monuments are one of the more archaeologically visible indicators of social memory and can often relate to movement.

My approach is also informed by contemporary understanding of cultural constructions that hold that identities are fluid, contextual, and situational (Hodder 1982; Jones 1997) and are most often only fully understood in relation to nonlocal things, people, and places (Helms 1993; Kopytoff 1987).

The "Big Bang" and a Mississippian Niche

The transition from Late Woodland to Mississippian is poorly understood in many regions, and my study area is no exception. In particular, we lack much information regarding the settlement system for the Late Woodland period in the study region (AD 400–1000). We currently recognize very few large sites, but we do not know how they formed, whether they were created by large groups of coresident populations or small ones over time. Villages *may have formed* during this time period, but if they did, we do not yet know how they were structured. There is the possibility that villages formed after the cultural reorganization that occurred after Hopewell cultures transitioned into Late Woodland cultures (ca. AD 400–700) (Dancey 1992; but see Clay and Creasman 1999 for an alternate view). There are a few Late Woodland candidates for circular villages with central plazas (see Pollack and Henderson 2000b), but these cases have not been sufficiently investigated to make a definitive determination. While we are not certain about the presence of large Late Woodland villages, we do know that the majority of sites at this time were small seasonally used sites and stone burial mounds. However, the spatial relationship between stone mounds and non-mound sites is not well known, although in some cases they are located near one another (e.g., Turpin). Two of the known potentially large Late Woodland sites are located relatively close to the mouths of the two major rivers (Great Miami [Haag], Little Miami [Turpin]), while the smaller sites are located throughout the study region. In general, stone mounds are located most often on river terraces, rather than on high hills (Kellar 1960:407), and sometimes contain stone box graves (Kellar 1960:406, 414) that are somewhat reminiscent of the earlier Adena culture log crypts (ca. 1000–100 BC) and Hopewell (ca. 100 BC–AD 400) stone box graves. However, many stone mounds lack central chambers, and the bodies are much more fragmentary and commingled than in the earlier cases. This may signify a shift toward more collective behavior and, possibly, more mobility and seasonal aggregation.

Part of the shift to Fort Ancient culture involved the incorporation of mortuary and ritual domains into one site plan. Becoming Fort Ancient meant integrating the small and scattered groups, several of which likely shared a single stone burial mound, together into a village that continued to share such a mortuary feature that was now integrated into the circular village plan with corporate groups associated with individual households. In an interesting twist, as burials became more individualized in the Fort Ancient culture, residential units may have become larger and more collective (villages).

Most Mississippian researchers are now in agreement that there was a foundational event in the Cahokia region at about AD 1050 that resulted in the restructuring of varying cultural groups into the largest and most complex Mississippian center ever to exist (e.g., Beck et al. 2007; Emerson et al. 2016; Pauketat 2007). This foundational event has been referred to as the Mississippian "big bang" (Pauketat 2007:146), a finding that I suggest fits well with macroevolutionary expectations regarding sudden culture change. This event at Cahokia involved dismantling much of the existing cultural landscape and then rapidly rebuilding it. At the center of the newly built settlement was a ritual and political precinct composed of many and often large burial and sub-structure mounds and dense neighborhoods of residential housing constructed in a new architectural style (walls made with trenches rather than single-set posts).

At about the time of this momentous transformation, an influx of peoples came from distant lands to Cahokia, and shortly after the rapid development at this major Mississippian mound center, an outpouring of people voyaged to distant lands (e.g., Pauketat et al. 2015). The outpouring of peoples is well expressed by the distribution of wall trench houses throughout a broad region of the Midwest and Southeast (Pauketat 2007:Figure 4.11). While the identification of such foreigners in either the Cahokia region or the distant lands has recently improved (Slater et al. 2014), specific social processes involved in these population movements remain poorly understood. However, there are certainly no shortages of possible scenarios, as people often migrate into or out of developing centers for all sorts of social, economic, and religious reasons. Below I offer specific scenarios regarding the incoming of people to the Fort Ancient region and find good application of the notion that the dramatic transformation in the Cahokia region affected peoples far and wide in both processual and historical terms. In essence, the Mississippian "big bang" fundamentally changed the cultural landscape, but the new cultures were constituted of reworked elements from both local and nonlocal traditions.

The mouth of the Great Miami River contains some of the largest and earliest Fort Ancient sites with clear and abundant material connections to neighboring Mississippian cultures. It has been argued that the lower Great Miami River topography created natural routes that facilitated cultural mixing (Black

Evolution of Fort Ancient Culture in the Miami Valleys · 145

1934:173). This area is also in the enviable position of being at the intersection of multiple ecozones and in close proximity to large floodplains, oxbows, and other wetlands that are attractive places to settle near, from a subsistence standpoint (Figure 5.7). Reidhead (1976:45) aptly describes this setting as "an environment which is exceedingly rich . . . the combined resources of the Great Miami River, its sloughs, backwaters, flood plain, terraces, adjacent slopes, up-

Figure 5.7. Artistic rendering of the lower Great Miami River illustrating the broad floodplains, oxbows, and wetlands targeted by Mississippian migrants and early Fort Ancient villagers (produced by Jeff Dilyard and Robert Cook).

lands . . . had the potential of reaching almost staggering proportions." The foregoing description of the type of environmental locale where the first Fort Ancient sites developed meets a strong environmental explanation of what can be considered to be the optimal Mississippian niche (*sensu* Smith 1978). Moreover, as one moves up the Ohio River, this region is the next large floodplain niche from where the Mississippian settlement systems of Angel (eleventh to fourteenth centuries [Monaghan and Peebles 2010]) and Prather (eleventh to twelfth centuries [Munson et al. 2006; Munson and McCullough 2004]) were located (in southwestern and south-central Indiana, respectively). While the foregoing environmental description was for the mouth of the Great Miami River, a similar conclusion could be reached on most counts for the lower portion of the Little Miami River.

Environmental change factors into our understanding of Mississippian and Fort Ancient development. There were two major climate changes for the main time period of interest in the study region. The beginning of Mississippian and Fort Ancient culture is marked by the Medieval Warm Period (AD 950 to 1250) (aka Medieval Climatic Anomaly), which was typified by warm and moist conditions, ideal for a burgeoning agricultural economy that indeed characterizes the earlier part of the Fort Ancient culture sequence in the region (Cook and Price 2015). Conversely, during the Little Ice Age (later AD 1300s to 1900) conditions cooled, rendering agricultural economies risky (Baerreis and Bryson 1965; Baerreis et al. 1976). In the study region, the Little Ice Age is associated with a time of new subsistence emphasis on bison (particularly after ca. 1550), a new pottery style (Madisonville type), and a shift in settlement location.

A more detailed view of this climate trend in temporal and geographic terms results when we consider moisture conditions in more detail in the study region. To this end, a recent study (Comstock 2017) considers the Palmer Drought Severity Index (PDSI), which is a reconstruction of soil moisture conditions as determined from tree ring data with the addition of correlations with historic moisture data when available and then extrapolated to the past. These data are based on two cumulative paleoclimate reconstructions. The first effort was the North American Drought Atlas (NADA), which uses reconstructed PDSI data to interpolate a continental climate model in a 2.5-×-2.5°-grid composed of 286 points based on 835 tree-ring chronologies (Cook et al. 2004), and the second and most current effort was a refinement referred to as the Living Blended Drought Atlas (LBDA). This model utilized additional tree ring data that allowed for a much higher-resolution continental map at a .5-×-.5° resolution of 11,396 grid points based on 1,845 tree-ring chronologies (Cook et al. 2010).

Above-average moisture conditions were present throughout much of the

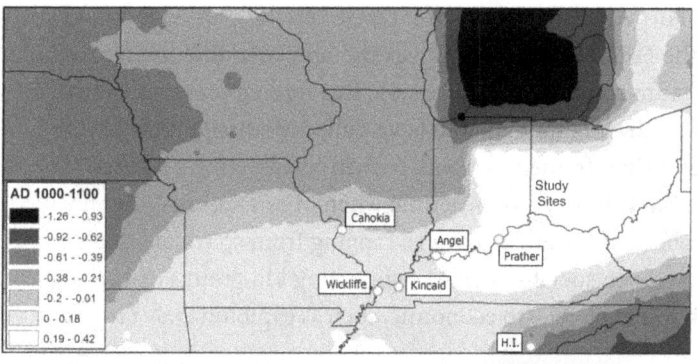
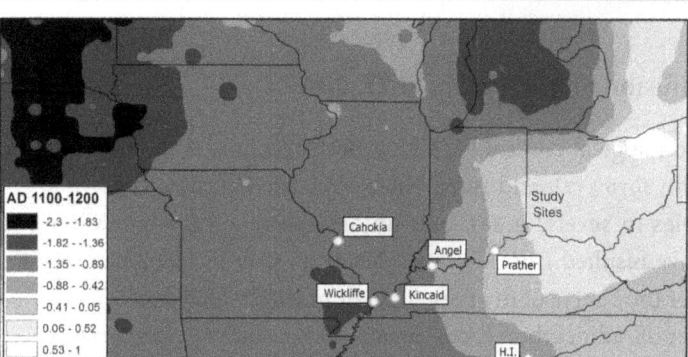
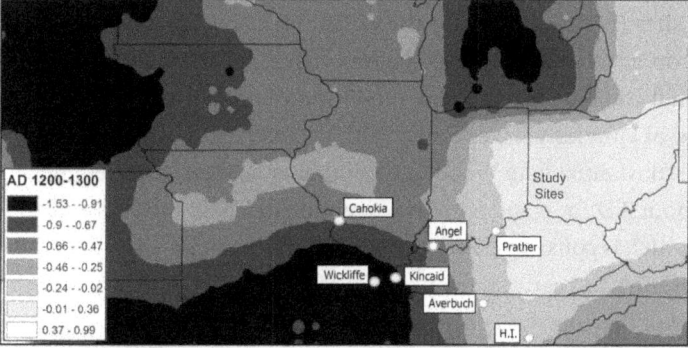
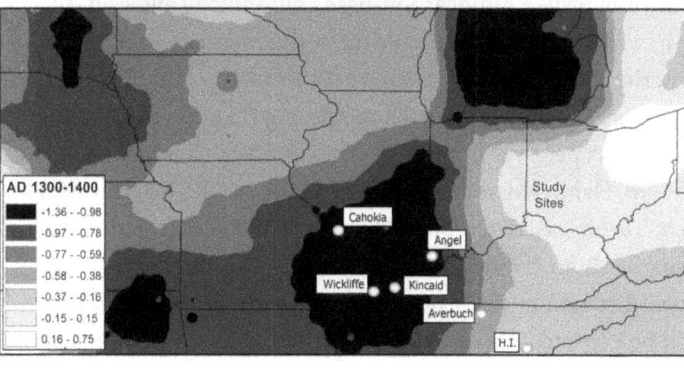

Figure 5.8. Changing drought conditions in the study area and adjacent regions. Darker shades indicate drought conditions, and lighter shades indicate non-drought conditions (produced by Aaron Comstock with data provided by Edward Cook).

Mississippian and Fort Ancient regions of interest here only until about AD 1100, after which the Fort Ancient region was the only area that maintained above-average moisture conditions (Figure 5.8). This finding provides us with an environmental constraint that may well have pulled Mississippians into the region and gives us a time frame to consider when interpreting evidence for human movement. But this may also be a time when Mississippian communities were being established for other reasons, ranging from spiritual—such as religious proselytizing—to social—such as segmenting kin groups or gaining leadership through war exploits—to economic, such as exploiting key raw material locations.

Time and the Diffusion of Mississippian Traditions

Problems with chronological control have long been recognized in Fort Ancient studies (Griffin 1978:557), and researchers have heeded the call by improving chronologies in several areas, but, unfortunately, relatively few radiocarbon dates have resulted from these studies (e.g., Cowan 1986; also see Drooker 1997). Over the course of my Fort Ancient research, I have more than doubled the number of radiocarbon dates for sites in the study region. Results clearly show that Guard, Haag, South Fort, State Line, and Turpin are very early Fort Ancient sites (Figure 5.9). With the exception of South Fort, these sites are all located on or relatively close to the mouths of the Great and Little Miami rivers. When it could be determined, these sites were found to be quite large and composed of circular village forms. With the exception of Haag and Turpin, which have substantial Late Woodland components, their histories effectively begin at about AD 1000 and with the exception of Haag, site uses end at about AD 1300, which is consistent with the general timespan for surrounding Mississippian origins and early developments. Most sites in the region are occupied by the end of this interval.

The new and firmly established radiocarbon-based chronology allows us to reassess the timing of villages, and along with them the presence of a series of key Mississippian criteria, such as wall-trench architecture (Alt and Pauketat 2011), maize agriculture (Griffin 1985), shell tempering (Holmes 1903), and people themselves. Eight (53 percent) of the Fort Ancient study sites have wall-trench structures (Guard, Hahn, Horseshoe Johnson, Madisonville, Schomaker, State Line, SunWatch, Turpin). Radiocarbon dates associated with five of these eight structures (Guard, Hahn, Horseshoe Johnson, SunWatch, Turpin) are temporally positioned throughout the sequence (Cook and Genheimer 2015) (Table 5.1). As would be expected, those nearer the Ohio River are more often

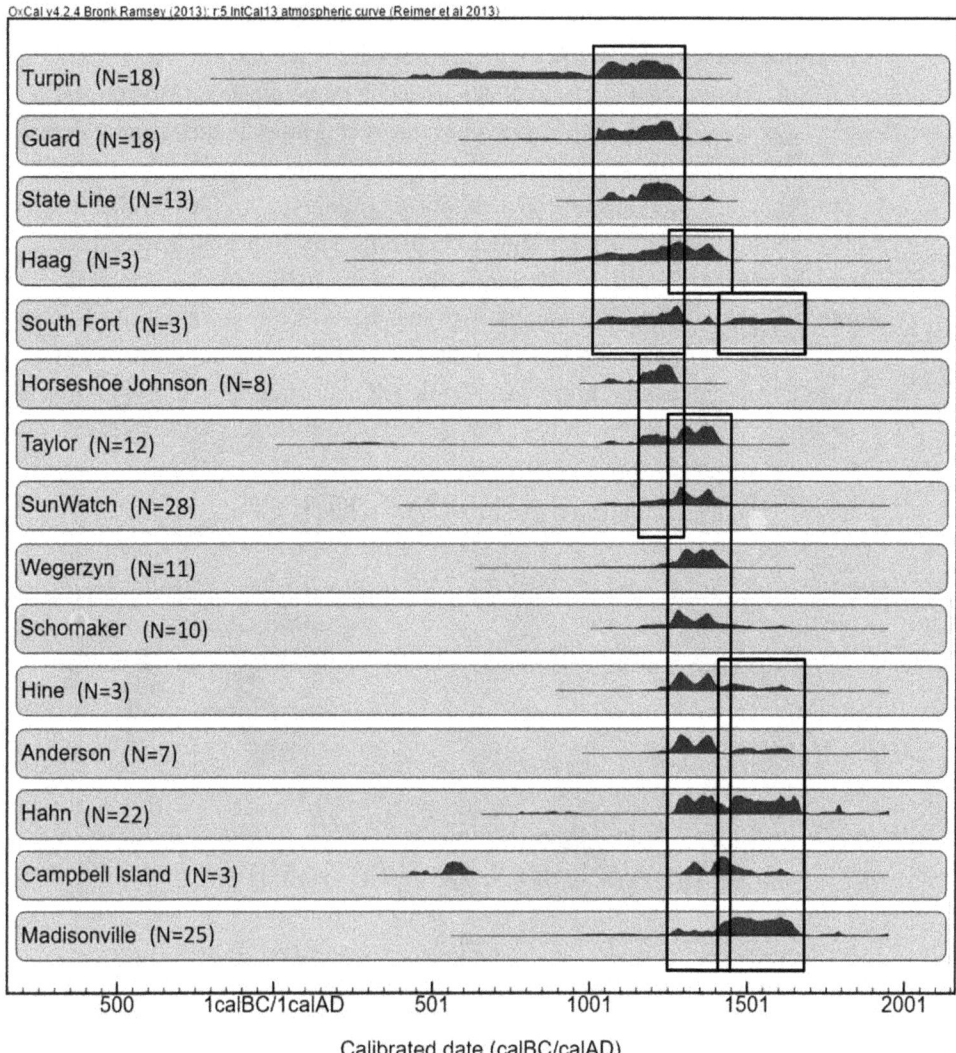

Figure 5.9. Summary ranges for radiocarbon dates (calibrated) from the study sites (produced by Aaron Comstock).

earlier, more abundant, and more complete forms, whereas those in upstream sites (SunWatch) or at sites on smaller streams (Horseshoe Johnson) are more often singular and hybrid forms, or structures that are mixes of post and trench construction styles (Figure 5.10). Such hybrids are what have been referred to as "faux" wall-trench houses, and such structures are not unusual in other "Mississippianized" regions (e.g., Alt 2006).

150 · Robert A. Cook

It is well known that many neighboring Mississippians consumed significantly more maize than Fort Ancient peoples when this assessment is based on carbon isotope levels, a direct measure of consumption (Schurr and Schoeninger 1995). But as data have accumulated, it is now apparent that there is also considerable dietary overlap between the regions. In particular, maize consumption is on par with several neighboring Mississippian site populations at the early sites with abundant higher occurrences of wall trench structures (Guard, State Line, Turpin) (Cook and Schurr 2009). In the one case that could be internally examined (SunWatch), higher maize consumption is linked to the area of the site containing the Mississippian hybrid house form, which was interpreted as evidence for migration (Cook and Schurr 2009).

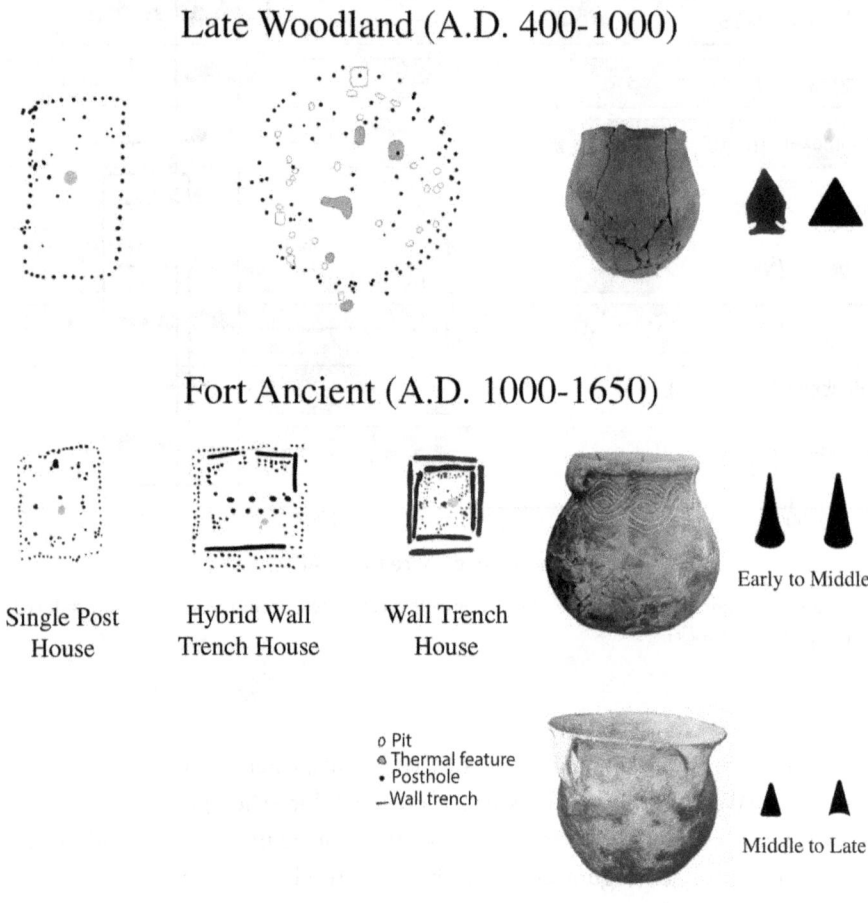

Figure 5.10. Selection of Woodland and Fort Ancient house, projectile point, and pottery forms. (Not to scale.)

Table 5.1. Radiocarbon Dates for Non-Local Individuals, People Buried with Mississippian Artifacts, and Wall Trench Houses

DATED NON-LOCAL INDIVIDUALS

Site	Burial	Lab Number	Sex	Age	Context	Body Position	Associated Artifacts	Radio-carbon Age	Two-sigma Calibrated Range	Heavy Maize Consumption
Turpin	952/91	AA100278	female	25–34	Late Woodland stone mound	?	?	1292±47	AD 651–865	no
Turpin	952/128	UCI 164712	female	35–44	Fort Ancient burial mound	extended	no	885±20	AD 1047–1216	yes
Turpin	952/244	AA100276	male	20–24	burial pattern around Fort Ancient burial mound	extended	no	983±46	AD 981–1161	yes
Turpin	952/156	AA100274	male	30–40	Fort Ancient burial mound	extended	flint knapping kit	923±45	AD 1024–1206	yes
Turpin	A25/060	AA100275	male	20–30	Fort Ancient burial mound?	?	"Old Village" Pottery Vessel	924±46	AD 1024–1207	yes
State Line	503-4	AA98042	?	?	Woodland mound reused by Fort Ancient culture	?	?	824±43	AD 1052–1277	?
Turpin	952/153	UCI 164711	female	35–44	Fort Ancient burial mound	extended	chunky stone	845±20	AD 1161–1248	yes
Guard	8	AA102763	female	18–20	south part of village	extended?	no	805±35	AD 1169–1273	yes
Turpin	952/117	AA100277	female	15–19	Fort Ancient burial mound	?	beads	763±46	AD 1169–1295	yes
State Line	503-4	AA100279	?	?	Woodland mound reused by Fort Ancient culture	?	?	745±47	AD 1189–1384	?

continued

Table 5.1—continued

DATED INDIVIDUALS THAT WERE BURIED WITH MISSISSIPPIAN ARTIFACTS

Site	Burial	Lab Number	Sex	Age	Context	Body Position	Associated Artifacts	Radiocarbon Age	Two-sigma Calibrated Range	Heavy Maize Consumption
Taylor	41592	AA98068	male	adult	mound	extended?	large knife	879±43	AD 1037–1245	yes
Guard	20	AA99941	male	20–25	south part of village	extended	Ramey knife	875±44	AD 1039–1251	yes
SunWatch	5/78	Beta 220062	male	35–40	ritual/leader area	extended	whelk shell pendant	700±40	AD 1248–1392	yes

DATED WALL TRENCH HOUSES

Site	Lab Number	Material	Context	Radiocarbon Age	Calibrated Date Range
Guard H. 4	UCI 164702	unid. wood charcoal	post hole in wall trench	990±20	AD 994–1148
Guard H. 2	AA 99946	unid. wood charcoal	post hole inside house	928±39	AD 1023–1201
Guard H. 3	AA 99947	unid. wood charcoal	structural timber on house floor	873±39	AD 1042–1250
Schomaker H. 1 (layer B)	AA98026	maize kernel	fill	850+34	AD 1050–1262
Horseshoe Johnson	AA 98050	maize kernel	midden in house	812±36	AD 1164–1271
Horseshoe Johnson	AA 98049	hickory or ash wood charcoal	structural timber on house floor	792±36	AD 1170–1279
Turpin	UCI 153694	unid. wood charcoal	post hole in wall trench	785±20	AD 1220–1271
SunWatch	OWU 448	unid. wood charcoal	structural timber on house floor	555±100	AD 1261–1625
Schomaker H. 1 (layer C)	AA98028	nutshell	original floor	657+35	AD 1276–1395
Hahn	Beta 259695	unid. wood charcoal	post hole in wall trench	641±38	AD 1282–1398
Hahn	Beta 259695	unid. wood charcoal	post hole in wall trench	590±40	AD 1296–1349
Schomaker H. 1	Beta 17994	?	?	516±60	AD 1296–1472
Schomaker H. 1	Beta 31965	?	?	482±50	AD 1314–1615

Shell-tempered pottery has also long been associated with Mississippians, again with very sporadic and low-frequency occurrences earlier in time, and the related issue being that most but not all Mississippians produced shell-tempered pottery. In the study area, shell-tempered pottery is abundant at the same early sites with numerous wall-trench structures and intense levels of maize consumption (Figure 5.11). Shell-tempered and other pottery with calcium car-

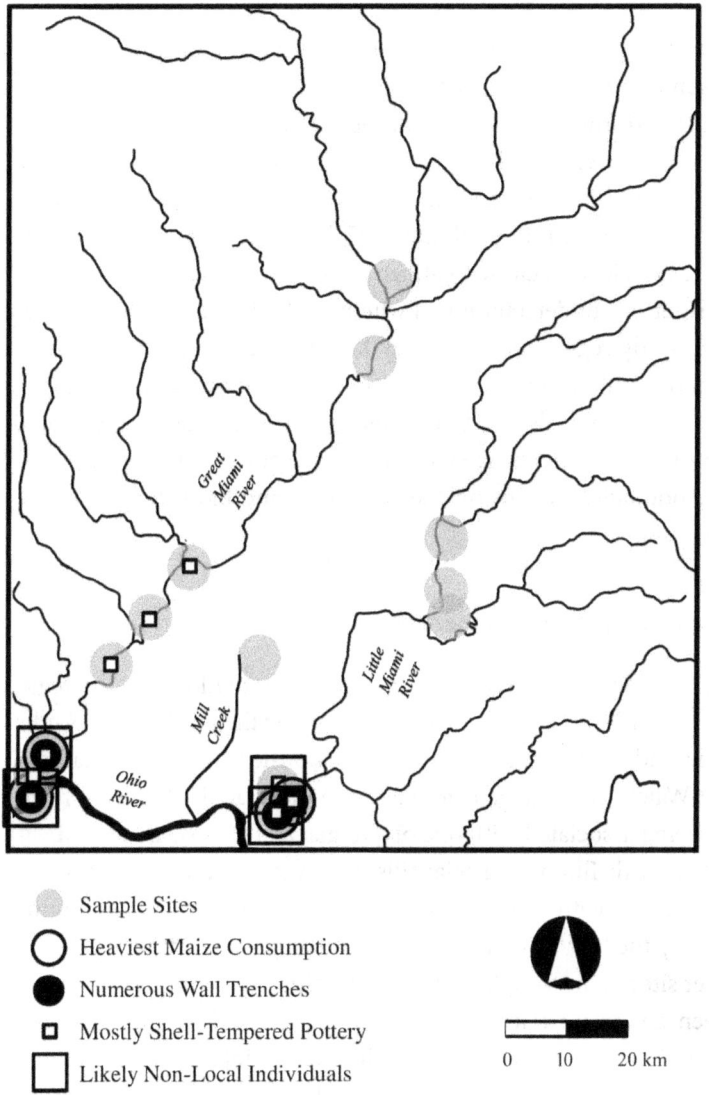

Figure 5.11. Map showing relationship between wall-trench houses, maize, shell-tempered pottery, and nonlocal individuals in the study area.

bonates (limestone) may well be related to maize consumption in ways we do not yet fully understand (e.g., Briggs 2016; Tankersley and Haines 2010; Upton et al. 2015). The frequency shift to shell temper and intensified maize consumption occurred, as far as we can tell at the present, almost simultaneously and early (AD 900–1100) in the lower parts of the Miami valleys (Greenlee 2002; Riggs 1998).

On the Identity of the Migrants

An approach well suited for the task of measuring human provenience is the comparison of strontium isotope ratios in human tooth enamel with local levels as derived from faunal assemblages (Price and Burton 2012). Tooth enamel is preferred over bone because it forms early in life, remains chemically unchanged, and is very resistant to postdepositional alteration (Cook and Price 2015; see also Budd et al. 2000; Kohn et al. 1999; Lee-Thorp and Sponheimer 2003). Hence, I chose to utilize strontium analysis of human tooth enamel to further our understanding of whether Mississippian migrants were present in the study region and how they factored into local developments. In order to more fully examine interregional population relationships observed in the strontium analysis, a biodistance study was focused on cemento-enamel junction (CEJ) metrics (see Cook and Price 2015 and Cook and Aubry 2014 for methodological details on the strontium and biodistance analyses, respectively).

Potential Mississippian Proveniences

A total of 27 (18 percent) individuals are potentially nonlocal to the region (Figure 5.12), with no significant difference in sex for the nonlocals at Anderson, State Line, and Turpin, but only females are non-local to Guard, Madisonville, and SunWatch. Ages range from young to older adult. The local region is defined as being associated with one of two glacial terrains, associated with Wisconsinan or with Illinoian glacial tills. SunWatch is the only site in the sample in the region with Wisconsinan till, which helps considerably in understanding why the $^{87}Sr/^{86}Sr$ values from that site are so distinct on average from the other sites in the sample. Other geographic proveniences with ranges that have been determined are where the Angel, Cahokia, Hiwassee Island, various Middle Cumberland sites, and Prather Mississippian sites are located. As expected, the majority of the samples fall within local ranges. The $^{87}Sr/^{86}Sr$ outliers for the Fort Ancient sample are attributable to a number of these Mis-

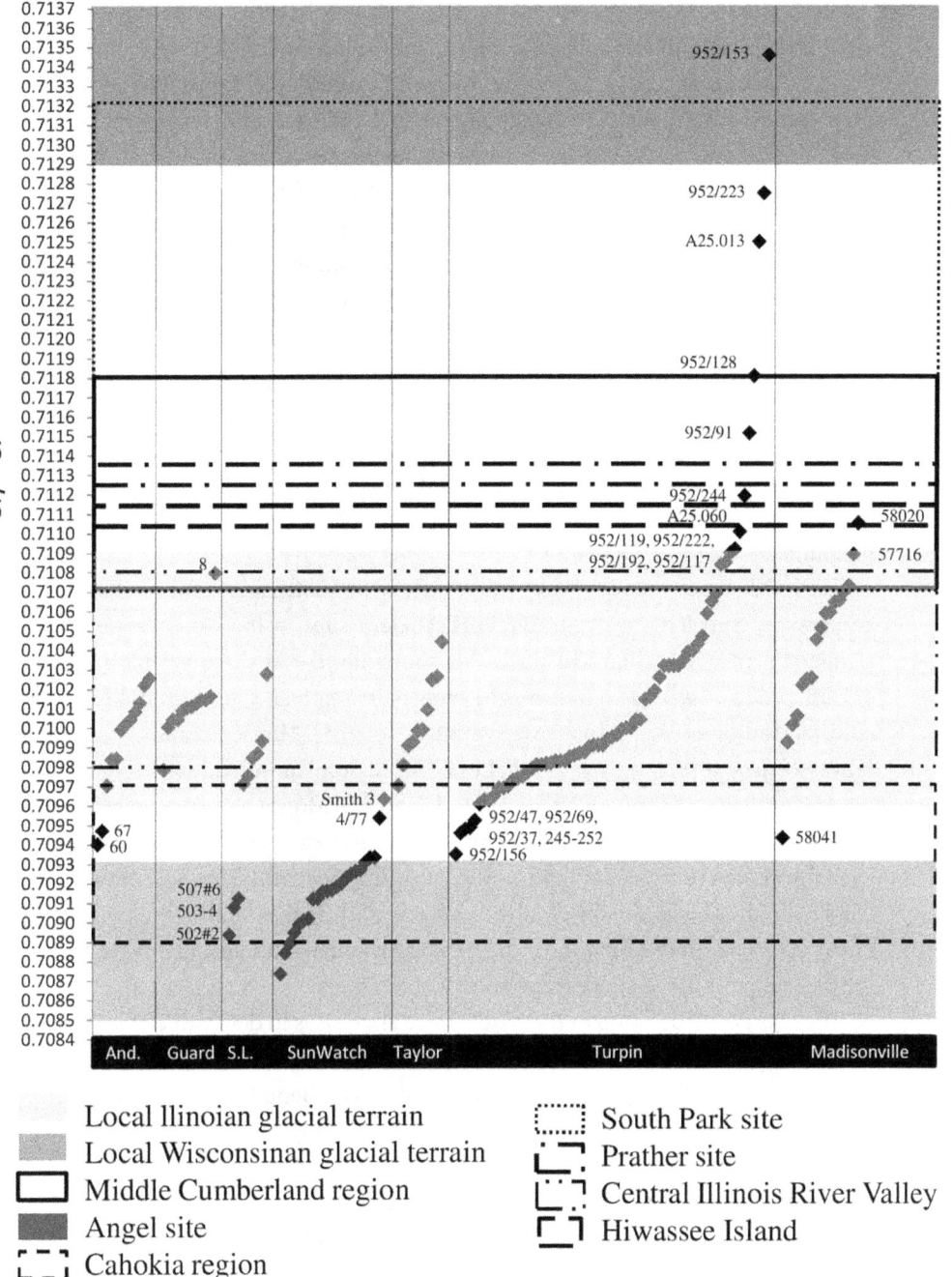

Figure 5.12. Strontium ratios for burials from study sites for first molars (and canines from a previous study at Turpin [McCall 2013]) with local strontium-ratio ranges, based on data from rodent remains (modified from Cook and Price 2015:Figure 8).

sissippian locales. The high outliers from Guard, Turpin, and Madisonville are most comparable to the rodent samples from the Middle Cumberland and Prather Regions of central Tennessee and southern Indiana, respectively. One of the outliers at Turpin best fits with the Angel site, located in southwest Indiana. While the bulk of the SunWatch samples were consistent with the range of values from the local Wisconsinan till, one individual buried at SunWatch better fits the nearby Illinoian till, suggesting they originated from a site on that terrain. Six individuals have $^{87}Sr/^{86}Sr$ values that are in a position of overlap between the local Illinoisan range and a nonlocal one (Middle Cumberland): Guard (n = 1), Turpin (n = 4), and Madisonville (n = 1). The State Line site individuals are split, with 67 percent in the Illinoian one and 33 percent in either the Wisconsinan one or Cahokia. Since there are many Mississippian objects and houses at State Line (Vickery et al. 2000), Cahokia remains a potential source area for these individuals (Cook and Price 2015). The low outliers from Anderson, SunWatch, Turpin, and Madisonville are also consistent with this possibility.

The biodistance analysis was undertaken with Scott Aubry and included adult males and females from five Fort Ancient sites in the study region—(Anderson [n = 32], Guard [n = 10], Madisonville [n = 105], SunWatch [n = 36], Turpin [n = 45])—and four neighboring Mississippian sites from different cultural traditions (Angel [n = 26], Averbuch [n = 168], Mouse Creeks [n = 27], Hiwassee Island [n = 44]) (note that only Mississippian individuals were included for the multicomponent Hiwassee Island and Mouse Creeks sites). Here I emphasize our finding that there was a lack of fit to a simple distance-decay model and then summarize significant relationships between Fort Ancient and Mississippian sites at the onset of the cultural tradition, as well as the period circa AD 1400, after which most of the Mississippian sites sampled were no longer being occupied (the exception is Mouse Creeks).

The main consideration of the biodistance analysis is to determine whether there was gene flow between Mississippian and Fort Ancient populations or whether drift better explains the resulting pattern. Gene flow should result in the lack of a significant relationship between biological and geographical distances (i.e., biological difference is not a product of geographical distance alone). In contrast, if drift best accounts for differences in biological relatedness, then there should be a significant relationship between biological and geographical distances. Preliminary results are that gene flow did occur between some Mississippian and Fort Ancient sites. Consideration of a multidimensional scaling map of Mahalanobis distances sheds light on which Fort Ancient sites are most biologically related to the Mississippian sites sampled.

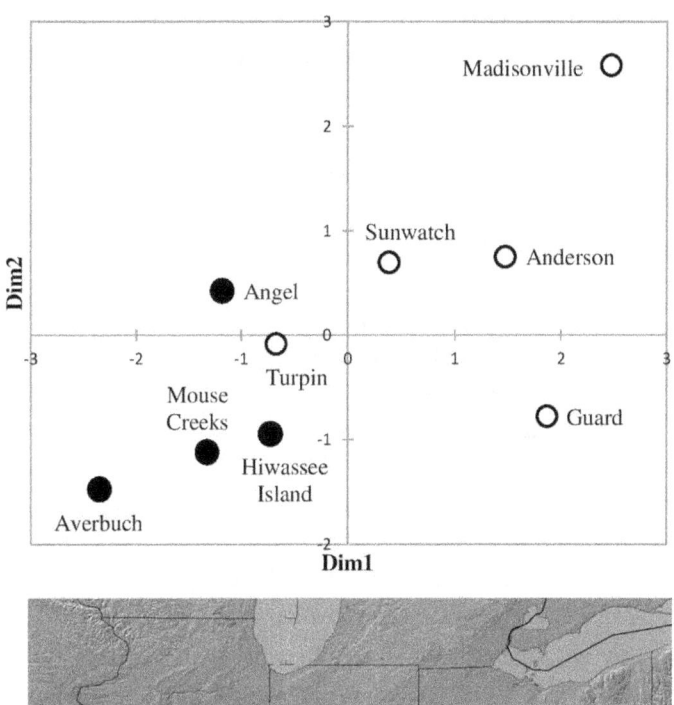
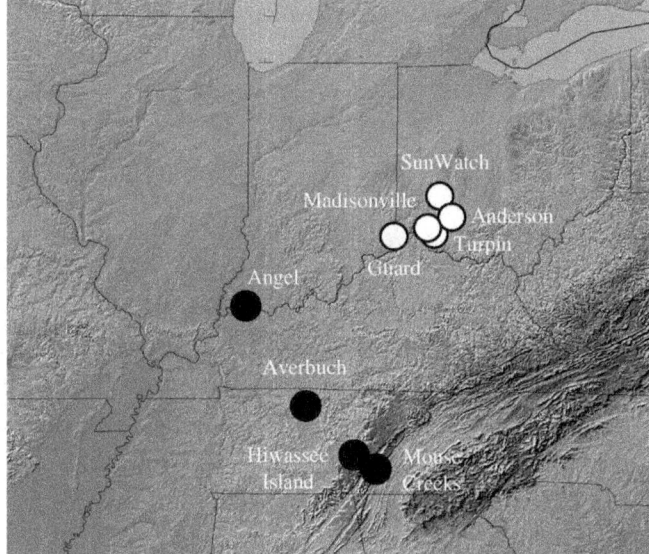

Figure 5.13. Multidimensional scaling plot showing preliminary biodistance results for key Early (Guard, Turpin), Middle (Anderson, SunWatch), and Late (Madisonville) Fort Ancient sites with neighboring Mississippian sites (Angel, Averbuch, Hiwassee Island, Mouse Creeks) (produced by Scott Aubry) (*top*). Location of sites in the biodistance study (*bottom*).

The closest biological distance regarding Fort Ancient to Mississippian is between Turpin and the Mississippian sites. Interestingly, despite considerable geographic distance between them, Angel, Averbuch, and Hiwassee Island are closely related biologically. The fact that there is gene flow and that Turpin is the closest of the Fort Ancient sites in terms of biodistance to the Mississippian sites is consistent with the strontium data (see above).

Mortuary, Temporal, and Dietary Considerations

The graves of two of the outliers at Turpin contain cultural objects thought to be Mississippian, a chunkey stone and a pottery vessel. The adult female with the chunkey stone is best associated with the Angel site, while the "Old Village" pottery vessel with an adult male is most likely from a different region. These two individuals were also regular consumers of maize. In contrast, the individual strontium outlier in the Late Woodland stone mound at Turpin had a diet with little maize.

The two female strontium outliers at Guard (one may be of a nonlocal origin) are young adults (late teens or early 20s) that date to AD 1043–1250 and AD 1169–1273. A single grave good accompanied one of these individuals, a modified femur from another individual. In the main and presumably local group at Guard, one individual (20–30-year-old male) was interred with a Ramey knife in his right hand. He was also directly dated (AD 1039–1251). Interestingly, the strontium ratio for this individual indicates he was local in birth.

Two adult males (one at SunWatch and one at Turpin) showed a marked shift in diet between the time when the first and third molars formed, with the former indicative of little to no maize, and the latter a diet heavy in maize. No artifacts are known to be associated with the Turpin individual, but the SunWatch individual was interred with a whelk shell pendant. This individual is particularly interesting, as he appears to be of local origin, based on strontium (but this is not conclusive, given the vagaries of similar strontium signatures in very distant locations [see above]), but was a village authority based on the occurrence of the Mississippian status symbol (Cook 2008). The individual at Turpin that transitioned to maize dates to AD 981–1162, while the individual at SunWatch with a marked uptake in maize consumption dates to AD 1248–1392.

Temporal indicators gained through direct AMS radiocarbon dating of human bone add important information for several outliers. The clearest pattern is that all of the directly dated individuals overlap in time with Mississippian beginnings and then continue as Mississippian cultures developed and spread.

Most are attributable to calibrated date ranges beginning at AD 981 and ending at AD 1278, with another set beginning at AD 1161 and ending at AD 1400 (see Table 5.1). This finding supports an earlier study that concluded on the basis of an evolutionary ecology model (processual-type theoretical orientation) that three time intervals were most likely to witness relaxed social boundary defense and long-distance migrations (AD 851–900, AD 1001–1050, and AD 1351–1400) (Nolan and Cook 2010).

Monumental Connections

At State Line, one individual in each of the two main strontium modes was located in a mound, although lack of further provenience information makes it impossible to determine whether or not they were in the same mound. These individuals are adult males and are associated with the Early Fort Ancient period. The mounds in which they were interred were likely constructed during Middle Woodland times (ca. 100 BC to AD 400), on the basis of local artifact collections (Vickery et al. 2000). If so, the inclusion of Fort Ancient burials in these mounds were subsequent acts, perhaps a means of nonlocals establishing a connection to local traditions (see Mann 2005). At Turpin, one of the outliers is an adult male in the Late Woodland stone mound that dates to the corresponding time period (AD 651–865), and two of the outliers are associated with the Fort Ancient mound (an adult male and female, dated to AD 1024–1206 and AD 1169–1295, respectively).

The individual at Taylor that consumed little to no maize has been directly dated (AD 138–385). In contrast to other dates from the site, this individual dates to the Middle Woodland period, which roughly spans 100 BC to AD 400. Furthermore, he was located in the only known mound at the site that was composed mainly of Fort Ancient burials. This individual had copper staining on his skull and mandible. The presence of a Middle Woodland individual suggests that these early Fort Ancient peoples reused an earlier mound; alternatively, it is possible that this earlier individual was curated and reinterred in a Fort Ancient mound. While I prefer the intrusive-mound scenario, it is difficult to fully evaluate, given the dearth of excavation documentation. However, there are several similarities between some Fort Ancient and Middle Woodland mounds (see Brady-Rawlins 2007) that may have more to do either with mound reuse or cultural continuity, an avenue of research that should be further investigated.

A distinct and large group of Fort Ancient burials at Taylor were interred in stone box graves and stratigraphically closer to the surface. The clustering of stone box graves in distinct locations within sites has been noted as a common occurrence (e.g., Cole 1951:57, 111, Plate XVIId; Thomas 1894: 134–140; Milner and Schroeder 1992). Shallower locations of stone box graves may be due to their being intrusive burials, not unlike cases observed elsewhere (e.g., Cole 1951:57, Plate XVIId).

Another hint at the invocation of ancestral memories comes from the Fort Ancient site itself. Two stone pavements located near the site, known as the Kern effigies, are thought to be serpent-shaped and aligned with the Fort Ancient site (Kardulias and White 1985; White 1987). The recently discovered Hopewell period post enclosure in the northern part of the Fort Ancient site (Riordan 2015) appears to line up with one of the Kern effigies on the summer solstice. While this possibility is interesting, two observations make it unlikely. First, the post circle would have long been gone, as it dates to at least 600 years earlier than the Early Fort Ancient culture. Second, based on a LiDAR analysis, the posts could have been seen only if they were more than 100 ft in height and there were no trees or other vegetation in the line of sight (Jarrod Burks, personal communication). While this alignment is more likely coincidental, the general referencing of the earlier Fort Ancient earthwork and cases for intrusive burials at the Taylor site located nearby makes it clear that we need to more closely consider the afterlife of earthen monuments.

A Tale of Two Villages

I consider in more detail two specific villages (SunWatch and Taylor) to further tease apart processual and historical aspects of Fort Ancient developments. Specifically, these two sites illustrate similarities and differences with respect to village formation. At each site, biodistance study disclosed the presence of a small cluster of two closely related adult males. One of the two males at each site was interred with a supralocal status object: a whelk shell pendant (*Busycon perversum*) at SunWatch (Burial 5/78), and a large chert knife at Taylor (Burial 41592) (Figure 5.15). These individuals can be interpreted as "big men" in the cultural sense of possessing a village-level authority position (Johnson and Earle 2000:32–36). Moreover, their outsider status on the basis of biological distance from other males at the site adds an important layer to their story, that being that they were not closely related to the local population. However, neither of these individuals was distinct from the local strontium signature at their respective sites, but this does not preclude the possibility that they could be from a geologically similar region outside of the study area. Interestingly, the SunWatch big man was also significantly taller than all other adults in the

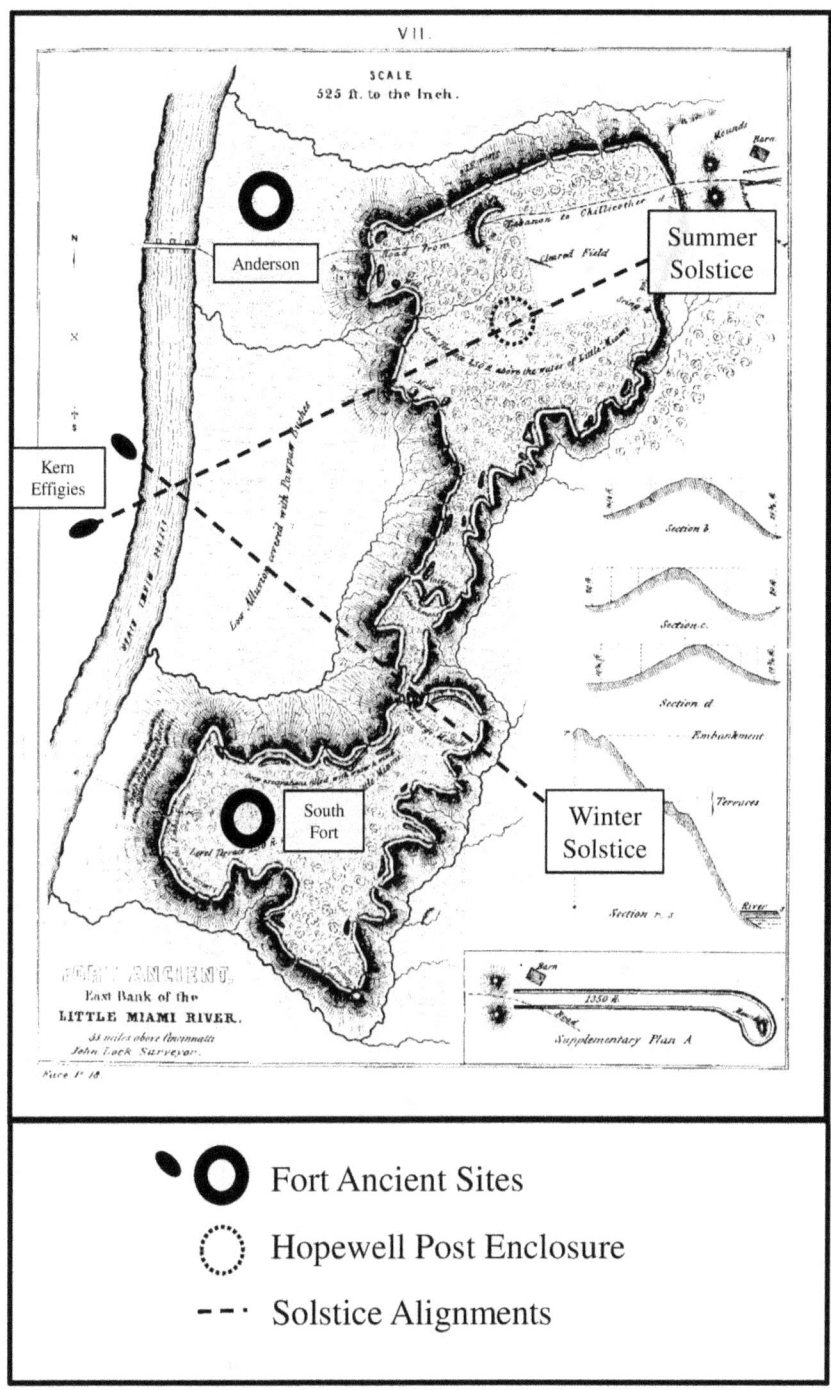

Figure 5.14. Solstice alignments between the Kern effigy sites and the Fort Ancient site (base map from Squier and Davis 1848:Plate VII; alignments after White 1987:Figure 1).

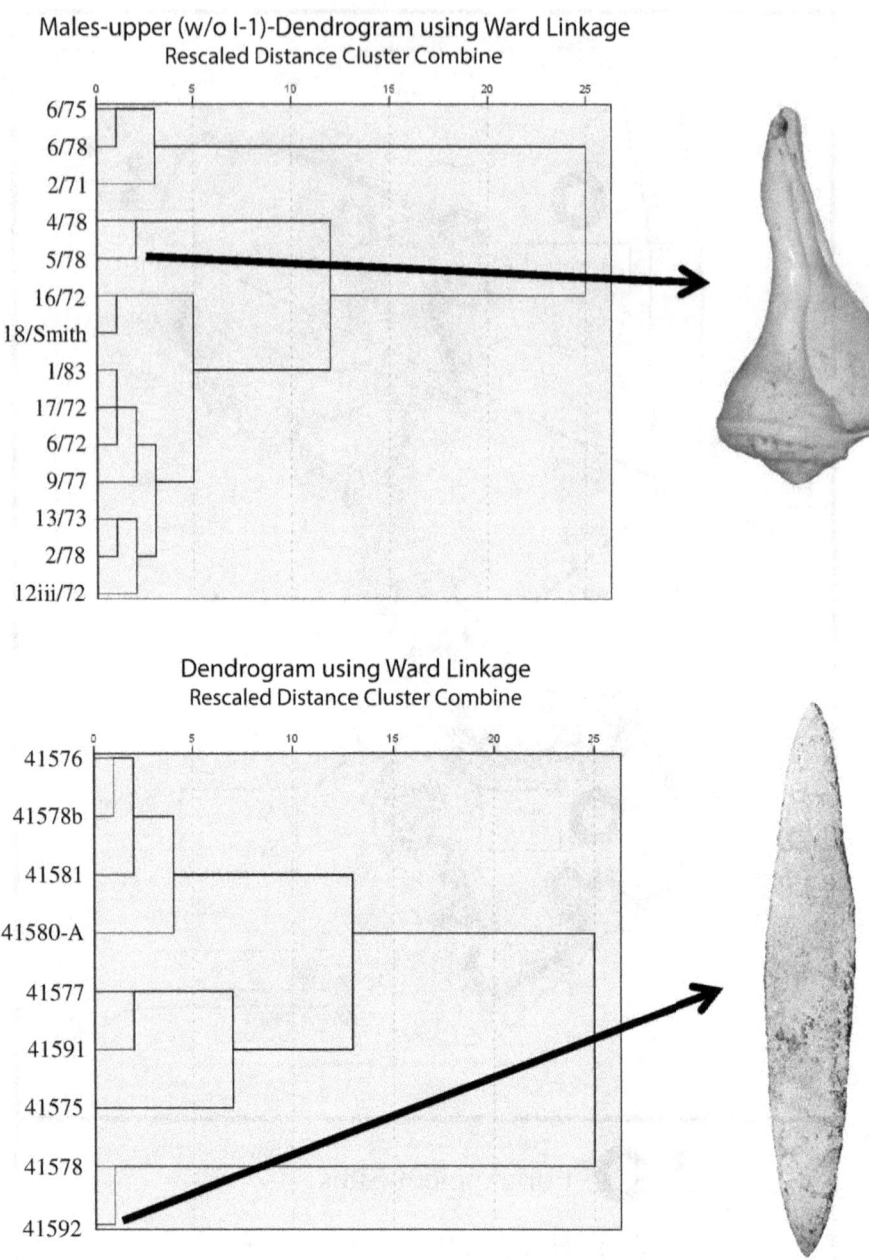

Figure 5.15. Biodistance dendrograms showing relationship of SunWatch burial with whelk shell pendant to rest of male burials at the site (*top*) and Taylor burial with large knife to rest of male burials at the site (*bottom*). Note that in each case the unique artifact is in a cluster of two closely related males. (Dendrograms produced by Scott Aubry. Photograph of knife after Griffin 1943:XLV.1; photograph of whelk shell pendant by author.)

village, rendering him literally the largest male in terms of height. Finding tall individuals in status positions is not uncommon, but this occurrence at SunWatch adds an important dimension for further understanding this individual's status that was originally recognized on the basis of possessing a Mississippian-style whelk shell pendant (Cook 2008). Unfortunately in the Taylor case, collection practices in the nineteenth century, when the site was excavated, were such that minimal skeletal materials were collected and curated from burial excavations. Hence, we could not adequately assess whether the adult male with the large knife at Taylor was unusually tall.

The two adult male authority figures at SunWatch and Taylor and their close biological male relatives reveal further clues regarding village formation. The SunWatch individual dates from AD 1248 to AD 1392, which is during the peak of that village sequence (Cook 2008), whereas the Taylor individual dates from AD 1037 to AD 1245, which is early in that village sequence. The SunWatch case appears to be a good illustration of a scalar threshold dynamic at the local site level (*sensu* Johnson 1982) where the outside leader served in part to organize a growing population. In contrast to the SunWatch scenario, Taylor is an example of what I consider to be a founding event. In this case, and assuming that the individual was buried in an earlier Middle Woodland mound, it was an act of social memory. Subsequently, the residential portions of the village formed around him, commemorating and monumentally marking/referencing this important event. In both cases, these important individuals were among the most biologically distant from the local population, indicating that they were outsiders. Being outsiders is a general characteristic (*sensu* Helms 1993) and is also characteristic of eighteenth-century Central Algonquians, where outsiders were often leaders, as they could reconcile the disputed and often quarreling lineages, because they were not members of any of them (White 1991:213). I further suggest that such leaders could have been from "apex families" at other sites around whom status differences began to develop in the new one (Alvaraz 1987; Anthony 1990). The Taylor case is also of interest in that it is located on a prominent topographic feature (high bluff) that became part of the overall settlement design in the region, perhaps similar to the Millstone Bluff case discussed earlier.

The Baby and the Bathwater

Fully integrating processual and historical dimensions of Fort Ancient culture change was not possible earlier due to a lack of adequate data, particularly those related to chronology, village layout, and provenience of artifacts and people. In this chapter I have briefly summarized my recent research efforts geared toward rectifying these deficiencies. The beginning of the Fort Ancient culture in the study area was abrupt, which I view as being consistent with macroevolutionary expectations regarding a major shift in *Baupläne*. Mississippian migration into the region was the punctuational event related to this development. The early AD 1000s seem appropriate to emphasize, for at about that time there was a clear frequency shift to maize and shell tempering (Greenlee 2002; Riggs 1998), and the first *definite* large villages date to this time, as do many of the nonlocal people. In addition to the early presence of Mississippian migrants, there was no progression from hamlets to villages in the study region, as is the case in other parts of the Fort Ancient culture region (e.g., Pollack and Henderson 1992, 2000a). The historical "kick" of Mississippian migration to the development of Fort Ancient culture was suggested by other researchers in the region years ago (Cowan 1987:11), and we now have conclusive data for it. The locales with clearest evidence for Mississippian migrants are nearest the mouths of the Great and Little Miami rivers. The environmental settings for each region satisfy the optimizing environmental definition for Mississippian settlement choice, as it contains oxbows, wetlands, and a diverse intersection of ecozones (Smith 1978). The timing was also keyed in part to environmental vagaries in most of the Mississippian homelands from which the migrants may have come.

The timing of Mississippian movements into the Fort Ancient region is much earlier than previously thought, at the dawn rather than the dusk of the cultural sequence (median dates cluster between AD 1071–1105 and AD 1231–1251). This finding supports the early conclusion that Mississippian people were instrumental in the origins of Fort Ancient culture (Griffin 1943) and were coeval with the rapid changes at Cahokia at about AD 1050 (Beck et al. 2007; Pauketat 2007; see also Slater et al. 2014). As expected, the majority of these individuals were regular consumers of maize and were sometimes interred with Mississippian-style artifacts. However, this was not always the case, revealing complex historical relationships between objects, people, and diet. It is also noteworthy that many of the non-locals at Cahokia (see Slater et al. 2014:Figure 5.5) are consistent with the local Illinoian glacial terrain examined here. While there are certainly other geographic locations that fit this range, it is possible that some of the non-locals at Cahokia were from the Middle Ohio Valley. Undoubtedly, movements between regions went both ways (see Anthony 1990). The presence of Fort Ancient pottery at the Angel (Black 1967) and Kincaid sites (Cole 1951), and likely elsewhere, further supports this pattern.

Mississippian interactions and movements were entangled with Fort Ancient origins and development in complex ways. Undoubtedly, as has been shown around the world, power was at times gained locally by befriending, hosting, and marrying non-local individuals. Parts of the Mississippian repertoire included quotidian things like household architecture, diet, and pottery temper, as well as community organization principles and other elements of site and household structure. But also key aspects of Mississippian myth were being incorporated, perhaps as the spread of a Mississippian founder's cult through materiality, citationality, and enchainment of cultural practices (Pauketat 2008:62–63; see also Butler 1993; Chapman 2000; Gell 1998; Joyce 2000; Meskell 2004, 2005; Strathern 1988). The two cases of village-level leadership discussed in detail (SunWatch, Taylor) are similar in that both individuals were marked in death with a key Mississippian status symbol, one of them with a large knife and the other with a whelk-shell pendant and shell discs

Figure 5.16. Drawing of a Middle Mississippian gorget from the Hixon site (located a few miles from the Hiwassee Island site) showing depictions of items similar to those found in key mortuary contexts in Fort Ancient villages (shell pendant and ear ornament from the SunWatch site, flint blade from the Guard site; gorget drawing modified from Lewis and Kneberg 1946:Figure 25).

worn as ear adornment. I suggest that these items are specific Mississippian references, drawing on the mythic corpus associated with the "bird man" and two males locked in combat. The individuals at SunWatch and Taylor were each closely biologically associated with only one other male in their respective local populations (of those analyzed). This scene and the Fort Ancient selections thereof are best illustrated on a gorget from the Hixon site (near the Hiwassee Island site) in eastern Tennessee (Figure 5.16), which is not a random choice, given the potential links to this region in both the strontium and biodistance analyses.

Another aspect regarding Fort Ancient origins revealed in the present study is what now seems to be a fairly regular act of links with earlier mounds. It remains unclear if and how Fort Ancient and earlier Late Woodland and Middle Woodland period groups were biologically related, but this may not be the most interesting question. Newcomers and/or those following a new tradition were clearly connecting with them in terms of monument usage. Ancestral memories were regularly invoked through mound reuse. Varying degrees of evidence have been presented, ranging from clear cases of Fort Ancient interments in Middle Woodland–age (Taylor) and Late Woodland–age (Turpin) mounds, to less clear cases of Fort Ancient interments in what are thought to be Middle Woodland mounds (State Line). On a larger scale, a case can be made at the Fort Ancient site for early Fort Ancient peoples linking some of their ceremonial sites (serpent effigies) with the earlier Middle Woodland earthwork along major solstice alignments.

Having refined the regional chronology and carried out appropriate tests to identify Mississippian migrants, it is now clear that the process of becoming Fort Ancient culture involved the direct presence of Mississippians that then formed hybrid relationships with local Woodland populations (Figure 5.17). These data couple well with the material connections between several sites in the study area and several Mississippian regions (Cowan 1987; Drooker 1997; Oehler 1973; Vickery et al. 2000). Instead of being viewed as somewhat unique, the hybrid nature of Fort Ancient is really true nearly everywhere Mississippians went, so I remain in favor of the conclusion that Fort Ancient in the study region is best understood as a Mississippian variant that generally lacks some of the classic Mississippian indicators, such as substructure mounds and complex hierarchical social organization (see Cook 2008). However, such "deficiencies" are not unusual in the Mississippian world, demanding that we rethink such definitional criteria (Blitz 2010; Cobb 2003).

The identification of Mississippian migrants brings us full circle, back to the earlier historical model (Griffin 1943, 1967; see also Prufer and Shane 1970) but

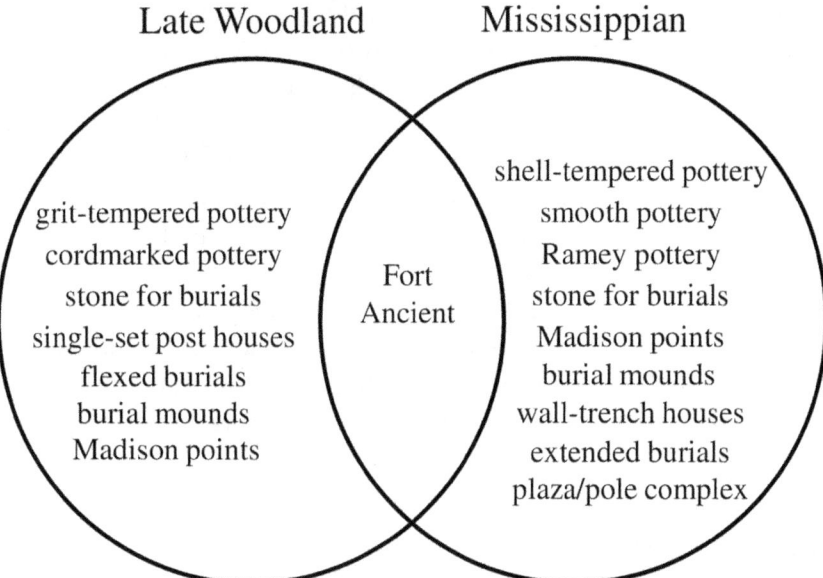

Figure 5.17. Venn diagram showing several key aspects of Mississippian and Late Woodland cultures that were blended together in the creation of Fort Ancient culture.

with the ability for much more nuanced understanding. Fort Ancient culture is not wholly attributed to Mississippian migrants, although it is likely that they factored heavily into their origins, making it vital to closely consider this in our understanding of the fabric of Fort Ancient culture. Reasons for a Mississippian presence in the Middle Ohio Valley are likely related to a variety of factors associated with both the environmental push of seeking less drought-prone regions as well as the spread of a new way of life and could well have included would-be leaders, marriage alliances, religious proselytizers, captives, and/or a search for distant markets or resources (Cook and Price 2015). Major changes such as migration likely involve many variables that mutually reinforce one another. Importantly, there is little evidence that major centers such as Angel or Kincaid were intensively occupied by large residential populations at this early point in time (Butler et al. 2011; Monaghan and Peebles 2010). In other words, the origin of Fort Ancient appears largely to have been coeval with that of neighboring Mississippian places such as Angel, Cahokia, Hiwassee Island, Middle Cumberland, and Prather.

That there are Mississippians in Fort Ancient villages and that this was early seems incontrovertible; the weight of the evidence is simply too great to explain otherwise. However, the issue is complex and really answerable only by linking biological and archaeological information at multiple scales, and we are just beginning to fully untangle the complexity of the various data sets. It should now be clearer that after examining variability in this case, the result has been a further blurring of a boundary that was not likely to have been very rigid to start with, illustrating the complex webs of human cultures. Clearly, we need to continue examining ancient movements and cease drawing boundaries around entities that may have never been bounded. In doing so, we can examine both culture process and history as I have just begun to do in the present chapter. There is no need to throw out the baby with the bathwater of a sometimes excessive reliance on migration to explain culture change from theories focused on processual interests. In doing so, we can more fully understand how the networks of external relations factored into local cultural constructions.

Acknowledgments

I thank Greg Wilson for inviting me to participate in the SEAC session and working with me to sharpen the focus of the finished product. Funding for various parts of the study was provided by the National Geographic Society, the National Science Foundation, Ohio State University, and the Illinois State Archaeological Survey. Access to materials analyzed was granted by the former American Indian Advisory Council, Cincinnati Museum Center, Cleveland Museum of Natural History, Dayton Society of Natural History, Field Museum of Natural History, Harvard University Peabody Museum, Indiana University Glenn Black Museum, Kentucky Archaeological Survey, and the Ohio History Connection. Comments from two anonymous reviewers helped strengthen the final manuscript.

References Cited

Alt, Susan M.
   2006   The Power of Diversity: Settlement in the Cahokian Uplands. In *Leadership and Polity in Mississippian Society*, edited by Brian M. Butler and Paul D. Welch, pp. 289–308. Center for Archaeological Investigations, Occasional Paper No. 33. Southern Illinois University, Carbondale.

Alt, Susan M., and Timothy R. Pauketat
   2011   Why Wall Trenches? *Southeastern Archaeology* 30:108–122.

Alvarez, Robert R. Jr.
   1987   *Familia: Migration and Adaptation in Baja and Alta California, 1800–1975*. University of California Press, Berkeley.

Anthony, David W.
  1990   Migration in Archeology: The Baby and the Bathwater. *American Anthropologist* 92:895–914.
Baerreis, David A., and Reid A. Bryson
  1965   Climatic Episodes and the Dating of Mississippian Cultures. *Wisconsin Archeologist* 46:203–220.
Baerreis, David A., Reid A. Bryson, and J. E. Kutzbach
  1976   Climate and Culture in the Western Great Lakes Region. *Midcontinental Journal of Archaeology* 1:39–58.
Barrett, John C.
  1999   The Mythical Landscapes of the British Iron Age. In *Archaeologies of Landscape: Contemporary Perspectives*, edited by Wendy Ashmore and A. Bernard Knapp, pp. 253–265. Blackwell, Oxford.
Barth, Fredrik
  1969   Introduction. In *Ethnic Groups and Boundaries*, edited by Fredrik Barth, pp. 9–38. Little Brown, Boston.
Beck, Robin A. Jr., Douglas J. Bolender, James A. Brown, and Timothy K. Earle
  2007   Eventful Archaeology: The Place of Space in Structural Transformation. *Current Anthropology* 48:833–860.
Black, Glenn A.
  1934   Archaeological Survey of Dearborn and Ohio Counties. *Indiana History Bulletin* 11(7):173–260.
  1967   *Angel Site: An Archaeological, Historical, and Ethnological Study*. 2 vols. Indiana Historical Society, Indianapolis.
Blitz, John H.
  2010   New Perspectives in Mississippian Archaeology. *Journal of Archaeological Research* 18:1–39.
Brady-Rawlins, Katherine
  2007   The O. C. Voss Site: Reassessing What We Know about the Fort Ancient Occupation of the Central Scioto Drainage and Its Tributaries. Unpublished PhD dissertation, Department of Anthropology, Ohio State University, Columbus.
Briggs, Rachel V.
  2016   The Civil Cooking Pot: Hominy and the Mississippian Standard Jar in the Black Warrior Valley, Alabama. *American Antiquity* 81:316–332.
Budd, Paul, Janet Montgomery, Barbara Barreiro, Richard G. Thomas
  2000   Differential Diagenesis of Strontium in Archaeological Human Dental Tissues. *Applied Geochemistry* 15:687–694.
Buikstra, Jane E., and Douglas K. Charles
  1999   Centering the Ancestors: Cemeteries, Mounds, and Sacred Landscapes of the Ancient North American Midcontinent. In *Archaeologies of Landscape: Contemporary Perspectives*, edited by Wendy Ashmore and H. Bernard Knapp, pp. 201–228. Blackwell, Oxford.
Burks, Jarrod, and Robert A. Cook
  2011   Beyond Squier and Davis: Rediscovering Ohio's Earthworks Using Geophysical Remote Sensing. *American Antiquity* 76:667–689.

Butler, Judith
 1993 Bodies That Matter: On the Discursive Limits of "Sex." Routledge, London.
Butler, Brian M., R. Berle Clay, Michael L. Hargrave, Staffan D. Peterson, John E. Schwegman, John A. Schwegman, and Paul D. Welch
 2011 A New Look at Kincaid: Magnetic Survey of a Large Mississippian Town. *Southeastern Archaeology* 30:20–37.
Chapman, John
 2000 Fragmentation in Archaeology: People, Places, and Broken Objects in the Prehistory of South Eastern Europe. Routledge, New York.
Church, Flora
 1987 An Inquiry into the Transition from Late Woodland to Late Prehistoric Cultures in the Central Scioto Valley, Ohio, circa AD 500 to AD 1250. PhD dissertation, Department of Anthropology, Ohio State University, Columbus.
Church, Flora, and John Nass
 2002 Central Ohio Valley during the Late Prehistoric: Subsistence-Settlement Systems' Response to Risk. In *Northeast Subsistence-Settlement Change, A.D. 700–A.D. 1300*, edited by John P. Hart and Christine Reith, pp. 11–42. New York State Museum Bulletin 496. New York State Department of Education, Albany.
Clay, R. Berle, and Steven D. Creasman
 1999 Middle Ohio Valley Late Woodland Nucleated Settlements: "Where's the Beef?" *West Virginia Archeologist* 51:1–10.
Cobb, Charles R.
 2003 Mississippian Chiefdoms: How Complex? *Annual Review of Anthropology* 32:63–84.
Cobb, Charles R., and Brian M. Butler
 2006 Mississippian Migration and Emplacement in the Lower Ohio Valley. In *Leadership and Polity in Mississippian Society*, edited by Brian M. Butler and Paul D. Welch, pp. 328–347. Center for Archaeological Investigations, Occasional Paper No. 33. Southern Illinois University, Carbondale.
Cole, Fay-Cooper
 1951 Kincaid: A Prehistoric Illinois Metropolis. University of Chicago Press, Chicago.
Comstock, Aaron R.
 2017 Climate Change, Migration, and the Emergence of Village Life on the Mississippian Periphery: A Middle Ohio Valley Case Study. Unpublished Ph.D. diss., Department of Anthropology, Ohio State University, Columbus.
Cook, Robert A.
 2008 *SunWatch: Fort Ancient Development in the Mississippian World*. University of Alabama Press, Tuscaloosa.
 2012 Dogs of War: Social Institutions of Conflict, Healing, and Death in a Fort Ancient Village. *American Antiquity* 77:498–523.
 2017 *Continuity and Change in the Native American Village: Multicultural Origins and Descendants of the Fort Ancient Culture*. Cambridge University Press, Cambridge. In press.
Cook, Robert A., and B. Scott Aubry
 2014 Aggregation, Interregional Interaction, and Postmarital Residence Patterns: A Study of Biological Variation in the Late Prehistoric Middle Ohio Valley. *American Journal of Physical Anthropology* 154:270–278.

Cook, Robert A., and Lane Fargher
2007 Fort Ancient–Mississippian Interaction and Shell-Tempered Pottery at the SunWatch Site. *Journal of Field Archaeology* 32:1–12.
2008 The Incorporation of Mississippian Traditions into Fort Ancient Societies: A Preliminary View of the Shift to Shell-Tempered Pottery Use in the Middle Ohio Valley. *Southeastern Archaeology* 27:222–237.

Cook, Robert A., and Robert Genheimer
2015 Wall Trench Structures in Fort Ancient Villages of Southwest Ohio and Southeast Indiana: Temporal and Formal Considerations. In *Building the Past: Studies of Prehistoric Wooden Post Architecture in the Ohio Valley–Great Lakes Region*, edited by Brian Redmond and Robert Genheimer. University Press of Florida, Gainesville.

Cook, Robert A., and T. Douglas Price
2015 Maize, Mounds, and the Movement of People: Isotope Analysis of a Mississippian/Fort Ancient Region. *Journal of Archaeological Science* 61: 112–128.

Cook, Robert A., and Mark Schurr
2009 Eating between the Lines: Mississippian Migration and Stable Carbon Isotope Variation in Fort Ancient Populations. *American Anthropologist* 111:344–359.

Cowan, C. Wesley
1986 *Fort Ancient Chronology and Settlement Evaluation in the Great Miami Valley, Volume II: Excavations and Chronology*. Report submitted to the Ohio Historic Preservation Office, Columbus.
1987 *First Farmers of the Middle Ohio Valley: Fort Ancient Societies, A.D. 1000–1670*. Cincinnati Museum of Natural History, Cincinnati.

Crumley, Carole L.
1979 Three Locational Models: An Epistemological Assessment of Anthropology and Archaeology. *Advances in Archaeological Method and Theory* 2:141–173.

Dancey, William S.
1992 Village Origins in Central Ohio: The Results and Implications of Recent Middle and Late Woodland Research. In *Cultural Variability in Context: Woodland Settlements of the Mid-Ohio Valley*, edited by Mark F. Seeman, pp. 24–29. Midcontinental Journal of Archaeology Special Paper No. 7. Kent State University Press, Kent.

Dillehay, Tom D.
2007 *Monuments, Empires, and Resistance: The Araucanian Polity and Ritual Narratives*. Cambridge University Press, Cambridge.

Drooker, Penelope B.
1997 *The View from Madisonville: Protohistoric Western Fort Ancient Interaction Patterns*. Museum of Anthropology, Memoirs No. 31. University of Michigan, Ann Arbor.

Drooker, Penelope B., and C. Wesley Cowan
2001 Transformation of the Fort Ancient Cultures of the Central Ohio Valley. In *Societies in Eclipse: Archaeology of the Eastern Woodlands Indians, A.D. 1400–1700*, edited by David S. Brose, C. Wesley Cowan, and Robert C. Mainfort Jr., pp. 83–106. Smithsonian Institution Press, Washington, D.C.

Emerson, Thomas E., Kristin M. Hedman, Eve A. Hargrave, Dawn E. Cobb, and Andrew R. Thompson
2016 Paradigms Lost: Reconfiguring Cahokia's Mound 72 Beaded Burial. *American Antiquity* 81:405–425.

Emerson, Thomas E., and R. Barry Lewis
 1991   *Cahokia and the Hinterlands*. University of Illinois Press, Urbana.

Erickson, Clark L.
 2006   The Domesticated Landscapes of the Bolivian Amazon. In *Time and Complexity in Historical Ecology: Studies in the Neotropical Lowlands*, edited by William Balée and Clark L. Erickson, pp. 235–278. Columbia University Press, New York.

Essenpreis, Patricia S.
 1978   Fort Ancient Settlement: Differential Response at a Mississippian–Late Woodland Interface. In *Mississippian Settlement Patterns*, edited by Bruce D. Smith, pp. 141–167. Academic Press, New York.

Gell, Alfred
 1998   *Art and Agency: An Anthropological Theory*. Clarendon Press, Oxford.

Gillespie, Susan D.
 2008   History in Practice: Ritual Deposition at La Venta Complex A. In *Memory Work: Archaeologies of Material Practices*, edited by Barbara J. Mills and William H. Walker, pp. 109–136. School for Advanced Research, Santa Fe.

Greenlee, Diana M.
 2002   Accounting for Subsistence Variation among Maize Farmers in Ohio Valley Prehistory. Unpublished Ph.D. dissertation, Department of Anthropology, University of Washington, Seattle.

Griffin, James B.
 1943   *The Fort Ancient Aspect: Its Cultural and Chronological Position in Mississippi Valley Archaeology*. University of Michigan Press, Ann Arbor.
 1967   Eastern North American Archaeology: A Summary. *Science* 156:175–191.
 1978   Late Prehistory of the Ohio Valley. In *Handbook of North American Indians: Northeast*, edited by Bruce G. Trigger, pp. 547–559. Smithsonian Institution Press, Washington, D.C.
 1985   Changing Concepts of the Prehistoric Mississippian Cultures of the Eastern United States. In *Alabama and the Borderlands: From Prehistory to Statehood*, edited by Reid R. Badger and Lawrence A. Clayton, pp. 40–63. University of Alabama Press, Tuscaloosa.

Gupta, Akhail, and James Ferguson
 1997   Culture, Power, Place: Ethnography at the End of an Era. In *Culture, Power, Place: Explorations in Critical Anthropology*, edited by Akhail Gupta and James Ferguson, pp. 1–29. Duke University Press, Durham.

Hegmon, Michelle
 2003   Setting Theoretical Egos Aside: Issues and Theory in American Archaeology. *American Antiquity* 68:213–243.

Helms, Mary W.
 1993   *Craft and the Kingly Ideal*. University of Texas Press, Austin.

Henderson, A. Gwynn
 1998   Middle Fort Ancient Villages and Organizational Complexity in Kentucky. Unpublished Ph.D. dissertation, Department of Anthropology, University of Kentucky, Lexington. University Microfilms, Ann Arbor.

Hodder, Ian
 1982   *Symbols in Action*. Cambridge University Press, Cambridge.

Holmes, William H.
   1903   *Aboriginal Pottery of the Eastern United States*. Bureau of American Ethnology 20th Annual Report. Smithsonian Institution, Washington, D.C.

Ingold, Tim
   1993   The Temporality of the Landscape. *World Archaeology* 25:152–174.

Johnson, Allen W., and Timothy Earle
   2000   *The Evolution of Human Societies*. 2nd ed. Stanford University Press, Stanford.

Johnson, Gregory A.
   1982   Organizational Structure and Scalar Stress. In *Theory and Explanation in Archaeology: The Southampton Conference*, edited by Colin Renfrew, M. Rowlands, and Barbara Abbott Segraves-Whallon, pp. 397–421. Academic Press, New York.

Jones, Siân
   1997   *The Archaeology of Ethnicity: Constructing Identities in the Past and Present*. Routledge, London.

Joyce, Rosemary A.
   2000   Heirlooms and Houses: Materiality and Social Memory. In *Beyond Kinship: Social and Material Reproduction in House Societies*, edited by Rosemary A. Joyce and Susan D. Gillespie, pp. 189–212. University of Pennsylvania Press, Philadelphia.
   2004   Unintended Consequences? Monumentality as a Novel Experience in Formative Mesoamerica. *Journal of Archaeological Method and Theory* 11:5–29.

Kardulias, Nick, and John R. White
   1985   Analysis of the Kern Effigy (33WA372) Lithics: A Fort Ancient Affiliation. *Midcontinental Journal of Archaeology* 10:3–19.

Kellar, James H.
   1960   The C. L. Lewis Stone Mound and the Stone Mound Problem. *Prehistory Research Series*, Volume 3, No. 4: 356–481. Indiana Historical Society, Indianapolis.

Kohn, Matthew J., Margaret J. Schoeninger, and William W. Barker
   1999   Altered States: Effects of Diagenesis on Fossil Tooth Chemistry. *Geochimica et Cosmochimica Acta* 63:2737–2747.

Kopytoff, Igor
   1987   The Internal African Frontier: The Making of African Political Culture. In *The African Frontier: The Reproduction of Traditional African Societies*, edited by Igor Kopytoff, pp. 3–84. Indiana University Press, Bloomington.

Kuijt, Ian
   2001   Place, Death, and the Transmission of Social Memory in Early Agricultural Communities of the Near Eastern Pre-pottery Neolithic. In *Social Memory, Identity, and Death: Anthropological Perspectives on Mortuary Rituals*, edited by Meredith S. Chesson, pp. 80–99. Archeological Papers of the American Anthropological Association No. 10. American Anthropological Association, Arlington.

Lee-Thorp, Julia, and Matt Sponheimer
   2003   Three Case Studies Used to Reassess the Reliability of Fossil Bone and Enamel Isotope Signals for Paleodietary Studies. *Journal of Anthropological Archaeology* 22:208–216.

Mann, Rob
   2005   Intruding on the Past: The Reuse of Ancient Earthen Mounds by Native Americans. *Southeastern Archaeology* 24:1–10.

Meskell, Lynn
  2003 Memories Materiality: Ancestral Presence, Commemorative Practice, and Disjunctive Locales. In *Archaeologies of Memory*, edited by Ruth Van Dyke and Susan Alcock, pp. 34–55. Blackwell Press, Oxford.
  2004 *Object Worlds in Ancient Egypt: Material Biographies Past and Present*. Berg, London.
  2005 Introduction: Object Orientations. In *Archaeologies of Materiality*, edited by Lynn Meskell, pp. 1–17. Blackwell, Oxford.

Milner, George R., and Sissel Schroeder
  1992 The Guy Smith Site and Stone Box Graves: New Perspectives from Old Collections. *Illinois Archaeology* 4:49–73.

Monaghan, G. William, and Christopher S. Peebles
  2010 The Construction, Use, and Abandonment of Angel Site Mound A: Tracing the History of a Middle Mississippian Town through Its Earthworks. *American Antiquity* 75:935–953.

Munson, Cheryl Ann, and Robert G. McCullough
  2004 *Archaeological Investigations at the Prather Site, Clark County, Indiana: The 2003 Baseline Archaeological Survey*. Indiana Department of Natural Resources, Division of Historic Preservation and Archaeology, Indianapolis.

Munson, Cheryl Ann, Michael Strezewski, and C. Russell Stafford
  2006 *Archaeological Investigations at the Prather Site, Clark County, Indiana: The 2005 Survey and Excavations*. Report of Investigations No. 602. IPFW Archaeological Survey, Fort Wayne.

Nass, John P. Jr., and Richard W. Yerkes
  1995 Social Differentiation in Mississippian and Fort Ancient Communities. In *Mississippian Communities and Households*, edited by J. Daniel Rogers and Bruce D. Smith, pp. 58–80. University of Alabama Press, Tuscaloosa.

Nelson, Ben A.
  2007 Crafting of Places: Mesoamerican Monumentality in Cerros de Trincheras and Other Hilltop Sites. In *Trincheras Sites in Time, Space, and Society*, edited by Suzanne K. Fish, Paul R. Fish, and Elisa Villalpando, pp. 230–246. University of Arizona Press, Tucson.

Nolan, Kevin C., and Robert A. Cook
  2010 An Evolutionary Model of Cultural Change in the Middle Ohio Valley. *Journal of Anthropological Archaeology* 29:62–79.

Oehler, Charles
  1973 Turpin Indians. *Journal of the Cincinnati Museum of Natural History* 23:1–65.

Pauketat, Timothy R.
  2004 *Ancient Cahokia and the Mississippians*. Cambridge University Press, Cambridge.
  2007 *Chiefdoms and Other Archaeological Delusions*. AltaMira Press, Lanham.
  2008 Founders' Cults and the Archaeology of *Wa-kan-da*. In *Memory Work: Archaeologies of Material Practices*, edited by Barbara J. Mills and William H. Walker, pp. 61–80. School for Advanced Research, Santa Fe.

Pauketat, Timothy R., and Susan M. Alt
  2003 Mounds, Memory, and Contested Mississippian History. In *Archaeologies of Memory*, edited by Ruth Van Dyke and Susan Alcock, pp. 149–179. Blackwell Press, Oxford.

Pauketat, Timothy R., Robert F. Boszhardt, and Danielle M. Benden
  2015   Trempealeau Entanglements: An Ancient Colony's Causes and Effects. *American Antiquity* 80:260–289.
Pollack, David, and A. Gwynn Henderson
  1992   Toward a Model of Fort Ancient Society. In *Fort Ancient Cultural Dynamics in the Middle Ohio Valley*, edited by A. Gwynn Henderson, pp. 281–294. Prehistory Press, Madison.
  2000a Insights into Fort Ancient Culture Change: A View from South of the Ohio River. In *Cultures before Contact: The Late Prehistory of Ohio and Surrounding Regions*, edited by Robert A. Genheimer, pp. 194–215. Ohio Archaeological Council, Columbus.
  2000b Late Woodland Cultures in Kentucky. In *Late Woodland Societies: Tradition and Transformation across the Midcontinent*, edited by Thomas E. Emerson, Dale L. McElrath, and Andrew C. Fortier, pp. 613–641. University of Nebraska Press, Lincoln.
Pollack, David, A. Gwynn Henderson, and Christopher T. Begley
  2002   Fort Ancient/Mississippian Interaction on the Northeastern Periphery. *Southeastern Archaeology* 21:206–220.
Prentiss, Anna Marie, Ian Kuijt, and James C. Chatters
  2009   Introduction. In *Macroevolution in Human Prehistory*, edited by Anna Marie Prentiss, Ian Kuijt, and James C. Chatters, pp. 1–19. Springer, New York.
Price, T. Douglas, and James H. Burton
  2012   *An Introduction to Archaeological Chemistry.* Springer, New York.
Prufer, Olaf H., and Orrin C. Shane
  1970   *Blain Village and the Fort Ancient Tradition in Ohio.* Kent State University Press, Kent.
Reidhead, Van
  1976   Optimization and Food Procurement at the Prehistoric Leonard Haag Site, Southeastern Indiana: A Linear Programming Approach. Ph.D. dissertation, Department of Anthropology, Indiana University, Bloomington.
Renfrew, Colin
  1986   Introduction. In *Peer Polity Interaction and Sociopolitical Change*, edited by Colin Renfrew and John F. Cherry, pp. 1–18. Cambridge University Press, Cambridge.
Riggs, Rodney E.
  1998   *Ceramics, Chronology and Cultural Change in the Lower Little Miami River Valley, Southwestern Ohio, circa 100 BC to circa AD 1650.* Ph.D. dissertation, Department of Anthropology, University of Wisconsin, Madison. University Microfilms, Ann Arbor.
Riordan, Robert
  2015   The End. In *Building the Past: Studies of Prehistoric Wooden Post Architecture in the Ohio Valley–Great Lakes Region*, edited by Brian Redmond and Robert Genheimer, pp. 126–145. University Press of Florida, Gainesville.
Robbins, Louise M., and Georg K. Neumann
  1972   *The Prehistoric People of the Fort Ancient Culture of the Central Ohio Valley.* Anthropological Papers No. 47. Museum of Anthropology, University of Michigan, Ann Arbor.
Robertson, James A.
  1980   Chipped Stone and Socio-cultural Interpretations. Master's thesis, Department of Anthropology, University of Illinois at Chicago Circle, Chicago.

Schlanger, Sarah H.
- 1992 Recognizing Persistent Places in Anasazi. In *Space, Time, and Archaeological Landscapes*, edited by Jacqueline Rossignol and LuAnn Wandsnider, pp. 91–113. Plenum Press, New York.

Schroeder, Sissel
- 2004 Current Research on Late Precontact Societies of the Midcontinental United States. *Journal of Archaeological Research* 12:311–372.

Schurr, Mark R., and Margaret J. Schoeninger
- 1995 Associations between Agricultural Intensification and Social Complexity: An Example from the Prehistoric Ohio Valley. *Journal of Anthropological Archaeology* 14:315–339.

Seeman, Mark F.
- 1992 The Bow and Arrow, The Intrusive Mound Complex, and a Late Woodland Jack's Reef Horizon in the Mid-Ohio Valley. In *Cultural Variability in Context: Woodland Settlements of the Mid-Ohio Valley*, edited by Mark F. Seeman, pp. 41–51. Midcontinental Journal of Archaeology Special Paper No. 7. Kent State University Press, Kent.

Slater, Phillip A., Kristin M. Hedman, and Thomas E. Emerson
- 2014 Immigrants at the Mississippian Polity of Cahokia: Strontium Isotope Evidence for Population Movement. *Journal of Archaeological Science* 44:117–127.

Smith, Bruce D.
- 1978 Variations in Mississippian Settlement Patterns. In *Mississippian Settlement Patterns*, edited by Bruce D. Smith, pp. 479–503. Academic Press, New York.
- 1990 Introduction. In *The Mississippian Emergence*, edited by Bruce D. Smith, pp. 1–8. Smithsonian Institution Press, Washington, D.C.

Stark, Miriam T., Brenda J. Bowser, and Lee Horne
- 2008 Why Breaking Down Boundaries Matters for Archaeological Research on Learning and Cultural Transmission: An Introduction. In *Cultural Transmission and Material Culture: Breaking Down Boundaries*, edited by Miriam T. Stark, Brenda J. Bowser, and Lee Horne, pp. 1–16. University of Arizona Press, Tucson.

Strathern, Marilyn
- 1988 *The Gender of the Gift: Problems with Women and Problems with Society in Melanesia.* University of California Press, Berkeley.

Tankersley, Kenneth B., and Angela L. Haines
- 2010 Was Newtown a Fort Ancient Progenitor? *North American Archaeologist* 31:201–220.

Thomas, Cyrus
- 1894 Report on the Mound Explorations of the Bureau of Ethnology. *Bureau of Ethnology Annual Report* 12:1–735.

Thomson, Victor, and Thomas Pluckhahn
- 2012 Monumentalization and Ritual Landscapes at Fort Center in the Lake Okeechobee Basin of South Florida. *Journal of Anthropological Archaeology* 31(1):49–65.

Trigger, Bruce G.
- 1991 Distinguished Lecture in Archaeology: Constraint and Freedom—A New Synthesis for Archaeological Explanation. *American Anthropologist* 93:551–569.

Upton, Andrew J., William A. Lovis, and Gerald R. Urquhart
- 2015 An Empirical Test of Shell Tempering as an Alkaline Agent in the Nixtamalization

Process. *Journal of Archaeological Science* 62:39–44.Vermilion, Mary R., Mark P. S. Krekeler, and Lawrence H. Keeley

2003 Pigment Identification on Two Moorehead Phase Ramey Knives from the Loyd Site, a Prehistoric Mississippian Homestead. *Journal of Archaeological Science* 30: 1459–1467.

Vickery, Kent D., Theodore S. Sunderhaus, and Robert A. Genheimer

2000 Preliminary Report on Excavations at the Fort Ancient State Line Site, 33Ha 58, in the Central Ohio Valley. In *Cultures before Contact: The Late Prehistory of Ohio and Surrounding Regions*, edited by Robert A. Genheimer, pp. 272–328. Ohio Archaeological Council, Columbus.

White, John R.

1987 Kern Effigy #2: A Fort Ancient Winter Solstice Marker? *Midcontinental Journal of Archaeology* 12:225–242.

White, Richard

1991 *The Middle Ground: Indians, Empires, and Republics in the Great Lakes Region, 1650–1815*. Cambridge University Press, Cambridge.

Wilson, Greg

2010 Community, Identity, and Social Memory at Moundville. *American Antiquity* 75:1–18.

Zeder, Melinda A.

2009 The Neolithic Macro-(R)evolution: Macroevolutionary Theory and the Study of Culture Change. *Journal of Archaeological Research* 17:1–63.

6

The Relationship between Becoming Caddo and Becoming Mississippian in the Middle Red River Drainage

AMANDA REGNIER

Since the earliest days of archaeology in the Caddo region, archaeologists have considered sites occupied between AD 1000 and 1550 to be the westernmost extension of the Mississippian pattern. A shallow look at broadly shared material traits reveals obvious connections with the broader Mississippian world. The prehistoric Caddo who lived in southeast Oklahoma, northeast Texas, southwest Arkansas, and northwest Louisiana built mounds, cultivated maize, participated in the wide-scale exchange of marine shell, copper, and other exotic artifacts, staged elaborate mortuary rituals to connect with the supernatural, and made shell-tempered ceramics. A deeper look at prehistoric Caddo archaeology reveals a number of these Mississippian material traits were selectively adopted, in many cases centuries after their spread across much of the Southeast. More importantly, fundamental differences in landscape use and settlement and, most importantly, ideology and ritual set the prehistoric Caddo apart from the Mississippian world.

Using the middle Red River as my case study, in this chapter I examine the emergence of prehistoric Caddo culture via the Late Woodland (AD 900–1050) to the Early Caddo (AD 1050–1200) transition. The middle portion of the Red River forms the boundary between northeast Texas and southeast Oklahoma, above the Great Bend region. The middle Red River cuts across in the Western Gulf Coastal Plain, south of the Ouachita Mountains, along the boundary of the Eastern Woodlands and the southern Plains, the very western edge of the Caddo area (Figure 6.1).[1] During the Early Caddo period, markers of early Caddo ritual first appeared on the landscape across the broader Caddo region, eventually making their way into the middle Red. The beginning of these shared Caddo cultural traditions is correlated with emergence of a broadly dis-

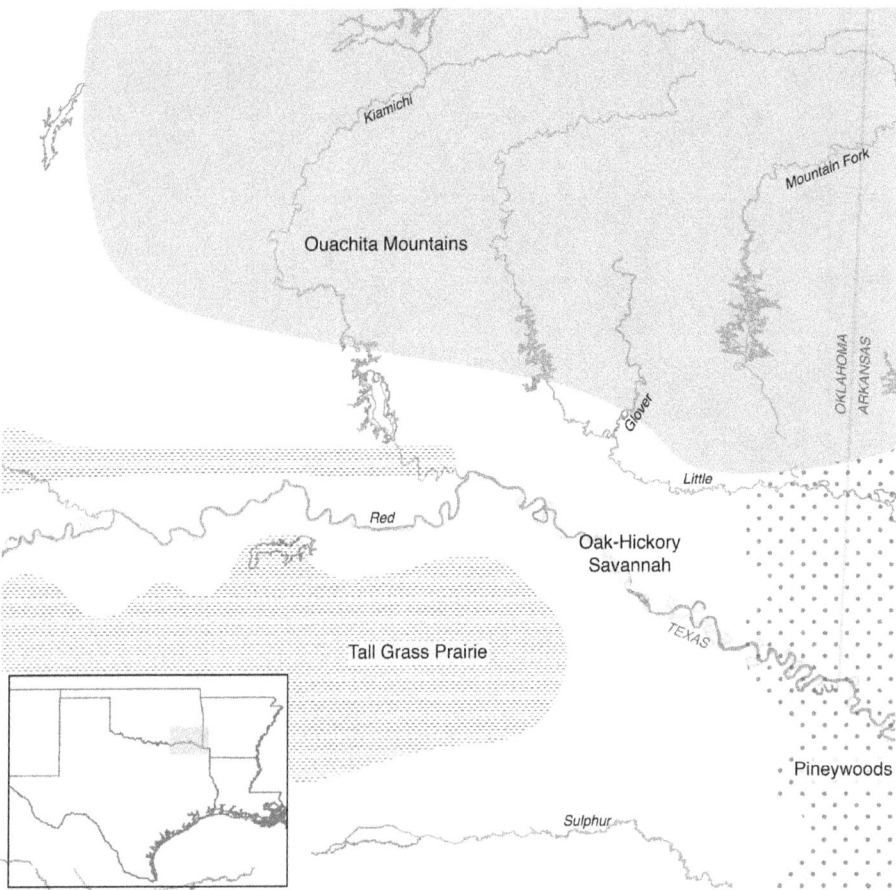

Figure 6.1. Physiographic/vegetation zones along the middle Red River drainage. (Adapted from Bruseth 1998:48, Figure 3.1)

tributed ceramic horizon, consisting most notably of three engraved fineware types best known from whole vessels—Hickory, Holly Fine, and Spiro Engraved—and one incised and punctate type, Crockett Curvilinear Incised.[2] The fineware types are known primarily from whole vessels recovered from burials, although they are found in other contexts.

Because this chapter deals with the emergence of the Early Caddo tradition from the preceding Late Woodland stage, I analyzed ceramics from the 1979 and 1985 excavations at the Bud Wright site (34Mc216), one of only a handful of excavated Late Woodland sites in the middle Red area, and reanalyzed ceramics from 1977 excavations at the Mahaffey site (34Ch1) (Figure 6.2). Excavations at both sites were conducted by Greg Perino of the Museum of the Red River

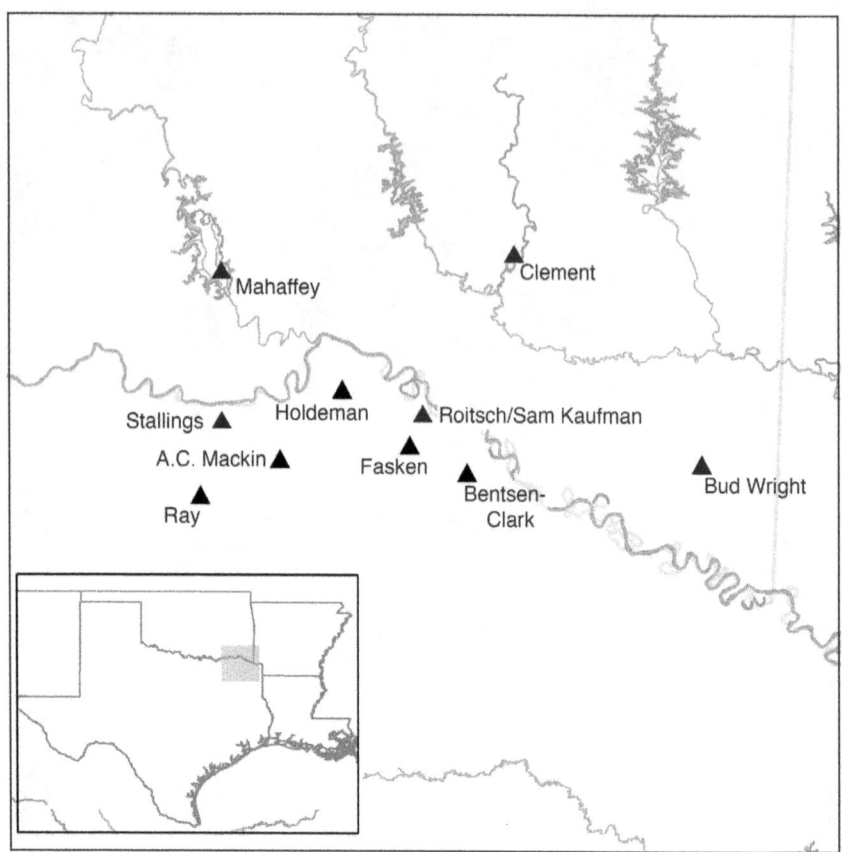

Figure 6.2. Locations of sites in the study.

in Idabel, Oklahoma. Ceramics from WPA excavations at the Clement site (34Mc8), reanalyzed between 2009 and 2014, also inform the study. I combine these new analysis with published information from seven Late Woodland/Early Caddo sites, including A. C. Mackin (41LR36) (Mallouf 1976), Bentsen-Clark (41RR41) (Banks and Winters 1975), Dan Holdeman (41RR11) (Perino 1995), Fasken (41RR14) (Prikryl 2008), Ray (41LR135) (Bruseth et al. 2001), Roitsch/Sam Kaufman (41RR16) (Perttula 2008a, 2008b; Skinner et al. 1969), and Stallings (Perttula 2008d), to describe the emergence of a *distinctly Caddo* tradition in the middle Red and beyond, over the 400-year period spanning AD 900–1250. While Caddo traditions may have drawn on the same set of broader cosmological models as the rest of the Mississippian world, people across the Caddo area were linked by a distinct, shared set of religious and ceremonial traditions that appeared and spread across the Caddo area between

AD 1000 and 1100, roughly contemporaneous with, but with a different trajectory than, the AD 1050 Mississippian Big Bang at Cahokia (Pauketat 1994). As I discuss below, adoption of the cultural traits that define the Mississippian cultural tradition came later and occurred at different times in the middle Red River Valley and the broader Caddo area.

The Late Woodland to Early Caddo Transition: Ceramic Evidence

Only a few Late Woodland and Early Caddo sites have been excavated along the middle Red River. From those sites only a handful of descriptions of excavated sherd assemblages are available; in some cases only whole vessels from burial contexts are described. To get a better handle on the Caddo emergence along the middle Red, I first examine the nature of Early Caddo ceramic assemblages at eight different sites. While all of these assemblages include Early Caddo utilitarian types, not every assemblage includes engraved finewares. The significant differences in the representations of different ceramic types and variety in ceramic pastes at each of the sites provide some clues about the nature of Late Woodland/Early Caddo societies along the middle Red, a point to which I return below.

In the Caddo area, Woodland occupations are grouped with the Fourche Maline cultural tradition, as described by Schambach (1982). The hallmark of Fourche Maline, broadly dated between 1000 BC and AD 900, is large, thick, flowerpot-shaped plain ceramic vessels tempered with grog, bone, and/or grit assigned to the type Williams Plain, and ubiquitous contracting-stemmed, rounded-base Gary points. In his description of Fourche Maline ceramic assemblages, Schambach (1982:141) noted the presence of Lower Mississippi Valley (LMV) Coles Creek and French Fork Incised ceramics. As both Schambach (1991) and Kidder (1998:131) have pointed out, Coles Creek Incised sherds from Caddo sites have substantially different pastes and were executed on different forms than their LMV counterparts. Leith's (2011) analysis of Oklahoma Fourche Maline ceramics demonstrated a very low percentage of decorated sherds recovered from Woodland sites north of the Ouachita Mountains but did not cover sites along the middle Red River.

Archaeological evidence indicates late Fourche Maline groups in southeast Oklahoma cultivated starchy seeds and were largely sedentary (Leith 2011). In eastern Oklahoma the best-known Fourche Maline sites are along the creek of the same name, north of the Ouachita Mountains. These sites consist of a series of intentionally constructed black midden mounds containing multiple burial interments, many of which were excavated by the WPA in the 1930s. Because their investigations focused largely on the mounds, until Leith's (2011) excavations in 2010, no Fourche Maline domestic buildings had been excavated in Oklahoma.[3]

The Mahaffey site (34Ch1), located along the lower Kiamichi River just above its junction with the Red, provides a good example of a typical Fourche Maline occupation from the middle Red. Charles Rohrbaugh (Rohrbaugh et al. 1971) conducted initial excavations at the site with the Oklahoma River Basin Survey in the late 1960s, and Perino conducted additional excavations in 1977. Perino's excavations included a Late Woodland cemetery, identified by the presence of 44 burials largely lacking grave goods (Perino and Bennett 1978).[4] Excavations also encountered 17 features, although as the authors note, "it was extremely difficult to establish clear cut dimensions for the cultural features of the Mahaffey site" (Perino and Bennett 1978:10). The 1,502 sherds recovered from the excavations are curated at the Sam Noble Museum of Natural History in Norman. Many of these are plain Late Woodland sherds or are related to the later Caddo occupation, but roughly 300 decorated and/or vessel landmark sherds can be associated with the Late Woodland/Early Caddo occupation. The assemblage includes a number of Williams Plain rims and bases; only a handful (n = 4) have bone inclusions in the grog-tempered paste. Decorated types in the Perino assemblage include Canton Incised, East Incised, and Hollyknowe Ridge Pinched. The assemblage from the ORBS testing (Rohrbaugh et al. 1971:54, Plate XXXIII) includes several utilitarian types associated with Early Caddo components, including Canton, East, Kiam, and Pennington Punctate Incised.

At the Ray site (41LR135) in northeast Texas, Bruseth and Banks (1992; Bruseth 1998) excavated two possible structures and a midden. Unfortunately, the 95 recorded posts failed to form a coherent pattern. Because a later Caddo occupation was present, it was not possible to establish these posts as contemporaneous with the Late Woodland/Early Caddo occupation. Bruseth et al. (2001:200) reported the assemblage from Ray was made up of 98.3 percent plain sherds with typical Williams Plain vessel forms, including thick, flat-bottomed jars with distinctive "keels" along the exterior of the base. The small decorated assemblage included Woodland Coles Creek and French Fork Incised types, and the Caddo fineware type Crockett Curvilinear Incised. Radiocarbon dates published by Bruseth et al. (2001:207) suggest that occupation at the site spanned the period of AD 800 to 1000. Given the ceramic types, it may be more appropriate to assign a slightly later occupation end date of AD 1100 for this assemblage.[5] The most interesting feature of the site assemblage is the mixture of artifacts, including not just ceramics, but also projectile points and pipes, associated with both Late Woodland Fourche Maline [following Schambach's (1982) work] and Caddo culture, suggesting that Ray was occupied during the Late Woodland/Early Caddo transition.

The large ceramic assemblage from the Bud Wright site (34Mc216) offers another opportunity to study the Caddo emergence along the middle Red River. The site is located off the main channel of the Red at the confluence of McKinney and Yellow creeks in the southeasternmost corner of Oklahoma. Just upstream along McKinney Creek are a number of later Caddo sites, including a small mound site, clustered around a salt spring dating to the Late Caddo McCurtain phase (AD 1300–1650). Gregory Perino from the Museum of the Red River in Idabel directed two sets of excavations at the site, in 1979 and 1985. Notes from those excavations are frustratingly sparse, consisting of only a few burial and feature forms and an incomplete map showing a few features and piece-plotted artifacts.

Based on the ceramic assemblage and sherd distribution, the most extensive occupation component at Bud Wright dates to the Late Woodland/Early Caddo transition. No report of the excavations exists; the only written narrative describing the excavations is a two-page letter Perino wrote to Frank Schambach, in which he describes working in 10-×-10-foot units excavated in six-inch levels. The incomplete site map and handful of feature and burial forms indicate that 27 burials, most with only a few grave goods, were excavated (Figure 6.3). Of the 27 burials on the map, seven are described as cremations, three are drawn as flexed, two are drawn as extended, and 15 are simply drawn as small circles or scattered skeletal elements, possibly due to poor preservation. A cluster of burials in the center of the site might have been part of a small cemetery. The recorded features included a series of burned rock clusters interpreted as hearths, four pits, and a single post mold. The notes do not reference any potential buildings, and the site map does not show any post patterns.

Despite the state of the notes, the Bud Wright site has a provenienced sherd collection useful for providing valuable information about Late Woodland/Early Caddo sites in the middle Red River. For the initial analysis, I spent a week at the Museum of the Red River documenting 420 decorated vessels and landmark sherds from this collection. The most common plain Fourche Maline ceramic type in the Woodland assemblage is Williams Plain (n = 39), followed by Williams Boneware (n = 20), and LeFlore Plain (n = 10) (Figure 6.4). The frequency of these typical thick Fourche Maline flat-based vessels with huge chunks of bone temper is somewhat surprising.[6] Other decorated utilitarian types include a number of Caddo area versions of Coles Creek Incised (n =

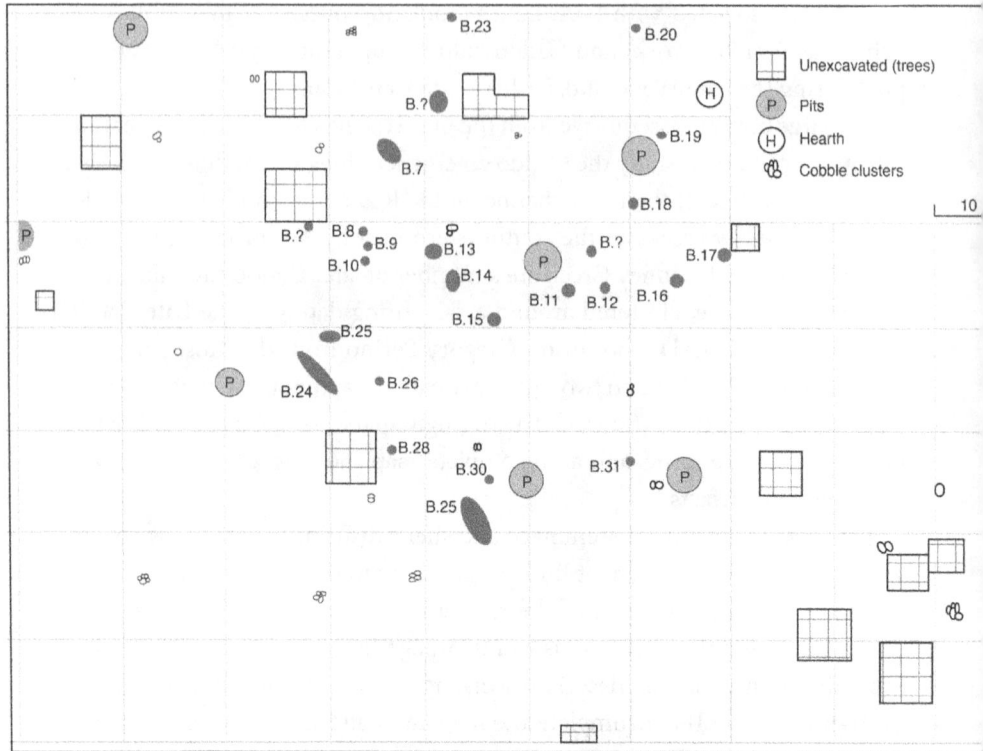

Figure 6.3. Digitized version of incomplete map of the Bud Wright site on file at the Museum of the Red River, Idabel, Oklahoma.

43), as well as Early Caddo types Harrison Bayou Incised (n = 40), Weches Fingernail Impressed (n = 3), Davis and East Incised (n = 13), Kiam Incised (n = 10), Crockett Curvilinear and Pennington Punctate Incised (n = 28), and Hollyknowe Ridge Pinched (n = 8). The Coles Creek Incised sherds are made on the same grog-tempered local paste typical of the rest of the assemblage. Early Caddo engraved finewares are absent, but sherds from Crockett Curvilinear Incised vessels were present.

Excavation at the Bud Wright site yielded no evidence that mortuary or other ritual that defined Early Caddo life took place there. The burials did not display the typical Caddo pattern of extended interment of individuals with multiple whole vessels. Numerous examples of fineware engraved sherds have been recovered from contemporaneous sites in southeast Oklahoma in ritual-associated contexts. The ceramic assemblage from WPA excavations at Clement (34Mc8), located along the lower Glover drainage in the piedmont zone between the Coastal Plain and the Ouachita Mountains (see Figure 6.1),

Figure 6.4. Sherds from the Bud Wright site assemblage: (*a*) Williams Plain thick, flat base, (*b*) Williams Boneware base sherd, (*c–e*) Coles Creek Incised, (*f*) Crockett Curvilinear Incised, (*g*) Weches Fingernail Impressed, (*h*) Hollyknowe Ridge Pinched, (*i–j*) Harrison Bayou Incised.

includes a number of engraved Early Caddo fineware sherds from non-burial contexts, as well as utilitarian types reminiscent of Coles Creek Incised and red-slipped Kiam Incised. The decorated sherds occur alongside fragments of very thick, grog-tempered bases from Williams Plain jars.

Bell and Baerreis (1951) reported three mounds at Clement; two, Mounds A and B, have been investigated. Ceramic assemblages from both indicate the bulk of mound construction dates to the later Sanders and McCurtain phases (Hammerstedt et al. 2010; Regnier et al. 2013). The Early Caddo sherds, which are restricted to one area of the site (Figure 6.5), roughly 100 m north of the larger Mound A, include Spiro and Holly Fine Engraved (Figure 6.6). Because of WPA recovery techniques, this context cannot be securely dated, and no notes exist for the excavations in this area. Given the careful WPA recording

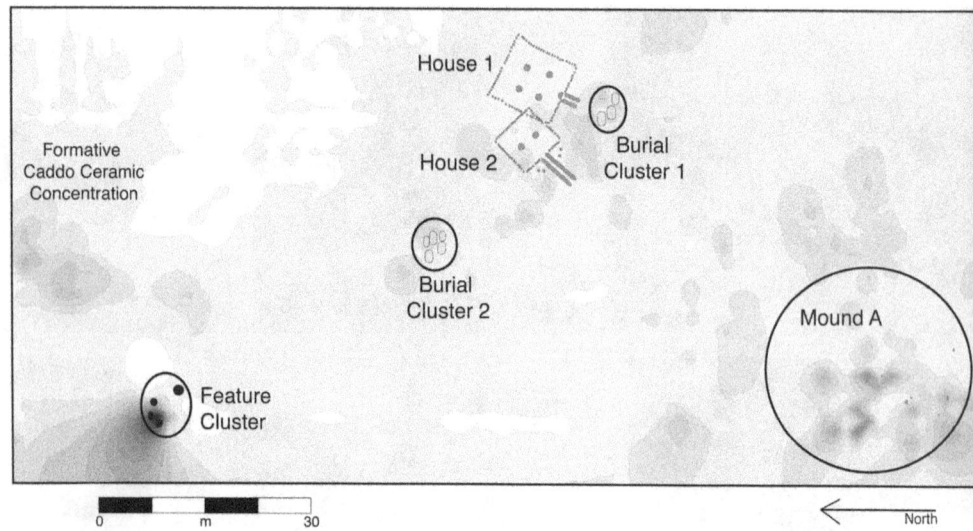

Figure 6.5. Map of 1941 WPA excavations at the Clement site, showing locations of Mound A and concentration of Formative Caddo sherds.

Figure 6.6. Selected Formative Caddo sherds from the 1941 WPA excavations at the Clement site, (*a–b*) Holly Fine Engraved bottle, red slipped, (*c*) red-slipped Williams Plain-like base sherd, (*d–f*) Coles Creek Incised, (*g*) Spiro Engraved with red pigment in engraved lines (*h*) Spiro Engraved, red slipped, (*i*) Pennington Punctate Incised, red slipped, (*j*) East Incised, red slipped, (*k*) Spiro Engraved with red pigment in engraved lines.

of burials, whole vessels, features, and houses elsewhere on the site, it seems unlikely these engraved fineware sherds came from a burial or domestic context. Prior to the recent reanalysis of WPA ceramics, Clement was thought to serve as a ritual precinct for groups living upstream along the terraces of the Glover between AD 1200 and 1450. The presence of these sherds suggests Clement served as a ritual center deeper into prehistory than was previously thought. The Early Caddo component certainly represents a very small portion of the overall activity in the mound precinct. The long-term use of Clement for ritual is supported by a charcoal sample taken from the base of the smaller mound at the site during the 2008 excavations, which returned a calibrated intercept of AD 1050, with a two-sigma range of AD 1034–1215 (Hammerstedt et al. 2010:287). This suggests that initial mound construction began when this area of the Clement site initially was occupied during the Early Caddo. Unfortunately, none of the sherds recovered from this context during the 2008 excavations had chronologically diagnostic attributes.

Engraved Caddo finewares also occur at several other sites on the Texas side of the Middle Red, most notably the Roitsch (41RR16), Stallings, (41LR297), Bentsen-Clark (41RR41), and Holdeman sites (41RR11). Whole vessels recovered from the multiple interment shaft tomb (Feature 1) at Bensen-Clark include a number of Spiro, Hickory, and Holly Fine Engraved vessels, as well as examples of nearly every Caddo utilitarian ware type. Like the sherds at Clement, several of the Spiro and Holly Fine Engraved vessels were red-filmed (Banks and Winters (1965:75). Perttula (2008d) documented a small assemblage of 88 decorated sherds from the Stallings site (41LR297), also located in northeast Texas, which included examples of Holly Fine or Hickory Engraved bottles and Crockett Curvilinear Incised sherds. This assemblage also included utilitarian ware types Coles Creek Incised, possibly *var. Greenhouse*, Hollyknowe Ridge Pinched, Dunkin Incised, and Weches Fingernail Impressed (Perttula 2008b:3–6). The assemblage of plain rim sherds includes a number of thick rim sherds reminiscent of Williams Plain, although since base sherds were excluded from the analysis, it was not possible to confirm these as thick-based Fourche Maline jars (Perttula 2008b:11). Much as with Bud Wright, the Stallings assemblage also included a high percentage of bone-tempered wares. Perttula (2008d:16) estimates the assemblage from the Stallings site to date prior to AD 1150 and suggests that two occupation components, associated with the Woodland and Early Caddo, may be present, given the occurrence of sherds from both series, although the combined weight of evidence from all of the assemblages points to a single occupation component.

Based on the ceramic data from the newly analyzed assemblages, there was a period of time during which people living in the middle Red made and used vessels associated with both Late Woodland and Early Caddo ceramic traditions. At Holdeman, a mound site along the Red, Perino (1995) documented a double burial (Burial 40/41) that contained both Spiro Engraved vessels and local copies of Coles Creek Incised on Caddo vessel forms. At Roitsch, Skinner et al. (1969) reported utilitarian types like East, Kiam, Canton, Pennington Punctate, Crockett Curvilinear, Coles Creek, and French Fork Incised from a midden below the East Mound. Calibrated dates from a nearby house, assumed to be contemporaneous, range between AD 1008 and 1206 (Perttula 1998:334; Skinner et al. 1969:21).

As Table 6.1 shows, four of the sites covered here have engraved finewares in their assemblages, and four do not. All but one have Crockett Curvilinear Incised. This is quite possibly the result of a sampling problem inherent in comparing whole vessels from burial assemblages with small assemblages from domestic or ritual contexts. It may also be the case that engraved fineware types were initially made somewhat later than utilitarian Caddo types in the middle Red. Based on the radiocarbon dates at Clement and Kaufman and the ceramic sequence in east Texas and northwest Louisiana (Girard 2009; Perttula 2011),

Table 6.1. Pottery Types Present at Late Woodland/Formative Caddo Sites in Study

Site	Williams Plain	Harrison Bayou Incised	Coles Creek Incised	French Fork Incised	Kiam Incised	Davis/East Incised	Dunkin Incised	Canton Incised
Mahaffey	X				X	X		X
Ray	X		X	X		X		
Bud Wright	X	X	X		X	X		X
Roitsch / Sam Kaufman	X		X	X	X	X		X
Stallings			X				X	
Holdeman*			X			X		X
Bentsen-Clark*					X	X		
Clement	X		X			X		

Note: * Whole burial vessels only included in type counts.

the utilitarian types certainly were in use by at least AD 1050. The presence of red filming, which was not common on any Caddo sites until after AD 1100, on engraved fineware sherds and vessels at Clement and Bentsen-Clark does imply these fineware types were made well into the twelfth century in the middle Red.

As Perttula (2008d:16) has pointed out, the differences in ceramic assemblages at middle Red sites may be the result of distinct local ceramic and ritual traditions at these widely distributed sites. This is true across the broader Caddo area, and well documented in the Sabine (Perttula 2011) and Neches (Perttula 2009b) drainages of east Texas, as well as in northwest Louisiana (Girard 2009). The distances between the Oklahoma sites Clement, Mahaffey, and Bud Wright are too large to expect that the occupants interacted regularly, which may account in part for the variation in ceramic assemblages. This assemblage diversity also implies that Early Caddo culture in the middle Red River was adopted by resident local groups, rather than the result of an influx of people moving in from major Caddo centers to the south and east. Based on the ceramic assemblages, sometime after AD 1050 the Woodland occupants of the middle Red adopted both the ceramic

			Pottery Types			
Hollyknowe Ridge Pinched	Weches Fingernail Impressed	Pennington Punctate Incised	Crockett Curvilinear Incised	Holly Fine Engraved	Hickory Engraved	Spiro Engraved
X			X			
			X			
X	X	X	X			
		X	X			
X	X		X	X	X	
	X	X	X	X		X
			X	X	X	X
		X		X		X

assemblages and, more importantly, the cultural practices that made them identifiable as the prehistoric Caddo. While this was concurrent with the Big Bang that jumpstarted the Mississippian emergence, the Caddo culture that emerged concurrently along the middle Red had a distinctly different trajectory, as I demonstrate below.

The Early Caddo Emergence in the Middle Red River

Based on the ceramic evidence, after AD 1050 the middle Red and the rest of the Caddo area witnessed the emergence of a widespread, shared set of ritual traditions. The best-known ceremonial centers associated with this Early Caddo tradition were the George C. Davis site in east Texas, the Crenshaw site in southwest Arkansas, and the Gahagan and Mounds Plantation sites in northwest Louisiana (Figure 6.7). While the diverse set of Caddo groups who constructed these centers and the smaller contemporaneous sites in the middle Red River were most certainly not politically consolidated, they shared a similar set of ceremonial and religious practices fundamentally distinct from other contemporaneous cultural developments from the Mississippi Valley, including the American Bottom and the LMV. While Coles Creek ceramics are found in varying frequencies at Early Caddo sites, the relationship between Early Caddo developments and LMV Coles Creek groups remains unclear (Girard 2009:53). Looking at this question from the western edge of the Caddo area, along the middle Red, I tend to agree with both Story's (1990) and Girard's (2009:54) notions that the Early Caddo arose out of several distinct cultural groups with relatively fluid social and territorial boundaries. Some of these groups apparently had much more extensive contact with Coles Creek groups, by virtue of proximity and other nebulous factors, but, even as they interacted more heavily with their neighbors, they remained a part of a broader religious and ceremonial tradition that distinguished them as Caddo.

Following Schambach (1982, 2002), in the middle Red, the cultural antecedents of the Caddo were resident Fourche Maline groups. However, I must reject Schambach's (2002:112) notion that Early Caddo mortuary ritual, particularly in a relative backwater such as the middle Red, is tied to developments at Cahokia. In that sense, I argue here that the adoption of Caddo ideology, rituals, and material traits at sites outside the four major centers occurred much earlier than the selective adoption of aspects of Mississippian ideology and material culture across the Caddo world. Archaeologists working in the Caddo region have identified a series of archaeological markers of religious and ceremonial practices that are distinctly Caddo, all of which can be found at Early Caddo

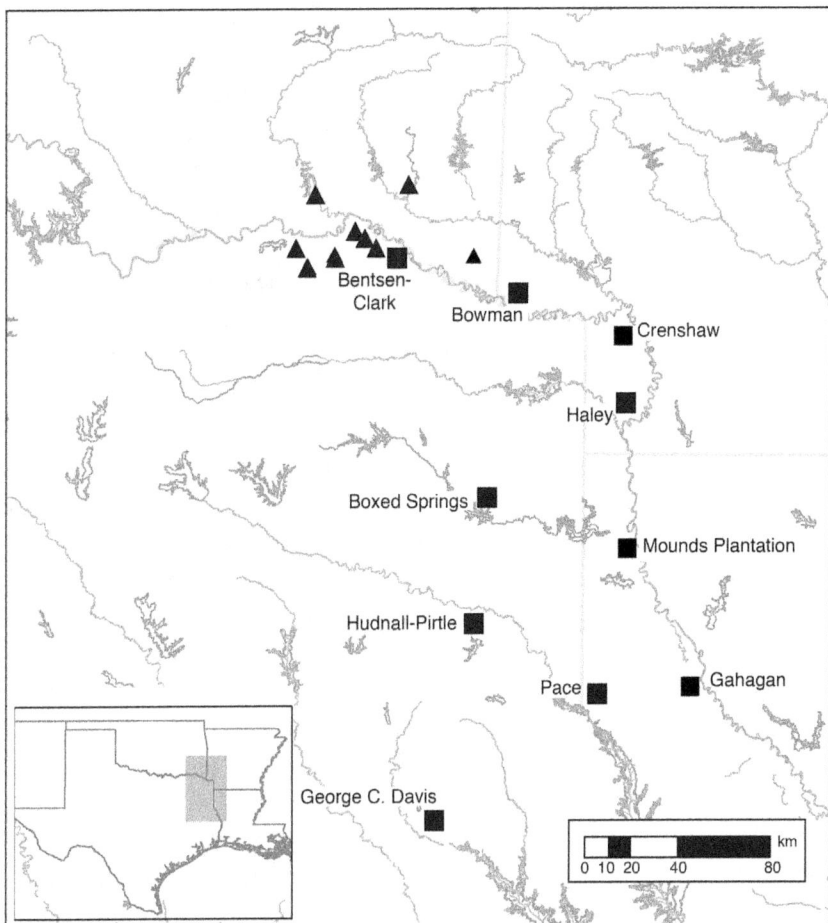

Figure 6.7. Locations of major centers in the Caddo area with respect to middle Red Formative Caddo sites.

sites in the middle Red River and other areas at the edge of the Caddo world, such as the Ouachita Mountains of southeast Oklahoma.

The most broadly distributed archaeological marker of Caddo ritual on the landscape is the buried structure mound, which also has been referred to as a "house mound." Trubitt's (2009) summary of mound structures in southwest Arkansas demonstrated that in most, but not all, cases these structures were burned and subsequently covered with earth. Whether this cycle of destruction and renewal coincided with prescribed cyclical calendar events or special occurrences, such as mortuary rituals, is unknown (Story 1990:341, 1998:39), although Kay and Sabo's (2006) suggestion that the smoke from these burnings represent an axis mundi for conveying souls to the world of the dead is compelling. Dowd's (2012) research on post–AD 1300 Caddo settlements in the Mountain Fork drainage of southeast Oklahoma has made it abundantly clear that, whatever their purpose, the rituals and underlying symbolism inherent in burying structures was not necessarily tied to any other trappings of political consolidation.[7] There is abundant evidence that burying and burning of structures began during the Early Caddo in the middle Red. Mounds at both the A. C. Mackin and Holdeman sites began with burned rectangular structures with extended entryways covered with layers of earth. Both mounds were added to and used as platform mounds during the subsequent Sanders (AD 1200–1300) phase.

The Caddo built both rectangular and circular structures, and special-purpose structures typically had enclosed extended entryways represented by paired end posts, a series of posts set in trenches, or a combination of the two (Perttula 2009a:31). Following Kay and Sabo's (2006) analysis of Harlan-style charnel houses in the Arkansas Valley, Perttula (2009a) compiled a study to determine the predominant orientation for these buildings and found that in the central Caddo area, which includes the middle Red, entryways of special-purpose buildings opened predominantly to the southeast, south, and southwest. These semicardinal directions may be tied to the winter solstice sunrise and sunsets. The entryway of the rectangular structure under the mound at Holdeman opened to the southwest.

Caddo platform mounds also express a distinct material symbolism, which George Sabo (Kay et al. 1989; Sabo 1985) has broken down into five attributes. These include (a) selective use of homogeneous soils in mound layers, (b) the use of contrasts in soil color in successive mound stages, (c) the special preparation of building surfaces, (d) the use of berms to enclose sacred space, and (e) the vertical alignment of mound features, including berms, hearths, and wall patterns. DeeAnn Story (1998) has extensively documented each attribute of mound symbolism associated with Early Caddo ritual practices at George C. Davis. Because so few Early Caddo sites are known in the middle Red, less evidence is available. At the Fasken site, Mound B began during the Early Caddo period as a prepared clay floor placed on an 88-cm-high rise (Prikryl 2008:165). As with the mounds at A. C. Mackin and Holdeman, additional mound stages were added during the subsequent occupations. While evidence from mound construction stages is lacking, color symbolism does seem to have been important at Early Caddo sites; three of 17 adult burials at the Holdeman site had associated vessels containing red pigments and green clay (Perino 1995). The multiple-interment burial at the Bentsen-Clark site also contained concentrations of green clay and red pigments in a configuration that has been interpreted as deliberate (Banks and Winters 1965:15–17).

Caddo mortuary ritual reached its most spectacular form via multiple-interment shaft tombs and mass burial pits. The burial pits for shaft tombs, which were single-episode interments of multiple individuals, were dug through previously existing mound levels into subsoil, where remains and grave goods were interred. Many shaft tombs also included upright poles that served as spatial markers. Like the smoke rising from buried burned structures, the re-use of poles also likely references the cosmological centering concept of the axis mundi (Brown 1996:94; Dowd 2012:173). Based on the presence of Early Caddo engraved finewares, the earliest shaft tombs were constructed after AD 1050. Shaft tombs excavated into mounds are documented all four of the major Early Caddo centers, and at other sites across the Caddo area. The spread of shaft tombs across the Caddo area occurred contemporaneously with a region-wide intensification of mound construction. Grave goods in these shaft tombs include numerous examples of whole Early Caddo fineware vessels, exotic artifacts, such as copper plates at Gahagan, ground-stone spatulate celts, and Gahagan bifaces.

The carefully constructed mass burials at Crenshaw and at George C. Davis may have been the precursors to later shaft tombs. The distinct differences between the two sites once again underscore the diversity of cultural practices across the Caddo area. At Crenshaw, Durham and Davis (1975) documented two mass burials, Burials A and H, with 27 and 43 adults, respectively, laid out on the Mound C surface and subsequently covered with earth. While the ceramics associated with each burial are Coles Creek Incised vessels, as Girard (2009:56–57) pointed out, these neat arrangements of individuals with grave goods are unlike mass Coles Creek burials from the LMV, where individual remains are jumbled, with skeletal elements frequently missing. The presence of Coles Creek vessels in the burial pits implies the mass burials at Crenshaw can be dated to sometime prior to AD 1000 (Girard 2009:57). Story (1998:17–26) described a pre-mound burial pit (Feature 134) with eight individuals placed below Mound C at George C. Davis. The pit, which contained six upright posts and possibly some sort of roof structure, was set off with a surrounding clay berm, intentionally built with an inverse stratigraphic profile from the alluvial terrace upon which the site is located. While grave goods, including swordlike chipped-stone Gahagan bifaces, were placed in concentrations along the north edge of the burial pit below Mound C, no ceramics are present in this early mass burial. Unlike at Crenshaw, Mounds Plantation, and Gahagan, Coles Creek sherds are extremely rare at George C. Davis, making up less than .01

percent of the total assemblage, a pattern that holds true more broadly across East Texas (Perttula 2011:70–71). A radiocarbon date run on corn from the early George C. Davis mass burial returned a calibrated date with an intercept of AD 960, and a two-sigma range of AD 870 to 1050 (Story and Valastro 1977:73, 86), which places it in a roughly contemporaneous position with the mass burial at Crenshaw.

Two Early Caddo mass burials are documented along the middle Red at the Bentsen-Clark site (Banks and Winters 1965). The larger of the two, Feature 1, was eroding into the rapidly shifting Red River channel, and only about a quarter remained. At least five individuals were interred in the main pit, where they were laid upon a floor covered with twilled cane matting. Grave goods in the pit consisted of numerous Spiro, Hickory, and Holly Fine Engraved whole vessels, a single plain conch shell drinking cup, mussel and marine shell beads, a number of Red River–style pipes, stone earspools with copper overlay, a carved limestone human effigy pipe, three Gahagan bifaces, nine celts, a copper strip, various bone awls, and black bear and mountain lion canines made into pendants. A second mass burial (Feature 3) was later placed about 10 feet away from the original tomb. The unknown number of individuals interred in this pit were buried with Spiro and Hickory Engraved vessels and at least one copper object. Despite the fact that the burials at Bentsen-Clark were not associated with mounds, the burials of multiple individuals with this assemblage of grave goods are clearly similar to the shaft tombs at other Early Caddo centers, and are indicative of the regional shared sphere of mortuary ritual.

The construction of shaft tombs continued well into the fifteenth century in the middle Red, a fact that further underscores their central role in Caddo ritual. In the middle Red, the overwhelming majority of exotic artifacts recovered from archaeological contexts are concentrated in these interments, leading to the natural question of who may have merited burial in these tombs. Are shaft tombs the final resting place of Caddo priest-chiefs, documented in the ethnographic record as *xinesis*, or are they another example of mortuary tableaus in which individual personhood is less important than the display, as Brown (2012) has recently posited for the Great Mortuary at Spiro, albeit on much a smaller scale? Based upon the way in which shaft tombs were deliberately dug through the center of burial mounds deep into subsoil, I suggest that the mounds with shaft tombs may have served as cosmograms, with mounds referencing the earth island (e.g., Knight 1989:280), and the shaft tomb a physical manifestation of the centering axis mundi that figured so prominently in the Caddo ritual sphere. If this was the case, the staging and ceremony surrounding these mass burials may have been paramount to the individuals interred. To that extent, it is probably overreaching to view the existence of these richly appointed graves at widely spaced centers as representative of the centers of highly stratified chiefdoms, a point to which I will return later.

My aim in presenting this brief summary of the vast Caddo ritual sphere has been to demonstrate that between AD 900 and 1200, the emergence that resulted in the construction of a number of the earliest mound sites in the Red River drainage and the southern Caddo area occurred simultaneously with developments in the Mississippian world. Excavations at the major Early Caddo centers at George C. Davis, Crenshaw, Mounds Plantation, and Gahagan and the smaller sites of the middle Red have demonstrated that, while individual differences may be present among the sites, the builders were participants in a broader shared ritual horizon. This is not to say the Caddo world and the American Bottom region were entirely disconnected. Gahagan, in particular, shows a strong connection with the American Bottom, in the form of flint clay pipes, copper objects, long-nosed god maskettes, and ceramics recovered from the mass burials dating to the twelfth century AD (Emerson and Girard 2004). It may well be the case that the ideology underpinning the explosion of Caddo ritual in the eleventh and twelfth centuries was spurred by Cahokia, as Girard et al. (2014:132) have suggested. It is also important to note that while these artifacts may have originated in the American Bottom, they became part of a distinctly Caddo ritual context when they were placed in the mass burials. What is clear is that the Caddo ritual program that spread beyond the major Early Caddo centers into hinterlands like the middle Red in the eleventh century had its own distinct differences from Cahokian ritual and lacked most of the classic material hallmarks of Mississippian culture.

The locations of major Early Caddo in the Caddo area reflect the differences in Caddo ritual centers and Early Mississippian political centers. The four major centers are widely distributed across the landscape, and in the middle Red, Bentsen-Clark is the only known Early center with evidence of elaborate mortuary ritual for nearly 80 km along the river.[8] Despite the contemporaneous ramping up in mound construction at Early Caddo and LMV Coles Creek sites, Kidder (1998:133) pointed out that Coles Creek mound centers in the LMV are spaced closely enough to indicate a series of petty chiefdoms, while Caddo centers are so distant from one another as to suggest these Early Caddo centers were "a vertically ranked society with territorially distinct authority over large area." Based on what is known from sites in the middle Red, I am disinclined to think that the evident social ranking among the Early Caddo translated into large-scale political integration of sites. Unlike Mississippian sites to the east, the placement of Caddo mounds on the landscape does not seem to reflect the waxing and waning political fortunes of a particular chiefly lineage.

One of the most remarkable aspects of many of the Early Caddo centers in the middle Red is the lengthy duration of so many of these mound sites; every Early Caddo site was expanded or reoccupied during subsequent phases, for as long as five centuries. Story (1998:39) documented the same lengthy use at George C. Davis, noting that the reuse of the site may indicate the existence of a powerful, possibly kin-based group of elites who maintained their authority over four centuries. While an unbroken political lineage may have been responsible for this, it may also be that Caddo elites legitimated their authority in a slightly different manner than Mississippian elites. While Mississippian elites both constructed new mound centers as a means of beginning a new chiefly lineage and appropriated older mound centers (following Anderson 1994 and Blitz 1999), Caddo leaders seem to have established their authority by returning to the same ceremonial space used by their predecessors for mortuary and renewal rituals. It seems that Caddo mound sites were more important as religious centers than they were as political centers. While religion and politics certainly were enmeshed across both the Caddo and the Mississippian worlds, the Caddo made a clear distinction between the two spheres, a distinction reflected in the very structure of their settlements.

From the ethnographic record, we know that the Caddo recognized two distinct offices of authority, the *xinesi*, who served as the chief priest and mediated relations with the spirit realm, and the *caddi*, who served as the political chief (Wyckoff and Baugh 1980). This may also explain why, on the 1691–1692 Teran map of the Kadohadacho village at the Great Bend of Red River, the ceremonial precinct, which includes an earthen mound, is situated on the edge of the polity. To enter the community, the Spanish party had to first pass through the temple complex, an area Sabo (2012:442) described as the gateway between the human and the spiritual worlds. The chief's residence was located in the very center of the string of dispersed households, which Sabo (2012:445) interpreted as the center of the human community. This split arrangement of space within Caddo polities explains why the spacing of sites in the middle Red does not match up with the typical arrangement of Mississippian chiefdoms described by Hally (1993). For example, the Clement and Grobin Davis (34Mc253) sites are multiple-mound sites along the lower Glover and Little rivers, with only sparse occupation located just six km apart. Both are located at the geographic edges of clusters of farmsteads; the largely vacant ritual complexes may in fact serve as a buffer between the two polities, bolstering the notion that Caddo mound centers played a fundamentally different role in the political-religious system than their Mississippian equivalents.

Mississippian Culture in the Caddo World

The Caddo did not live in a vacuum, however, and eventually cultural traditions from the broader Mississippian world did begin to creep in along the middle Red River. While maize is found on Caddo sites in contexts dated as early as AD 800, it did not become a staple of Caddo subsistence until AD 1300 (Perttula 2008c). Likewise, the extensive use of shell as a tempering agent was not adopted by Caddo potters in the middle Red until after AD 1300; even then, shell-tempered wares represent only about 40–70 percent of known Late Caddo ceramic assemblages in the middle Red (Perttula et al. 2011:251). By the mid-fifteenth century, the Caddo in southeast Oklahoma started to abandon the Ouachita Mountains and the piedmont zone and moved to the terraces of the middle Red, likely due to ongoing drought conditions (Perttula 2012b). As Perttula (2012b:97) pointed out, it is only after this shift that Caddo settlements are arranged in archaeologically recognizable polities. This time period witnessed an intensification in mound building as well; the largest Caddo mound site on the Red River, Battle Mound, was constructed during this period in the Great Bend region (McKinnon 2010). It is only after AD 1450 that we begin to see evidence of the Caddo of the middle Red participating in the more extensive circulation of Southeastern Ceremonial Complex goods, as evidenced by the engraved shell gorgets found in shaft burials at the Roden (Perino 1981) and Sam Kaufman sites (Skinner et al. 1969). Excavations of Titus phase cemeteries in the Big Cypress Creek basin, just south of the middle Red, finally show evidence of status expressed in *individual* cemetery burials, rather than just shaft tombs, including the burial of individuals on litters, with ear spools and caches of celts, blades, and arrowpoints (Perttula 2012a:403).

Across the Red River drainage and its tributaries, a shared ritual tradition, marked by a series of broadly shared religious practices and an accompanying ceramic horizon emerged and spread between AD 1000 and 1150. By AD 1100 the shared ritual and ceramic complexes had spread across the ancestral Caddo world, including the marginal middle Red drainage. The emergence of prehistoric Caddo culture during the Early period was part of a cultural trajectory that may have been influenced by the Mississippian emergence in the American Bottom but resulted in a distinctly different ritual expression. Before at least AD 1450, the elaborate religious displays in the Caddo world were not accompanied by the trappings of political inequality seen in the Mississippian world. While the Caddo shared the same cosmology as the rest of the Mississippian world, they chose to interact with the supernatural in distinctly different ways, reflected in their methods of house and mound construction, use of the landscape, and mortuary ritual.

Notes

1. As Albert (1985) has demonstrated, since at least 5500 BP, and probably earlier, this boundary has shifted based on climatic conditions. As rainfall totals and mean temperatures have fluctuated over the millennia, the location of the boundary between the drier, more climatically variable southern Plains grasslands and the wetter, more stable Eastern Woodlands has moved east and west across this portion of the Red River drainage.

2. For Caddo ceramic assemblages, fine and utilitarian wares are defined following Schambach and Miller's (1984) work at the Cedar Grove site, on the Arkansas side of the Great Bend of the Red River. Utilitarian wares have a coarser temper, lack burnishing or slipping, and may be decorated with incising, appliqué, punctuation, and brushing, or any combination thereof. Finewares consist of engraved and slipped sherds from bottles and bowls, which have smoothed and burnished exterior surfaces.

3. The only previous documented excavations of a Fourche Maline house are those at the Poole site, located in the Ouachita Mountains near Hot Springs, Arkansas. The house is a large oval-shaped building measuring 29.6 m long by 8.5 m wide with a single line of support posts down the center (Schambach 1982:144).

4. In this case, the lack of grave goods pinpoints the date for these burials. If they were later Formative Caddo burials, they would contain whole vessels.

5. Based on dates from the George C. Davis site, Perttula (2009:70) has suggested that, at least at the more southerly East Texas sites along the Neches and Sabine, Crockett Curvilinear Incised is rare prior to AD 1027, which could justify pushing the date for the Ray site at least 50 years, and probably later, at least into the twelfth century.

6. There was a higher-than-expected frequency of bone temper in the post–AD 1300 Caddo sherds recovered from Bud Wright as well, which may be indicative of an enduring, localized stylistic tradition among the prehistoric Caddo in this area.

7. Dowd's (2012) research demonstrated that the Woods Mound group, a series of nine house mounds on a terrace of the Mountain Fork in the southern Ouachita Mountains, was used by people living in dispersed settlements along the narrow stream terraces for communal ritual. Ceramics recovered from excavations into several of the mounds before the site was inundated by Broken Bow Lake showed evidence for communal feasting, but no evidence of social differentiation among feast participants. Woods seems to have been a vacant ceremonial center used for periodic rituals involving the destruction and burying of buildings.

8. The next-closest Formative Caddo center was at the Bowman site, located just over the Arkansas border. Unfortunately, the only excavations into the two mounds at the site were done by avocational archaeologists, and there are very few reliable notes about mound stratigraphy (Hoffman 1970).

References Cited

Albert, Lois M.
1981   *Ferndale Bog and Natural Lake: Five Thousand Years of Environmental Change in Southeastern Oklahoma.* Studies in Oklahoma's Past No. 7. Oklahoma Archeological Survey, Norman.

Anderson, David G.
1994   *The Savannah River Chiefdoms: Political Change in the Late Prehistoric Southeast.* University of Alabama Press, Tuscaloosa.

Banks, Larry D., and Joe Winters
1975   *The Bentsen-Clark Site: A Preliminary Report.* Special Publication No. 2. Texas Archeological Society, San Antonio.

Blitz, John H.
1999   Mississippian Chiefdoms and the Fission-Fusion Process. *American Antiquity* 64(4): 577–592.

Brown, James A.
1996   *The Spiro Ceremonial Center.* Memoirs of the University of Michigan Museum of Anthropology, No. 20, Vols. 1 and 2. Ann Arbor.
2012   Spiro Reconsidered: Sacred Economy at the Western Frontier of the Eastern Woodlands. In *The Archaeology of the Caddo,* edited by Timothy K. Perttula and Chester. P. Walker, pp. 117–138. University of Nebraska Press, Lincoln.

Bruseth, James E.
1998   The Development of Caddoan Polities along the Middle Red River Valley of Eastern Texas and Oklahoma. In *The Native History of the Caddo: Their Place in Southeastern Archeology and Ethnohistory,* edited by Timothy K. Perttula and James E. Bruseth, pp. 9–43. Studies in Archeology No. 30. Texas Archeological Research Laboratory, University of Texas, Austin.

Bruseth, James E., and Larry Banks
1992   Ray Site (41LR135). *Texas Archeology* 36(3):1, 7.

Bruseth, James E., Larry Banks, and Jimmy Smith
2001   The Ray Site (41LR135). *Bulletin of the Texas Archaeological Society* 72:197–213.

Dowd, Elsbeth Linn
2012   Alternative Conceptions of Complexity: Sociopolitical Dynamics of the Mountain Fork Caddo. Unpublished Ph.D. dissertation, Department of Anthropology, University of Oklahoma, Norman.

Durham, James H., and Michael K. Davis
1975   Reports on Burials Found at Crenshaw Mound "C," Miller County, Arkansas. *Bulletin of the Oklahoma Anthropological Society* 23:1–90.

Emerson, Thomas M., and Jeffrey S. Girard
2004   Dating Gahagan and Its Implications for Understanding Cahokia–Caddo Interactions. *Southeastern Archaeology* 23(1):57–64.

Girard, Jeffrey S.
2009   Comments on Caddo Origins in Northwest Louisiana. *Journal of Northeast Texas Archaeology* 31:51–60.

Girard, Jeffrey S., Mary Beth Trubitt, and Timothy K. Perttula
  2014   *Caddo Connections: Cultural Interactions within and beyond the Caddo World.* Rowman and Littlefield, Lanham.

Hally, David J.
  1993   The Territorial Sizes of Mississippian Chiefdoms. In *Archaeology of Eastern North America: Papers in Honor of Stephen Williams*, edited by James B. Stoltman, pp. 143–168. Archaeological Research Report No. 25. Mississippi Department of Archives and History, Jackson.

Hammerstedt, Scott W., Amanda L. Regnier, and Patrick C. Livingood
  2010   Geophysical and Archaeological Investigations at the Clement Site, a Caddo Mound Complex in Southeastern Oklahoma. *Southeastern Archaeology* 29(2):279–291.

Hoffman, Michael P.
  1970   Archaeological and Historical Assessment of the Red River Basin in Arkansas. In *Archeological and Historical Resources of the Red River Basin*, edited by Hester A. Davis, pp. 137–194. Research Series No. 1. Arkansas Archeological Survey, Fayetteville.

Kay, Marvin, and George Sabo III
  2006   Mortuary Ritual and Winter Solstice Imagery of the Harlan-Style Charnal House. *Southeastern Archaeology* 5(1):29–47.

Kay, Marvin, George Sabo III, and Ralph Merletti
  1989   Late Prehistoric Settlement Patterning: A View from Three Caddoan Civic Ceremonial Centers in Northwest Arkansas. In *Contributions to Spiro Archeology: Mound Excavations and Regional Perspectives*, edited by J. Daniel Rogers, Don Wyckoff, and Dennis Peterson, pp. 129–158. Studies in Oklahoma's Past No. 16. Oklahoma Archeological Survey, Norman.

Kidder, Tristram R.
  1998   Rethinking Caddoan–Lower Mississippi Valley Interaction. In *The Native History of the Caddo: Their Place in Southeastern Archeology and Ethnohistory*, edited by Timothy K. Perttula and James E. Bruseth, pp. 129–143. Studies in Archeology No. 30. Texas Archeological Research Laboratory, University of Texas, Austin.

Knight, Vernon J. Jr.
  1989   Symbolism of Mississippian Mounds. In *Powhatan's Mantle*, edited by Peter H. Wood, Gregory A. Waselkov, and M. Thomas Hatley, pp. 279–291. University of Nebraska Press, Lincoln.

Leith, Luther J.
  2011   A Re-conceptualization of the Fourche Maline Culture: The Woodland Period as a Transition in Southeast Oklahoma. Unpublished Ph.D. dissertation, Department of Anthropology, University of Oklahoma, Norman.

Mallouf, Robert J.
  1976   *Archeological Investigations at Proposed Big Pine Lake, 1974–1975: Lamar and Red River Counties.* Archeological Survey Report 18. Texas Historical Commission, Austin.

McKinnon, Duncan
  2010   Continuing the Research: Archaeogeophysical Investigations at the Battle Mound Site (3LA1) in Lafayette County, Arkansas. *Southeastern Archaeology* 29(2):250–260.

Perino, Gregory
  1981   *Archaeological Investigations at the Roden Site, McCurtain County, Oklahoma.* Potsherd Press Publication No. 1. Museum of the Red River, Idabel.

1995 The Dan Holdeman Site (41RR11), Red River County, Texas. *Journal of Northeast Texas Archaeology* 6:3–65.

Perino, Gregory, and W. J. Bennett

1978 *Archaeological Investigations at the Mahaffey Site, CH-1, Hugo Reservoir, Choctaw County, Oklahoma.* Museum of the Red River, Idabel.

Perttula, Timothy K.

2008a Archeological Survey of the Roitsch Farm and Adjoining Lands, 1991 and 1992 Texas Archeological Society Field School, Red River County, Texas. In *Collected Papers from Past Texas Archeological Society Field Schools*, edited by Timothy K. Perttula, pp. 152–172. Special Publication No. 5. Texas Archeological Society, Austin.

2008b The Archeology of the Roitsch Site (41RR16), an Early to Historic Caddo Period Village on the Red River in Northeast Texas. In *Collected Papers from Past Texas Archeological Society Field Schools*, edited by Timothy K. Perttula, pp. 313–628. Special Publication No. 5. Texas Archeological Society, Austin.

2008c Caddo Agriculture on the Western Frontier of the Eastern Woodlands. *Plains Anthropologist* 53(205):79–105.

2008d The Decorated Ceramic Sherds, Plain Rims, and Clay Pipe Sherds from the Stallings Site (41LR297), Lamar County, Texas. Manuscript on file at the Oklahoma Archeological Survey, Norman.

2009a Extended Entryway Structures in the Caddo Archeological Area. *Southeastern Archaeology* 28(1):27–42.

2009b Lake Naconiche Archaeology and Caddo Origins Issues. *Journal of Northeast Texas Archaeology* 31:61–86.

2011 *Archaeological and Archaeogeophysical Investigations at an Early Caddo Mound Center in the Sabine River Basin of East Texas.* Special Publication No. 15. Friends of Northeast Texas Archaeology.

2012a The Character of Fifteenth- to Seventeenth-Century Caddo Communities in the Big Cypress Creek Basin of Northeast Texas. In *The Archaeology of the Caddo*, edited by Timothy K. Perttula, pp. 363–410. University of Nebraska Press, Lincoln.

2012b Watershed Times for the Caddo People of the Far Southeast. *Caddo Archaeology Journal* 22:97–114.

Perttula, Timothy K., Mary Beth Trubitt, and Jeffrey S. Girard

2011 The Use of Shell-Tempered Pottery in the Caddo Area of the Southeastern United States. *Southeastern Archaeology* 30(2):242–267.

Prikryl, Daniel J.

2008 The 1991 and 1992 Texas Archeological Society Field School Investigations at the Fasken Site (41RR14), Red River County, Texas. In *Collected Papers from Past Texas Archeological Society Summer Field Schools*, edited by Timothy K. Perttula, pp. 125–172. Special Publication No. 5. Texas Archeological Society, Austin.

Regnier, Amanda, Patrick Livingood, and Scott Hammerstedt

2013 The End of the WPA in Oklahoma: The Clement and McDonald Sites. In *Shovel Ready: Archaeology and Roosevelt's New Deal for America*, edited by Bernard Means, pp. 110–128. University of Alabama Press, Tuscaloosa.

Rohrbaugh, Charles L., Robert J. Burton, Susan Sasse Burton, and Lura Joseph Rosewitz

1971 *Hugo Reservoir I.* Archaeological Site Report No. 22. Oklahoma River Basin Survey, University of Oklahoma Research Institute, Norman.

Sabo, George III
   1985   Mound-Building as Material Symbolism: An Example from the West Ozark Highland. Paper presented at the Annual Meeting of the Society for American Archaeology, Denver.
   2012   The Teran Map and Caddo Cosmology. In *The Archaeology of the Caddo*, edited by Timothy K. Perttula and Chester P. Walker, pp. 431–448. University of Nebraska Press, Lincoln.

Schambach, Frank R.
   1982   An Outline of Fourche Maline Culture in Southwest Arkansas. In *Arkansas Archaeology in Review*, edited by Neal L. Trubowitz and Marvin D. Jeter, pp. 132–197. Research Series No. 15. Arkansas Archeological Survey, Fayetteville.
   1991   Coles Creek Culture and the Trans-Mississippi South. *Caddoan Archeology* 2(3):2–8.
   2002   Fourche Maline: A Woodland Period Culture of the Trans-Mississippi South. In *The Woodland Southeast*, edited by David G. Anderson and Robert C. Mainfort Jr., pp. 91–112. University of Alabama Press, Tuscaloosa.

Skinner, S. Alan, R. King Harris, and Keith M. Anderson
   1969   *Archaeological Investigations at the Sam Kaufman Site, Red River County, Texas*. Contributions in Anthropology 5. Department of Anthropology, Southern Methodist University, Dallas.

Story, Dee Ann
   1990   Culture History of the Native Americans. In *The Archeology and Bioarcheology of the Gulf Coastal Plain*, edited by Dee Ann Story, Janice A. Guy, Barbara A. Burnett, Martha D. Freeman, Jerome C. Rose, D. Gentry Steele, Ben W. Olive, and Karl J. Reinhard, pp. 163–366. Research Series No. 38. Arkansas Archeological Survey, Fayetteville.
   1998   The George C. Davis Site: Glimpses into Early Caddoan Symbolism and Ideology. In *The Native History of the Caddo: Their Place in Southeastern Archeology and Ethnohistory*, edited by Timothy K. Perttula and James E. Bruseth, pp. 9–43. Studies in Archeology No. 30. Texas Archeological Research Laboratory, University of Texas, Austin.

Story, DeeAnn, and S. Valastro Jr.
   1977   Radiocarbon Dating and the George C. Davis Site, Texas. *Journal of Field Archaeology* 4(1):63–89.

Trubitt, Mary Beth
   2009   Burning and Burying Buildings: Exploring Variation in Caddo Archaeology in Southwest Arkansas. *Southeastern Archaeology* 28(2):233–247.

Wyckoff, Don G., and Timothy Baugh
   1980   Early Historic Hasinai Elites: A Model for the Material Culture of Governing Elites. *Midcontinental Journal of Archaeology* 5(2):225–288.

7

Early Mississippian in the North Carolina Piedmont

EDMOND A. BOUDREAUX III

Mississippian origins in the North Carolina Piedmont have been a topic of interest since Joffre Coe presented the region's first comprehensive cultural chronology in his contribution to the 1952 volume *Archeology of Eastern United States*. Coe (1952:308–309, Figure 164) interpreted Mississippian cultural practices in the Piedmont as an intrusive way of life brought in by an enclave of migrants from the south. This was based primarily on the fact that Mississippian ceramic assemblages in the Piedmont are dominated by complicated stamping, a surface treatment that was not found in earlier or contemporaneous Late Woodland ceramic traditions in the area (Coe 1952:309; Ferguson 1971). Mississippian peoples were seen as intruders who abandoned the Piedmont less than a century after they arrived, due to their constant conflict with the indigenous Late Woodland peoples they had displaced (Coe 1952:308). Coe (1952:309) eloquently stated his ideas about the short-lived duration of Mississippian culture in the Piedmont and its distinctiveness from other cultural practices in the region in the statement, "It appeared so suddenly and was gone so quickly that it resembles a beam of light flashing across a dark sky."

In some ways, our understanding of Mississippian culture in the North Carolina Piedmont has changed significantly since Coe's 1952 publication. For example, Mississippian culture can no longer be viewed as a phenomenon of short duration in the region, as it is now clear that Mississippian communities were present by around AD 1150 (Boudreaux 2007a; Mountjoy 1989), and this way of life persisted at least into the 1500s, when the area was traversed by Spanish expeditions led by De Soto and Pardo (Beck 2009; Hudson 1990). Another change is that we now know that the sites of the North Carolina Piedmont represent the northeastern edge of the Mississippian world, rather than an enclave (Boudreaux 2007a:32–35; Ferguson 1971; Hally 1994), which suggests that the movement of ideas is an explanation for Mississippian origins in the Piedmont that is equally plausible as the migration of new people into the region (Ward and Davis 1999:133).

The North Carolina Piedmont is a broad plateau of rolling hills located at the center of the state between the Appalachian Mountains to the west and the Atlantic coastal plain to the east (Bobyarchick and Diemer 2000:17–19). Although very little research has focused explicitly on Early Mississippian in the region, and the topic of Mississippian origins has not been investigated, this chapter pulls together information from various sources to explore several topics that are important for investigating the Piedmont's Early Mississippian societies, defined here as the time from AD 1150 to 1300. This chapter begins with a discussion of chronological issues. Several lines of evidence suggest that Mississippian lifeways appeared in the southern North Carolina Piedmont around AD 1150, which is later than the Early Mississippian period (AD 1000–1150) in the region's current cultural chronology (Boudreaux 2007a:Table 14;

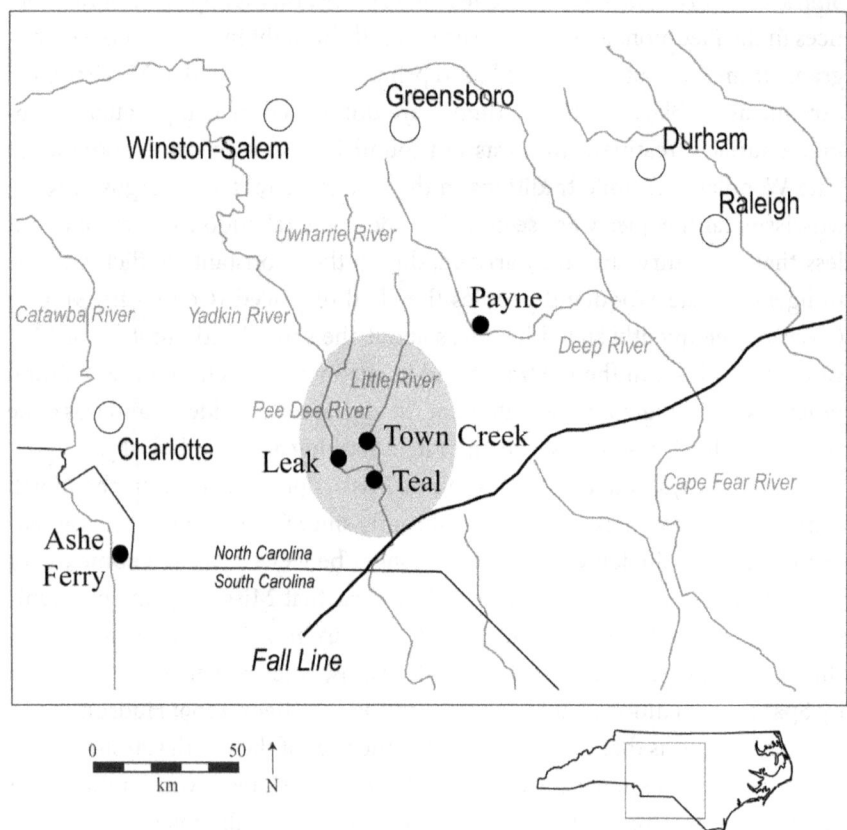

Figure 7.1. Regional map with sites discussed in text.

Oliver 1992:Figure 45; Ward and Davis 1999:Figure 1.5). Next, Early Mississippian architecture and site structure are discussed, especially as they relate to inferences about social organization at the household and community levels. Although this discussion includes information from multiple sites, it is necessarily dominated by architectural and mortuary information from the civic-ceremonial center at Town Creek (Figure 7.1), the Piedmont's largest settlement and one of the region's most extensively excavated sites (Boudreaux 2011; Coe 1995; Ward and Davis 1999:123). Architectural and mortuary patterns at Town Creek are used to develop some inferences about social organization and political economy within the Early Mississippian community there. Town Creek represented a significant departure from earlier forms of community organization in the Piedmont, and this new way of life would have required new strategies for organizing and integrating larger groups of people. It appears that these strategies included the development of enduring household groups and the integration of these households at multiple levels.

Chronology of Mississippian Origins in the North Carolina Piedmont

The North Carolina Piedmont's current cultural chronology (Table 7.1) divides the Mississippian period into three phases—Teal, Town Creek, and Leak—that span the interval approximately AD 1000–1500 (Boudreaux 2007a:25–34; Ward and Davis 1999:132–134).[1] Early Mississippian in the region has been associated with the Teal phase (AD 1000–1150) (Boudreaux 2007a:25; Oliver 1992:240), but there are several indications that Mississippian cultural practices were not present in the region until the early Town Creek phase (AD 1150–1250).

Little can be said about non-ceramic attributes of the Teal phase, and, as argued here, even our understanding of the ceramics may actually conflate pottery types from different phases. As currently defined, a Teal phase ceramic assemblage consists of large proportions of complicated stamping, cordmarking, and fine cordmarking or fine simple stamping in contexts that date between AD 1000 and 1150 (Boudreaux 2007a:25; Oliver 1992:204–206). This phase was defined based on materials excavated from the Teal site (see Figure 7.1), but it actually is a poorly understood, multiple-component site that has produced radiocarbon dates that range from AD 900 to 1600 (Oliver 1992:Figure 40).

While chronological issues cannot be resolved with existing materials from the Teal site itself, because the associations between ceramics and radiocarbon dates there are not always clear, information from two other sites in the region suggests that complicated stamping either was introduced or came to

Table 7.1. Dates for Mississippian Phases of the North Carolina Piedmont

Phase	Calibrated	Uncalibrated
Leak	1300–1500	1300–1550
Town Creek	1150–1300	1050–1300
Late	1250–1300	1250–1300
Early	1150–1250	1050–1250
Teal	1000–1150	900–1050

dominate assemblages no earlier than around AD 1150–1200. First, ceramics from the Ashe Ferry site (see Figure 7.1), a largely Late Woodland site complex located on the Catawba River in northern South Carolina (Riggs et al. 2014), are consistent with the appearance of complicated stamping in the area during the late AD 1100s to early 1200s. Radiocarbon dates from eight feature contexts at Ashe Ferry suggest a Late Woodland occupation span of AD 950–1150 associated with simple stamped and plain ceramics. Complicated stamping was not present in the Ashe Ferry ceramic sequence until after AD 1150–1200 (Riggs et al. 2014). Second, the Payne site is an Early Mississippian site located along the Deep River in North Carolina (see Figure 7.1) (Mountjoy 1989:8). The three radiocarbon dates from Payne have large error ranges, but their one-sigma distributions overlap around AD 1150–1175, suggesting that this may have been when the site was occupied (Table 7.2) (Boudreaux 2007a:Table 15). Complicated stamping is the most common surface treatment at Payne, while cordmarking is poorly represented and fine cordmarking is absent (Boudreaux 2007a:Table 1). The Payne site assemblage suggests that complicated stamping was the dominant surface treatment in the southern Piedmont by the beginning of the early Town Creek phase around AD 1150–1200.

While the relationship between the appearance of complicated stamping and the presence of other Mississippian traits in the North Carolina Piedmont is not known, the spread of Mississippian lifeways involved the acceptance of religious practices and an ideology that emphasized the importance of a cosmic center and the division of the cosmos into four portions (Anderson 1997:262–263; King 2010:63–64; Knight 1986:685; Lankford 2004:208–209). King (2010:64–65) has argued that this quadripartite organization was expressed at multiple scales, including in the patterns impressed into the surface of complicated stamped pottery in some parts of the Mississippian world. This is the case in the North Carolina Piedmont, where many of the patterns found on complicated stamped

Table 7.2. Early Mississippian Period Radiocarbon Dates from the North Carolina Piedmont

Sample Code	Site	Context	Age (BP)	Uncalibrated Date	Calibrated 1-Sigma[a]	Calibrated 2-Sigma[a]	Modeled Date[b]	References
Beta-201468	Town Creek	Structure 4a	820	AD 1130±40	1185–1260	1155–1275	1165–1270	Boudreaux 2005:157
FSU-184/FSU-174	Town Creek	Level A	745	AD 1205±140	1155–1395	1015–1440	1095–1260	Reid 1967:62[c]
Beta-201469	Town Creek	Structure 5a	940	AD 1010±40	1030–1160	1020–1185	1035–1215	Boudreaux 2005:157
Beta-18411	Payne	Feature	820	1060–1200	1160–1275	1040–1285	-	Mountjoy 1989:15[c]
Beta-18412	Payne	Feature	860	1020–1160	1050–1255	1030–1270	-	Mountjoy 1989:15[c]
Beta-18410	Payne	Feature	910	980–1100	1040–1175	1020–1250	-	Mountjoy 1989:15[c]
Uga-6047	Teal	Feature 47	950	950–1050	1025–1155	995–1210	-	Oliver 1992:209[c]
Uga-6048	Teal	Feature 49	950	950–1050	1025–1155	995–1210	-	Oliver 1992:209[c]
Uga-6046	Teal	Feature 46	1000	895–1005	985–1150	895–1165	-	Oliver 1992:209[c]

Notes: a. Calibrated dates generated with CALIB (Stuiver et al. 2005).
b. Bayesian model generated with OxCal 4.2 (Bronk Ramsey 2009).
c. Dates also discussed in Eastman 1994.

pottery are some variation of a design that has been divided into four parts (Reid 1967:Plates II–III; Ward and Davis 1999:Figure 4.24).

The assemblages and radiocarbon dates from the Teal, Payne, and Ashe Ferry sites suggest that complicated stamping either was not present or at least was not popular in the Piedmont until around AD 1150–1200. If the appearance of complicated stamped pottery in the region reflects the spread of Mississippian ideology, then the later appearance of complicated stamping suggests that Early Mississippian communities were not present in the North Carolina Piedmont until during the early Town Creek phase (AD 1150–1250), which is significantly later than what is recognized as Early Mississippian within existing cultural chronologies (Boudreaux 2007a:Table 14; Oliver 1992:Figure 45). This later time frame actually is more consistent with some ideas about the timing of the spread of Mississippian cultural practices across the Southeast. For example, Anderson (1997:262, 1999:225) argues that Mississippian first appeared in the central Mississippi Valley around AD 900 and then spread eastward, eventually reaching the Carolinas after AD 1100–1150.

Early Mississippian Sites and Communities in the North Carolina Piedmont

The entire Piedmont was characterized by similar ways of life until approximately AD 1150, when cultural practices characterized as Late Woodland developed across the northern and central Piedmont while Mississippian lifeways appeared in a small part of the southern Piedmont, primarily south of the confluence of the Pee Dee and Uwharrie rivers (see shaded area in Figure 7.1) (Oliver 1992:Figure 2; Ward and Davis 1999:98–99). North of this confluence, Late Woodland cultural practices persisted into the eighteenth century (Ward and Davis 1999). Mississippian sites in the Piedmont mostly are found along the Pee Dee River—the major waterway in the region—and its tributaries (Oliver 1992:54–84), and this association led Coe (1952) to name Mississippian in the Piedmont the Pee Dee culture. Pee Dee ceramics have been recognized as a local variant within the broader South Appalachian Mississippian ceramic tradition, which consists of complicated stamped, non-shell-tempered ceramics found across much of the eastern half of the Southeast (Caldwell 1958:34; Ferguson 1971:7–8; Griffin 1967:190).

Surface collections of Mississippian pottery suggest that small sites, presumably farmsteads or hamlets, were the typical kind of Early Mississippian settlement in the North Carolina Piedmont (Oliver 1992:48–84). Oliver (1992:53–54) notes that nearly all of the Mississippian sites in the Piedmont were located on soils that would have been good for farming, but it is not known how this pattern differs, if at all, from the settlement locations of earlier periods. Three sites—Leak, Teal, and Payne (Mountjoy 1989:12; Oliver 1992)—may represent larger settlements, but none of these sites has been sufficiently investigated to characterize site structure or determine what type of settlement they represent.[2]

The Early Mississippian period also saw the appearance around AD 1150 of the largest Native American settlement in the southern Piedmont, the civic-ceremonial center at Town Creek (Figure 7.2) (Boudreaux 2007b:49, 2013:484).

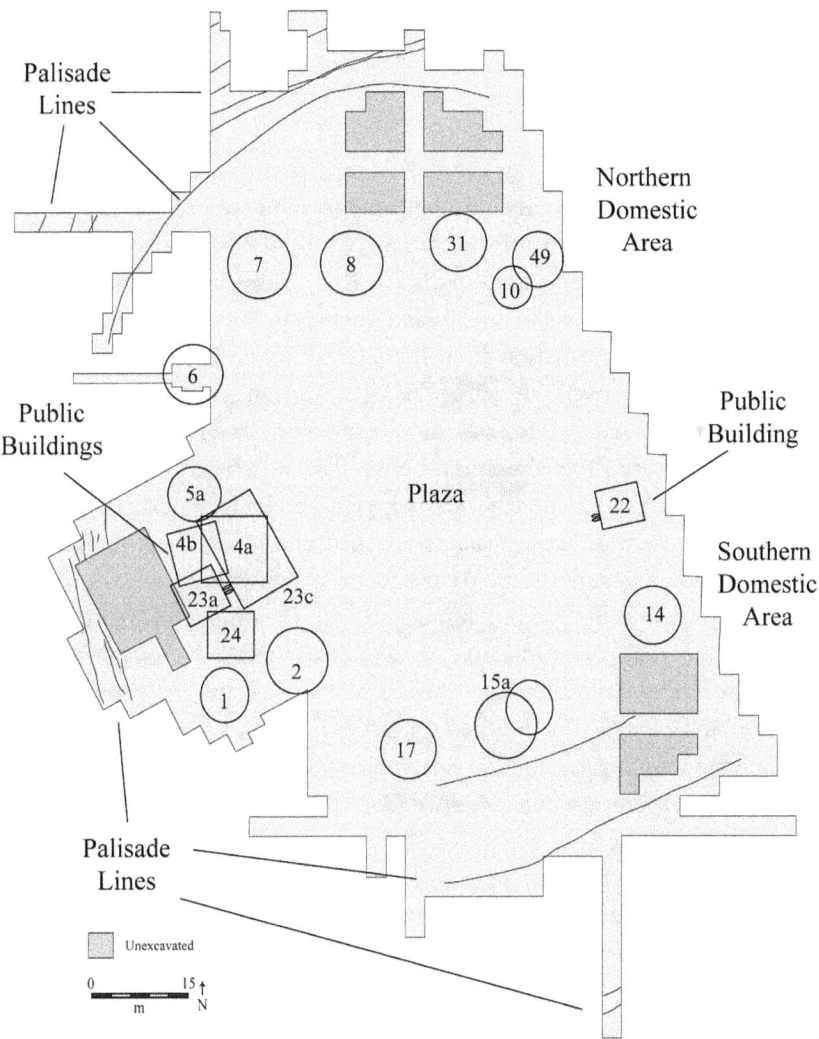

Figure 7.2. Select architectural elements at Town Creek with areas and structures discussed in text.

Multiple lines of evidence indicate that Town Creek was a relatively large town (ca. 1.5 ha) with a substantial residential population during the Early Mississippian period. This evidence includes ceramic deposition rates that peaked during that time and the presence of sizeable midden deposits, multiple palisade lines, and a number of domestic structures that date to the Early Mississippian period (Boudreaux 2013:491–492). Town Creek would have been the locus of regionally important ceremonial, social, and political events, based on its size and significant public architecture (see Blitz 1993:11; Hally 1996:93–95; Holley 1999:23; Lewis et al. 1998:11; Lindauer and Blitz 1997:185), so its establishment may indicate the presence of a multiple-community polity in the southern Piedmont during the Early Mississippian period.

Early Mississippian Architecture

Domestic and public buildings are important elements of the built environment that can provide insights into the composition of household groups and the interaction of social groups within a community. In this section, information from several sites is used to discuss Early Mississippian domestic and public architecture in the North Carolina Piedmont. This discussion is dominated, however, by information from Town Creek, where extensive, long-term excavations have uncovered much of the Mississippian settlement that existed there from around AD 1150 to 1400 (Boudreaux 2011; Coe 1995).

Circular buildings that measured between 7 and 10.5 m in diameter appear to have been used as Early Mississippian houses in the North Carolina Piedmont (Figure 7.3). These structures lacked interior roof supports, which suggests that they were flexed-pole constructions, consisting of posts that were individually set into the ground at one end with the other ends being lashed together to form a roof (Boudreaux 2005:209; Lewis and Lewis 1995:60).[3] These circular structures have been identified as houses, because they are the most common kind of structure at Town Creek (n = 14), and their size seems appropriate for a domestic structure relative to other buildings at the site (Boudreaux 2007b:Figures 2.5 and 2.6, 2013:489).[4] Similar circular structures have been identified at the Leak site in North Carolina (Oliver 1992:120) and at the Charles Towne Landing site in coastal South Carolina (South 2002:Figure 6.6H), with the latter suggesting that this type of structure may have been used by Early Mississippian groups across a large region.

Identifying and investigating Early Mississippian domestic architecture at Town Creek has been challenging, because the site's long history of use has produced a dense palimpsest of features from multiple occupations that

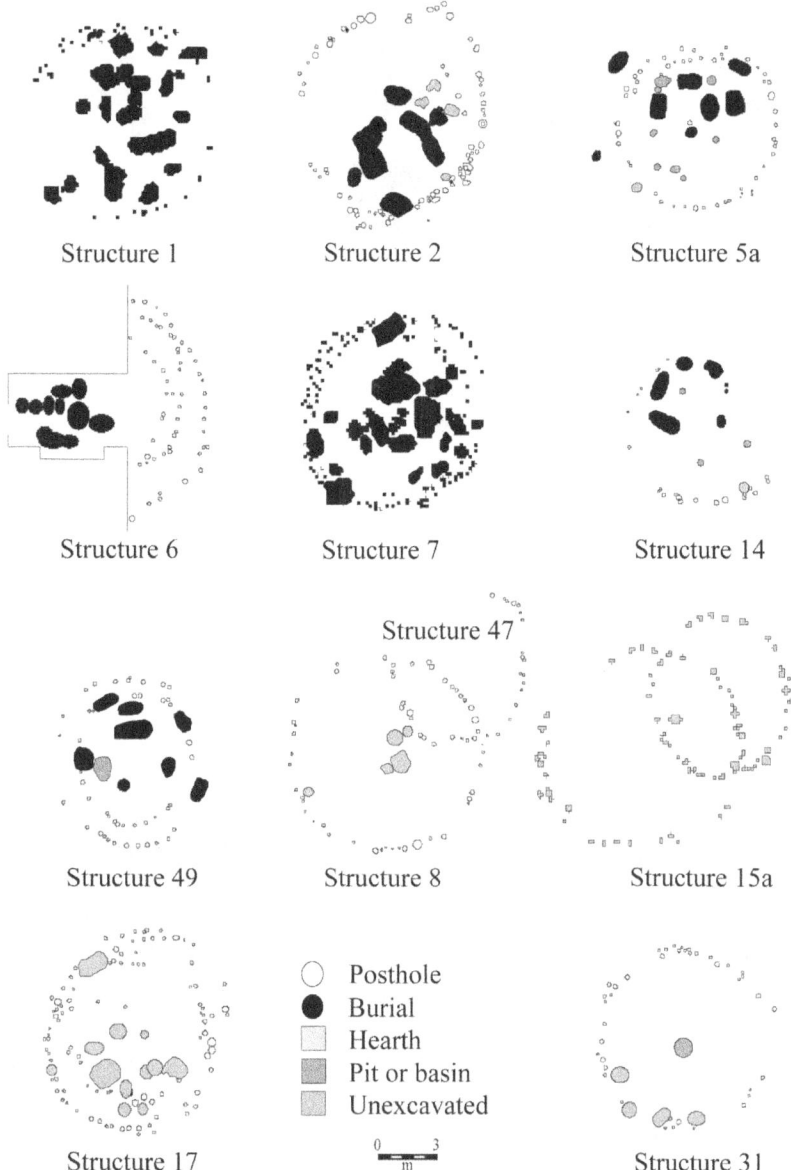

Figure 7.3. Probable Early Mississippian houses from the Town Creek site.

makes it difficult—often impossible—to isolate Early Mississippian features and structures (Boudreaux 2013:488–489). Early Mississippian houses at Town Creek are especially challenging to isolate, because several of them were transformed into large, enclosed cemeteries later in time, presumably by de-

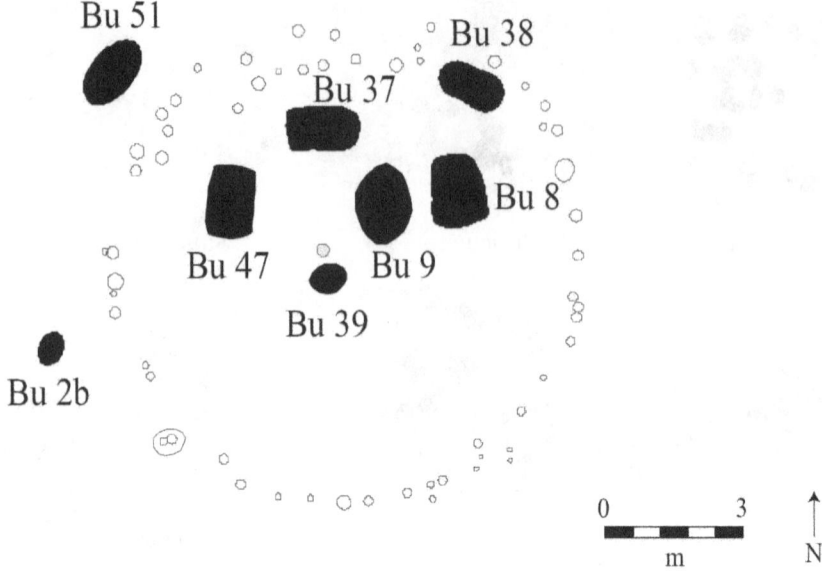

Figure 7.4. Structure 5a, an Early Mississippian domestic structure at the Town Creek site.

scendants of the family group that had once lived there (Boudreaux 2013:496). One example of an Early Mississippian circular house at Town Creek that was not disturbed by later activities is Structure 5a, a building that was covered by the northeastern edge of a platform mound that was built around AD 1300 (Figure 7.4). This not only prevented later Mississippian residents from disturbing this space but also protected this structure from plowing, a post-depositional disturbance that destroyed all but the deepest features in most non-mound contexts. Structure 5a was 8 m in diameter, with a hearth located near its center (Boudreaux 2005:121). Six burials, most of which were aligned to the cardinal directions, were located within the structure, and they were placed around an open space that contained the hearth. Two burials located outside the structure may have been associated with it, but this is not certain. Corn from a cob-filled pit (Mg2-Feature 54) within this structure produced a calibrated radiocarbon date of AD 900–1155 (2-sigma) (Boudreaux 2005:157). A Bayesian model of seven radiocarbon dates from stratified pre-mound and mound contexts produced a modeled date of AD 1035–1215 (2-sigma) for the Structure 5a sample, with the highest part of the probability curve corresponding to AD 1160, which is consistent with deposition during the Early Mississippian period (see Table 7.2).

The Early Mississippian circular houses at Town Creek and a single example from the nearby Leak site were large buildings with fully excavated examples ranging in area from 46 to 66 m². These large, circular buildings are very different from the small, rectilinear Early Mississippian houses found in many other parts of the Southeast (Lacquement 2007:4). In fact, the Early Mississippian houses of the North Carolina Piedmont are among some of the largest in the region (Table 7.3), which suggests that domestic groups there were larger than in many other places. While individual nuclear families may have occupied the smaller houses in other Mississippian communities (Smith 1995:236–238), extended families may have been the preferred co-residential group at Town Creek and Leak. The Early Mississippian houses in the Piedmont are large, but their size is not unique in the Southeast, as houses that were comparable in size have been identified at a number of late prehistoric through Contact period sites in North Carolina, South Carolina, Georgia, and Tennessee (Anderson and Schuldenrein 1985; Davis et al. 1998; Gougeon 2002; Hally 2008; Hatch 1995; South 2002:202; Sullivan 1987; Ward and Davis 1999). The geographic clustering of these sites in the northeastern part of the Southeast suggests that the large, Early Mississippian domestic structures in the North Carolina Piedmont may have been part of a more general adaptation or preference for larger domestic groups in this area. The reasons why larger domestic groups would have been preferred are not clear, but they could have included the ability of larger groups to perform subsistence activities more efficiently, advantages in pooling risk at a level above the nuclear family, or simply a cultural preference for larger households (Flannery 2002:424–425).[5]

Several square buildings that are comparable in size to the circular houses have been identified in the North Carolina Piedmont, but it is not clear if these also were domestic structures or if they were more public in nature. At the Teal site, Oliver (1992:232) identified a square structure that measured 7.6 m on a side with interior features that included a central hearth and four burials containing eight individuals.[6] This building was interpreted as a locus for special activities based on the presence of unusual objects that included four anthropomorphic faces made of fired clay and several stones with incised lines. Mississippian burials in the North Carolina Piedmont are almost always primary interments, so it is unusual that this structure contained the cremated remains of an adolescent and an adult that were buried within large ceramic jars (Oliver 1992:216, 222–223). The presence of multiple individuals in another grave is another unusual attribute of this structure's mortuary record. The initial interment within this grave was an adult male (25–35 years) who had an adolescent placed on his chest and the bundle burials of an adolescent and

Table 7.3. Attributes of Domestic Structures (sorted by size) from Selected Late Prehistoric and Contact Period Sites

Site	Phase or Period	Number of Structures	Average Size (m²)	Size Range (m²)	Total Number of Burials	Average Burial Density	Average Burials per Structure	Range of Burials per Structure	Source
Sugar Creek	Lamar	1	78.5	79	4	.05	4.00	4	Hatch 1995:Figure 7.8
Charles Towne Landing	Wilmington	1	74.7	75	-	-	-	-	South 2002:Figure 6.6H
Wall	Hillsboro	6	62.4	24–105	2	.03	.33	0–1	Davis et al. 1998:Table 49
Little Egypt	Barnett	3	59.3	41–89	5	.08	1.67	0–5	Gougeon 2002:32
Rucker's Bottom	Beaverdam	2	59.1	33–68	-	-	-	-	Anderson and Schuldenrein 1985:Figure 10.69
Leake	Town Creek	1	57.2	57	-	-	-	-	Oliver 1992:Figure 17
Ledford Island	Mouse Creek	11	56.5	28–112	21	.37	1.91	6–16	Lewis and Lewis 1995:Table 29.1 and Figure 29.2
King	Barnett	42	56.2	28–100	42	.75	1.00	0–6	Hally 2008:Table 5.1
Town Creek[a]	Early Town Creek	4	53.3	46–66	34	.64	8.50	7–10	Boudreaux 2013:Table 1
Lindsey	Lamar	1	54.1	54	7	.13	7.00	7	Hatch 1995:Figure 7.5
Sweetgum	Lamar	1	50.2	50	5	.10	5.00	5	Hatch 1995:Figure 7.11
Rymer	Mouse Creek	23	50.0	25–114	21	.42	.91	0–5	Lewis and Lewis 1995:Table 27.1 and Figure 27.5
Mouse Creeks	Mouse Creek	13	49.0	24–89	8	.16	.62	0–7	Lewis and Lewis 1995:Table 28.1 and Figures 28.2–28.3
Mouse Creeks	Dallas	4	47.5	20–107	1	.02	.25	0–1	Lewis and Lewis 1995:Table 28.1 and Figures 28.2–28.3
Ledford Island	Dallas	4	46.8	17–81	10	.21	2.50	0–8	Lewis and Lewis 1995:Table 29.1 and Figure 29.2
Toqua	Dallas	40	45.5	19–86	87	1.91	2.18	0–18	Polhemus 1987:Table 5.2

Site	Phase/Culture	N	Mean	Range					Reference
Davis	Hiwassee	1	44.6	45	-	-	-	-	Lewis and Lewis 1995:Table 25.1 and Figure 25.10
Toqua	Hiwassee Island	15	41.5	21–95	6	.14	.40	0–3	Polhemus 1987:Table 5.2
Hiwassee Island	Hiwassee Island	9	40.0	27–60	-	-	-	-	Lewis and Lewis 1946:Table 14
Rucker's Bottom	Rembert	3	38.5	33–42	-	-	-	-	Anderson and Schuldenrein 1985:560
Warren Wilson	Pisgah	10	38.1	30–56	21	.55	2.10	0–6	Dickens 1976:34–36
Ocoee	Mouse Creek	3	32.8	28–37	-	-	-	-	Lewis and Lewis 1995:Table 30.1 and Figures 30.3–30.4
Dallas	Dallas	22	31.5	18–54	-	-	-	-	Lewis and Lewis 1995:Table 23.3 and Figure 23.3
Brasstown Valley	Late Woodland/Etowah	13	28.6	15–39	NR[b]	-	-	-	Cable 2000:Figure 42
Turner	Powers	45	26.0	7–56	NR	-	-	-	O'Brien and Cogswell 2001:Table 6.2
Snodgrass	Powers	93	23.6	7–52	NR	-	-	-	O'Brien and Cogswell 2001:Table 6.2
Moundville	Moundville I	66	22.8	8–47	NR	-	-	-	Wilson 2008:Appendix 1
Hixon	Dallas	1	22.3	22	-	-	-	-	Lewis and Lewis 1995:Table 24.2 and Figures 24.25, 24.27–24.28
Dallas	Mouse Creek	2	16.9	16–18	-	-	-	-	Lewis and Lewis 1995:Table 23.3 and Figure 23.3
Sale Creek	Hiwassee Island	5	15.7	8–28	4	.25	.80	0–4	Lewis and Lewis 1995:Table 26.1 and Figure 26.4
Hixon	Hiwassee Island	4	12.5	10–17	-	-	-	-	Lewis and Lewis 1995:Table 24.2 and Figures 24.25, 24.27–24.28

Notes: a. The Town Creek data are limited to completely excavated structures that were occupied only during the Early Mississippian period.
b. NR = not reported.

an infant placed near his feet. The adult male and the adolescent at his chest both wore shell bead necklaces, and the adolescent also was associated with a square-cross shell gorget (Oliver 1992:222, Plate 52), a style associated with Early Mississippian contexts in east Tennessee that date to the late twelfth century AD (Brain and Phillips 1996:21; Sullivan 2007:Figure 5.7). Four square structures (Structures 9a, 16, 21a, and 28) in domestic areas at Town Creek are similar in size (ca. 8 m) to the Early Mississippian square structure at the Teal site, but only one of these buildings (Structure 28) has been excavated, so their chronology and function still are not clear.[7]

Several Early Mississippian public buildings have been identified at the Town Creek site. They are distinctive from domestic structures based on attributes that include their size, construction techniques, and low density of interior burials (Boudreaux 2007b:53, 55, 57). These buildings are important because their spatial arrangement, mortuary associations, and associated activities all provide insights into the nature of Early Mississippian leadership and political economy. Physically, the Town Creek community consisted of two domestic spaces to the north and south of a public axis that bisected the entire settlement (see Figure 7.2). This public axis consisted of public buildings at the eastern and western ends of a central plaza. Isolating Early Mississippian contexts in the public area on the east side of the plaza has been challenging, because later activities were not separated stratigraphically, and no radiocarbon dates are associated with this area, but at least one likely Early Mississippian public building has been identified in this area. The identification of Early Mississippian contexts at the west end of the plaza has been facilitated by the fact that a platform mound built there around AD 1300 sealed earlier deposits and stratigraphically separated them from later ones (Boudreaux 2005:114–132). These pre-mound contexts include an extensive midden deposit and the remains of three, superimposed sets of public buildings that were used at different times during the Early Mississippian period (Figure 7.5).[8] Dates from a Bayesian model of radiocarbon dates from these stratified deposits, especially the first set of public buildings (AD 1165–1270, 2-sigma) and an extensive pre-mound midden deposit (AD 1095–1260, 2-sigma) (see Table 7.2), indicate that public architecture and public events were in place by the mid-1100s to early 1200s.

Several of the Early Mississippian public buildings at Town Creek contained burials, and the interment of these individuals in public buildings instead of within one of the houses along the plaza where most people were buried indicates that different statuses were being expressed by burial location. Furthermore, the lower burial densities for these public buildings relative to the

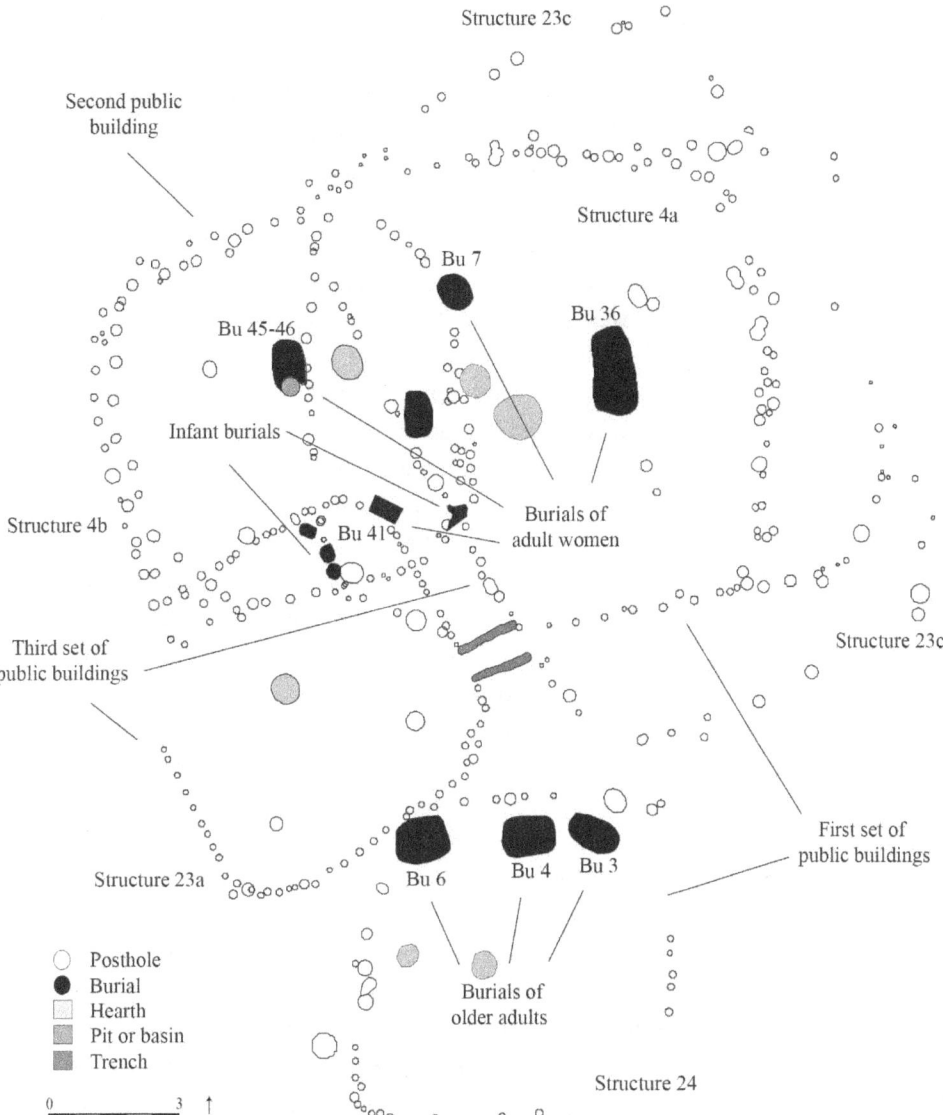

Figure 7.5. Early Mississippian public buildings located along the west end of the plaza at the Town Creek site.

circular houses in the domestic areas suggest that the criteria used for inclusion in the former were more exclusive than those used for the latter. As such, who these people were and what they were buried with may provide some insights into activities and attributes that were considered important within the context of community leadership during the Early Mississippian period at Town Creek.

The burials of seven adults and two children were associated with the first two sets of public buildings (Structures 4a, 4b, and 24) (Boudreaux 2005:273–280, 2010a:204–212). The smaller building (Structure 24) in the first set of public structures contained the burials of three older adults (> 35 years), two males and a female, which suggests that older individuals, perhaps those who had distinguished themselves through their achievements, were esteemed and that they played prominent roles within the community (Boudreaux 2007b:82–83, 2010a:213). One of these individuals—an older adult male—was buried with six bone needles that likely were part of a ceremonial skin scratcher like those used by historic native groups (Boudreaux 2005:Figure 5.5, 2007b:70; Coe 1995:Figure 13.6). Ceremonial scratchers were used for scratching, scarification, and tattooing as part of ritual activities that often were associated with political or ritual leaders and high-status individuals (Coe 1995:240; Dye 2000:8; Hudson 1976:415–416; Lefler 1967:49; Speck 1979:121; Swanton 1979:564; Waselkov and Braund 1995:71, 122, 144). The two larger structures (Structures 4a and 4b) in the first two sets of public buildings contained the burials of four adult females.[9] The absence of adult males from these buildings is interesting, because men are often associated with public contexts in Mississippian communities (Hally 1994:241–245; Sullivan 2001:110). If matrilineality was important during the Early Mississippian period at Town Creek, as it is assumed to have been in late prehistoric societies across the Southeast (Hally 2008:309; Hudson 1976:189; Knight 1990:5–6), then the presence of these women in public buildings may reflect their status as prominent members of their own kin groups, a role that also may have been associated with influence or authority at a community-wide scale (Boudreaux 2007b:82, 2010a:212–213).

The third set of Early Mississippian public buildings on the west side of the plaza are those that were in use immediately before the mound was built. These structures have not been associated with any radiocarbon dates, but they likely were in use between ca. AD 1250–1300 based on modeled dates associated with stratigraphically earlier and later public buildings. This set of buildings consisted of a large structure and a small, earth-embanked structure that were joined by an entrance trench. The large (152 m^2) building (Structure 23c), which appears to have been a pavilion or ramada, overlaps with at least two other structures, so it is not clear which internal features were associated with it. The size of the large structure and its location adjacent to the plaza suggest that activities associated with it were accessible, or at least visible, to large segments of the community. In contrast, access to the structure that it was paired with (Structure 23a) probably was more limited, based on its smaller size (49 m^2), restricted entrance, and location away from the plaza. Adult burials were not associated with either structure, but a cluster of four infant burials may have been (Boudreaux 2005:128–131, 2007b:70).

The smaller, earth-embanked structure in the third set of public buildings (Structure 23a) was relatively well preserved beneath the first construction stage of the mound (Boudreaux 2005:126–131). Materials recovered from inside this structure include several ornaments, a fragment of copper, and the bowl of a ceramic pipe (Armour 2012:84–85), objects that are consistent with this structure having been a special context. Several bone artifacts—including a needle, an awl, and the dentary of a longnose gar—also were found in this structure (Armour 2012:85). While these objects could have been used for some kind of craft production, Armour (2012:84–85) speculates that they, along with a lump of graphite also from the structure, might have been used for ritual scratching and tattooing (see Deter-Wolf 2013; Marcoux 2010:159). The presence of bone tools that could have been used for scarification and tattooing is reminiscent of the bone needles found with the older adult male buried in the earlier small public building (Structure 24), and suggests that similar activities were associated with these small, public buildings throughout the Early Mississippian period.

Faunal remains from inside Structure 23a indicate the consumption of deer, turkey, and passenger pigeon (Armour 2012:85; Scott 2012). The presence of passenger pigeon is especially intriguing, because this species has been associated at other Mississippian sites with special contexts that include high-status burials and residences, ritual buildings, and mound contexts (Jackson and Scott 1995:110 and 116, 2003:554). Passenger pigeon at Town Creek (n = 111) has a limited distribution as well, with nearly all specimens being found either in the public areas on the west side of the plaza (n = 52), in both mound and pre-mound contexts, or in the largest cemetery in the domestic area (n = 52) (Structure 7).[10] Structure 23a's small size, narrow entrance, and association with a special food all suggest that access to the activities that took place in this building was more restricted. An emphasis on limited access and small groups is consistent with an analysis of ceramic vessels that showed that the smaller Early Mississippian public buildings in sub-mound contexts were associated with a high proportion of small vessels (Boudreaux 2007b:100, 2010b:26–27). These Early Mississippian archaeological patterns at Town Creek are reminiscent of the distinction in some ethnohistorically documented Cherokee and Creek towns between public spaces that were relatively more accessible and public spaces that were more exclusive in nature (Rodning 2002:12–13; Schroedl 1986:219–224; Waselkov and Braund 1995:102–105).

At the east end of Town Creek's plaza, another earth-embanked building (Structure 22) appears to have been in use at the end of the Early Mississippian period, around AD 1250. Unfortunately, nothing can be said about the activities that took place within Structure 22, because plowing has obliterated everything but its postholes and entrance trench. It is likely, though, that Structures 22 and 23a faced each other across the plaza, because they are very similar in size, shape, orientation, and construction (Boudreaux 2007b:49). The presence of two very similar, possibly contemporaneous structures that face each other on opposite ends of Town Creek's public axis is interesting, given the presence of two discrete domestic areas located on either side of this public axis. This suggests the existence during the Early Mississippian period of an intermediary social grouping such as a moiety between the level of the household group and that of the entire community (see Means 2007:45–48). It is possible that Structures 22 and 23a—very similar structures that likely faced each other across the plaza—represent public buildings associated with the two major social segments that constituted the Town Creek community at the end of the Early Mississippian period.

Discussion

It is likely that Mississippian lifeways did not appear in the North Carolina Piedmont until around AD 1150–1200, a process that coincided with the appearance of complicated stamped pottery, the design elements of which expressed fundamental aspects of Mississippian ideology. The majority of Mississippian sites in the Piedmont likely were small farmsteads or hamlets, but several larger, more intensively occupied settlements also developed. The largest of these new communities was the civic-ceremonial center at Town Creek, with 10–15 large houses and multiple areas that contained distinctive elements of public architecture. Town Creek represented a very different kind of settlement relative to the smaller settlements that previously existed in the region (Davis and Ward 1991:52; Ward and Davis 1999:101).

The processes that shaped the development of the center at Town Creek are not known, but it is likely that a number of factors played some role in pushing and pulling people into this large settlement. The creation of the Early Mississippian settlement at Town Creek may have been related to changing subsistence practices, such as the intensification of corn agriculture (Anderson and Sassaman 2012:158–159). Based on ethnographic examples, a nucleated settlement like Town Creek could develop if farming involved multiple social groups cooperating in different agricultural tasks (Flannery 2002:431).

Nucleation could also result if farmers used a scattered-fields strategy to minimize risk and settled in a location that was central to their multiple fields (Flannery 2002:431). Corn does not appear to have become a staple in the North Carolina Piedmont until AD 1000 or later, although little actually is known about the timing and tempo of its appearance and intensification in the region (Anderson 1989:113; Ward 1983:72–73). Corn remains are present, and in some cases ubiquitous, at the largest Early Mississippian sites in the North Carolina Piedmont (Mountjoy 1989:19; Oliver 1992:Figure 38, Table 4; Trinkley 1995:129).

Another factor in the development of the large Early Mississippian settlement at Town Creek could have been inter-community conflict. If raiding and warfare was a concern, then the benefits of mutual protection offered by a large settlement would have been a significant reason for aggregation (Anderson and Sassaman 2012:160; Blitz 1999:589). One indication that defense was important throughout the Early Mississippian period at Town Creek is that the town was encircled by a palisade that was rebuilt multiple times. At least five palisade lines are present at Town Creek, and all of them appear to predate ca. AD 1300 (see Figure 7.2) (Boudreaux 2013:492). More direct evidence for violence comes from the fact that some of the burials at Town Creek—13 of 92 (14 percent) complete enough to be fully analyzed—exhibit traumatic injuries (Driscoll 2001:Table 5.15–5.16). Injuries include long-bone fractures, skull fractures, and a projectile point embedded in the vertebra of an adult male (Driscoll 2001:Table 5.15–5.16). While trauma patterns unique to the Early Mississippian period community cannot be determined, because the proportion of Early Mississippian burials within Town Creek's overall burial population is not known, the overall patterns indicate that men were much more likely than women to exhibit traumatic injuries and that individuals with trauma were more likely to be associated with artifacts (Driscoll 2001:152–153). These patterns are consistent with the conducting of warfare by men in Mississippian societies and participation in warfare as a means to enhance one's status (Hally 2008:493–494; Sullivan 2001:124).

Some of the most visible elements of Town Creek's archaeological record are the spaces that were associated with household groups. Rebuilding houses in place and burying people within household spaces may have been important practices that helped to establish and maintain household-group identity and cohesion within the civic-ceremonial center at Town Creek, a place that would have represented a new kind of social milieu where individuals from different groups may have been in regular contact for the first time, where groups would have been competing to attract and retain members, and where groups would have been competing to acquire and defend resources (Brown 2007; Knight 1990:6; Muller 1997:190).

Although houses at Town Creek were not unique in the Southeast because of their size, they certainly were distinctive based on the number of burials that they eventually contained. Several structures (Structures 1, 7, 10, and 15b) appear to have started as circular houses during the Early Mississippian period, but they evolved into enclosed cemeteries that were used beyond AD 1300 (Boudreaux 2007b:Figure 2.5, 2013:489–490). The regular arrangement of the burials within Structure 5a is informative, because it suggests that the dense, seemingly chaotic clusters of burials in other domestic-area cemeteries at Town Creek may have started as orderly, organized burial spaces within the floors of Early Mississippian houses. This idea is supported by Rosenwinkel's (2013) analysis of the Structure 7 cemetery—the largest at Town Creek, with 50 individuals buried in 40 graves—which indicates that this large, complex burial space began as four graves arranged around a central, open area.

The placement of burial clusters within household spaces in prominent locations around Town Creek's plaza—which may reflect the creation of ancestors as a way to emphasize group identity and continuity through time (Hally and Kelly 1998:61; McAnany 1995:8; Wilson 2010)—suggests that corporate groups played important roles in Town Creek's social, political, and economic life from the time of its founding during the Early Mississippian period. The presence at Town Creek of discrete, dense clusters of burials associated with large domestic structures—something that was not seen before in the North Carolina Piedmont—suggests that even if corporate groups had existed in the region prior to the Early Mississippian period, something new was occurring at Town Creek. Corporate groups may have developed, or at least became more formally organized—and hence, more archaeologically visible—within the Early Mississippian town at Town Creek as a way to structure social interactions as part of a strategy to efficiently organize, control, and distribute labor and resources (see Ensor 2011:205). These changes may have been a reaction to life within this new kind of settlement, an adaptation to the changing lifeways associated with the intensification of corn agriculture, or partly a reaction to both.

The division of the Early Mississippian domestic areas at Town Creek into two parts suggests that dual organization, the division of society into two major sections, may have been an important structuring principal within this community. Among a number of Historic period southeastern Indian groups, the roles played by the two social divisions varied considerably, but they included marriage regulation and responsibility for complementary aspects of ritual practices (Hudson 1976:234; Knight 1990:6; Swanton 1979:663; Urban and Jackson 2004:697). The practice of dual organization also was used as a way to incorporate into an existing community groups that previously had been politically autonomous or of a different ethnicity (Blitz 1999:584–585; Johnson et al. 2008:8–9). It is possible that dual organization served a similar purpose during the Early Mississippian period at Town Creek, when it would have been necessary to incorporate different corporate groups into the large community that had developed there (see Blitz 1999:585).

Summary and Conclusions

Mississippian lifeways appeared in the southern Piedmont of North Carolina around AD 1150, as indicated by the spread of complicated stamped ceramics. Although the full range of Mississippian cultural practices that accompanied this change in ceramics is not known, the nucleation of people into the Early Mississippian community at Town Creek represented a significant departure from earlier settlements, and it appears that new social and ceremonial practices were developed or adopted as well. New social practices included the formation of household groups, probably corporate kin groups, which likely served as efficient units for organizing people, labor, and resources and for regulating social relationships within this new kind of settlement. The development and persistence of these household-group spaces and the emphasis on mortuary activities within them may reflect efforts by group members to maintain group identity and compete for resources within a context of increased interaction and competition within a new kind of community, the civic-ceremonial center at Town Creek. Household groups appear to have been integrated at multiple levels above that of the individual group. The presence of two discrete domestic areas suggests that multiple corporate groups may have been integrated as moieties in a dual organization system similar to that used by southeastern Indian groups during the Historic period. Also, ceremonial activities that took place in Town Creek's public areas likely helped to integrate corporate groups at a community-wide scale. Some public ceremonial activities appear to have been truly communal and integrative in nature, possibly involving large groups of people as participants or spectators. Other activities that occurred in public spaces appear to have been more exclusive in nature.

Very little research has focused explicitly on investigating Early Mississippian societies and Mississippian origins in the North Carolina Piedmont, so there is still much that is not known about these topics. A few suggestions for future research are offered here. The large dataset from the extensive excavations at Town Creek dominates the interpretations presented in this chapter, and, although there is still much to learn about Town Creek itself, future research should explore beyond that site to try and understand Mississippian origins in the southern Piedmont from a more regional scale. The importance of a more regional perspective is indicated by the fact that such a view was necessary for developing the argument presented in this chapter that Mississippian cultural practices likely appeared later than originally thought. Also, although it is speculated that the spread of Mississippian cultural practices, the appearance of larger settlements, and the intensification of corn agriculture were related processes in the Piedmont, more information from many sites across the region will be needed because little is actually known about the timing of sedentism, the intensification of corn agriculture, or the full range of settlement types that existed within pre-Mississippian and Early Mississippian societies in the region. Another direction for future research should be to develop and test models for various ways in which Mississippian cultural practices could have spread into the region (see Blitz and Lorenz 2002; Pauketat 2003). For many years, Mississippian origins in the North Carolina Piedmont have been characterized as "[o]ne of the best archeological records of the movement of a people in the southeast" (Coe 1952:308). Although current interpretations emphasize the spread of ideas rather than people (Boudreaux 2007b:65; Ward and Davis 1999:133), how Mississippian cultural practices spread into the North Carolina Piedmont remains unresolved. A related question is why this new way of life, whether it was brought by new people or new ideas, was isolated to a relatively restricted area in the southern Piedmont. Why did those people or ideas not continue to spread to the north or east, where contemporaneous societies exhibited very different cultural practices? Hopefully, the questions raised and the topics discussed in this chapter will help relate Early Mississippian in the North Carolina Piedmont to developments in other regions and prompt new research directions into the origins of these societies at the northeastern edge of the Mississippian world.

Notes

1. Dates in this chapter are based on calibrated radiocarbon dates derived from the CALIB (Stuiver et al. 2005) and OXCAL (Bronk Ramsey 2009) calibration software packages.

2. Both Leak and Teal show strong Early Mississippian occupations, but they exhibit later components as well.

3. Similar circular, flexed-pole houses were built by the Caddo of the trans-Mississippi Southeast (see Swanton 1996:148–154).

4. The total number of circular houses present during the Early Mississippian period is

not clear for several reasons. Several circular structures have been only tentatively identified because they have not been fully excavated (Boudreaux 2007b:20–22). Also, while all of the circular structures identified as houses are assumed to date to the Early Mississippian period, only a few of them have been dated based on superposition or an association with diagnostic ceramics (Boudreaux 2005:219–225). Furthermore, it is not clear if the structures that have been identified represent all of the Early Mississippian houses that were present at Town Creek. Palisade lines extend some distance to the north and south away from the core of the site, which suggests that additional Early Mississippian structures may be present in uninvestigated areas at the margins of the site.

The structures at Town Creek identified as circular houses include Structures 2, 5a, 6, 8, 14, 15a, 17, 31, and 49. Additional circular houses are indicated by the interior circular posthole patterns of Structures 1, 7, 10, and 15b. These four structures have been interpreted as houses that evolved into enclosed cemeteries later in Town Creek's history (Boudreaux 2007b:19–20, 2013:490). Additionally, a cluster of eight burials (Burial Cluster 40) located at the west end of the domestic area on the south side of the plaza is assumed to represent the burials within an Early Mississippian domestic structure whose pattern of circular postholes could not be identified (Boudreaux 2005:188). Several other structures (Structures 12, 21b, and 36) previously identified as circular houses (Boudreaux 2005:Figure 3.70) are not considered here, because their existence either is in doubt or has been disproved (Boudreaux et al. 2009).

5. It must be emphasized that the structure data used for comparison are those that were easily accessible through available publications, reports, and dissertations. They do not constitute a representative sample of structures from across the Southeast.

6. Oliver (1992:232) interprets three of these burials as postdating the use of the structure, but the basis for this interpretation is not clear.

7. These structures originally were attributed to the Late Mississippian period (Boudreaux 2007b:26), but this designation should be reevaluated.

8. This pre-mound midden, designated Level A by the excavators at Town Creek (Boudreaux 2005:55; Coe 1995:Table 4.1), is at least 800m^2 in area.

9. These two structures overlap, so it is not possible to determine with which structure individual burials were associated.

10. Inferences about the distribution of passenger pigeon are based on my examination of the analysis sheets for individual contexts compiled by Homes Hogue and Jack Wilson in their analysis of the faunal remains at Town Creek for a chapter (Wilson and Hogue 1995) in Coe's (1995) book on the site. These analysis sheets are part of the Joffre Lanning Coe Papers curated by the North Carolina State Archives in Raleigh.

References Cited

Anderson, David G.
- 1989 The Mississippian in South Carolina. In *Studies in South Carolina Archaeology: Essays in Honor of Robert L. Stephenson*, edited by Albert. C. Goodyear III and Glen. T. Hanson, pp. 101–131. Anthropological Studies, Occasional Paper 9. South Carolina Institute of Archaeology and Anthropology. University of South Carolina, Columbia.
- 1994 *The Savannah River Chiefdoms: Political Change in the Late Prehistoric Southeast.* University of Alabama Press, Tuscaloosa.

1997   The Role of Cahokia in the Evolution of Southeastern Mississippian Society. In *Cahokia: Domination and Ideology in the Mississippian World*, edited by Timothy R. Pauketat and Thomas E. Emerson, pp. 248–268. University of Nebraska Press, Lincoln.

1999   Examining Chiefdoms in the Southeast: An Application of Multiscalar Analysis. In *Great Towns and Regional Polities in the Prehistoric American Southwest and Southeast*, edited by Jill E. Neitzel, pp. 215–241. University of New Mexico Press, Albuquerque.

Anderson, David G., and Kenneth E. Sassaman

2012   *Recent Developments in Southeastern Archaeology*. Society for American Archaeology Press, Washington, D.C.

Anderson, David G., and Joseph Schuldenrein

1985   *Prehistoric Human Ecology along the Upper Savannah River: Excavations at the Rucker's Bottom, Abbeville, and Bullard Site Groups, Volume II*. Russell Papers. Archeological Services Branch, National Park Service, Atlanta.

Armour, Daryl W.

2012   Comparison of Artifacts and Activities among Mound Area Contexts at Town Creek, a Mississippian Site in Piedmont North Carolina. Unpublished master's thesis, Department of Anthropology, East Carolina University, Greenville.

Beck, Robin A. Jr.

2009   Catawba Coalescence and the Shattering of the Carolina Piedmont, 1540–1675. In *Mapping the Mississippian Shatter Zone: The Colonial Indian Slave Trade and Regional Instability in the American South*, edited by Robbie Ethridge and Sheri M. Shuck-Hall, pp. 115–141. University of Nebraska Press, Lincoln.

Blitz, John H.

1993   *Ancient Chiefdoms of the Tombigbee*. University of Alabama Press, Tuscaloosa.

1999   Mississippian Chiefdoms and the Fission-Fusion Process. *American Antiquity* 64(4): 577–592.

2010   New Perspectives in Mississippian Archaeology. *Journal of Archaeological Research* 18:1–39.

Blitz, John H., and Karl G. Lorenz

2002   The Early Mississippian Frontier in the Lower Chattahoochee–Apalachicola River Valley. *Southeastern Archaeology* 21(2):117–135.

Bobyarchick, Andy R., and John A. Diemar

2000   Land Regions and Geology. In *The North Carolina Atlas: Portrait for a New Century*, edited by Doug M. Orr Jr. and Alfred W. Stuart, pp. 10–21. University of North Carolina Press, Chapel Hill.

Boudreaux, Edmond A. III

2005   The Archaeology of Town Creek: Chronology, Community Patterns, and Leadership at a Mississippian Town. Unpublished Ph.D. dissertation, Department of Anthropology, University of North Carolina, Chapel Hill.

2007a   A Mississippian Ceramic Chronology for the Town Creek Region. *North Carolina Archaeology* 56:1–57.

2007b   *The Archaeology of Town Creek*. University of Alabama Press, Tuscaloosa.

2010a   Mound Construction and Change in the Mississippian Community at Town Creek. In *Mississippian Mortuary Practices: Beyond Hierarchy and the Representationist Perspec-*

tive, edited by Robert C. Mainfort Jr. and Lynne P. Sullivan, pp. 195–233. University Press of Florida, Gainesville.
2010b   A Functional Analysis of Mississippian Ceramic Vessels from Town Creek. *Southeastern Archaeology* 29(1):8–30.
2011   The Current State of Town Creek Research: What Have We Learned after the First 75 Years? In *The Archaeology of North Carolina: Three Archaeological Symposia*, edited by Charles R. Ewen, Thomas R. Whyte, and R. P. Stephen Davis Jr. Publication Number 30. North Carolina Archaeological Council, Raleigh.
2013   Community and Ritual within the Mississippian Center at Town Creek. *American Antiquity* 78(3):483–501.

Boudreaux, Edmond A. III, R. P. Stephen Davis Jr., and Brett H. Riggs
2009   *2009 Archaeological Investigations at Town Creek Indian Mound State Historic Site*. Research Report No. 30. Research Laboratories of Archaeology, University of North Carolina, Chapel Hill.

Brain, Jeffrey P., and Philip Phillips
1996   *Shell Gorgets: Styles of the Late Prehistoric and Protohistoric Southeast*. Peabody Museum Press, Cambridge.

Bronk Ramsey, C.
2009   Bayesian Analysis of Radiocarbon Dates. *Radiocarbon* 51(1):337–360.

Brown, James A.
1981   The Search for Rank in Prehistoric Burials. In *The Archaeology of Death*, edited by Robert Chapman, Ian Kinnes, and Klavs Randsborg, pp. 25–37. Cambridge University Press, Cambridge.
2007   The Social House in Southeastern Archaeology. In *The Durable House: House Society Models in Archaeology*, edited by Robin A. Beck Jr., pp. 227–247. Center for Archaeological Investigations, Occasional Paper No. 35. Southern Illinois University, Carbondale.

Butler, Ruth Lapham
1934   *Journal of Paul Du Ru [February 1 to May 8, 1700]: Missionary Priest to Louisiana*. Caxton Club, Chicago.

Cable, John S.
2000   Late Woodland and Etowah Occupations. *Early Georgia* 28(2):102–111.

Caldwell, Joseph R.
1958   *Trend and Tradition in the Prehistory of the Eastern United States*. Memoir No. 88. American Anthropological Association, Springfield, Illinois.

Cobb, Charles R.
2003   Mississippian Chiefdoms: How Complex? *Annual Review of Anthropology* 32:63–84.

Coe, Joffre L.
1952   The Cultural Sequence of the Carolina Piedmont. In *Archeology of Eastern United States*, edited by James B. Griffin, pp. 301–311. University of Chicago Press, Chicago.
1964   *The Formative Cultures of the Carolina Piedmont*. Transactions of the American Philosophical Society, Vol. 54, Part 5. The Society, Philadelphia.
1995   *Town Creek Indian Mound: A Native American Legacy*. University of North Carolina Press, Chapel Hill.

Davis, R. P. Stephen Jr., Patrick Livingood, H. Trawick Ward, and Vincas P. Steponaitis
1998   *Excavating Occaneechi Town: Archaeology of an Eighteenth-Century Indian Village in North Carolina*. University of North Carolina Press, Chapel Hill.

Davis, R. P. Stephen Jr., and H. Trawick Ward
1991 The Evolution of Siouan Communities in Piedmont North Carolina. *Southeastern Archaeology* 10(1):40–53.

Deter-Wolf, Aaron
2013 Needle in a Haystack: Examining the Archaeological Evidence for Prehistoric Tattooing. In *Drawing with Great Needles: Ancient Tattoo Traditions of North America*, edited by Aaron Deter-Wolf and Carol Diaz-Granados, pp. 43–72. University of Texas Press, Austin.

Dickens, Roy S.
1976 *Cherokee Prehistory: The Pisgah Phase in the Appalachian Summit Region*. University of Tennessee Press, Knoxville.

Driscoll, Elizabeth Monahan
2001 Bioarchaeology, Mortuary Patterning, and Social Organization at Town Creek. Unpublished Ph.D. dissertation, Department of Anthropology, University of North Carolina, Chapel Hill.

Dye, David H.
2000 The Accoutrements of High Office: Elite Ritual Paraphernalia from Pickwick Basin. Paper presented at the 57th Annual Meeting of the Southeastern Archaeological Conference, Macon.

Eastman, Jane M.
1994 The North Carolina Radiocarbon Date Study (Part 1). *Southern Indian Studies* 42:1–63.

Ensor, Bradley E.
2011 Kinship Theory in Archaeology: From Critiques to the Study of Transformations. *American Antiquity* 76(2):203–227.

Ferguson, Leland G.
1971 South Appalachian Mississippian. Unpublished Ph.D. dissertation, Department of Anthropology, University of North Carolina, Chapel Hill.

Flannery, Kent V.
2002 The Origins of the Village Revisited: From Nuclear to Extended Households. *American Antiquity* 67(3):417–433.

Goldstein, Lynne G.
1980 *Mississippian Mortuary Practices: A Case Study of Two Cemeteries in the Lower Illinois Valley*. Scientific Papers No. 4. Northwestern University Archeological Program, Evanston.

Gougeon, Ramie A.
2002 Household Research at the Late Mississippian Little Egypt site (9MU102). Unpublished Ph.D. dissertation, Department of Anthropology, University of Georgia, Athens.

Griffin, James B.
1985 Changing Concepts of the Prehistoric Mississippian Cultures of the Eastern United States. In *Alabama and the Borderlands: From Prehistory to Statehood*, edited by R. Reid Badger and Lawrence A. Clayton, pp. 40–63. University of Alabama Press, Tuscaloosa.

Hally, David J.
1994 An Overview of Lamar Culture. In *Ocumulgee Archaeology, 1936–1986*, edited by David J. Hally, pp. 144–174. University of Georgia Press, Athens.
1996 Platform-Mound Construction and the Instability of Mississippian Chiefdoms. In

Political Structure and Change in the Prehistoric Southeastern United States, edited by John F. Scarry, pp. 92–127. University Press of Florida, Gainesville.

2008 *King: The Social Archaeology of a Late Mississippian Town in Northwestern Georgia.* University of Alabama Press, Tuscaloosa.

Hally, David J., and Hypatia Kelly

1998 The Nature of Mississippian Towns in Georgia: The King Site Example. In *Mississippian Towns and Sacred Spaces: Searching for an Architectural Grammar*, edited by R. Barry Lewis and Charles Stout, pp. 49–63. University of Alabama Press, Tuscaloosa.

Hatch, James W.

1995 Lamar Period Upland Farmsteads of the Oconee River Valley, Georgia. In *Mississippian Communities and Households*, edited by J. Daniel Rogers and Bruce D. Smith, pp. 135–155. University of Alabama Press, Tuscaloosa.

Holley, George R.

1999 Late Prehistoric Towns in the Southeast. In *Great Towns and Regional Polities in the Prehistoric American Southwest and Southeast*, edited by Jill E. Neitzel, pp. 22–38. University of New Mexico Press, Albuquerque.

Howell, Todd L., and Keith W. Kintigh

1996 Archaeological Identification of Kin Groups Using Mortuary and Biological Data: An Example from the American Southwest. *American Antiquity* 61(3):537–554.

Hudson, Charles

1976 *The Southeastern Indians.* University of Tennessee Press, Knoxville.

1990 *The Juan Pardo Expeditions: Exploration of the Carolinas and Tennessee, 1566–1568.* Smithsonian Institution Press, Washington, D.C.

Jackson, H. Edwin, and Susan L. Scott

1995 The Faunal Record of the Southeastern Elite: The Implications of Economy, Social Relations, and Ideology. *Southeastern Archaeology* 14(2):103–119.

2003 Patterns of Elite Faunal Utilization at Moundville, Alabama. *American Antiquity* 68(3):552–572.

Johnson, Jay K., John W. O'Hear, Robbie Ethridge, Brad R. Lieb, Susan L. Scott, and H. Edwin Jackson

2008 Measuring Chickasaw Adaptation on the Western Frontier of the Colonial South: A Correlation of Documentary and Archaeological Data. *Southeastern Archaeology* 27(1):1–30.

King, Adam

2010 Multiple Groups, Overlapping Symbols, and the Creation of a Sacred Space at Etowah's Mound C. In *Mississippian Mortuary Practices: Beyond Hierarchy and the Representationist Perspective*, edited by Lynne P. Sullivan and Robert C. Mainfort Jr., pp. 54–73. University Press of Florida, Gainesville.

Knight, Vernon J. Jr.

1986 The Institutional Organization of Mississippian Religion. *American Antiquity* 51(4):675–687.

1990 Social Organization and the Evolution of Hierarchy in Southeastern Chiefdoms. *Journal of Anthropological Research* 46(1):1–22.

1998 Moundville as a Diagrammatic Ceremonial Center. In *Archaeology of the Moundville Chiefdom*, edited by Vernon J. Knight Jr. and Vincas P. Steponaitis, pp. 44–62. Smithsonian Institution Press, Washington, D.C.

2001 Feasting and the Emergence of Platform Mound Ceremonialism in Eastern North America. In *Feasts: Archaeological and Ethnographic Perspectives on Food, Politics, and Power*, edited by Michael Dietler and Brian Hayden, pp. 311–333. Smithsonian Institution Press, Washington, D.C.
2004 Characterizing Elite Midden Deposits at Moundville. *American Antiquity* 69(2):304–321.

Lacquement, Cameron H.
2007 Typology, Chronology, and Technological Changes of Mississippian Domestic Architecture in West-Central Alabama. In *Architectural Variability in the Southeast*, edited by Cameron H. Lacquement, pp. 49–72. University of Alabama Press, Tuscaloosa.

Lankford, George E.
2004 World on a String: Some Cosmological Components of the Southeastern Ceremonial Complex. In *Hero, Hawk, and Open Hand: American Indian Art of the Ancient Midwest and South*, edited by Richard F. Townsend and Robert V. Sharp, pp. 207–217. Yale University Press, New Haven.

Lefler, Hugh T.
1967 *A New Voyage to Carolina*. University of North Carolina Press, Chapel Hill.

Lewis, R. Barry, Charles Stout, and Cameron B. Wesson
1998 The Design of Mississippian Towns. In *Mississippian Towns and Sacred Spaces: Searching for an Architectural Grammar*, edited by R. Barry Lewis and Charles Stout, pp. 1–21. University of Alabama Press, Tuscaloosa.

Lewis, Thomas M. N., and Madeline D. Kneberg Lewis
1946 *Hiwassee Island: An Archaeological Account of Four Tennessee Indian Peoples*. University of Tennessee Press, Knoxville.
1995 *The Prehistory of the Chickamauga Basin in Tennessee*, edited by Lynne P. Sullivan. University of Tennessee Press, Knoxville.

Lindauer, Owen, and John H. Blitz
1997 Higher Ground: The Archaeology of North American Platform Mounds. *Journal of Archaeological Research* 5(2):169–207.

Marcoux, Jon B.
2010 The Materialization of Status and Social Structure at Koger's Island Cemetery, Alabama. In *Mississippian Mortuary Practices: Beyond Hierarchy and the Representationist Perspective*, edited by Lynne P. Sullivan and Robert C. Mainfort Jr., pp. 145–173. University Press of Florida, Gainesville.

McAnany, Patricia A.
1995 *Living with the Ancestors: Kinship and Kingship in Ancient Maya Society*. University of Texas Press, Austin.

Means, Bernard K.
2007 *Circular Villages of the Monongahela Tradition*. University of Alabama Press, Tuscaloosa.

Mountjoy, Joseph B.
1989 Early Radiocarbon Dates from a Site on the Pee Dee–Siouan Frontier in the Piedmont of Central North Carolina. *Southern Indian Studies* 38:7–21.

Muller, Jon
1997 *Mississippian Political Economy*. PlenumPress, New York.

O'Brien, Michael J., and James W. Cogswell
  2001   The Construction and Abandonment of Powers Phase Structures. In *Mississippian Community Organization: The Powers Phase in Southeastern Missouri*, edited by Michael J. O'Brien, pp. 141–180. Kluwer Academic, New York.
Oliver, Billy L.
  1992   Settlements of the Pee Dee Culture. Unpublished Ph.D. dissertation, Department of Anthropology, University of North Carolina, Chapel Hill.
Pauketat, Timothy R.
  2003   Resettled Farmers and the Making of a Mississippian Polity. *American Antiquity* 68(1):39–66.
Pluckhahn, Thomas
  2010   The Sacred and the Secular Revisited: The Essential Tensions of Early Village Society in the Southeastern United States. In *Becoming Villagers: Comparing Early Village Societies*, edited by Matthew S. Bandy and Jake R. Fox, pp. 100–118. University of Arizona Press, Tucson.
Polhemus, Richard R.
  1987   *The Toqua Site: A Late Mississippian Dallas Phase Town*. Report of Investigations No. 41. Department of Anthropology, University of Tennessee. Publications in Anthropology 44. Tennessee Valley Authority, Knoxville.
  1990   Dallas Phase Architecture and Sociopolitical Structure. In *Lamar Archaeology: Mississippian Chiefdoms in the Deep South*, edited by Mark Williams and Guy Shapiro, pp. 125–138. University of Alabama Press, Tuscaloosa.
Reid, James J. Jr.
  1967   Pee Dee Pottery from the Mound at Town Creek. Unpublished master's thesis, Department of Anthropology, University of North Carolina, Chapel Hill.
Riggs, Brett H., R. P. Stephen Davis Jr, and Duane Esarey
  2014   Archaeology at Ashe Ferry: The Late Woodland Period in the Lower Catawba River Valley. Draft final report submitted to the South Carolina Department of Transportation. Research Laboratories of Archaeology, University of North Carolina, Chapel Hill.
Rodning, Christopher B.
  2002   The Townhouse at Coweeta Creek. *Southeastern Archaeology* 21(1):10–20.
Rosenwinkel, Heidi A.
  2013   A Mortuary Analysis of the Structure 7 Cemetery at Town Creek, a Mississippian Site in the Piedmont of North Carolina. Unpublished master's thesis, Department of Anthropology, East Carolina University, Greenville.
Rudolph, James L.
  1984   Earthlodges and Platform Mounds: Changing Public Architecture in the Southeastern U.S. *Southeastern Archaeology* 3(1):33–45.
Saxe, Arthur A.
  1970   Social Dimensions of Mortuary Practices in a Mesolithic Population from Wadi Halfa, Sudan. Unpublished Ph.D. dissertation, Department of Anthropology, University of Michigan, Ann Arbor.
Schroedl, Gerald F.
  1986   Structures. In *Overhill Cherokee Archaeology at Chota-Tanasee*, edited by Gerald F. Schroedl, pp. 217–272. Report of Investigations 38. Department of Anthropology, Uni-

versity of Tennessee. Publications in Anthropology 42. Tennessee Valley Authority, Knoxville.

1998   Mississippian Towns in the Eastern Tennessee Valley. In *Mississippian Towns and Sacred Spaces: Searching for an Architectural Grammar*, edited by R. Barry Lewis and Charles Stout, pp. 64–92. University of Alabama Press, Tuscaloosa.

Scott, Susan
2012   Faunal Assemblages within the Mound at Town Creek. Manuscript on file, Department of Anthropology, East Carolina University, Greenville.

Smith, Bruce D.
1995   The Analysis of Single-Household Mississippian Settlements. In *Mississippian Communities and Households*, edited by J. Daniel Rogers and Bruce D. Smith, pp. 224–249. University of Alabama Press, Tuscaloosa.

South, Stanley
2002   *Archaeological Pathways to Historic Site Development*. Kluwer Academic/Plenum, New York.

Speck, Frank G.
1979   *Ethnology of the Yuchi Indians*. Reprinted. Humanities Press, Atlantic Highlands. Originally published 1909. Anthropological Publications of the University Museum, Vol. 1, No. 1. University of Pennsylvania, Philadelphia.

Steponaitis, Vincas P.
1986   Prehistoric Archaeology in the Southeastern United States, 1970–1985. *Annual Review of Anthropology* 15:363–404.

Stuiver, Minze, Paula J. Reimer, and Ron Reimer
2005   CALIB Radiocarbon Calibration. Electronic document. http://radiocarbon.pa.qub.ac.uk/calib, accessed March 18, 2005.

Sullivan, Lynne P.
1987   The Mouse Creek Phase Household. *Southeastern Archaeology* 6(1):16–29.
1995   Mississippian Household and Community Organization in Eastern Tennessee. In *Mississippian Communities and Households*, edited by J. Daniel Rogers and Bruce D. Smith, pp. 99–123. University of Alabama Press, Tuscaloosa.
2001   Those Men in the Mounds: Gender, Politics, and Mortuary Practices in Late Prehistoric Eastern Tennessee. In *Archaeological Studies of Gender in the Southeastern United States*, edited by Jane M. Eastman and Christopher B. Rodning, pp. 101–126. University Press of Florida, Gainesville.
2007   Shell Gorgets, Time, and the Southeastern Ceremonial Complex in Southeastern Tennessee. In *Southeastern Ceremonial Complex: Chronology, Content, Context*, edited by Adam King, pp. 88–106. University of Alabama, Tuscaloosa.

Swanton, John R.
1911   *Indian Tribes of the Lower Mississippi Valley and Adjacent Coast of the Gulf of Mexico*. Bulletin 43. Bureau of American Ethnology, Smithsonian Institution, Government Printing Office, Washington, D.C.
1979   *The Indians of the Southeastern United States*. Reprinted. Smithsonian Institution Press, Washington, D.C. Originally published 1946. Bulletin Number 137. Bureau of American Ethnology, United States Government Printing Office, Washington, D.C.
1996   *Source Material on the History and Ethnology of the Caddo Indians*. Reprinted. Uni-

versity of Oklahoma Press, Norman. Originally published 1942. Bulletin Number 132. Bureau of American Ethnology, Smithsonian Institution, Washington, D.C.

Trinkley, Michael B.
1995 Plant Resources. In *Town Creek Indian Mound: A Native American Legacy*, by Joffre L. Coe, pp. 117–135. University of North Carolina Press, Chapel Hill.

Urban, Greg, and Jason B. Jackson
2004 Social Organization. In *Southeast* edited by Raymond D. Fogelson, pp. 697–706. Handbook of North American Indians, Vol. 14, William C. Sturtevant, general editor, Smithsonian Institution Press, Washington, D.C.

Ward, H. Trawick
1983 A Review of Archaeology in the North Carolina Piedmont: A Study of Change. In *The Prehistory of North Carolina: An Archaeological Symposium*, edited by Mark A. Mathis and Jeffrey J. Crow, pp. 53–81. Division of Archives and History, North Carolina Department of Cultural Resources, Raleigh.

Ward, H. Trawick, and R. P. Stephen Davis Jr.
1999 *Time before History: The Archaeology of North Carolina*. University of North Carolina Press, Chapel Hill.

Waselkov, Gregory A., and Kathryn E. Holland Braund
1995 *William Bartram on the Southeastern Indians*. University of Nebraska Press, Lincoln.

Wilson, Gregory D.
2008 *The Archaeology of Everyday Life at Early Moundville*. University of Alabama Press, Tuscaloosa.
2010 Community, Identity, and Social Memory at Moundville. *American Antiquity* 75(1):3–18.

Wilson, Jack H., and S. Homes Hogue
1995 Animal Remains. In *Town Creek Indian Mound: A Native American Legacy*, edited by Joffre L. Coe, pp. 136–150. University of North Carolina Press, Chapel Hill.

8

The Hollywood Site (9RI1) and the Foundations of Mississippian in the Middle Savannah River Valley

ADAM KING, CHRISTOPHER L. THORNOCK, AND KEITH STEPHENSON

Bruce Smith's *Mississippian Emergence* volume published in 1990 both summarized and focused new intellectual efforts on understanding the beginnings of Mississippian societies (Smith 1990). The papers in that volume largely focused on issues of chronology, scale, and organization and offered explanations based in ecological models and evolutionary approaches. Since its publication, our field has more widely embraced historically contingent perspectives that focus explanatory efforts on labor, agency, and practice (Blitz 2010; Cobb 2003; Pauketat 2007). In this chapter we turn that same general lens on the emergence of Mississippian in the middle Savannah River valley of South Carolina and Georgia (Figure 8.1) by exploring the role that the Hollywood site (9RI1) played in that process. Mississippian emergence in this region begins later than in surrounding areas and is characterized by a material diversity suggestive of cultural diversity. The actual appearance of Mississippian societies is closely associated with the appearance of nonlocal materials and presumably ideas at the Hollywood site and the creation of a unique mortuary deposit in Mound B. We argue that differences between local and nonlocal traditions were negotiated through the manipulation of people and objects during mortuary ritual. The end result was a unique variant of Mississippian political culture that became Mississippian in the middle Savannah River valley.

Mississippian Beginnings, Pluralism, and Entanglement

In his recent consideration of chiefdoms in the Southeast, Pauketat (2007) makes a strong case for the fact that great social changes, like the emergence of

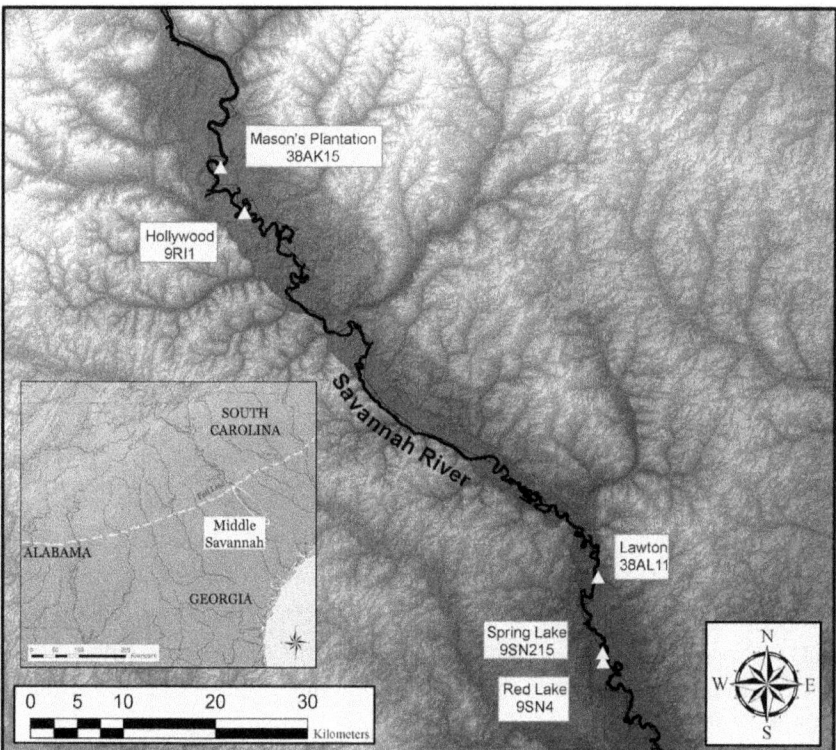

Figure 8.1. Mississippian mound sites in the middle Savannah River valley.

complex polities around the world, involved a mixing of people, practices, histories, and identities spurred at least in part by the movement of new people. He and colleagues have marshaled evidence supporting this for the emergence of Mississippian at the great site of Cahokia in the American Bottom. As we will discuss, it is clear that foreign objects and practices appeared in the middle Savannah River valley around AD 1250. We think this meeting of difference was the catalyst for the emergence of a distinctive version of Mississippian political culture.

Archaeologists have used the concept of hybridity to explore this and similar processes (Alt 2006; Loren 2010). While we like the emphasis hybridity places on the generative nature of the meeting of differences, we also recognize the critique that hybridity can lose its explanatory power when it is used outside of the political and social imbalances implied in colonial and postcolonial contexts (Silliman 2015; Stockhammer 2013). In the middle Savannah River valley, we have no reason to impose those notions of inequality on the local and the foreign. As an alternative, we focus on the relationship between people and things, and how the creation and use of things are avenues through which differences are contested and new practices and material traditions negotiated. These are core ideas of entanglement (Hitchcock and Maeir 2013; Hodder 2011, 2012).

Entanglement focuses on the intertwining of things, people, and practices, and in particular allows for things to be agents of change. Entanglement recognizes that social life is defined and practiced through relations with things as well as people. It also recognizes that the meaning and role of things are defined by their relationships with people, as well as with other things. Meaning, identity, and history are continually defined through the entangled relations of people and things. We will argue that foreign objects, practices, and people came to the Hollywood site early in the site's history. Those objects, ideas, and people were integrated into local ritual activities associated with death. The unique mortuary feature created at Hollywood (Mound B) actively and willfully placed those foreign objects and people in a model of the cosmos that united them with local practices and objects. In so doing, the inhabitants of Hollywood effectively re-created their world, and by extension their society, in a form that melded the local and nonlocal into a unique version of Mississippian.

The Mississippian Emergence in the Middle Savannah River Valley

The Savannah River is a major watershed of the South Atlantic Slope that forms most of the boundary between the modern states of Georgia and South Carolina. Like other major rivers in the region, it traverses three physiographic provinces, with its tributary headwaters starting in the Blue Ridge, flowing through the Piedmont and Coastal Plain, and ultimately emptying into the Atlantic Ocean. Based on topographic and geologic characteristics, the river can be divided into three sections, upper, middle, and lower (Seabrook 2006). The middle Savannah River is the physiographic section under consideration in this study (Figure 8.1), and it flows from the Piedmont Fall Line zone across the Upper Coastal Plain, or Fall Line Sandhill region, to the confluence of Brier Creek (the only major tributary of the Savannah River on the Georgia Coastal Plain) in Screven County, Georgia.

The Mississippian sequence of the middle Savannah River valley has been the object of fairly intense study, thanks primarily to the work of David Anderson (1994, Anderson et al. 1986). Archaeological research in the middle part of the valley has been driven over the past 40 years by the Savannah River

Table 8.1. Middle Savannah River Valley Ceramic Phase Chronology

Date AD	Local Phase
900–1200	Savannah I
900–1100	Sleepy Hollow
1100–1250	Lawton
1250–1350	Hollywood
1350–1450	Silver Bluff
1450–1550	Unoccupied

Source: Stephenson et al. 2015.

Archaeological Research Program funded by the Department of Energy (Sassaman et al. 1990). Our understanding of the Mississippian beginnings in this part of the valley (Table 8.1) builds upon the work of Anderson but adds another two decades of research (Stephenson et al. 2015).

In some ways the beginnings of Mississippian in the middle Savannah River valley follow a path that is different from a similar process in other regions. During the Late Woodland–Mississippian transition in this region, we see a diversity of material culture, particularly in pottery assemblages. Between AD 900 and 1200, the regional landscape was occupied by people with three different pottery traditions. From AD 900 and 1100, a cordmarking tradition of the Savannah I phase is represented by a large number of sites, while a smaller set of different sites contain complicated stamped pottery of the Sleepy Hollow phase bearing Pisgah design motifs (Brummitt 2007; DePratter 1979). The former is a coastal tradition extending across the Coastal Plain (Sassaman et al. 1990:203), while the latter is a tradition with connections to the Piedmont and Appalachian Summit of the Carolinas (Dickens 1976). After AD 1100, the Pisgah-related assemblages of the Sleepy Hollow phase are replaced by sites possessing Etowah complicated stamped pottery of the Lawton phase. The latter is a pottery tradition common in the Ridge and Valley, Piedmont, and Blue Ridge provinces of Georgia and South Carolina (Anderson 1994; Anderson et al. 1986).

This overlap of complicated stamped and cordmarked pottery traditions in the middle Savannah River valley is traditionally considered to be the time of the Late Woodland to Early Mississippian transformation. While associating pottery assemblages with ethnic groups is fraught with difficulty, the presence of these distinct traditions on distinct sites suggests that a certain level of cultural diversity characterized the region at this time. Based on the numbers of sites associated with each ceramic tradition, there were fewer people associated with the Sleepy Hollow and succeeding Lawton phases living in the region than were associated with the Savannah I phase. However, site location choices made by the people creating each distinct ceramic assemblage used the landscape in essentially the same way. Upland and riverine areas were occupied on both seasonal and sometimes year-round bases by small and likely single-family settlements. Larger, nucleated communities were absent. Although the presence of corncob impressed pottery in the Lawton phase suggests access to the products of agriculture, there is no evidence apparent in settlement locations that farming was a significant part of subsistence. In other areas of northern Georgia and South Carolina, the hallmarks of Mississippian began to appear. However, on the middle Savannah platform mounds, elaborate grave offerings and compact communities were not yet present.

After the beginning of the thirteenth century, the middle Savannah River valley experienced a fairly dramatic social reorganization. The ceramic assemblage diversity that had persisted for three centuries disappeared, as the only identifiable component is that of the Hollywood phase. Hollywood pottery represents a regional variant of Savannah period assemblages found across Georgia and South Carolina (Hally and Rudolph 1986). It has long been argued that the Savannah pottery tradition is a direct descendant of the earlier Etowah period complicated stamped pottery traditions (Fairbanks 1950; Hally and Rudolph 1986) associated with phases such as the Lawton phase.

At the very beginning of the Hollywood phase, the first Mississippian mound in the area was constructed at the Hollywood site. Before the turn of the fourteenth century, mounds were constructed at four other sites, both near the Fall Line (Mason's Plantation) and farther south (Lawton, Red Lake, and Spring Lake) along the Savannah River (Anderson 1994; Stephenson 2011; Wood 2009). While all of these sites were founded during the Hollywood phase, seriation studies of associated pottery collections and radiocarbon dates indicate that they were not strictly contemporary but instead may have been built sequentially (Stephenson 2011; Stephenson et al. 2015).

Based on what we have learned, the Mississippian emergence happened around AD 1250 in the middle Savannah River valley, probably at the Hollywood site. This is fairly late compared to other areas of South Appalachia. This is an interesting time in the wider region, because it marks the period when big centers arose in several different parts of Georgia and South Carolina. It also is a time when elaborate ritual objects and regalia made from non-local materials and decorated with meaning-laden symbols are found with small segments of Mississippian societies. We recognize these objects as part of what has been called the Southeastern Ceremonial Complex (SECC), which is now understood to be a set of symbols drawn from a broadly shared conception of the cosmos expressed in various styles and themes across the Southeast and Midwest (King 2007a; Reilly and Garber 2007; Reilly et al. 2011). The interesting thing about these objects is that they were moved across wide regions, and their styles and meanings can tell us a great deal about where they came from and how they were used in particular archaeological contexts.

There is only one context in the middle Savannah River valley where these kinds of goods have been found, and that is in Mound B of the Hollywood site (9RI1)—the place we understand to be the first Mississippian center on the middle Savannah. It has long been recognized that those SECC objects were made somewhere else and brought to the site, creating the possibility that foreign objects, ideas, and possibly even people were involved in the beginnings of Mississippian during the Hollywood phase. Given this potential, understanding the Hollywood site may hold the key to understanding the Mississippian emergence in this region.

The Hollywood Site and Mound B

Hollywood is a Mississippian period site with two earthen platform mounds located 20.5 km below the Fall Line on the Savannah River floodplain near Augusta, Georgia (Figure 8.2). Like so many other Mississippian mound sites, Hollywood became well known after it was investigated by one of Cyrus Thomas' field assistants, Henry Reynolds, during the Bureau of American Ethnology's Mound Builders project (King and Stephenson 2012; Thomas 1894; Williams and Stephenson 2012). Reynolds' 1889 excavations in Mound B at the site revealed an impressive collection of elaborate pots, embossed copper, stone, copper celts, and pipes in a series of graves. Those objects figured prominently in the original definition of the SECC (Muller 1989; Waring and Holder 1945).

Reynolds claimed to have completely excavated Mound B, the smaller of the two mounds present at the site. He described Mound B as conical in form, 3 m in height, 21 m in diameter, and located 85 m due north of the large mound (Thomas 1894:317–326). Reynolds noted that atop this mound were the remains of a cattle barn that had been destroyed during recent flooding of the Savannah River. He initiated his excavation with two trenches, each 3 m wide, crosswise through the center in cardinal directions and down to the base of the mound. As Thomas (1894:318) put it, "the segments that remained were then cut down several feet beyond the radius that covered the interments found in the trenches. In this manner the mound was thoroughly excavated and all

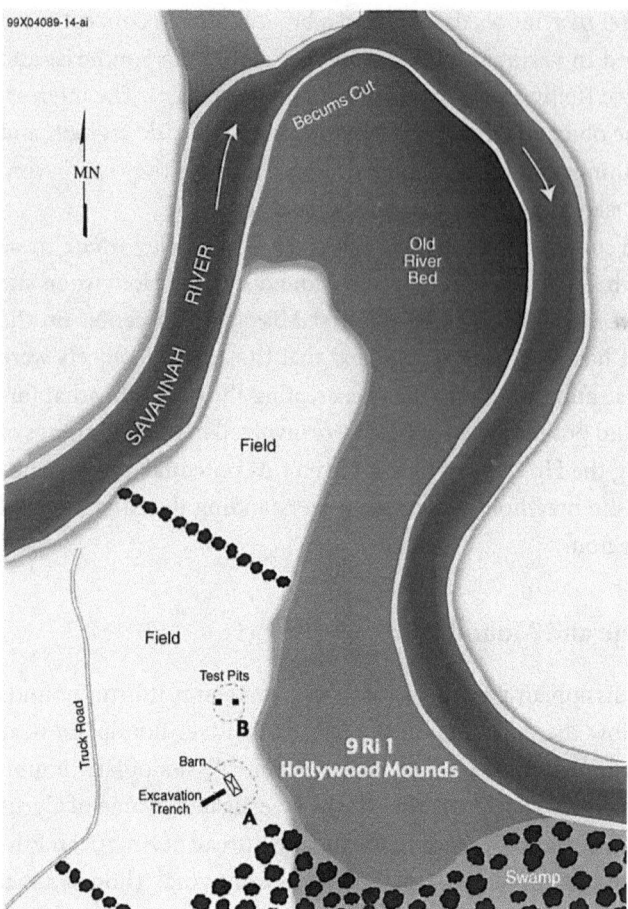

Figure 8.2. Map of the Hollywood site (9RI1).

its buried contents exposed." These efforts revealed the mound as stratified (Figure 8.3), consisting of an upper stratum about 1 m thick and composed of a sandy micaceous loam (most likely an accumulation of floodplain alluvium) containing historic period (ca. AD 1800) artifacts, and a lower stratum some 2 m thick and composed of compact, silty-clay sediments including human burials and accompanying grave goods. The burials within the lower stratum were grouped into two layers, with the upper burial group between .3 and .6 m below the top of the stratum, and the lower group at the base of the mound within the initial .45 m of fill. These superimposed burial groups were separated by 1 m of nondifferentiated mound fill. Reynolds further observed that the burials were not intrusive into the mound, noting that the soil above them showed no indication of disturbance.

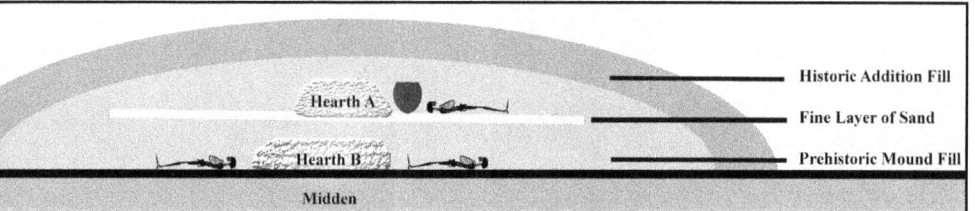

Figure 8.3. Idealized profile of Hollywood's Mound B.

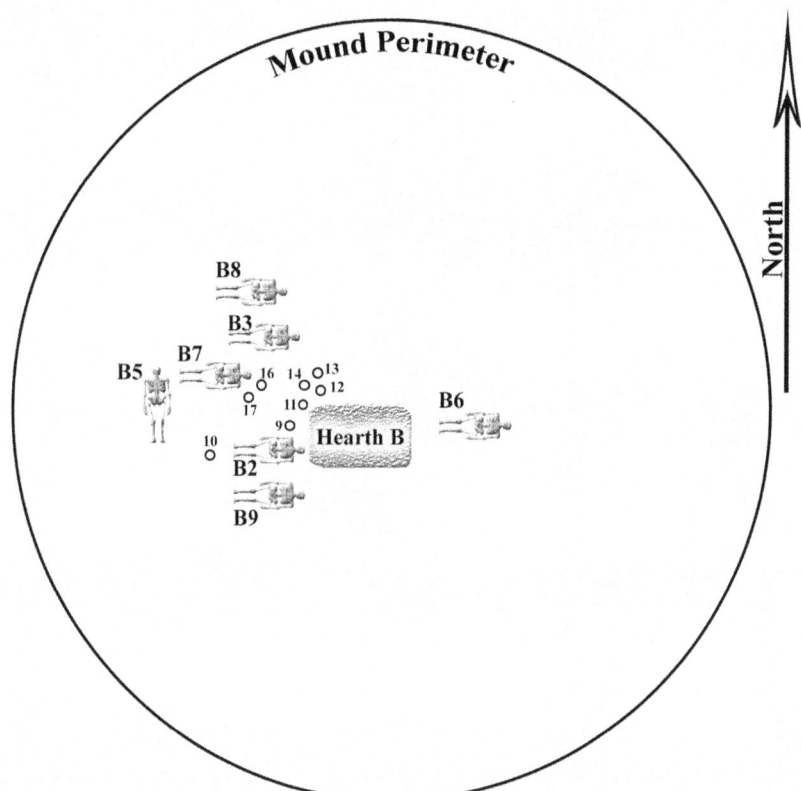

Figure 8.4. Plan map of the lower burial deposit in Mound B, the Hollywood site.

The lower burial grouping (Figure 8.4) included seven extended burials and discrete bundles of objects laid out on a surface and arranged around a hearth. Prominent among the extended burials was Burial 2, which included the extended remains of a person along with two ceramic vessels and a ceramic pipe (Thomas 1894:323). One of the ceramic vessels (Figure 8.5) was described by Thomas (1894:323) as "a bottle standing on a tripod of human heads," while the second, found at the foot of the skeleton, is a check stamped jar with puncta-

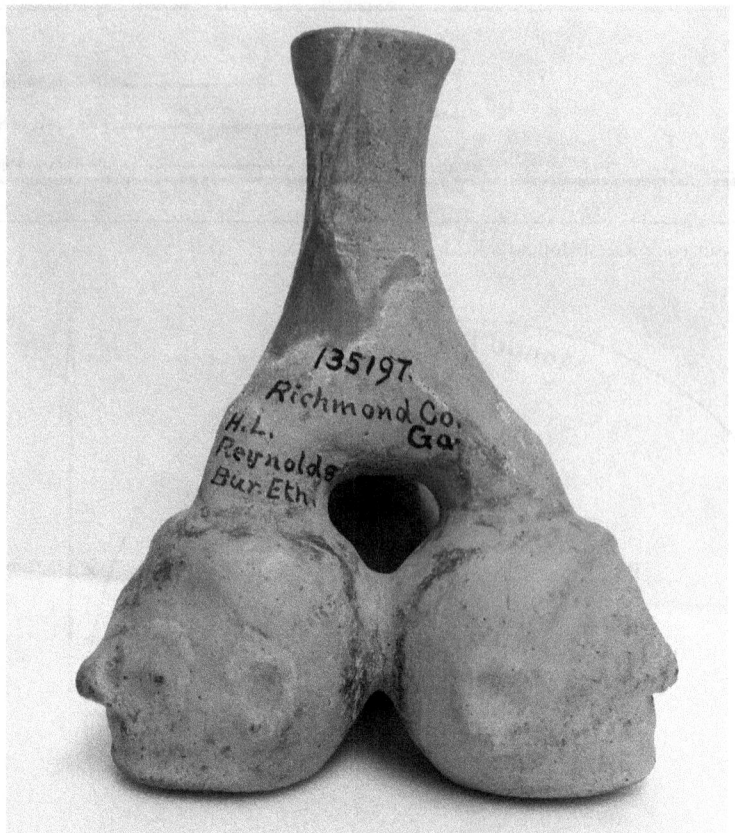

Figure 8.5. Tripod-form bottle, lower burial deposit, Mound B, Hollywood, (Acc. #135197) Department of Anthropology, Smithsonian Institution.

tions at the rim and opposed punctated nodes. As we will discuss below, this is the only vessel in the lower burial deposit that is made in the local Hollywood phase tradition.

Burial 3 included a single individual associated with a large quantity of shell beads and perforated disks as well as a copper-sheathed ornament of wood. Burial 5 included another extended skeleton along with a ceramic pipe, one decayed shell ornament, three ground-stone celts, and five chunkey stones. The ceramic pipe was made in the image of an owl facing the smoker. With the remains of Burial 6 was found a ground-stone celt, while the individual in Burial 8 was associated with many shell beads, a copper ax encased in wood, and the decayed remains of a shell columella.

In addition to the obvious burials, a series of clusters of artifacts also were found in the lower burial deposit. Some have evidence that they were wrapped

Foundations of Mississippian in the Middle Savannah River Valley · 243

or placed in a container, leading us to consider them bundles. Northeast of Burial 2, situated on the western edge of the central fire, sat a bundle of artifacts composed of a carafe-form ceramic bottle, six pipes, three ceramic cups, and a copper axe head wrapper in cloth and bark (Thomas 1894:322–323). While five of the pipes were ceramic and represent various forms found throughout the Southeast, the sixth was made of soapstone and took the form of a kneeling human holding a pottery vessel (Figure 8.6). The three ceramic cups were similar in size, but two were engraved with a distinctive entwined, human-headed snake image (Figure 8.7).

To the west of this bundle lay a second bundle of artifacts associated with Burial 7. It was composed of two ceramic bottles, a quartz chunkey stone, two copper celts, sheets of mica, and a headdress made of repoussé copper, mica, and shell wrapped in leather. One of the bottles had a negative painted image depicting a cross-in-circle with a petaloid surround (Figure 8.8). The second bottle lacked decoration but is similar in form to the first. The headdress appears to be

Figure 8.6. Anthropomorphic soapstone pipe, lower burial deposit, Mound B, Hollywood, (Acc. #135216) Department of Anthropology, Smithsonian Institution.

Figure 8.7. Engraved ceramic cup, lower burial deposit, Mound B, Hollywood, (Acc. #135204) Department of Anthropology, Smithsonian Institution.

the same type identified by Larson (1959) in Etowah's Mound C. In addition to a frontal-facing feline plate (Figure 8.9), it also contains multiple copper cut-outs made in the shape of plumes and arrows (Corsi 2012).

The upper burial deposit (Figure 8.10) had a distinctly different material assemblage. It consisted primarily of locally made pottery vessels, most functioning as burial urns for cremations. As in the lower deposit, six urns as well as four extended burials were arranged around a central hearth. Unlike in the lower deposit, no bundles of objects were placed on this second surface.

One of the extended burials in this upper deposit was located along the northern side of Hearth A. The report (Thomas 1894:322) states that "the remains were so remarkably meager as to give the impression that all the bones of the body could not have been buried," and because there was so little non-skeletal material left, the report goes on to propose "that the bones were buried after having been denuded of flesh." This observation seems to suggest that the people interred in the upper burial context were kept, and possibly defleshed, elsewhere before finally coming to rest in the upper burial deposit.

Another of the extended burials was notable for its association with frag-

Figure 8.8. Plain (left, Acc. #135203) and negative painted bottle (right, Acc. #135202), lower burial deposit, Mound B, Hollywood, Department of Anthropology, Smithsonian Institution.

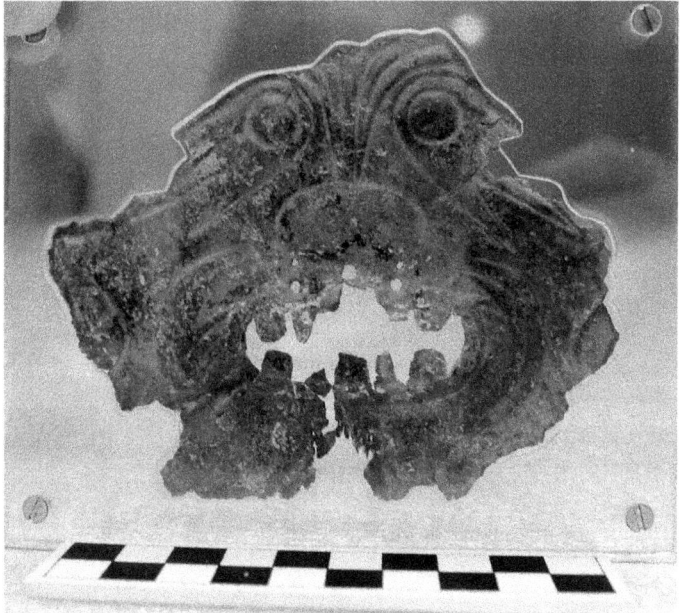

Figure 8.9. Frontal-facing feline copper plate, lower burial deposit, Mound B, Hollywood, (Acc. #135227) Department of Anthropology, Smithsonian Institution.

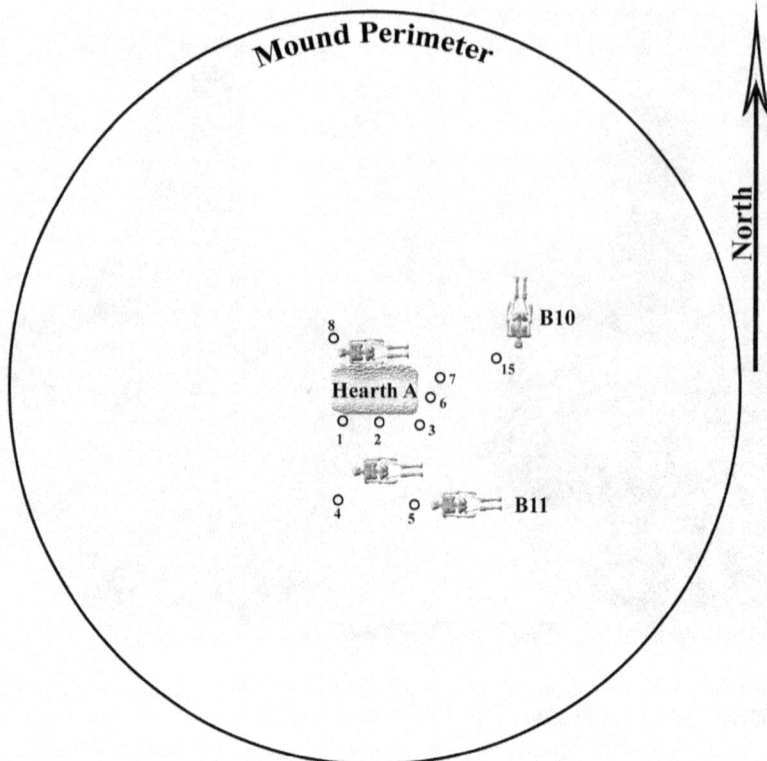

Figure 8.10. Plan map of the upper burial deposit in Mound B, the Hollywood site.

ments of embossed copper. This is the only burial in the upper burial deposit with objects associated with the SECC and clearly of non-local origin. While fragmentary, at least some of the pieces of this plate exhibit enough of its original embossed image to indicate that it once depicted a raptor, like those found at Etowah and other sites in the Southeast. In fact, there is enough of the image present to support the inference that the plate was executed in the Classic Braden style like some of the plates found at Etowah (Thornock 2016).

It is important to emphasize that both series of interments were collectively arranged around a central area of "burnt earth and ashes" (Thomas 1894:319). The central hearth on the lower burial surface (Hearth B, Figure 8.4) was 3.05 m in diameter and had been used multiple times. As Thomas (1894:322–323) described Hearth B, it "consisted of four layers of pure white ashes each one-half inch thick, separated by red burnt earth averaging an inch in thickness. Ashes formed the bottom as well as the top most layers." It is surely no accident that the hearth went through four cycles, because the number four is sacred to many native peoples of the Southeast. As Thomas (1894:323) stated, "there seems to have been more than one ceremony attendant upon the burial of these articles." It is noteworthy that the last burning of the hearth overlapped part of Burial 2, indicating that its last use took place after at least some of the burials were put onto the lower surface. This at least suggests that the people and objects buried in the lower burial context may have been interred as individuals or in groups over an extended period of time.

Equally interesting is the fact that Hearth B was not in the center of the mound but instead was positioned in the center of a sub-mound midden. As Thomas (1894:323) describes it, the hearth "rested on the curious black mold at the bottom. This black mold did not penetrate to the north and east border of the mound, but lay only over an area of which the hearth was the center." Earlier in the account, the sub-mound soil is described by Thomas (1894:319) as "a very black and rich vegetable mold, permeated throughout with innumerable small pieces of burnt pottery, charcoal, shell, mica, chipped flint, and charred and decayed bones too small for identification. The surface of the black mold appears to be the original surface upon which the mound was built." The fact that this sub-mound soil, or midden, was bounded and contained a large central hearth suggests that this may have been the location of a large pre-mound structure, possibly even a charnel house. Perhaps the lower burial surface represents the placement of people and objects on the floor of this house as part of its final use and closing.

The central hearth of the upper burial context, Hearth A, was smaller, measuring 1.5 m in diameter. It appears to have been used once, producing .61 m of ash and charcoal resting on reddish burnt earth. Given that the hearth shows only a single use, and most of the people interred on this surface were cremated, it is possible that this second burial deposit is populated with people who were once processed and stored in the charnel house. Recall that at least one of the extended burials on this surface was so poorly preserved as to lead Thomas to suggest it was secondarily deposited.

Dating the Hollywood Site (9RI1)

Understanding when the Hollywood site was occupied is key to understanding its role in the beginnings of Mississippian as it manifested in the middle Savannah River valley. Traditionally, the Hollywood site was thought to have been occupied between AD 1250 and 1350, thereby lending its name to the Hollywood phase and pottery from sites in the region during that period. Anderson and colleagues (1986:40–41) defined the components of the Hollywood phase pottery assemblage based on the Mound A excavations of Clemens de Baillou (1965), and the date range of the Hollywood phase based on the similarities of the pottery assemblage to the neighboring Beaverdam, Rembert, and Pee Dee phases. The relatively high frequency of fylfot motif stamping, along with the use of unthickened jar rims with cane punctations and punctated nodes, led the authors to place the Hollywood phase between the Beaverdam phase (radiocarbon-dated to AD 1200–1300) and the slightly later Rembert and Pee Dee phases, suggesting a date range of AD 1250–1350. This was the commonly accepted date range for the Hollywood site over the next decade (e.g., Anderson 1994), until Brain and Phillips (1996) argued for a later, protohistoric, occupation of the site.

In an attempt to resolve the conflict between these interpretations, King and Stephenson (2012) examined and dated the pottery vessels from each of the two mortuary deposits in Hollywood's Mound B. An examination of the vessels themselves confirmed that both burial deposits in Mound B contained

Table 8.2. The Radiocarbon Dates from the Hollywood Site

Sample No.	Mound Context	Sample	Calibrated Date (1 sigma)	Calibrated Date (2 sigma)
Beta-134794	Mound A	Soot from check stamped sherd	AD 1310–1360 and AD 1385–1410	AD 1300–1425
Beta-144165	Mound A	Soot from check stamped sherd	AD 1234–1280	AD 1205–1290
Beta-145333	Mound A	Soot from check stamped sherd	AD 1280–1300	AD 1270–1320 and AD 1350–1390
Beta-320926	Mound B, upper	Soot from complicated stamped burial urn	AD 1280–1300 and AD 1370–1380	AD 1280–1320 and AD 1350–1390
Beta-320927	Mound B, upper	Soot from complicated stamped burial urn	AD 1320–1350 and AD 1390–1410	AD 1300–1360 and AD 1380–1420
Beta-320928	Mound B, lower	Soot from check stamped vessel	AD 1400–1430	AD 1320–1340 and AD 1390–1440
Beta-322825	Mound B, lower	Soot from ceramic effigy pipe	AD 1270–1290	AD 1260–1300 and AD 1370–1380
Beta-322826	Mound B, lower	Cane from back of copper plate	AD 1260–1280	AD 1250–1290
Beta-322827	Mound B, lower	Wood from haft of copper celt	AD 1300–1360 and AD 1380–1400	AD 1290–1410

Source: Stephenson 2011; Stephenson et al. 2015.

vessels that were local to the middle Savannah River valley and belonged to the Hollywood phase. As a means of confirming the accepted dates for the phase, radiocarbon samples were obtained from soot adhering to three of the pottery vessels and an owl-effigy pipe, as well as from a fragment of cane matting associated with a copper plate, and wood from the haft of a copper celt. The results presented in Table 8.2 confirm that the samples, which span both mortuary deposits in Mound B, fall within the commonly accepted range of the Hollywood phase.

These radiocarbon results are supported by cross-dates derived from artifact links between the Hollywood site's Mound B and Mound C at the Etowah site (9Br1), located in northwestern Georgia (King 2007b). In the lower deposit of Hollywood's Mound B, an embossed copper plate was recovered that exhibits the frontal depiction of a feline creature that Lankford (2007) identifies as the Underwater Panther (Figure 8.9). This plate has a stylistic counterpart excavated by Larson from Burial 48 in Etowah's Mound C (Brain and Phillips 1996:156; King and Stephenson 2012). Brain and Phillips (1996:156) describe the plate as "identical in style (and probably subject) to the feline plate from Burial 7 at the Hollywood site." The carved soapstone anthropomorphic pipe (Figure 8.6), also excavated from the lower deposit at Hollywood's Mound B, has a similar stylistic counterpart excavated from Etowah's Mound C (Brain and Phillips 1996:192). King (2007b:132) has concluded that Mound C was constructed entirely during the Early and Late Wilbanks phases at Etowah, between AD 1250 and AD 1375, a period that corresponds directly with the Hollywood phase.

Outside of Mound B, radiocarbon dates also are available from three sooted pottery sherds excavated by Clemens de Baillou in 1965 from Mound A (Table 8.2) (Stephenson 2011:117–118). The sherd types include two check stamped sherds and a complicated stamped sherd bearing a cross-in-circle motif. As Table 8.2 shows, all three returned dates consistent with the dating of Mound B.

Given the evidence presented above, it is clear that both the Hollywood site and its Mound B date to the Hollywood phase. We stated earlier, based on detailed ceramic studies and recent radiocarbon dates, that each of the other mound sites in the middle Savannah River valley also dates to the same phase. Recently, Stephenson and colleagues (Stephenson 2011; Stephenson et al. 2015) have attempted to determine whether those mound sites were all occupied sequentially or at the same time. Employing ceramic seriation informed by radiocarbon dates, it was determined that all regional mounds sites were occupied sequentially. Further, of those mound sites, Hollywood formed earliest in the occupational sequence (Stephenson 2011:117–119). This places Hollywood and the construction of Mound B at the beginnings of Mississippian in this region.

The Local and the Non-Local in Mound B

It has long been recognized that some of the artifacts recovered in the Mound B burial deposits were not made at Hollywood (Waring and Holder 1945). Recently, King and Stephenson (2012) examined all objects recovered from Mound B graves at the Smithsonian Institution's Museum Support Center. With a better understanding of how these objects fit with regional styles and their dating, it is now clear that many of the source areas for these non-local objects found at Hollywood are located to the west—from the Mississippi River Valley to the Nashville Basin and northern Georgia. Included in these exotic artifacts are the vast majority of items placed in the lower burial deposit. Interestingly, and no doubt intentionally, the vast majority of artifacts located in the upper deposit were produced locally. As we will discuss below, the deliberate grouping of specific items of non-local (regions to the west) in the lower burial deposit and items of local (eastern) manufacture in the upper burial deposit suggests that the origins of the artifacts placed in Mound B were on the minds of its creators.

Among the objects found with the extended individual in Burial 2 of the lower burial deposit was a tripod-form bottle with human-headed feet (Figure 8.5). This vessel type is known to appear only in the Central Mississippi Valley (Hatchcock 1976; David Dye personal communication 2012) and is likely either a product of that area or a locally made copy. To the northeast of Burial 2, Reynolds found a bundle of objects that included several pipes, engraved ceramic cups, a copper celt, and a ceramic bottle. This bottle takes the carafe form (King and Stephenson 2012), which is another distinctive vessel form found in the Central Mississippi Valley (Hatchcock 1976; David Dye personal communication 2012). Also in this same bundle was the carved soapstone anthropomorphic pipe (Figure 8.6), which, as discussed previously, is a close stylistic match to other pipes found at the Etowah site in Georgia and the Greenwood site in Tennessee (Brain and Phillips 1996:192) and likely was made in northern Georgia or eastern Tennessee. Finally, the two engraved ceramic cups (Figure 8.7) found in this same set of objects are engraved in the recently defined Holly Bluff style whose place of origin is the Lower Mississippi Valley (Corsi 2012:44; Jim Knight, personal communication 2012).

Another bundle of artifacts was found in the lower burial deposit associated with Burial 7. One of the bottles found in this bundle (Figure 8.8) is negative painted with a cross-in-circle surrounded by a petaloid motif (Thomas 1894:323, Figure 200). This bottle is characteristic of Nashville Negative Painted vessels made in the southern Appalachians, most likely from northern Alabama or southeastern Tennessee (Kevin Smith, personal communication 2012). A second bottle in the bundle is either unpainted or, more likely, a second Nashville Negative Painted vessel whose decoration has faded. It also was most likely made in the Cumberland Valley around Nashville, Tennessee (Kevin Smith, personal communication 2012). Finally, this bundle contained a headdress with the frontal-facing feline copper plate (Figure 8.9). Because a virtually identical plate was found in Etowah's Mound C, this site may serve as its source.

The exotic origins of objects in the lower burial deposit are in stark contrast to the objects found in the upper burial deposit, which were decidedly local in character. All of the ceramic vessels found in the upper burial deposit are Hollywood phase vessels that appear to have been produced locally (King and Stephenson 2012). In fact, the only nonlocal object found in the upper burial deposit was associated with the burial form more commonly found in the lower burial deposit—an extended burial. It consisted of fragments of an embossed copper plate with avian imagery. Although only fragments of the image exist, it appears to be executed in the Classic Braden style (Thornock 2016), whose place of origin is the American Bottom (Brown and Kelly 2000).

In summary, we can see that many of the objects found in the lower burial deposit were made in areas to the west of the Hollywood site. The Holly Bluff phase ceramic cups, the carafe-form bottle, and the tripod bottle were all made in the Central Mississippi Valley, while the negative painted vessels were likely made in central Tennessee. The carved stone human figural pipe and feline copper plate appear to have come from the Southern Appalachian area around North Georgia and Eastern Tennessee. In contrast, the upper burial deposit was dominated by local Hollywood phase vessels. The lone exception to the local character of the upper burial deposit is an embossed copper plate with stylistic connections to the Mississippi River Valley.

Two additional observations are in order regarding the objects found in Mound B, especially those from regions outside of the middle Savannah River valley. The first is that many are not simply elaborate objects buried with important people. They are decorated with imagery or made in forms that clearly show they were specialized objects with symbolic meaning. This may be most apparent with objects like the stone anthropomorphic pipe, the feline copper plate headdress, and the avian copper plate. It is equally apparent that the negative painted bottles, carafe-form bottles, human-head effigy bottle, and engraved cups are vessels whose use was specialized. Even the copper celts, which should be viewed as sociotechnic weapons, were symbolically loaded objects. The second observation is that many of these objects were not placed with people but instead were wrapped and placed on the first burial surface separately. Given this, we think these objects should be considered regalia and equipment for conducting ritual. They also may have been markers of particular statuses, but those statuses were defined by control of ritual. The fact that this regalia and equipment are dominated by foreign objects suggests that the rituals and their practitioners were brought to Hollywood from places to the west.

The Mound B Tableau

The description of the Mound B archaeological record suggests it was more than a set of graves. It was a very intentional arrangement of people and objects designed for a purpose that transcended the burial of individuals. For reasons we outline below, we think it is best to consider the Mound B mortuary set as a tableau.

It appears that the Mound B area initially was occupied by a building in which the dead were processed and possibly even curated. When that facility was closed, bundled objects and people were positioned in reference to the central hearth. It is possible to argue that those people and objects once occupied the structure and therefore represent venerated ancestors with their regalia, as well as bundles of sacred objects.

It is important to remember that the objects found with the individual interments, as well as those in the bundles, were made in areas outside of Hollywood. As such, we think they represent nonlocal people and the objects they needed to conduct ritual. The people, the objects, and the activities (rituals) associated with the regalia and bundles all represent ideas and practices foreign to the Hollywood site. These could have arrived at Hollywood with their foreign owners or as bundles acquired by inhabitants of the site. We suspect the former.

Although this is an assumption, we think the regalia and sacred objects found on this floor were used in mortuary rituals conducted inside the structure to prepare the dead. The presence of a large hearth and substantial ash deposits suggests those rituals may have included cremation. This form of burial treatment appears to have been the most common in the middle Savannah River valley, starting as early as the Late Woodland period. If this series of propositions is accepted, then in Mound B non-local ritual objects, and presumably non-local ritual, were used to prepare the dead, ultimately resulting in a local and long-standing burial form.

With the cessation in use of the pre-mound mortuary structure, bundled sacred objects and people were carefully arranged around its hearth and covered with a layer of earth. Upon this newly created surface, the inhabitants of Hollywood placed a new hearth and used it. We can assume that, like the previous hearth, this one was used in mortuary processing. Also arranged on this surface were four extended burials and six cremations placed in pottery vessels. Unlike the lower burial deposit, this one included mostly local burial goods and local burial forms. As noted previously, one of the extended skeletons was poorly preserved and apparently incomplete. This led Reynolds to hypothesize that it had been allowed to decay elsewhere and was placed in the Mound B deposit later. As with the lower burial deposit, it is possible that this upper deposit contained the remains of people that once lay in the pre-mound mortuary structure. It may have also contained the cremated remains of people who received mortuary treatment in that structure or on the surface of this upper burial deposit. Eventually, this second burial deposit was covered by another layer of earth, effectively closing the entire facility.

As discussed previously, there are some clear patterns in the ways people and objects were positioned in the upper and lower burial deposits of Mound B. These reveal a clear complementarity between the two deposits (Figures 8.4 and 8.10). In the lower burial deposit, people and objects were placed on a prepared surface and positioned so as to be on the western side of the central fire. Many objects were not buried directly with people but were placed in discrete piles, and excavation data indicate that some of those objects were bundled. In this lower layer all of the objects interred were nonlocal in origin, with the exception of one Hollywood phase vessel. In the upper deposit, people and objects were positioned on a second prepared surface, but this time they were positioned to the north, east, and south of the central fire. The majority of the upper-deposit interments were placed in burial urns made using local Hollywood phase vessels. Only one burial in the deposit contained the remains of a person accompanied by a non-local object, an avian copper plate.

The directional associations revealed by the positioning of people and objects in each burial deposit are mirrored in the imagery found in those deposits. As noted above, the imagery found in the lower deposit—the Underwater Panther and the horned serpent—is associated with the Beneath World realm of the cosmos as seen by Native Americans of eastern North America (Lankford 2007; Reilly 2004). The direction associated with the Beneath World is west, the same direction that captures the origins of the non-local material interred in the deposit. The identifiable imagery from the upper deposit is avian in character, which is associated with the opposing Above World realm of the cosmos (Lankford 2007; Reilly 2004). East and the rising sun are associated with the Above World and the source of the local grave goods dominating the upper deposit.

While the two deposits complement one another spatially, symbolically, and geographically (in terms of origins of objects interred in each), it also is apparent that they are connected temporally. The description of the Mound B stratigraphy seems to make it clear that not a great deal of time passed between the creation of the two burial deposits. The chronological evidence we present here supports that inference. Given this, the two burial deposits should be considered to be parts of a single, symbolic whole.

Using iconography and ethnographic information, scholars like Reilly (2004) and Lankford (2007) have shown that Mississippian imagery and ritual behavior can be linked to still-living Native American belief traditions about the nature of the cosmos and its organizing principles. Using their arguments, it is possible to view Hollywood's Mound B as a model of the cosmos. We know from ethnographic sources that the sacred fire served as both the center of the earthly plane (This World) and a link to those realms of the cosmos above and below. We believe it is possible to view the two fire pits located near the center of each burial layer in Mound B as a similar kind of organizational anchor. In the same way that elements of the cosmos are arranged around the sacred fire, people and objects symbolically connected to different realms of the cosmos are arranged around the central fire basins of Mound B.

If this perspective is accepted, then the creation of Mound B was a re-creation of the cosmos or, in the eyes of the creators, a reenactment of creation itself. In that model of the cosmos, foreign people and practices were symbolically linked to local people and practices. We have argued that mortuary processing was a key function of the initial pre-mound structure and that the people and objects on the first burial deposit were integral parts of the rituals conducted there. If this is accepted, then those rituals were not of local origin, but they appear to have been used to create local burial forms (burial urns containing cremated remains). By employing foreign objects and rituals in local burial practices, those new ideas and material traditions became entangled with local ideas and practices. What resulted was a new way of doing things. That new way was enshrined in the landscape of Hollywood and the middle Savannah River valley when the pre-mound mortuary structure was closed and the set of events that led to the building of Mound B was completed.

Hollywood and the Mississippian Emergence in the Middle Savannah River Valley

As discussed above, it was during the Hollywood phase that mound sites and a particular variant of Mississippian political culture abruptly appeared at the Fall Line of Georgia and South Carolina, at Hollywood (9RI1) and Mason's Plantation (38AK11), and farther south, into the Upper Coastal Plain at Lawton (38AL11), Red Lake (9SN4), and Spring Lake (9SN215). It was at the beginning of this phase that non-local ritual objects appeared at Hollywood, and a new kind of mortuary deposit was created. We have little doubt that the correspondence in timing of the appearance of foreign goods and ideology and the rapid emergence of Mississippian in the region means that the two processes are causally linked. In fact, we argue that the ritual acts creating Hollywood's Mound B were a key part of the process that led to the establishment of Mississippian polities in the middle Savannah River valley.

We find it useful to view the emergence of Mississippian in the middle Savannah River valley as its own unique historical process. The presence of non-local goods in Hollywood's Mound B clearly shows that this process was impacted in no small way by external forces. In fact, we propose that the use of non-local practices and objects to create local burial forms was part of a process whereby difference (local and foreign) was met and negotiated through ritual action, creating a new set of practices and material traditions. Those new practices and traditions went beyond simply the creation of Mound B to include a new way of organizing society and understanding its place in the larger cosmos. The set of events that led to the completion of Mound B embedded those newly created practices and traditions into the landscape of the Hollywood site and the middle Savannah River valley.

As it is the earliest center in the middle Savannah River valley, we argue that the changes that culminated in Mound B inspired a broader set of transformations. Those led to the building of other mounds in the middle Savannah River valley and the reorganization of settlement systems. Dispersed settlement throughout the upland and riverine areas was refocused on the newly created centers. The degree to which other hallmarks of Mississippian lifeways were part of this is unclear. Direct evidence of corn cultivation has been recovered in recent excavations at the Lawton site, but the intensity of that cultivation remains unexplored (Nelson 2005). Outside of the elaborate burials in Hollywood's Mound B, no other evidence has been found indicating that social ranking was materialized through burial treatment and access to specialized objects. Testing of mounds at Lawton, Red Lake, and Spring Lake, including the excavation of old looters' trenches, has produced no evidence for the kind of elaborate mortuary ceremonialism found at Hollywood (Nelson 2005; Dale 2007; Wood 2009). The most common burial form in the area is the unaccompanied urn burial containing cremated remains placed in natural sand ridge cemeteries along the Savannah River (Stephenson 2011:33–37; King and Stephenson 2012).

The result of these changes was a unique version of Mississippian. In terms of material traditions, Mississippian in the middle Savannah River valley looks similar to Mississippian societies in the surrounding regions. However, there is little evidence for social ranking, at least as visible in mortuary treatment. Despite arguments to the contrary (Hally 1996; Wood 2009), the polities that developed in the middle Savannah River valley appear to have been smaller and less centralized than those in the surrounding areas of Georgia and South Carolina (King 2012; Stephenson 2011; Stephenson et al. 2015). They also were not as stable, as they appear to have collapsed as quickly as they formed. By the end of the Hollywood phase, all of the mound centers in the middle Savannah River valley were abandoned and, with the start of the fifteenth-century, settlement no longer focused on those mound centers.

References Cited

Alt, Susan
  2006   The Power of Diversity: Settlement in the Cahokian Uplands. In *Leadership and Polity in Mississippian Society*, edited by Brian M. Butler and Paul D. Welch, pp. 289–308. Center for Archaeological Investigations, Occasional Paper No. 33. Southern Illinois University, Carbondale.
Anderson, David G.
  1994   *The Savannah River Chiefdoms: Political Change in the Late Prehistoric Southeast*. University of Alabama Press, Tuscaloosa.
Anderson, David G., David J. Hally, and James L. Rudolph
  1986   The Mississippian Occupation of the Savannah River Valley. *Southeastern Archaeology* 5(1):32–51.
Bhabha, Homi K.
  1994   *The Location of Culture*. Routledge, New York.
Blitz, John H.
  2010   New Perspectives in Mississippian Archaeology. *Journal of Archaeological Research* 18(1):1–39.
Brain, Jeffrey P., and Philip Phillips
  1996   *Shell Gorgets: Styles of the Late Prehistoric and Protohistoric Southeast*. Peabody Museum Press, Cambridge.
Brown, James, and John Kelly
  2000   Cahokia and the Southeastern Ceremonial Complex. In *Mounds, Modoc, and Meso-*

america: Papers in Honor of Melvin L. Fowler, edited by Steven R. Ahler, pp. 469–510. Scientific Papers 55. Illinois State Museum, Springfield.

Brummitt, Aaron G.
2007   The Sleepy Hollow Phase: Mississippian Emergence in the Middle Savannah Valley. Unpublished master's thesis, Department of Anthropology, University of South Carolina, Columbia.

Cobb, Charles R.
2003   Mississippian Chiefdoms: How Complex? *Annual Review of Anthropology* 32:63–84.

Cobb, Charles, and Adam King
2005   Re-inventing Mississippian Tradition at Etowah. *Journal of Archaeological Method and Theory* 12(3):167–190.

Corsi, Alexander Dean
2012   Reverence for the Dead: Identifying and Interpreting Patterns in Mortuary Objects within the Hollywood Mound Site. Unpublished master's thesis, Department of Anthropology, Texas State University, San Marcos.

Dale, Emily L. K.
2007   *The Red Lake Site (9SN4): A Middle Mississippian Mound Town in the Central Savannah River Valley*. Unpublished master's thesis, Department of Anthropology, University of South Carolina, Columbia.

De Baillou, Clemens
1965   A Test Excavation of the Hollywood Mound (9 Ri 1), Georgia. *Southern Indian Studies* 17:3–11.

DePratter, Chester B.
1979   Ceramics. In *The Anthropology of St. Catherines Island: 2. The Refuge-Deptford Mortuary Complex*, edited by D. H. Thomas and C. S. Larsen, pp. 109–132. Anthropological Papers of the American Museum of Natural History 56, Part I. American Museum of Natural History, New York.

Dickens, Roy S.
1976   *Cherokee Archaeology: The Pisgah Phase of the Appalachian Summit Region*. University of Tennessee Press, Knoxville.

Fairbanks, Charles H.
1950   A Preliminary Segregation of Etowah, Savannah, and Lamar. *American Antiquity* 16(2): 142–151.

Hally, David J.
1996   Platform-Mound Construction and the Instability of Mississippian Chiefdoms. In *Political Structure and Change in the Prehistoric Southeastern United States*, edited by J. F. Scarry, pp. 92–127. University Press of Florida, Gainesville.

Hally, David J., and James B. Rudolph
1986   *Mississippi Period Archaeology of the Georgia Piedmont*. Laboratory of Archaeology Series Report 24. Department of Anthropology, University of Georgia, Athens.

Hatchcock, Roy
1976   *Ancient Indian Pottery of the Mississippi Valley*. Hurley Press, Camden.

Hitchcock, Louise, and Aren M. Maeir
2013   Beyond Creolization and Hybridity: Entangled and Transcultural Identities in Philistia. *Archaeological Review of Cambridge* 28:51–73.

Hodder, Ian
   2011   Human-Thing Entanglement: Towards an Integrated Archaeological Perspective. *Journal of the Royal Anthropological Institute* 17:154–177.
   2012   *Entangled: An Archaeology of the Relationships between Humans and Things.* Wiley and Blackwell, London.

King, Adam
   2007a   *Southeastern Ceremonial Complex: Chronology, Content, Context.* University of Alabama Press, Tuscaloosa.
   2007b   Mound C and the Southeastern Ceremonial Complex in the History of the Etowah Site. In *Southeastern Ceremonial Complex: Chronology, Content, Context*, edited by Adam King, pp. 107–133. University of Alabama Press, Tuscaloosa.

King, Adam, and Keith Stephenson
   2012   Archival Research of the Hollywood Mound Site. *Early Georgia* 40(1):87–101.

Lankford, George E.
   2007   The "Path of Souls": Some Death Imagery in the Southeastern Ceremonial Complex. In *Ancient Objects and Sacred Realms: Interpretations of Mississippian Iconography*, edited by F. Kent Reilly III and James F. Garber, pp. 174–212. University of Texas Press, Austin.

Lankford, George E., F. Kent Reilly III, and James F. Garber
   2011   *Visualizing the Sacred: Cosmic Visions, Regionalism, and the Art of the Mississippian World.* University of Texas Press, Austin.

Larson, Lewis H.
   1959   A Mississippian Headdress from Etowah, Georgia. *American Antiquity* 25(1):109–112.

Loren, Diana Dipaolo
   2010   *The Archaeology of Clothing and Bodily Adornment in Colonial America.* University Press of Florida, Gainesville.

Moorehead, Warren K. (editor)
   1932   *Etowah Papers.* Yale University Press, New Haven, for the Phillips Academy, Andover.

Muller, Jon
   1989   The Southern Cult. In *Southeastern Ceremonial Complex: Artifacts and Analysis*, edited by Patricia A. Galloway, pp. 11–26. University of Nebraska Press, Lincoln.

Nelson, Michael
   2005   Understanding Lawton (38AL11): The Social and Political Functions and Occupational History of a Middle Mississippian Chiefdom Capital. Unpublished master's thesis, Department of Anthropology, University of South Carolina, Columbia.

Pauketat, Timothy
   2007   *Chiefdoms and Other Archaeological Delusions.* AltaMira Press, Lanham.

Reilly, F. Kent III
   2004   People of Earth, People of Sky: Visualizing the Sacred in Native American Art of the Mississippian Period. In *Hero, Hawk, and Open Hand: American Indian Art of the Ancient Midwest and South*, edited by Robert V. Sharp, pp. 125–138. Yale University Press, New Haven.

Reilly, F. Kent III, and James F. Garber (editors)
   2007   *Ancient Objects and Sacred Realms: Interpretations of Mississippian Iconography.* University of Texas Press, Austin.

Reilly, F. Kent III, James F. Garber, and George E. Lankford
   2011   Introduction. In *Visualizing the Sacred: Cosmic Visions, Regionalisms, and the Art of*

the Mississippian World, edited by George E. Lankford, F. Kent Reilly III, and James F. Garber, pp. xi–xviii. University of Texas Press, Austin.

Sassaman, Kenneth E., Mark J. Brooks, Glen T. Hanson, and David G. Anderson.
- 1990 *Native American Prehistory of the Middle Savannah River Valley: A Synthesis of Archaeological Investigations on the Savannah River Site, Aiken and Barnwell Counties, South Carolina*. Research Papers No. 1. Savannah River Archaeological Research Program, South Carolina Institute of Archaeology and Anthropology, University of South Carolina, Columbia.

Seabrook, Charles
- 2006 Savannah River. In *The New Georgia Encyclopedia*. Electronic document http://www.georgiaencyclopedia.org/articles/geography-*environment/savannah-river*, accessed January 29, 2015.

Silliman, Stephen W.
- 2015 A Requiem for Hybridity? The Problem with Frankensteins, Purées, and Mules. *Journal of Social Archaeology* 15(3):277–298.

Smith, Bruce D. (editor)
- 1990 *The Mississippian Emergence*. Smithsonian Institution Press, Washington, D.C.

Stephenson, Keith
- 2011 Mississippi Period Occupational and Political History of the Middle Savannah River Valley. Unpublished Ph.D. dissertation, Department of Anthropology, University of Kentucky, Lexington.

Stephenson, Keith, Adam King, and Karen Y. Smith
- 2015 Space and Time: The Culture Historical Setting for the Hollywood Phase of the Middle Savannah River Valley. In *Archaeological Perspectives on the Southern Appalachians: A Multiscalar Approach*, edited by Ramie A. Gougeon and Maureen S. Meyers, pp. 171–198. University of Tennessee Press, Knoxville.

Stockhammer, Philipp W.
- 2013 From Hybridity to Entanglement, from Essentialism to Practice. *Archaeological Review of Cambridge* 28:11–28.

Thomas, Cyrus
- 1894 *Report of the Mound Explorations of the Bureau of Ethnology*. Annual Report 12. Bureau of Ethnology, Washington, D.C.

Thornock, Christopher L.
- 2016 The Hollywood Site (9RI1): Meaningful Archaeological Analysis through Complementary Interpretive Frameworks. Unpublished Ph.D. dissertation, Department of Anthropology, University of South Carolina, Columbia.

Waring, Antonio J., and Preston Holder
- 1945 A Prehistoric Ceremonial Complex in the Southeastern United States. *American Anthropologist* 47(1):1–34.

Williams, Mark, and Keith Stephenson
- 2012 Henry L. Reynolds, Jr.: Georgia's Greatest 19th Century Archaeologist. *Early Georgia* 40(1):69–85.

Wood, M. Jared
- 2009 Mississippian Chiefdom Organization: A Case Study from the Savannah River Valley. Unpublished Ph.D. dissertation, Department of Anthropology, University of Georgia, Athens.

9

Fort Walton Mississippian Beginnings in the Apalachicola–Lower Chattahoochee River Valley of Northwest Florida, Southwest Georgia, and Southeast Alabama

JEFFREY P. DU VERNAY AND NANCY MARIE WHITE

Fort Walton is the Mississippian cultural variant in northwest Florida–southwest Georgia–southeast Alabama that spans from the Choctawhatchee Bay on the west to the Aucilla River on the east, and north from the Gulf of Mexico approximately 160 river miles up the Apalachicola–lower Chattahoochee River (Marrinan and White 2007:292–294). Within this geographical area, the Tallahassee Red Hills and Apalachicola–lower Chattahoochee River valley are recognized as being the major loci of Fort Walton activity (Figure 9.1). In his monumental synthesis of the archaeology of the Gulf Coast, Gordon Willey (1949) first identified the defining attributes of Fort Walton culture, the core of which still are relevant today (Marrinan and White 2007:292–294). Since Willey, the subject of Fort Walton beginnings has been of great research interest, with most now recognizing an in situ emergence out of local Late Woodland populations (e.g., Blitz and Lorenz 2002; Brose and Percy 1978; Marrinan and White 2007; Scarry 1984, 1990; White 1982; White et al. 2012). Over the past 35 years, in situ models for Fort Walton emergence have been proposed, emphasizing population growth, resource stress, maize intensification, and the rise of elites to manage these issues (Brose and Percy 1978; Scarry 1984, 1990; White 1982). More recently, Blitz and Lorenz (2002:131, 2006) have hypothesized that Fort Walton was the result of local Late Woodland period groups responding to "the real or perceived threat" following the arrival of Rood Mississippian pioneers with shell-tempered pottery and other typical Mississippian traits just to the north up the Chattahoochee around AD 1100.

Recently completed and previously underreported field and collections

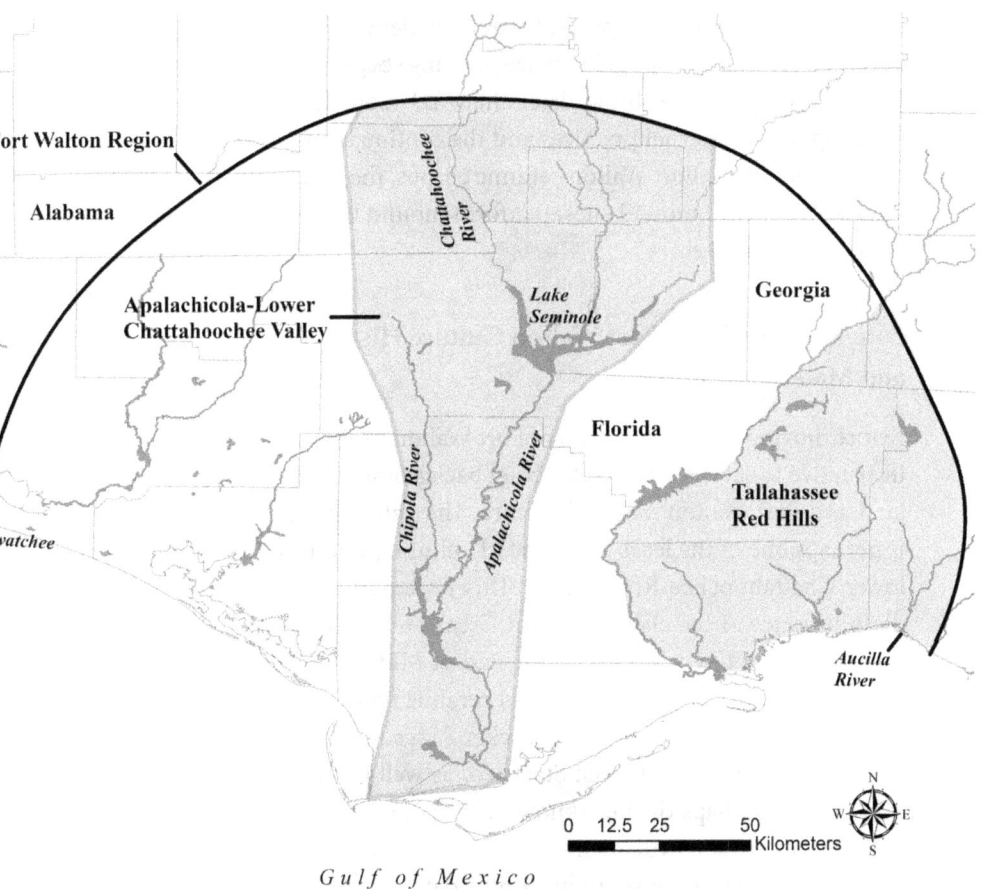

Figure 9.1. The Fort Walton region, with the Apalachicola–lower Chattahoochee and Tallahassee Red Hills areas highlighted (adapted from Marrinan and White 2007:293).

work done by the authors and students at University of South Florida (USF) has produced data useful for characterizing and refining our understanding of Fort Walton beginnings in the Apalachicola–lower Chattahoochee River valley. In this chapter, we discuss these data in an effort to enhance interpretations of Fort Walton origins. We argue that Fort Walton development in this region involved local Late Woodland (late Weeden Island) groups negotiating the retention of their local traditions in conjunction with an influx of outside Mississippian practices, which resulted in an emergence of a Mississippian culture with great regional distinctiveness. This view of in situ development with outside influence is not new (e.g., Brose 1984), but now we can add finer detail and also can better contrast coastal and interior settlement and subsistence in Fort Walton emergence. Current evidence suggests that components of this cultural shift (especially maize growing) began slightly before AD 1000 and were fully realized by no later than AD 1200. This shift included both the adoption of external practices and the continuation of old ones—particularly evident in the Fort Walton ceramic corpus, the reoccupation of Early and Middle Woodland mound sites, platform mound building, and variability in subsistence practices.

Late Woodland and Fort Walton Culture History and Material Culture

Before moving into a discussion of Fort Walton beginnings in this region, it is instructive to set the stage with a brief background discussion of Late Woodland and Fort Walton material culture. The Late Woodland (AD 700–1000) is perhaps one of the least-investigated cultural periods of the Apalachicola–lower Chattahoochee River valley. This time period here is marked by the disappearance of the elaborate Swift Creek and early Weeden Island ceramics and fancy effigy vessels with the end of Middle Woodland, and the continuation of a few late Weeden Island ceramic types, including Keith Incised, Carrabelle Incised and Punctate, Tucker Ridge Pinched, and, with the greatest frequency, Wakulla Check Stamped, as well as sand- and grit-tempered plain wares. Perhaps the best-known example of this ceramic pattern is seen at the Sycamore site (Milanich 1974) (Figure 9.2). Here, a seasonally occupied late Weeden Island house, radiocarbon-dated to AD 860 with a two-sigma calibrated range date of AD 712–1154 (Table 9.1), produced 9083 sherds, 48 percent (n = 4325) of which were Wakulla Check-Stamped (Milanich 1974:16, Table 4). Similar ceramic frequency trends have been documented at other sites in the region (Percy and Jones 1975:104, 1976), including at the Sunstroke site (8Li217). Since the 1980s, White has completed multiple surface collection surveys at Sunstroke, as well as a test excavation in 1990, but until recently not all of these data were fully examined. A recent tabulation of the ceramic data from these investigations indicates that Wakulla Check Stamped sherds account for approximately 49 percent (n = 1,300) of the total assemblage (n = 2,644) (Table 9.2). A charcoal sample recovered during the Sunstroke test excavation produced a radiocarbon date of 1220 ± 90 BP (Beta-116361) (see Table 9.1). The intercept point of this date with the calibration curve is AD 800 (with a 2-sigma range of AD 650–1005), making it nearly contemporaneous with Sycamore.

Notably, the ceremonial burial mound construction so characteristic of

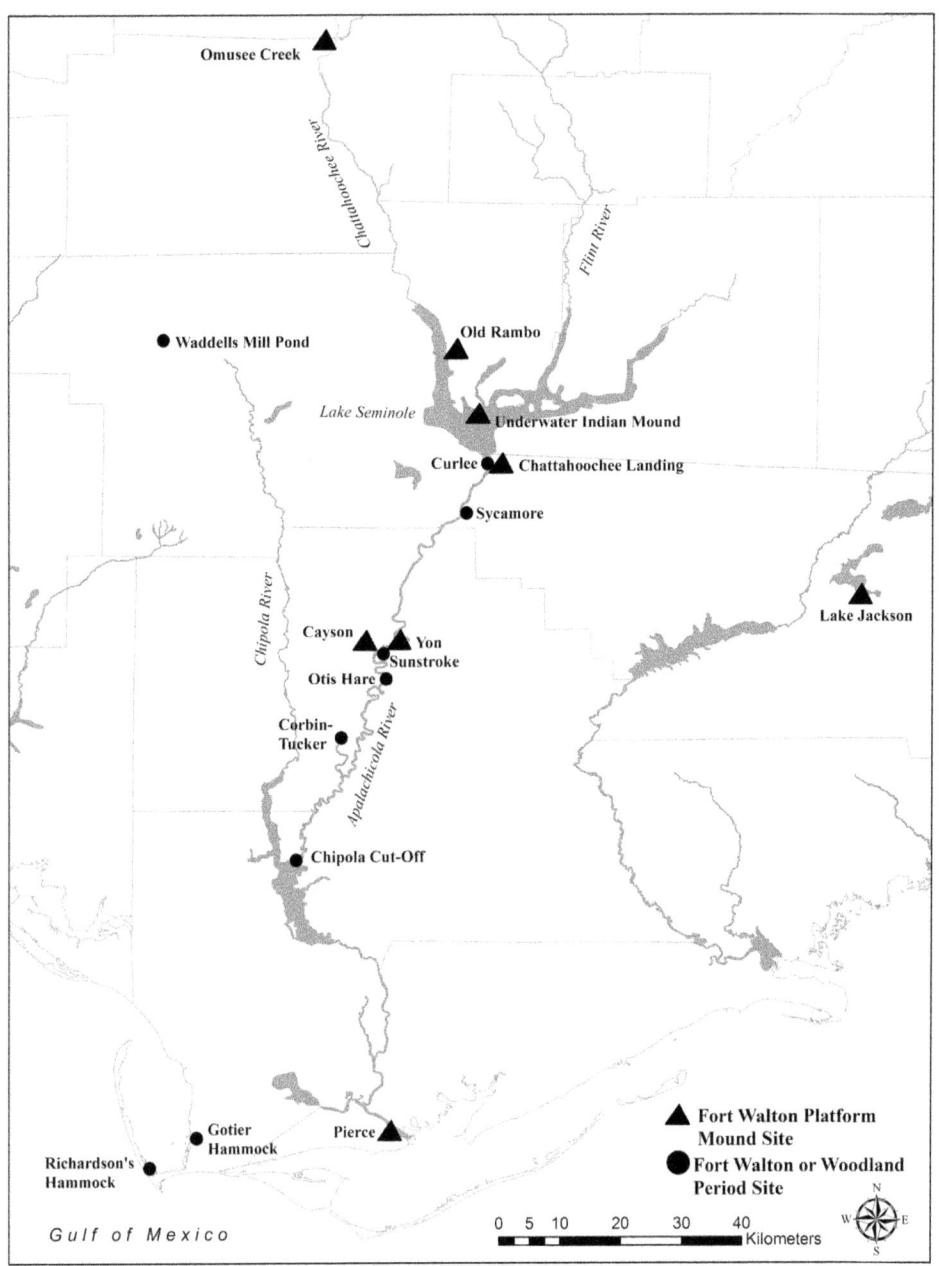

Figure 9.2. Fort Walton and Woodland sites discussed in chapter.

Table 9.1. Radiometric Data

Site	Lab #	Provenience	Conventional Radiocarbon Age	Calibrated Date Range (1 sigma)	Calibrated Date Range (2 sigma)	Calibrated Intercept
Sycamore[a]	I-7253	Area around hearth inside house	1090 ± 85 BP	AD 778–1025	AD 712–1154	AD 860
Sunstroke	Beta-110361	TUA, Floor 6	1220 ± 90 BP	AD 690–950	AD 650–1005	AD 800
Chattahoochee Landing	Beta-306923	Mound 1, profile, Stratum IV	1510 ± 30 BP	AD 550–600	AD 540–620	AD 570
Corbin-Tucker	Beta-30633	Feature 1	1080 ± 90 BP	AD 880–1030	AD 770–1170	AD 990
Corbin-Tucker	Beta-68757	Feature 1	1060± 90 BP	AD 900–1030	AD 800–1170	AD 1000
Pierce	Beta-221908	Core, 100 cm, 200 m SE of Mound H	750 ± 40 BP	AD 1260–1290	AD 1220–1300	AD 1270
Cayson[b]	DIC-46	Unknown village unit/ "Level 8"	770 ± 40 BP	AD 1224–1276	AD 1054–1386	AD 1260
Cayson[b]	DIC-45	"edge of mound"	840 ± 65 BP	AD 1058–1264	AD 1040–1276	AD 1180
Cayson[b]	DIC-94	"low mound"	900 ± 100 BP	AD 1035–1214	AD 903–1284	AD 1020 AD 1100 AD1160
Cayson[b]	DIC-44	Village unit, "Feature 3"	940 ± 145 BP	AD 981–1249	AD 775–1380	AD 1050
Cayson[b]	DIC-93	Village unit, "wall trench"	1000 ± 70 BP	AD 976–1154	AD 893–1206	AD 1010

Notes: a. Data from Milanich (1974:35, Table 8).
b. Data from Scarry (1990:236, Table 26) and available radiocarbon submittal form summaries. Sycamore and Cayson dates recalibrated with Oxcal online calibration program.

Early and Middle Woodland groups in the valley also disappeared by Late Woodland times. Researchers have long interpreted the Late Woodland here as a time of socioeconomic instability, population growth, and the coalescence of populations at perhaps more densely populated sites and into diverse ecological zones, but with particular interest given to those locations that were agriculturally advantageous (Brose and Percy 1978:105; Brose 1984; White 1986:207). A tabulation of sites in the valley indicated that a total of 122 Late Woodland sites are known, identified based on the presence of diagnostic late Weeden Island ceramic types (Schieffer 2012), and with most being situated on the fertile alluvial riverbank soils. The Late Woodland period marks the initial appearance of maize growing in the valley, known from the recovery of maize kernels or cob-impressed pottery from late Weeden Island contexts at a few sites, including the aforementioned Sycamore site (Milanich 1974).

The number of sites in the Apalachicola–lower Chattahoochee River valley increased during Fort Walton times over what it was during the Late Woodland period. To date, 201 Fort Walton sites have been recorded here, including mound centers, small probable farmsteads and cemeteries, and, near the coast, dense shell middens (Du Vernay 2011; Schieffer 2012; White et al. 2012). As brought out in two thorough syntheses of Fort Walton, our understanding of the chronology of most of these sites is poor, and this has hindered our ability to model Fort Walton along many fronts (Marrinan and White 2007; White et al. 2012). Fort Walton ceramic phases have been proposed (Scarry 1984, 1990) but are problematic (Blitz and Lorenz 2006; Marrinan and White 2007), so here and elsewhere (Du Vernay 2011; White et al. 2012) we use the general time periods of early (AD 1000–1200), middle (AD 1200–1400), and late (AD 1400–1600) Fort Walton (Table 9.3) that were first defined by White (1982) and were subsequently updated (Marrinan and White 2007), based upon an improved understanding of general shifts in ceramic trends through time.

Four Fort Walton platform mound centers, including some with earlier cultural components, are known from the Apalachicola valley proper (Moore 1902, 1903), including Pierce (8Fr14) (White et al. 2012) at the river mouth, Yon (8Li2) (Du Vernay 2011, 2014; White 1996), and Cayson (8Ca3) (Brose 1975; Brose et al. 1976) in the middle valley, and Chattahoochee Landing (8Gd4) (White 2011a) just below the Flint–Chattahoochee confluence, where the Lake Seminole reservoir is today. For many years the Curlee (8Ja7) site, located across the river from Chattahoochee Landing, also was believed to have at one time contained a Fort Walton period platform mound, but now it

Table 9.2. Late Weeden Island and Fort Walton Site Ceramic Tabulations Discussed in Chapter

Site	Carrabelle Incised		Tucker Ridge Pinched		Keith Incised		Check-Stamped		Cob-Marked		Fort Walton Incised		Lake Jackson	
	N	Wt (g)	N	Wt (g)	N	Wt (g)	N	Wt (g)	N	Wt (g)	N	Wt (g)	N	Wt (g)
Sunstroke[a]	2	9	3	52	0	0	1,300	22,659	3	33	16	192	18	453
	0%	0%	0%	0%	0%	0%	49%	69%	0%	0%	1%	1%	1%	1%
Corbin-Tucker[b]	0	0	0	0	0	0	1,480	6,989	0	0	11	76	8	59
	0%	0%	0%	0%	0%	0%	58%	72%	0%	0%	0%	1%	0%	1%
Chattahoochee	0	0	0	0	0	0	454	4,805	13	154	15	193	25	254
	0%	0%	0%	0%	0%	0%	34%	37%	1%	1%	1%	2%	2%	2%
Landing[c]	1	7	1	3	0	0	132	1,114	0	0	129	996	94	758
	0%	0%	0%	0%	0%	0%	10%	13%	0%	0%	9%	12%	7%	9%
Pierce[d]	0	0	0	0	0	0								
	0%	0%	0%	0%	0%	0%								
Yon[e]	0	0	2	23	23	182	191	3,737	91	1,326	366	4,037	218	2,637
	0%	0%	0%	0%	0%	0%	1%	4%	1%	1%	2%	4%	1%	3%

Site	Marsh Island Incised		Point Washington Incised		Cool Branch Incised		Shell-Tempered Wares		Other Types in Assemblage		Total	
	N	Wt (g)	N	Wt (g)	N	Wt (g)	N	Wt (g)	N	Wt (g)	N	Wt (g)
Sunstroke[a]	1	25	3	22	1	3	27	111	1,270	9,327	2,644	32,887
	0%	0%	0%	0%	0%	0%	1%	0%	48%	28%	100%	100%
Corbin-Tucker[b]	0	0	3	41	0	0	2	16	1,053	2,477	2,557	9,658
	0%	0%	0%	0%	0%	0%	0%	0%	41%	26%	100%	100%
Chattahoochee Landing[c]	1	8	0	0	0	0	2	3	845	7,411	1,355	12,828
	0%	0%	0%	0%	0%	0%	0%	0%	68%	61%	100%	100%
Pierce[d]	3	35	8	40	5	59	56	377	937	5,272	1,366	8,661
	0%	0%	1%	0%	0%	1%	4%	4%	69%	61%	100%	100%
Yon[e]	155	3,900	65	1,053	27	508	253	1,519	16,757	78,713	18,148	97,287
	1%	4%	0%	1%	0%	0%	1%	1%				

Notes: a. n.d., USF archaeology lab; ceramics recovered from single test unit and surface.
b. White 1994; White et al. 2012; ceramics recovered from village area test excavation units.
c. White 2011a; ceramics recovered from surface, subsurface testing, and exposed mound profiles.
d. White 2013; ceramics recovered from subsurface testing, exposed mound profile, and surface; ceramics included in table collected for Fort Walton area of site only (discussed below).
e. Du Vernay 2011; White 1996; ceramics collected from test excavation units, manual core surveys, and surface.

Table 9.3. Fort Walton Ceramic Chronology

Period	Ceramic Trends
Early Fort Walton (AD 1000–1200)	Large proportion of check stamped sherds (~ 20 to 25%; frequency sometimes higher if site has preceding late Weeden Island component) The presence of some late Weeden Island types Small proportion of shell-tempered sherds (~ 2 to 5%) Cob-marked sherds All Fort Walton types
Middle Fort Walton (AD 1200–1400)	Very small proportion of check stamped sherds (~ 1%) Very small proportion of shell-tempered sherds (~ 1%) All Fort Walton types
Late Fort Walton (AD 1400–1600)	Very small proportion or absence of check stamped sherds All Fort Walton types Appearance of Lamar types (or they could also be post–Fort Walton)

Source: Adapted from Marrinan and White 2007:293.

is recognized as being strictly a cemetery and village site occupied from transitional Late Woodland to early–middle Fort Walton (White et al. 2012:233). In addition, a number of Early or Middle Woodland period burial mound sites have demonstrated Fort Walton components, including the Pierce and Chattahoochee Landing sites, as well as Chipola Cutoff (8Gu5), which was once situated near the confluence of the Chipola and Apalachicola Rivers but has been completely washed away (White 2011b), and the Waddell's Mill Pond (8Ja65) site located upstream from Chipola Cutoff, which has a Middle Woodland mound and a Fort Walton component (Gardner 1966; Tesar and Jones 2009). Along the southern reaches of the lower Chattahoochee are two sites with platform mounds (Belovich et al. 1982; Blitz and Lorenz 2006; Moore 1907; Neuman 1961; White 1981): Old Rambo (9Se15), on the east bank, and Omussee Creek mound (1Ho27), on the west bank at about the northernmost extent of Fort Walton culture area (Blitz and Lorenz 2006; Marrinan and White 2007:293). A possible Fort Walton mound that is now submerged in Lake Seminole, the Underwater Indian Mound (9Se27), also contained an earlier Middle Woodland component (White 1981; White et al. 2012:233–234).

Since Willey's initial definition of Fort Walton, ceramics have been the primary focus in the discussions of Fort Walton diagnostic elements, and today Willey's Fort Walton ceramic types (1949:452–468) still are recognized as valid

(Marrinan and White 2007:292–293). The complex is known to contain only very small percentages of shell-tempered wares (Willey's Pensacola ceramic series), which are a cultural marker for the Pensacola Mississippian variant located to the west of the Fort Walton region. Ceramic type revisions have been proposed, including some with subtypes (Bullen 1958; Griffin 1950) and some using the type-variety system (Scarry 1984:417–470, 1985); both systems have problems (Blitz and Lorenz 2006; Marrinan and White 2007). Over the past 25 years, the USF archaeology lab has developed a sorting guide that is founded on Willey's typology and refined based on subsequent USF fieldwork to have non-overlapping types (White 2009).

The diagnostic Fort Walton ceramic types include Fort Walton Incised, Lake Jackson (a name that once included overlapping types "Plain" and "Incised"), Marsh Island Incised, and Point Washington Incised. In addition, generic (or non-diagnostic) types, including red-painted, black-painted, and engraved ceramics, also appear at Fort Walton sites, but in extremely low numbers, possibly due to their nonutilitarian, ceremonial use. Blitz and Lorenz (2006:114–118) have argued that these generic types (as well as effigy vessels, bottles and beakers) may have been associated with an interregional style of ceramics shared among Rood and Fort Walton mound polities along the lower Chattahoochee and Apalachicola rivers. The Wakulla Check Stamped pottery so prevalent in the preceding Late Woodland also is present, typically in earlier Fort Walton deposits (White 1982), as are cob-marked sherds. Additionally, sherds belonging to the later Lamar ceramic complex also occasionally appear at Fort Walton sites very late in the stratigraphic sequence. But because this complex has its origins in central Georgia (Hally 1994; Wauchope 1966; Williams 2008; Williams and Shapiro 1990), it represents one that was introduced to the Fort Walton region, likely sometime following initial European contact, as our newest data indicate (Du Vernay 2011). Other ceramic types found at Fort Walton sites but with probable origins outside of the region include shell-tempered Pensacola wares noted above and Cool Branch Incised (Sears 1967:32). Curiously, shell-tempered plain and occasionally incised, which by definition here must be called Pensacola Incised until proven otherwise, appear early in the Fort Walton sequence, and only in very small percentages. Interestingly, this pattern is similar for cob-marked pottery as well. Cool Branch Incised has been included in some discussions of diagnostic Fort Walton ceramics (Marrinan and White 2007:293), but its predominance among Middle Mississippian Rood II phase (AD 1200–1300) sites of the lower Chattahoochee (Blitz and Lorenz 2006:106), just north of the Fort Walton area, suggests it probably has its origins there.

Retaining Local Practices and Adopting Outside Traditions

Externally derived Mississippian influences on local Late Woodland groups in the Apalachicola–lower Chattahoochee River valley resulted in the emergence of a distinct regional cultural tradition that displayed both the continuation of some centuries-old practices and the incorporation of new Mississippian ideas. This mix is particularly evident in the ceramics. Most diagnostic Fort Walton ceramic types and forms, from the earliest Fort Walton deposits through post-European contact times, are recognizable as being a product of intersecting externally derived Mississippian and local traditions (Figure 9.3).

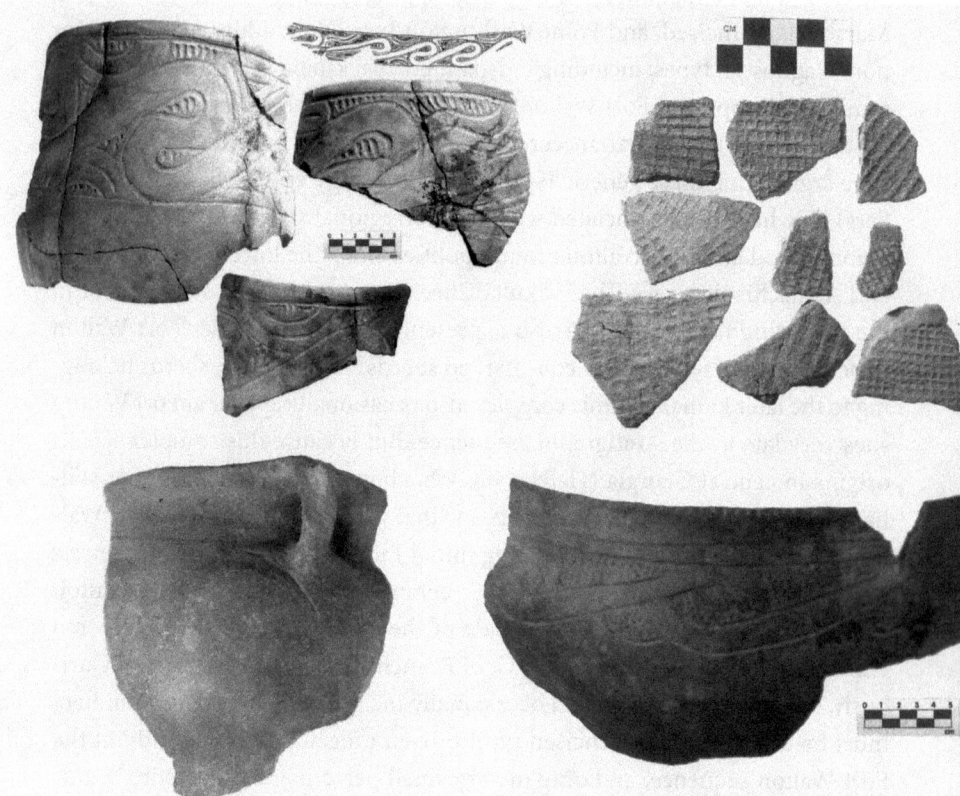

Figure 9.3. Sample of some of the ceramic types discussed. *Upper left*: Basin Bayou Incised jar, showing traditional scroll/loop type pattern (from Middle Woodland Gotier Hammock Mound, radiocarbon-dated soot on exterior to AD 650) (White 2010); *upper right*: Wakulla Check Stamped (Late Woodland and early Fort Walton—*top row*, from Curlee site, 8Ja7; *middle and bottom rows*, from Otis Hare site, 8Li172); *lower left*, Lake Jackson Jar (from Curlee site, 8Ja7) (White 1982); *lower right*, Fort Walton Incised bowl (from Corbin-Tucker, 8Ca142).

The Lake Jackson type is morphologically similar to Mississippi Plain jars; the type Fort Walton Incised has slightly more distinctive characteristics, with incised scrolls or lines and punctations, but often on typical Mississippian carinated bowls, and also bottles/beakers (Marrinan and White 2007:293). Point Washington Incised is characterized with scrolls but no punctations, and Marsh Island Incised with parallel diagonal incised lines on the vessel neck only; both are usually open bowl shapes, sometimes with attached head and tail adornos (White 2009:9–11; White et al. 2012:237–239). These typical Fort Walton designs (especially scrolls) resemble those found on local Woodland types (e.g., Basin Bayou Incised; see Figure 9.3) (White et al. 2012:249), but the precursors to the Mississippian vessel forms, particularly handled jars, do not exist here, suggesting at least the introduction of the shape from an external source (Blitz and Lorenz 2002:128). Most important and distinctive, however, is that Fort Walton potters preferred tempering their ceramics with grit and/or with lesser amounts of grog and sand, ceramic tempers used since Early Woodland times; this practice set them apart from most of the Mississippian world, where crushed shell was the preferred tempering agent (Marrinan and White 2007:292–293). Additionally, we see the appearance of distinctive fine serving wares in the form of the six-pointed (or occasionally five-pointed) open bowl, often found in burial contexts. The shallow, flared-rim open soup bowl/plate shape is known elsewhere in Mississippian times but typically with shell temper and a round rim. Its manifestation with the six-pointed rim shape and grit temper is apparently confined to the Fort Walton region (although a shell-tempered version exists within Pensacola material culture to the west) and may represent the Fort Walton adoption and subsequent adjustment and redesign of a common Mississippian form.

The presence of check stamped pottery along with Fort Walton types has long been used as the primary evidence for the existence of a regional continuity between the Late Woodland and early Fort Walton periods (Blitz and Lorenz 2002; Brose 1984; Scarry 1984, 1990; White 1982), and the sites in the valley demonstrating this ceramic continuity are many. A particularly well-documented example is seen at the Curlee site (8Ja7), the transitional late Weeden Island–early to middle Fort Walton village and cemetery mentioned above, on the west bank of the Apalachicola River just south of the river confluence. Here, 22 percent of the ceramic assemblage from the earliest Fort Walton zones consisted of check stamped sherds in the same strata as the Mississippian-style Lake Jackson jars with handles (White 1982). A well-dated but underreported example of this ceramic mix is seen at the Corbin-Tucker site (8Ca142), a village and cemetery located in the middle Apalachicola valley investigated by

USF during the 1990s (White 1994; White et al. 2012). At Corbin-Tucker, two charcoal samples from a refuse pit replete with Wakulla Check Stamped and plain sherds dated to cal. AD 880–1030 (see Table 9.1). The village area located around the feature produced additional Wakulla Check Stamped sherds (n = 1,480), composing 58 percent of the total ceramic assemblage (n = 2,557), in addition to diagnostic Fort Walton and a couple of shell-tempered sherds (see Table 9.2). In the cemetery area of the site, which likely is associated with late Fort Walton activity, there were among the grave goods a *Busycon* shell cup and greenstone celts, copper discs, and other materials coupled with distinctive Fort Walton ceramics, such as six-pointed bowl sherds (White 1994; White et al. 2012). Taken together, these data suggest a very late ninth-century, late Weeden Island village settlement at Corbin-Tucker that flowed into an early Fort Walton one, and a late Fort Walton component as well.

We argue that the continuation of check stamped pottery and the characteristics defining diagnostic Fort Walton ceramic types, including extant decorative elements, tempering, and vessel forms, demonstrate a negotiation between the retention of traditional ceramic technologies and the incorporation of externally derived ideas. The continued manufacture of check stamped ceramics and the traditional and distinctive non-shell temper reflect a strong Woodland pottery-making practice that smoothly transformed into an early Fort Walton practice that was accompanied by the adoption of externally derived Mississippian vessel forms. We believe that the significance of maintaining grit tempering and only negligible use of shell tempering among emerging Fort Walton groups is significant, especially when considering the abundance of shell available in the region and the high frequency of shell tempering occurring just to the north among the contemporaneous Rood I groups of the lower Chattahoochee valley. We agree with others (e.g., Alt 2006:292; Fortier 2001:186–187) who regard ceramic temper as an identity marker as much as a technological necessity. The few shell-tempered sherds that do exist in Fort Walton assemblages may have come from outside sources; this hypothesis is now more testable with modern instrumentation for trace element studies, so the research continues.

From this perspective, the cultural processes involved with pottery production and use would have been important in the building and combining of tradition and social identity (Pauketat 2001:82). The selection among early Fort Walton communities (as well as those who followed them) of materials other than shell to temper their pottery, while coincidentally adopting other broader Mississippian practices from vessel forms to maize agriculture to flat-topped pyramidal mounds, can be understood as an effort to maintain a sense of identity within the context of the wider Mississippian world (Marrinan and White 2007:293). Shell-tempered sherds are present at Fort Walton sites in the valley only in negligible amounts, and as discussed above, generally are found in greater frequency in early Fort Walton contexts, which may represent early external Mississippian influences from Rood I groups to the north of Fort Walton and Pensacola groups to the west, the more typical Mississippian manifestations with shell-tempered pottery (Blitz and Lorenz 2002, 2006; Harris 2012). A possible caveat for a Pensacola-derived influence is the current (and limited) radiometric data for that region that suggest that this tradition might be more contemporaneous with middle and late Fort Walton than early Fort Walton (e.g., Harris 2012:282). However, it is reasonable to argue that when Pensacola culture is better dated, we will likely see earlier dates there.

It has long been recognized that a general characteristic indicating change through time in Fort Walton is the decreasing frequency and eventual disappearance of Wakulla Check Stamped pottery from Fort Walton contexts (Marrinan and White 2007:293; Willey 1949:438; White 1982:109). Given the apparent role that this type had in continuation of local practices in the face of external influences since the Early Woodland two millennia previously, it is worthwhile to discuss this topic in light of new data and what they potentially reveal about Fort Walton beginnings. A recently completed analysis of ceramic, stratigraphic, and radiocarbon data from investigations at the Yon mound and village site has shed additional light on the fading of Wakulla Check Stamped pottery manufacturing (Du Vernay 2011, 2014). To date, Yon represents the most thoroughly studied Fort Walton mound center in the Apalachicola River Valley, with multiple investigations completed by USF (White 1996; Du Vernay 2011) and various other researchers, including John Scarry (1978), Matthew Stirling (see Willey 1949:262), and Clarence Bloomfield Moore (1903:393), as well as James Miller, Daniel Penton, George Percy, David Phelps, Bennie Keel, and L. Ross Morrell (Du Vernay 2011:67–79).

Yon has a single, flat-topped mound, 7.3 m high, which is surrounded by a dense village midden area. Ceramic and stratigraphic data and multiple radiocarbon dates for the primary Fort Walton village midden zone and the earliest basket-loaded mound layer indicate that mound construction and a domestic occupation started at the beginning of the middle Fort Walton period, between AD 1200 and 1250, with little stratigraphic or ceramic evidence of any substantial late Weeden Island or early Fort Walton activity preceding it (Du Vernay 2011, 2104). Over 18,000 sherds from the multiple Yon investigations were examined. All Fort Walton types (and later Lamar sherds) were present, dominating the site's diagnostic ceramic assemblage, but only a mere 191 check stamped sherds were identified, amounting to about one percent of the total assemblage (Du Vernay 2011) (see Table 9.2). None of these were identifiable as Leon Check Stamped, the type associated with the site's protohistoric component. Taken together, these data indicate that the Wakulla Check Stamped pottery production so prevalent among local late Weeden Island and early Fort Walton groups lost much steam in the region as early as circa AD 1200–1250 at the beginning of middle Fort Walton, perhaps indicating that, on the level of daily practice, a more robust Fort Walton identity had emerged by this time.

Coincident with the fading of Wakulla Check Stamped pottery and what we interpret as a more fully realized Fort Walton emergence was the appearance in the valley of a new and external ceramic type—Cool Branch Incised—that we argue demonstrates a blending of cultural traditions with distinct origins. This type predominates among contemporaneous Rood II Mississippian sites farther up the lower Chattahoochee River Valley (Blitz and Lorenz 2006:109). It exists in low frequencies at Fort Walton sites—about two to three percent among diagnostic types—including at Yon (Du Vernay 2011). This type is characterized by incised arches accompanied by punctations or ticks ("eyelashes") at the top and is the grit-tempered equivalent of the shell-tempered Moundville Incised, the diagnostic type in the Rood region 100 years earlier (Blitz and Lorenz 2002; Blitz and Lorenz 2006:106, Table 1). Cool Branch Incised in Fort Walton suggests a communication at the level of domestic practice with Rood II groups but also may represent the creation of a new "hybrid" ceramic type resulting from the intersection of Rood and Fort Walton traditions that likely began during early Fort Walton times.

Recently, the concepts of hybrid cultural forms and "hybridity" have been considered by many researchers (e.g., Alt 2006; Card 2013a; Stockhammer 2013) and represent an important theoretical focus of this volume. Specifically, as detailed by Card (2013b:4), these concepts are best understood as "the incorporation, blending, adoption, or other form of mixing of discrete elements from different cultural sources" to generate new cultural forms and identities. From this perspective, hybridity as a process involves the modification of cultural traditions by such sources (or groups) as a form of accommodation (Alt 2006). As such, hybridity creates change and generates new cultural traditions from the shifting social relations among interacting groups with disparate origins (Alt 2006:292) and involves the "production of material objects incorporating elements of multiple existing stylistic or technological traditions" (Card 2013b:1).

We argue that Cool Branch Incised fits within the purview of a new hybrid cultural form or "material entanglement" (Stockhammer 2013:18) in that it combines elements from different types, namely, the decorative motifs originally featured on shell-tempered Moundville Incised, with the decidedly Fort Walton grit temper. Although Cool Branch Incised represents a ceramic type with origins outside of the Fort Walton region, its innovation likely is in part the result of interaction with emerging Fort Walton groups; and its appearance in the Fort Walton region circa AD 1200, albeit a comparatively minimal one, we suggest, represents a unique brand of receptiveness to an external ceramic tradition. This interpretation may appear contrary to the position by Blitz and Lorenz (2006:109–110) that Rood and Fort Walton had a buffer zone between them at this time. The move to grit tempering from shell among Rood groups shortly after their arrival to the upper part of the lower Chattahoochee River area and coming into contact with developing Fort Walton communities to the south can be understood as an initial step in the disintegration of this possible buffer zone.

Platform Mound Building and the Reoccupation of Woodland Burial Mound Sites

Earthen platform mounds have long been recognized as a defining feature of the Mississippi period, although it is now well known that they were constructed at a number of sites in the Southeast and Midwest regions prior to Mississippian times, but in a much lower frequency (Lindauer and Blitz 1997:172–173). As succinctly summarized by Blitz and Livingood (2004:292), these earthen structures were sociopolitically significant, serving as high-status residence and mortuary locales, markers of regional political capitals, a means to legitimize status through the control of construction and use, and other purposes (although White [2011a, 2013] has suggested that platforms were also sometimes built simply to raise people and/or structures above floodplain levels). As noted, it appears that the Late Woodland–early Fort Walton transition in the valley involved an increase in population and the number of sites, as well as a settlement shift to a concentration of larger riverbank settlements, possibly for continued agricultural and communication intensification. It is also during this time that initial platform-mound building appeared and earlier burial mound sites were reoccupied. The platform mound sites in the valley have been briefly introduced above. Among them, Chattahoochee Landing, Pierce, and Cayson are the ones with the best evidence for pre–Fort Walton activity and probable early Fort Walton platform mounds (Figure 9.4). The remaining two sites with platform mounds—Yon and Omussee Creek—presently lack evidence of pre–Fort Walton mound-building episodes or very minimal evidence for any earlier occupation (Du Vernay 2011; Blitz and Lorenz 2006:59).

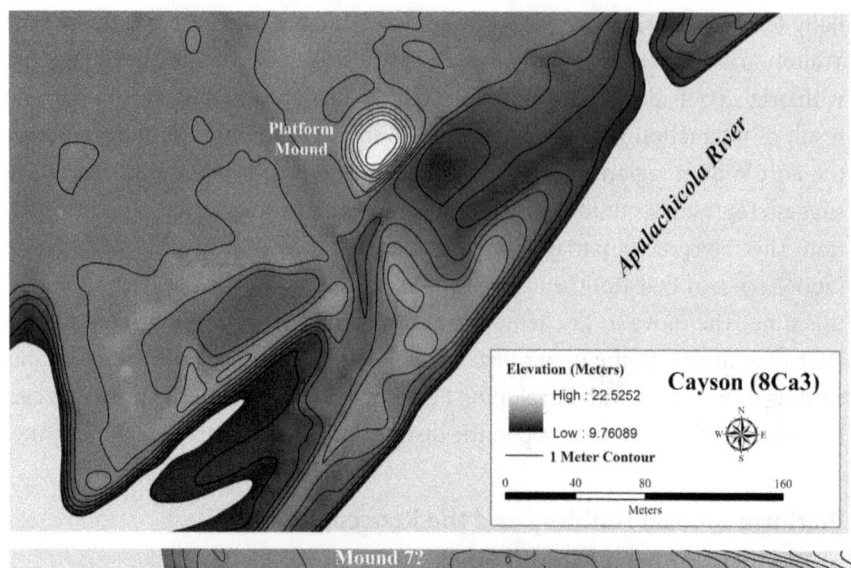

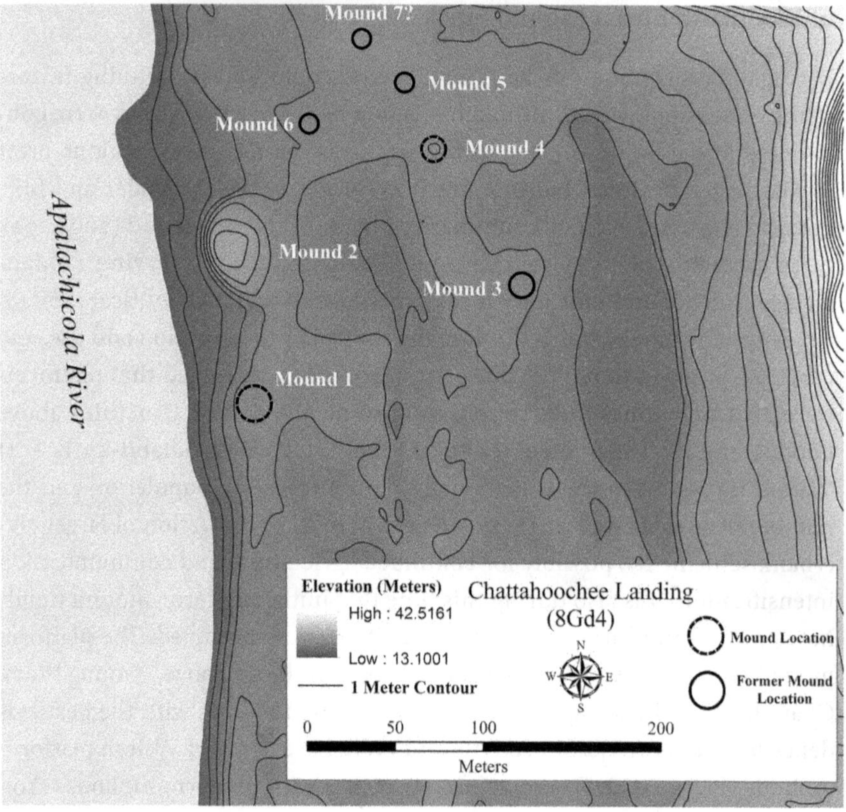

Figure 9.4. Contour and digital elevation maps (DEM) of the Cayson (*a*), Chattahoochee Landing (*b*), and Pierce (*c, opposite*) sites derived from National Elevation Dataset (NED) aerial LiDAR data.

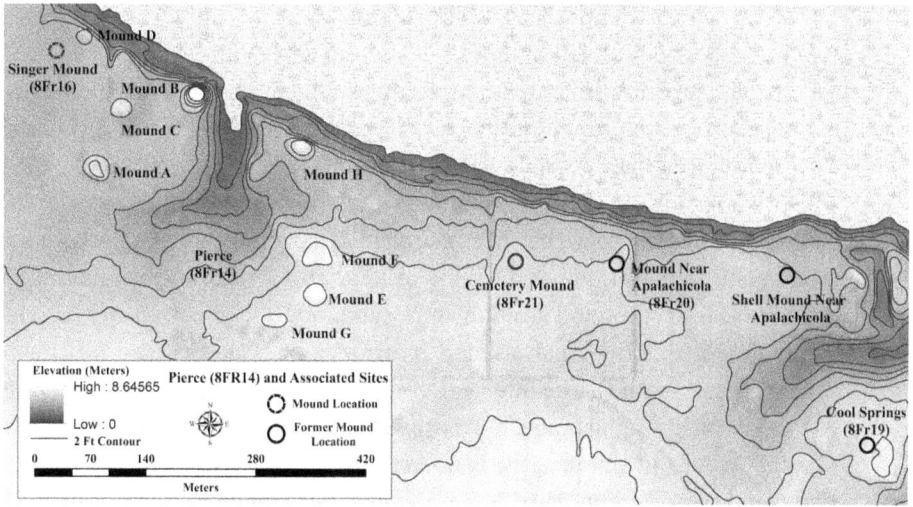

(c)

Chattahoochee Landing and Pierce are the multiple-mound Fort Walton centers; both have Woodland mounds dating to one or two millennia before Fort Walton. Recent fieldwork by USF at both these sites, as well as reexaminations of previous work and collections, has improved our understanding of their layouts, compositions, and occupational histories, and enhanced our understanding of processes operating during the early Fort Walton period (White 2011a, 2013). The Chattahoochee Landing site was initially recorded over a century ago by Moore (1903:491–492), and while the site initially contained seven earthen mounds, today only portions of three remain, although the locations of those destroyed recently have been identified (White 2011a). Chattahoochee Landing sits at the strategic location of the confluence of the Chattahoochee and Flint rivers, at the top of the Apalachicola, a locality undoubtedly selected in part for its subsistence advantages and regional and interregional travel possibilities. The diminished state of the site poses some obvious interpretive challenges, particularly in the way of firmly dating the various mound construction episodes. The recent work (White 2011a) has helped to shed new light on the site's occupational components, which began over 2,000 years ago, and their probable significance to local populations living in the initial wake of Mississippian influences. This work included the examination and tabulation of materials previously collected by Case Western Reserve University and the Florida Bureau of Archaeological Research (both surface and excavated), as well as additional subsurface testing and surface collection by USF in 2011. The combined ceramic tabulations derived from these investigations are presented in Table 9.2.

The various Chattahoochee Landing mound, midden, and surface-collected ceramic materials and data synthesized showed that mound building and site activity here probably initially occurred during the Early Woodland, circa 100 BC to AD 200, seen in the presence of Deptford ceramics. This initial activity was followed by a possible Late Woodland occupation. During the 2011 USF investigation, an exposed profile at Mound 1 was cleaned to reveal a midden stratum characterized by check stamped and plain ceramics lying beneath three mound-building zones. Organic residues from a feature encountered in the second-lowest mound stratum were submitted to Beta Analytic, Inc., by White for radiocarbon analysis, and returned a date of 1510 ± 30 BP (Beta-306923) (see Table 9.1). The intercept of this date with the calibration curve is AD 570 (with a 2-sigma range of AD 540–620). Although this date sits within Middle Woodland times, there is no ceramic evidence suggesting a Middle Woodland period component at the site. Additionally, Beta Analytic, Inc., indicated to White the likelihood of the organic residues submitted returning a date range older than what is reflected in the surrounding cultural material. Together with the ceramic composition of the midden zone, White took it as probable evidence for a Late Woodland foundation for the Fort Walton mound center. No diagnostic Fort Walton ceramic types were encountered during the limited Mound 1 profile cleaning.

The most platform-mound-building activity at Chattahoochee Landing was associated with Mound 2, an approximately 3-m-high mound that was likely enlarged from an Early Woodland mound. Unfortunately, radiometric dates do not presently exist for Mound 2, but the extant ceramic evidence hints that an early Fort Walton context is most probable. This evidence includes the recovery of check-stamped sherds during Case Western Reserve University (CWRU) investigation from a shallow mound provenience as well as the presence of cob-marked pottery and additional check stamped pottery and diagnostic Fort Walton types, including Fort Walton Incised, Lake Jackson, and Point Washington Incised from the mound surface and adjacent areas (White 2011a:38). It is important to point out that some of the check stamped sherds associated with Mound 2 and other areas that derive from a surface context could be associated with the site's Early Woodland component, and not Late Woodland or early Fort Walton activities.

At the other end of the Apalachicola River from Chattahoochee Landing are Pierce mounds, where an early Mississippian influence also is evident. Pierce is composed of a long *Rangia* and oyster-shell midden ridge running around the west side of the river mouth, a sizeable village area, and at least a dozen (possibly 13) mounds, seven of which are arranged in an oval with a possible plaza in the middle (see Figure 9.4). Combined, these landscape features make Pierce the most geographically expansive site in the Apalachicola–lower Chattahoochee River valley. The strategic location gave access to east–west movement along the Gulf and a north–south travel and information corridor up the Apalachicola River and far into the interior Southeast. Like Chattahoochee Landing, Pierce was initially recorded by Moore (1902:217–219), and his and subsequent investigators' data were recently synthesized with information from recent USF investigations, providing an improved understanding of the site's extensive occupational history as well as correcting mistakes in interpretations (such as mound names) that have been compounded over several decades (White 2013).

Pierce burial mound construction and domestic activity were initiated on the west side of the site during the Early Woodland period, temporally identified by the presence of Deptford ceramics in both mound fill and surrounding occupation area. Mound building and site activity expanded during the following Middle Woodland period to include a variety of burial types replete with copper, shell, and other exotic materials that are well known from Moore's (1902:217–219) investigation, as well as an abundance of Swift Creek and early Weeden Island ceramics. Middle Woodland burial-mound ceremonialism evident there showed clear connections with contemporaneous sites from across the Southeast and Midwest, with many of the Pierce artifacts and raw materials (such as bison bone, copper, and silver) having been acquired from faraway places. Pierce has long been known as a preeminent Middle Woodland burial mound complex, but most researchers are unaware that it has an important Fort Walton component as well, on the east side. This reality is largely the by-product of Moore's investigation and the absence of any Fort Walton descriptions in his summary.

Pierce's Fort Walton component centers on Mound H, an approximately 2.5-m-high platform mound built of shell from (and on) the midden ridge, with an adjacent village area to the south-southeast (see Figure 9.4). Much of what is presently known of Mound H and its associated village derives from data collected during USF investigations from exposed mound areas in looter holes and from the mound surface, coupled with previously unreported data from these areas that were collected by the Florida Bureau of Archaeological Research in the 1970s and 1990s and recently examined by White (2013). Ceramic tabulation for Pierce Mound H and adjacent village area from all of these collections is summarized in Table 9.2 and includes all standard Fort Walton ceramic types, and a comparably higher frequency of check stamped sherds as well as a few Late Woodland sherds (Carrabelle Incised and Tucker

Ridge Pinched). Using surface-collected materials for interpretive purposes has obvious problems, but we argue that these ceramic data do suggest early Fort Walton occupation. Notably absent on the Fort Walton side of the site are any Early or Middle Woodland materials, with the exception of one possible Middle Woodland Weeden Island Incised sherd. This absence is interesting given the high level of activity the site experienced prior to Fort Walton times, and it might suggest that the local emerging Fort Walton groups opted to build their platform mound adjacent to the earlier mounds as opposed to on top of one of them. A core with a 4-inch bucket auger taken in the Fort Walton village area, just east of Mound H, revealed a thick midden zone extending a meter deep, and charcoal that returned a radiocarbon date of 750 ± 40 BP (Beta-221908) (see Table 9.1). The intercept for this date is AD 1270 (with a 2-sigma range of AD 1220–1300), suggesting that the Fort Walton occupation at Pierce likely continued into middle Fort Walton times.

The Cayson site has a large platform mound and a probable small burial mound and is situated in the middle Apalachicola River valley at the likely strategic location of the northern extent of the Gulf Coastal Lowlands. The site was first recorded by Moore (1903:468), but because he was unable to obtain permission to excavate there, he did not give it an official name, instead simply referring to it as "Mound near Blountstown." Multiple excavations in the mound and village areas were completed at Cayson by CWRU and Florida State University (FSU) during the 1970s. Most of the data derived from these investigations remain underreported, although we have begun to examine these materials at the USF archaeology lab. In two short reports, Brose (1975) and Brose et al. (1976) presented some initial findings, ceramic frequency tabulations, and radiocarbon dating results, and other preliminary results have been presented by Scarry (1980). The Cayson ceramic tabulations given in Brose (1975) and Brose et al. (1976) suggest that Cayson experienced Middle Woodland period activity, seen in the presence of Weeden Island Incised and Weeden Island Plain pottery, although it is difficult to discern from the reports whether these ceramic types were associated with mound contexts (Brose 1975:Table 1). A minimal number of Middle to Late Woodland ceramics, including Carrabelle Punctate and Carrabelle Incised, also were recovered, as was a relatively significant amount of Wakulla Check Stamped pottery, amounting to 23 percent of the total number of sherds reported (n = 2,648). In the greatest frequency were Fort Walton sherds, with all Fort Walton types represented.

Although the existing Cayson ceramic data are extremely preliminary, they do suggest that the site had both a Middle Woodland component and a Late

Woodland–early Fort Walton occupation. This latter component is largely corroborated by the extant radiocarbon data derived from the CWRU investigations, although the provenience documentation for these dates is poor (see Table 9.1). These dates were originally corrected by Scarry (1990:236, Table 26) (using Klein et al. 1982 and Ralph et al. 1973) but recently were recalibrated with a refined radiocarbon calibration dataset (Reimer et al. 2009) electronically available through Oxcal, although the recalibrations generated only a negligible difference. With the exception of one sample, the calibrated intercepts all fall within early Fort Walton (AD 1000–1200), although the preferred calibrated range (2 sigma) clearly spans from late Weeden Island to middle Fort Walton times (see Table 9.1). Coupled with the reported Wakulla Check Stamped ceramic frequency, this suggests that an early Fort Walton occupation is probable, and that local populations selected for their platform mound a location with links to earlier Middle Woodland activity. We continue our review of field notes, maps, and materials from the CWRU and FSU Cayson investigations to try to determine the degree to which Middle Woodland peoples used this location for mound building and whether their early Fort Walton descendants elected to construct their platform mound on top of such an earlier construction.

Although limited, the data suggest that early Fort Walton groups were drawn to Early and Middle Woodland mounds and habitation sites, establishing villages and sometimes building their own mounds near or possibly on top of them. Such practices may have been oriented toward paying homage to or claiming the distinctive heritage of their (or any) ancestors while simultaneously establishing new Mississippian traditions. Whatever the case, this pattern suggests that connecting with pasts as manifested in Woodland period monuments likely was important for emerging Fort Walton groups in the wake of Mississippian influences.

The Role of Maize Agriculture in Fort Walton Beginnings

Intensified maize production has long been considered one of the defining characteristics of Mississippian, and an absence of it has served as a "common denominator" in the designation of other contemporaneous cultures as being outside of this cultural realm (Ashley and White 2012:14). As recently brought out by Ashley and White (2012:14–15), this scenario is particularly acute in Florida, where the lack of an agricultural tradition among St. Johns, Safety Harbor, and Pensacola cultures, for example, frequently has pushed these regional cultural variants to the fringe in discussions of things Mississippian. In the Apalachicola–lower Chattahoochee River valley, the importance of maize agriculture in explanations of Fort Walton emergence has long been emphasized (Brose 1984; Brose and Percy 1974, 1978; Scarry 1981, 1990; White 1982, 1986). As noted, maize was introduced to the region during the Late Woodland period, with the best evidence for it (both botanical and radiometric) deriving from the Sycamore site in the upper Apalachicola River valley (Milanich 1974). Beginning in the 1970s, such evidence was coupled with regional settlement data suggesting that local Late Woodland groups expanded into diverse yet ecologically restricted locales advantageous for cultivation. It was argued that competition for arable land and population growth forced the transition to a more intensive cultivation system and a more efficient mechanism of social control (i.e., chiefdoms), both of which ultimately stemmed from knowledge of external Mississippian communities (Brose and Percy 1974, 1978; Scarry 1990).

The presence of Late Woodland maize in the valley suggests that agriculture was likely an important component (among others) for emerging Fort Walton communities. Moreover, Fort Walton beginnings in part may have represented the expansion of local Late Woodland gardening of this productive crop into full-blown farming. However, there is little evidence that this expansion resulted in overcrowding or an exhaustion of arable lands (Marrinan and White 2007:300). Current evidence of maize here during both the Late Woodland and Mississippian periods has come from sites situated well inland from the Gulf Coast, likely because the sandy, salty, and swampy soils of the lower valley may have made farming more difficult, coupled with the possibly more abundant and easily obtainable wild wetland and aquatic resources. To date, six Fort Walton sites in the valley have well-documented direct evidence for maize in the form of cobs or kernels (Bullen 1958; Neuman 1961; White 1982; also see White et al. 2012:264, Table 10.3, for a list of all known maize evidence at Fort Walton sites). Perhaps the best evidence is seen at the Curlee site in the upper Apalachicola River valley, with its late Weeden Island–early Fort Walton occupation containing charred cobs (White 1982). Brose (1975) and Brose and colleagues (1976) reported the presence of maize pollen from multiple soil samples taken from the middle Apalachicola River valley Cayson and Yon sites, but the contextual information regarding these samples is poorly documented. Cob-marked pottery constitutes additional (albeit indirect) evidence for maize production. Cob-marked pottery occurs with the greatest frequency during the early Fort Walton period and with some frequency during the preceding late Weeden Island period, when maize first appeared (e.g., Milanich 1974), together suggesting the relatively important subsistence role of maize growing during these times. Stamping cobs onto wet clay to impress vessel surfaces may have had some symbolic importance as well.

Both macrobotanical remains and cob-marked pottery demonstrate the presence of maize in the middle and upper Apalachicola and lower Chattahoochee area, but such evidence is so far absent in the southern reaches of the valley (see White et al. 2012:264, Table 10.3). Currently, the southernmost maize is known from the middle valley at the Yon (Du Vernay 2008, 2011; White 1996) and Cayson (Brose 1975; Brose et al. 1976) sites. Below here and into the coastal areas, Fort Walton sites have produced no evidence of maize growing or indications of agricultural production of any kind. In the middle valley, Yon and Cayson are at the northern extent of the Gulf Coastal Lowlands physiographic region, possibly the southernmost locations in the valley where intensive agricultural production would have been more easily achieved. Below here in the lower delta wetlands and coastal regions, the subsistence data for Fort Walton sites of any period, primarily known from the investigation of shell middens (e.g., White 2005, 2012, 2014; White et al. 2002), show a heavy reliance on aquatic resources, a food pathway employed here since at least the Middle Archaic (Ashley and White 2012:17). To the west, around Choctawhatchee Bay, maize has been reported at a few coastal sites characterized by a mix of Fort Walton and Pensacola Mississippian traditions (Harris 2012:284). The most extensive Gulf Coast maize evidence is at the Pensacola-Mississippian Bottle Creek site, in the swampy Mobile delta of Alabama, where it may have been imported already processed (Gremillion 1993; Scarry 2003a, 2003b). It is of course possible that a similar scenario of maize importation existed for Fort Walton (early or later) sites situated in the lower Apalachicola River valley and adjacent coastal areas (Marrinan and White 2007:297). However, multiple years of USF investigations in these locales have included efforts to recover such materials, including through systematically collected flotation samples.

The apparent absence of farming in the lower reaches of the valley has implications for refining our understanding of Fort Walton beginnings. Specifically, it calls into question the long-standing and geographically blanketed primacy given to maize intensification in discussions of Fort Walton emergence that has given little consideration to the diverse ecological zones characterizing the region, particularly the important differences between coastal and inland environments (White 1999). This long-held perspective stems from the decades of archaeological investigations that largely focused on inland Fort Walton sites with the solid evidence of maize. More recent coastal lowland investigations (e.g., Harke 2012; White 2005, 2013; White et al. 2002) improve our understanding of Fort Walton subsistence and the intraregional variability that likely characterized it. These investigations have suggested that coastal Fort Walton groups, including at Pierce (White 2013) and Richardson's Hammock located along St. Joseph Bay (White 2005; Harke 2012), likely resided in the region year-round, largely subsisting on the region's abundant bay and estuarine resources. For Fort Walton beginnings, this subsistence variability and pattern has particular implications for the Pierce site, with its likely early Fort Walton platform-mound building and occupation that emerged in situ from local Late Woodland groups. Here, present evidence suggests these emerging Fort Walton coastal groups possibly opted to embrace only some externally derived Mississippian practices, such as ceramics and platform-mound building, but not agriculture like the contemporaneous populations upriver with whom they interacted. Thus, we suggest this possible important variation within Fort Walton itself and its beginnings.

Discussion and Concluding Remarks

As stated by Blitz (2010:13), "Mississippian in its diverse forms was the product of intersecting local and external factors that defy isolation." The evidence for Fort Walton Mississippian beginnings from the Apalachicola–lower Chattahoochee River valley discussed herein is compatible with this perspective. When we characterize these beginnings, we hypothesize an in situ transition, shaped by external relations and existing local traditions, into a new lifestyle and distinctive material culture. From this perspective, the historical process of a Late Woodland–early Fort Walton Mississippianization involved the successors of long-established groups solidifying leadership through the continuation of some existing local traditions and the resettling and expanding of the sacred mound sites of their predecessors while at the same time adding a new and externally derived Mississippian flavor to the local cultural milieu. Perhaps this transition initially may have been slow moving, as indicated by the continuation of check stamped and cob-marked pottery into early Fort Walton; but we argue that, by no later than AD 1200, Fort Walton had fully emerged within the Mississippian world.

There is little doubt that early Fort Walton people and their descendants were organized into communities headed by chiefs, much like the rest of the Mississippian world, although whether such leaders simply had social ranks or wielded real political and economic power is not yet known. Recent Mississippian discussions have emphasized the high degree of sociopolitical variability and diversity that characterized these societies (e.g., Blitz 2010; Smith 2007). Unfortunately, the extant datasets for the Apalachicola–lower Chattahoochee region presently are too limited to make robust interpretations along this front. The well-known elite female and male burials at the Lake Jackson site in the Tallahassee Red Hills region (Jones 1982; Marrinan 2012), which show strong connections with other well-known Southeastern Ceremonial Complex (SECC) sites in the Southeast (e.g., Etowah), are not yet equaled by anything known from the Apalachicola–lower Chattahoochee valley. Additionally, there is no evidence to suggest that Fort Walton beginnings in any way involved new people intruding into the region to establish a new suite of practices or traditions, nor is there any evidence so far that Fort Walton emergence was the result of conflict or warfare; definitive evidence for fortifications presently does not exist (White et al. 2012:272).

At inland locations it is clear that an intensified level of maize growing was a central component to Fort Walton beginnings, so this evidence can be combined with factors ranging from population growth to political or social influences from the wider Mississippian world to explain the emergence of a more complex society here. Clearly, subsistence practices on the coast that emphasized the continuation of wild (aquatic and terrestrial) resource collection instead of food production may have had social implications as well, but we do not yet know what these were. It is possible that the settlement pattern change from widespread, ecologically diverse locales during the Late Woodland to more concentrated settlements along the inland riverbanks by early Fort Walton times might reflect not only a shift to accommodate maize intensification but also a movement toward a more "corporate" organizational structure (e.g., Smith 2007:xvii–xxviii). The probable early Fort Walton platform-mound construction tentatively proposed here for Pierce, Cayson, and Chattahoochee Landing likely was the result of centralized or directed labor projects and presently represents the best evidence for the existence of a more corporate type of organization, although many more data are needed from each of these sites to confirm such an interpretation. Mississippian mound building as a ritual activity, potentially with a theme of unification for those who participated, has long been recognized (Blitz and Lorenz 2006; Blitz and Livingood 2004; Knight 1986:678; Pauketat and Alt 2003:152; Steponaitis 1978). As stated by Blitz (2010:15), platform mound building "helped to create and essentialize . . . new identities and social relationships required to expand political and social integration." We argue that early Fort Walton platform-mound building may have served this function, and because it initially occurred often at sites with existing earlier mounds, we interpret such labor projects as promoting group cohesion for early Fort Walton groups that were incorporating new cultural practices within the context of their own histories and a shared geographic place.

Much of Fort Walton material culture reflects what we think is an assertion of local identity while simultaneously participating in the wider Mississippian world to greater or lesser extent. The burial practices (although known from only a few sites) of including valued goods such as conch shell cups, copper, disks, and jars with handles (Shahramfar 2008), as well as the platform mound–village site pattern and the evidence of farming, at least in the inland riverine environments, show direct participation in Mississippian patterns of both daily life and special ritual. But other differences from the traditional understanding of what "Mississippian" really was can be seen in the unusual ceramic styles and tempers that can only be interpreted as identity markers. In sum, we argue that the material record of early (and later) Fort Walton is clearly Mississippian but with a distinctive regional flavor. Explanations of why emerging Fort Walton groups and their descendants preferred non-shell tempers for their ceramics likely do not lie in any technological, functional, or environmental realm alone. We argue that they also are linked to the maintenance of a regional identity, one that is associated with a long-standing participation in the communal traditions that were established during the Woodland period or earlier, and were being transformed in the light of Mississippian influences from outside the region.

Fifteen years ago, Blitz and Lorenz (2002) argued that contact and interaction with Rood Mississippian pioneers farther up the Chattahoochee around AD 1100 inspired the cultural shifts that occurred among local groups in the valley during this time. Direct evidence for such contact or interaction can be seen in the presence of the Rood ceramic type Cool Branch Incised at Fort Walton sites. Additionally, we argue that interaction with Pensacola groups to the west (Harris 2012) should not be overlooked as a source of Mississippian influence in the valley either, particularly in light of the ceramic decorative motifs shared between the Fort Walton and Pensacola traditions (e.g., Pensacola Incised is the shell-tempered equivalent of the grit-tempered Fort Walton Incised). Although the present and limited radiocarbon data for the Pensacola region suggest activity contemporaneous with a middle-to-late Fort Walton timeframe, we argue that there is little reason to suggest that they were somehow exempt from the early Mississippian influences. The presence of both the Rood and Pensacola traditions adjacent to the Fort Walton area, we suggest, helps to demonstrate the existence of a Fort Walton people maintaining aspects of their own social identity while engaging in a Mississippian-influenced reorganization. Moreover, whatever the source(s) of the foreign Mississippian influences were to Late Woodland groups, it is apparent that efforts were made to retain aspects of local traditions as such influences entered the region. As such, while the Apalachicola–lower Chattahoochee valley region was open to the transmission of new ideas and practices across social boundaries, this transmission is best understood as being negotiated within the context of local histories and traditions, resulting in the generation of a distinctive Mississippian cultural variant in this relatively remote valley so far from the Mississippian heartland.

Acknowledgments

We would like to thank Greg Wilson for inviting us to participate in the 2012 SEAC symposium on Mississippian Beginnings and for including us in this publication. We also extend a sincere thank-you to Karl Lorenz for reviewing our chapter. His insightful comments and suggestions improved the content of the manuscript. Finally, we thank the USF students who have researched Fort Walton sites over the last several years and helped to collect and process some of the data discussed in this chapter.

References Cited

Alt, Susan M.
 2006 The Power of Diversity: The Roles of Migration and Hybridity in Culture Change. In *Leadership and Polity in Mississippian Society*, edited by Brian M. Butler and Paul D. Welch, pp. 289–308. Center for Archaeological Investigations, Occasional Paper No. 33. Southern Illinois University, Carbondale.

Ashley, Keith, and Nancy Marie White
 2012 Late Prehistoric Florida: An Introduction. In *Late Prehistoric Florida: Archaeology at the Edge of the Mississippian World*, edited by Keith Ashley and Nancy White, pp. 1–28. University Press of Florida, Gainesville.

Belovich, Stephanie J., David S. Brose, Russell M. Weisman, and Nancy Marie White
 1982 *Archaeological Survey at George W. Andrews Lake and Chattahoochee River*. Archaeological Report No. 37. Cleveland Museum of Natural History, Cleveland.

Blitz, John H.
 2010 New Perspectives in Mississippian Archaeology. *Journal of Archaeological Research* 18:1–39.

Blitz, John H., and Patrick Livingood
 2004 Sociopolitical Implications of Mississippian Mound Volume. *American Antiquity* 69:291–301.

Blitz, John H., and Karl G. Lorenz
 2002 The Early Mississippian Frontier in the Lower Chattahoochee–Apalachicola River Valley. *Southeastern Archaeology* 21:117–135.
 2006 *The Chattahoochee Chiefdoms*. University of Alabama Press, Tuscaloosa.

Brose, David
 1975 Case Western Reserve University Contributions to the Archaeological Investigation of

Two Early Fort Walton Sites in the Apalachicola River Valley, Northwest Florida: 1973. Manuscript on file, Department of Anthropology, Case Western Reserve University, Cleveland.

1984 Mississippian Period Cultures in Northwest Florida. In *Perspectives on Gulf Coast Prehistory*, edited by Dave Davis, pp. 165–197. University Press of Florida, Gainesville.

Brose, David, Patricia Essenpreis, John Scarry, Helga Bluestone, and Anna Forsythe

1976 Contributions to the Archaeology of Northwestern Florida: Investigation of Early Fort Walton Sites in the Middle Apalachicola River Valley. Manuscript on file, Department of Anthropology, Case Western Reserve University, Cleveland.

Brose, David, and George Percy

1974 An Outline of Weeden Island Ceremonial Activity in Northwest Florida. Paper presented at the 39th Annual Society for American Archaeology Meeting, Washington, D.C.

1978 Fort Walton Settlement Patterns. In *Mississippian Settlement Patterns*, edited by Bruce D. Smith, pp. 81–114. Academic Press, New York.

Bullen, Ripley P.

1958 Six Sites near the Chattahoochee River in the Jim Woodruff Reservoir Area, Florida. In *River Basin Survey Papers*, edited by Frank H. H. Roberts Jr., pp. 315–376. Bureau of American Ethnology Bulletin 169. Smithsonian Institution, Washington, D.C.

Card, Jeb J. (editor)

2013a *The Archaeology of Hybrid Material Culture*. Southern Illinois University Press, Carbondale.

2013b Introduction. In *The Archaeology of Hybrid Material Culture*, edited by Jeb J. Card, pp. 1–21. Southern Illinois University Press, Carbondale.

Du Vernay, Jeffrey P.

2008 Recent Investigations at the Yon Mound and Village Site. Paper presented at the 60th Florida Anthropological Society Meeting, Tampa.

2011 The Archaeology of Yon Mound and Village, Middle Apalachicola River Valley, Florida. Unpublished Ph.D. dissertation, Department of Anthropology, University of South Florida.

2014 Yon Mound and Village: A Fort Walton Center in Middle Apalachicola River Valley of Northwest Florida. *Florida Anthropologist* 67(1):37–61.

Fortier, Andrew C.

2001 The Tradition of Discontinuity: American Bottom Early and Middle Woodland Culture History Reexamined. In *The Archaeology of Traditions: Agency and History before and after Columbus*, edited by Timothy R. Pauketat, pp. 174–194. University Press of Florida, Gainesville.

Gardner, William M.

1966 The Waddells Mill Pond Site. *Florida Anthropologist* 19:43–64.

Gremillion, Kristen J.

1993 Prehistoric Maize from Bottle Creek. In *Bottle Creek Research: Working Papers on the Bottle Creek Site (1Ba2), Baldwin County, Alabama*, edited by Ian W. Brown and Richard S. Fuller, pp. 133–150. *Journal of Alabama Archaeology* 39(1–2).

Griffin, John W.

1950 Test Excavations at the Lake Jackson Site. *American Antiquity* 16:99–112.

Hally, David J.
1994   An Overview of Lamar Culture. In *Ocmulgee Archaeology: 1936–1986*, edited by David J. Hally, pp. 144–174. University of Georgia Press, Athens.

Harke, Ryan
2012   Stable Isotope Analysis of *Busycon sinistrum* to Determine Fort Walton-Period Seasonality at St. Joseph Bay, Northwest Florida. Master's thesis, Department of Anthropology, University of South Florida. Available online through the USF Library.

Harris, Norma
2012   Defining Pensacola and Fort Walton Cultures in the Western Panhandle. In *Late Prehistoric Florida: Archaeology at the Edge of the Mississippian World*, edited by Keith Ashley and Nancy White, pp. 274–295. University Press of Florida, Gainesville.

Jones, B. Calvin
1982   Southeastern Cult Manifestations at the Lake Jackson Site, Leon County, Florida: Salvage Excavation of Mound 3. *Midcontinental Journal of Archaeology* 7:3–44.

Klein, Jeffrey, J. C. Lerman, Paul E. Damon, and Elizabeth K. Ralph
1982   Calibration of Radiocarbon Dates: Tables Based on the Consensus Data of the Workshop on Calibrating the Radiocarbon Time Scale. *Radiocarbon* 24:103–150.

Knight, Vernon James Jr.
1986   The Institutional Organization of Mississippian Religion. *American Antiquity* 51:675–687.

Lindauer, Owen, and John H. Blitz
1997   Higher Ground: The Archaeology of North American Platform Mounds. *Journal of Archaeological Research* 5(2):169–207.

Marrinan, Rochelle A.
2012   Fort Walton Culture in the Tallahassee Hills. In *Late Prehistoric Florida: Archaeology at the Edge of the Mississippian World*, edited by Keith Ashley and Nancy White, pp. 186–230. University Press of Florida, Gainesville.

Marrinan, Rochelle A., and Nancy Marie White
2007   Modeling Fort Walton Culture in Northwest Florida. *Southeastern Archaeology* 26:292–318.

Milanich, Jerald T.
1974   Life in a 9th Century Indian Household, a Weeden Island Fall–Winter Site on the Upper Apalachicola River, Florida. *Bureau of Historic Sites and Properties Bulletin* 4:1–44.

Moore, Clarence Bloomfield
1902   Certain Aboriginal Remains of the Northwest Florida Coast, Part II. *Journal of the Academy of Natural Sciences of Philadelphia* 12:126–355.
1903   Certain Aboriginal Mounds of the Apalachicola River, Part III. *Journal of the Academy of Natural Sciences of Philadelphia* 12:430–442.
1907   Mounds of the Lower Chattahoochee and Lower Flint Rivers, Part III. *Journal of the Academy of Natural Sciences of Philadelphia* 13:426–456.

Neuman, Robert W.
1961   Domesticated Corn from a Fort Walton Site in Houston County, Alabama. *Florida Anthropologist* 14(3–4):75–80.

Pauketat, Timothy R.
2001   Practice and History in Archaeology: An Emerging Paradigm. *Anthropological Theory* 1:73–98.

Pauketat, Timothy R., and Susan M. Alt
  2003 Mounds, Memory, and Contested Mississippian History. In *Archaeologies of Memory*, edited by Ruth M. Van Dyke and Susan E. Alcock, pp. 151–179. Blackwell, Malden.

Percy, George W., and M. Katherine Jones
  1975 An Archaeological Survey of Upland Locales in Gadsden and Liberty Counties, Florida. Florida State University. Report submitted to the Florida Division of Historical Resources, Tallahassee.
  1976 An Archaeological Survey of Upland Locales in Gadsden and Liberty Counties, Florida. *Florida Anthropologist* 29:105–125.

Ralph, E. K., Ho No Michael, and Mo Co Han
  1973 Radiocarbon Dates and Reality. *MASCA Newsletter* 9:1–20.

Reimer, P. J., M. G. L. Baillie, E. Bard, A. Bayliss, J. W. Beck, P. G. Blackwell, C. Bronk Ramsey, C. E. Buck, G. S. Burr, R. L. Edwards, M. Friedrich, P. M. Grootes, T. P. Guilderson, I. Hajdas, T. J. Heaton, A. G. Hogg, K. A. Hughen, K. F. Kaiser, B. Kromer, F. G. McCormac, S. W. Manning, R. W. Reimer, S. A. Richards, J. R. Southon, S. Talamo, C. S. M. Turney, J. van der Plicht, and C. E. Weyhenmeyer
  2009 IntCal09 and Marine09 Radiocarbon Age Calibration Curves, 0–50,000 years cal BP. *Radiocarbon* 51(4):1111–1150.

Scarry, C. Margaret
  2003a Food Plant Remains from Excavations in Mounds A, B, C, D, and L at Bottle Creek. In *Bottle Creek: A Pensacola Culture Site in South Alabama*, edited by Ian W. Brown, pp. 103–113. University of Alabama Press, Tuscaloosa.
  2003b The Use of Plants in Mound-Related Activities at Bottle Creek and Moundville. In *Bottle Creek: A Pensacola Culture Site in South Alabama*, edited by Ian W. Brown, pp. 114–129. University of Alabama Press, Tuscaloosa.

Scarry, John F.
  1978 Yon National Register of Historic Places Nomination Summary.
  1981 Fort Walton Culture: A Redefinition. *Southeastern Archaeology Conference Bulletin* 24:18–21.
  1984 *Fort Walton Development: Mississippian Chiefdoms in the Lower Southeast*. Ph.D. dissertation, Case Western Reserve University, Cleveland. University Microfilms, Ann Arbor.
  1990 Mississippian Emergence in the Fort Walton Area: The Evolution of the Cayson and Lake Jackson Phases. In *The Mississippian Emergence*, edited by Bruce D. Smith, pp. 227–250. Smithsonian Institution Press, Washington, D.C.

Schieffer, Adam
  2012 Archaeological Site Distribution in the Apalachicola/Lower Chattahoochee River Valley of Northwest Florida, Southwest Georgia, and Southeast Alabama. Master's thesis, Department of Anthropology, University of South Florida. Available online through the USF Library.

Sears, William H.
  1967 The Tierra Verde Burial Mound. *Florida Anthropologist* 20:25–74.

Shahramfar, Gabrielle
  2008 Determining Fort Walton Burial Patterns and Their Relationship within the Greater Mississippian. Master's thesis, Department of Anthropology, University of South Florida. Available online through the USF Library.

Smith, Bruce D.
2007   Preface to the New Edition. In *Mississippian Emergence*, edited by Bruce D. Smith, pp. xiv–xxxi. University of Alabama Press, Tuscaloosa.

Steponaitis, Vincas P.
1978   Location Theory and Complex Chiefdoms: A Mississippian Example. In *Mississippian Settlement Patterns*, edited by Bruce D. Smith, pp. 417–453. Academic Press, New York.

Stockhammer, Philipp W.
2013   From Hybridity to Entanglement, from Essentialism to Practice. *Archaeological Review from Cambridge* 28(1): 11–28.

Tesar, Louis D., and B. Calvin Jones
2009   *The Waddells Mills Pond Site: 1973–1974 Test Excavation Results*. Florida Bureau of Archaeological Research. Report submitted to the Florida Division of Historical Resources, Tallahassee.

Wauchope, Robert
1966   *Archaeological Survey of Northern Georgia, with a Test of Some Cultural Hypotheses*. Memoir No. 21. Society for American Archaeology, Salt Lake City.

White, Nancy Marie
1981   *Archaeology at Lake Seminole*. Final report of the Cultural Resources Survey and Evaluation of Lake Seminole, Florida, Georgia, and Alabama. Archaeological Research Report No. 29. Cleveland Museum of Natural History, Cleveland.

1982   The Curlee Site (8Ja7) and Fort Walton Development in the Upper Apalachicola–Lower Chattahoochee River Valley, Florida, Georgia, Alabama. Unpublished Ph.D. dissertation, Department of Anthropology, Case Western Reserve University.

1986   Prehistoric Cultural Chronology in the Apalachicola Valley: The Evolution of Native Chiefdoms in Northwest Florida. In *Threads of Tradition and Culture along the Gulf Coast*, edited by Ronald Evans, pp. 194–215. Gulf Coast Humanities Conference, Pensacola, Florida.

1994   *Archaeological Investigations at Six Sites in the Apalachicola River Valley, Northwest Florida*. National Oceanic and Atmospheric Administration Technical Memorandum NOS SRD 26. Marine and Estuarine Management Division, Washington, D.C.

1996   Test Excavations at the Yon Mound and Village Site (8Li2), Middle Apalachicola Valley, Northwest Florida. Report to the Florida Division of Historical Resources, Tallahassee. Department of Anthropology, University of South Florida, Tampa.

1999   Coastal vs. Interior Adaptations in Late Prehistoric Societies of Northwest Florida, Southeastern United States. Paper presented at the World Archaeological Congress 4, University of Cape Town, South Africa. January 10–14.

2005   *Archaeological Survey of the St. Joseph Bay State Buffer Preserve, Gulf County, Florida*. University of South Florida. Report to the Apalachicola National Estuarine Research Reserve, East Point, and the Division of Historical Resources, Tallahassee.

2009   Northwest Florida Artifact Typology and Sorting Criteria. Manuscript on file, Department of Anthropology, University of South Florida. Revised version of 1982 guide from University of West Florida.

2010   Gotier Hammock Mound and Midden on St. Joseph Bay. *Florida Anthropologist* 63:149–182.

2011a   Archaeology at Chattahoochee Landing, Gadsden County, Northwest Florida. Ms. on file, Florida Division of Historic Resources, Tallahassee.

2011b Middle Woodland and Protohistoric Fort Walton at the Lost Chipola Cutoff Mound, Northwest Florida. *Florida Anthropologist* 64:241–274.
2013   Pierce Mounds, an Ancient Capital in Northwest Florida: Preliminary Report. Ms. on file, Florida Division of Historic Resources, Tallahassee.
2014   Apalachicola Valley Riverine, Estuarine, Bayshore, and Saltwater Shell Middens. *Florida Anthropologist* 67(2–3:77–104).

White, Nancy Marie, Nelson Rodriguez, Christopher Smith, and Mary Beth Fitts
2002   *St. Joseph Bay Shell Middens Test Excavations, Gulf County, Florida, 2000–2002.* University of South Florida. Report submitted to the Florida Division of Historical Resources, Tallahassee.

White, Nancy Marie, Jeffrey Du Vernay, and Amber Yuellig
2012   Fort Walton Culture in the Apalachicola Valley, Northwest Florida. In *Late Prehistoric Florida: Archaeology at the Edge of the Mississippian World*, edited by Keith Ashley and Nancy White, pp. 231–274. University Press of Florida, Gainesville.

Willey, Gordon R.
1949   *Archeology of the Florida Gulf Coast.* Smithsonian Miscellaneous Collections 115. Washington, D.C. Reprinted 1999 by University Press of Florida, Gainesville.

Williams, Mark
2008   The Lamar Tradition. *Early Georgia* 36(2):119–128.

Williams, Mark, and Gary Shapiro (editors)
1990   *Lamar Archaeology: Mississippian Chiefdoms of the Deep South.* University of Alabama Press, Tuscaloosa.

10

Mississippian Beginnings

Multiple Perspectives on Migration, Monumentality, and Religion in the Prehistoric Eastern United States

DAVID G. ANDERSON

Archaeological research directed to Mississippian sites and research themes has continued to dominate professional interest in the southeastern and lower midwestern United States since the last major statement on Mississippian origins examining case studies from across the region appeared in 1990 (Smith 1990). In the 30 years from 1982 to 2012, in fact, more articles on Mississippian period research were published in the regional and national flagship archaeological journals *Southeastern Archaeology* and *American Antiquity* than for all the previous periods of prehistory combined; when Contact era papers are added, the numbers are far higher (Anderson and Sassaman 2012:153–155). The current volume covers some of the same geographic areas examined in the 1990 volume, highlighting recent work that has occurred but, importantly, includes summaries of work in portions of the region all but unexplored two decades ago, particularly from the perspective of what Mississippian is and how it began. Approaches to Mississippian archaeology have changed dramatically in recent decades (Wilson and Sullivan, chapter 1), particularly in the past few years. Much of the specific information presented in this volume, in fact, was unknown or just beginning to be recognized as recently as 2012, when a regional synthesis appeared directed to "recent developments in southeastern archaeology," and that included a major section covering the Mississippian and Contact periods, ca. AD 1000 to 1800 (Anderson and Sassaman 2012:152–190).

Many of our research concerns remain the same as they were a quarter of a century ago, albeit examined from new theoretical perspectives and technologies. We are still wrestling with questions like what Mississippian is and how it appeared and changed over time, and the roles that variables like climate, intensive maize agriculture, population growth, religion, warfare, or migration played in the observed changes. What is new is how we are addressing these questions. Interest in variability and change in the historical trajectories of sites and societies, as well as the actions and roles of individuals, ideas, and materials in shaping these trajectories, has replaced the use of static descriptions or neoevolutionary constructs. While terms like "chiefdom" or "cycling" remain very much with us, they are now recognized as heuristics subsuming appreciable variability, and recognizing what was happening in individual or multiple cases is what is important, rather than generating new categories of societal forms or developmental processes (e.g., Anderson and Sassaman 2012:158–161; Blitz 1999; Cobb 2003; Pauketat 2001, 2007). Concepts like "Mississippian" and "Mississippianization" must themselves be understood on a case-by-case basis, and using them for other than broad temporal or cultural markers is as uninformative as using neoevolutionary stage terminology when characterizing specific archaeological cases. Much has changed from both methodological and theoretical perspectives: technologies like isotope geochemistry or remote sensing are widely and routinely used, as are theoretical perspectives emphasizing the role of religion and cultural interaction and entanglement in the Mississippian emergence, as discussed below (Wilson and Sullivan, this volume; Pauketat 2013). Our temporal resolution is improving markedly, given advances in absolute dating, particularly associated with the widespread use of AMS radiocarbon dating and, in some areas, use of dendrochronologically supported sequences (e.g., Emerson and Hedman 2016; Koerner et al. 2009). At some sites in the Mississippian world, temporal resolution—at least during those parts of their occupational history where extensive AMS dating has occurred, like Mound A, Shiloh, at the East Saint Louis complex, or Monks Mound, Cahokia—is now at the generational, ca. 15-to-25-year range, rather than the lifetime or half-century-to-century-level resolution we had using conventional radiocarbon dating or ceramic seriations (e.g., Anderson et al. 2013; Emerson and Hedman 2016; Hally 1993, 1996; Pauketat et al. 2013; Schilling 2010, 2012, 2013).

While cultural historical concerns and sequence development remain important, these goals are now commonly pursued in concurrence with the exploration of a wide array of subjects. Current research increasingly focuses on reconstructing fine-grained descriptive histories of sites and localities, and seeking commonalities and differences among them in the pursuit of explanations or factors shaping these historical trajectories. Analyses of older well-curated site collections have continued to yield impressive results in terms of understanding Mississippian societies first explored archaeologically decades to as much as a century and more ago (e.g., King et al., chapter 8; Sullivan et al. 1995; Sullivan et al. 2011; Welch 2006). Likewise, a lot of field archaeology has continued to occur, much of it sponsored by academic field schools or CRM project work. Wide-area stripping coupled with large-scale excavation and feature removal remains common on threatened sites, revealing whole community plans or extensive feature assemblages, a practice that dates back to the Great Depression era in the region, albeit now more commonly conducted using massive earthmoving machines rather than large numbers of laborers (e.g., Alt 2002, 2006; Emerson and Hedman 2016; Pauketat 2003; Pauketat et al. 2013; Riggs et al. 2015; Sullivan et al. 1995; Walthall et al. 1997; Webb 2002).

The role of remote sensing has also expanded markedly and is a critical part of contemporary research. The recognition of occupation clusters, structures and plazas, and other features such as marker posts or burials on Mississippian sites has changed dramatically, thanks to the use of this noninvasive technology, as seen in recent work at Cahokia (IL), Etowah (GA), Hiwassee Island (TN), Kincaid (IL), Macon Plateau/Ocmulgee (GA), Moundville (AL), Shiloh (TN), and Washausen (IL) (e.g., Baires 2014a, 2014b; Barrier 2014; Bigman 2012; Bigman et al. 2011; Butler et al. 2011; Davis et al. 2015; King et al. 2011; Lydick et al. 2013). We are now able to recognize feature assemblages unknown and unsuspected even a few years ago, like the early Mississippian community under the plaza at Moundville (Davis et al. 2015), and the technology, with ground-truthing excavation, is now routinely used to explore variation in status, house size, and neighborhoods within communities. Such analyses were inaccessible to all but the largest of research projects a generation ago, when exposing and documenting community plans required vast amounts of fieldwork. Stable isotope analyses of human skeletal remains are another area of research with great potential when allowed to occur and have proven critical to determining not only aspects of health, status, and diet, but also where individuals lived over the course of their lives, which with genetic evidence is useful to proving cultural identity and continuity or ancestry (e.g., Ambrose et al. 2003; Betzenhauser, this volume; Cook, this volume; Cook and Price 2015; Emerson et al. 2016; Rasmussen et al. 2015; Slater et al. 2014; Thompson et al. 2015). Residue analyses are showing what was used in vessels, with sometimes dramatic results, such as the recent demonstration that the black drink was likely consumed at Cahokia, well outside the native range of the holly plant species likely used, *Ilex vomitoria*, resulting in new thinking about the scope and nature of Mississippian exchange (Crown et al. 2012).

As global climate change occupies greater public as well as research attention, the role of drought, excessive rainfall, and flooding patterns on the trajectories of Mississippian societies, both individually and over large areas, is also receiving increasing emphasis (e.g., Anderson 1994; Anderson et al. 1995; Baires et al. 2015; Benson et al. 2009; Blitz and Lorenz 2006; Emerson and Hedman 2016; Meeks and Anderson 2013; Munoz, Gruley, Fike, Schroeder, and Williams 2015; Munoz, Gruley, Massie, Fike, Schroeder, and Williams 2015). The emergence and spread of intensive maize agriculture and Mississippian culture has long been associated with a period of warm climate known as the Medieval Warm Period (Anderson 2001:166; Griffin 1961:711–713), and how such broad patterns of global climate change played out in individual areas is beginning to be explored.

One important result from recent fieldwork has been that we know that great care and ceremony went into the construction of Mississippian mounds and plazas, as demonstrated by work at Cahokia (Alt et al. 2010; Dalan 1997; Dalan et al. 2003; Holley et al. 1993; Pauketat 2003, 2010; Sherwood and Kidder 2011), Moundville (Davis et al. 2015; Knight 2010), and Shiloh (Anderson 2012; Anderson et al. 2013; Sherwood and Kidder 2011), among many others (e.g., Pursell 2004, 2013). A vast effort, in fact, is directed to exploring Mississippian iconography, religion, and cosmology (e.g., Emerson 2003; Emerson et al. 2003; Knight 2012; Lankford et al. 2011; Pauketat 2013; Reilly and Garber 2007; Townsend and Sharp 2004). This is not directed solely to mound construction or aboveground objects and artifacts; we now know the ritual landscape of Mississippian peoples included remarkable artwork placed in a variety of settings, both open-air and underground, parietal and permanent (Diaz-Granados et al. 2015; Simek et al. 2013). Just as sites were constructed and imbued with meaning, so too were landscapes, in ways we are only beginning to recognize.

Examining Mississippian Beginnings

Two decades ago the Mississippian Emergence was thought to have been either (1) a spread from a single source or (2) a simultaneous and largely independent development in a number of areas, facilitated by interaction and competitive emulation, but primarily shaped by local reactions to common underlying conditions, such as climate change or population growth (Smith 1990). Most authorities at the time favored explanation (2), independent local developments. In recent years, however, we have become increasingly aware of the role played by the direct movement of ideas and people to and from the central Mississippi Valley, and within and between other parts of the region as well. This spread, furthermore, is no longer explained by using general terms like *migration* or *diffusion* but is instead examined in terms of the actions of people, ideas, and aspects of material culture in source, route, and destination areas. Mississippian beginnings, several chapters herein highlight, clearly involved not only the movement of Mississippian peoples into new areas and their interaction with local populations, what used to be subsumed under the rubric of migration, but also the movement of people from outlying areas to Mississippian centers and then returning home with new ideas, artifacts, and ways of doing things. Indeed, movement both ways, of ideas as well as of people and objects, was likely far more common than once thought, and categories of people who moved over the landscape now include pilgrims and proselytizers in addition to more traditional groups, like warriors, settlers, or traders, not that the latter weren't also important in some times and places. While it was once possible to argue that population movement was relatively unimportant in the Eastern Woodlands—itself a reaction to earlier frameworks that saw migration as widespread and the primary impetus for Mississippianization (e.g., Ford and Willey 1941:350–351; Griffin 1946, 1967:189; Smith 1984)—such a perspective is no longer widely accepted, not only in the Late Prehistoric and Contact periods, where evidence for movement for a range of reasons is widespread, but also during much earlier periods, like the Woodland, Archaic, and even Paleoindian eras (e.g., Anderson 1995, 1999; Anderson et al. 2015; Gilmore 2016; Kidder and Sassaman 2009; Pauketat 2007; Sassaman 1995, 2001, 2010, 2016). Local peoples interacted with outsiders or visited and returned from special places, producing new cultural constructs, and generating appreciable variability in what we consider Mississippian. The emphasis in research at present is on how these situations played out, in terms of individual historical events and trajectories.

Our theoretical approaches and associated metalanguage brought to the study of Mississippian lifeways have thus changed markedly, with terms like *ceremonial complex, chiefdom, diffusion, evolution, site unit intrusion,* or *trade* that served as foci for research now replaced by concepts of community, polity, history, hybridity, interaction, entanglement, religion, and cosmology. Our explanatory narratives have changed from broad process-oriented generalizations to specific event-centered histories, often with new terminology highlighting the change in approach. If an archaeologist used the phrase "Big Bang" twenty-five years ago, for example, people would have thought the reference was to cosmology, and not to the rapid appearance of Cahokia about AD 1050 (e.g., Pauketat 1997:31). Change is now commonly framed in terms of the actions and reactions of individuals and events in the shaping of history and practice (Anderson 2015; Beck et al. 2007; Gilmore and O'Donoughue 2015; Pauketat 2001, 2007, 2013; Pauketat, Alt, and Krutchen 2015; Sassaman 2012, 2016).

Other notable omissions or reductions in terminological usage are references to *trade sherds* or *prestige goods*, or even the expression *Emergent Mississippian* itself, which has fallen into disfavor due to its teleological implications (cf. Emerson 2002; Fortier and McElrath 2002; Kelly 1987, 1990). Likewise, the Southern Cult or Southeastern Ceremonial Complex are themselves no longer recognized as useful constructs (Wilson and Sullivan, this volume; King 2006; Knight 2006), even while the role of religion and iconography and its importance in shaping the Mississippian world has become a subject of great and sustained research (e.g., Lankford et al. 2011; Pauketat 2013; Reilly and Garber 2007; Townsend and Sharp 2004). Likewise, the adoption of new forms of subsistence, architecture, or pottery is now couched in how these were used and what they meant to people in terms of shaping identity, organization, and history, and not solely in terms of when they appeared or where they came from (as many of the chapters herein demonstrate). Becoming Mississippian involved more than the adoption of a few items of ritual or material culture, but rather, changes in many aspects of daily life and practice, the creation of a new identity that required appreciable effort.

We now acknowledge, far more than we did a generation ago, the importance and role of Cahokia in the emergence of Mississippian culture in the East. Mississippianization was a spread of ideas and religion, fostered by the movements of peoples to and from Cahokia as well as at secondary centers and autonomous societies farther afield. The emergence of Cahokia itself is actually part of a much larger story of the emergence and relationships between three closely spaced centers, the St. Louis, East St. Louis, and Cahokia mound groups—what Pauketat and Emerson (1997:9) call the Central Political-Administrative Complex. The rapid appearance and growth of this society or closely linked group of societies appears due to a coalescence or resettlement of peoples and cultures both locally and from across the region, perhaps from as far away as the lower Ohio and Mississippi River valleys, a "Big Crunch" that was part and parcel of the "Big Bang" (Alt 2006, 2010; Pauketat 2007, 2009). The Big Bang, while it happened quickly, was not instantaneous but likely played out over a few decades or generations. Recent analyses, for example, show that the construction of much or all of Monks Mound may have occurred fairly quickly, perhaps in a few decades' time or less (Schilling 2010, 2012, 2013). This was not a localized phenomenon, furthermore, but involved peoples from many differing parts of the continent. The beginnings of the Mississippian world, we are seeing, are becoming increasingly entangled.

Case Studies

An excellent summary of past and contemporary thinking on the origins of Mississippian in what is currently recognized by many archaeologists as the heartland of this cultural tradition/civilization (*sensu* Pauketat 2007), in the American Bottom of Illinois and immediately adjoining areas, is provided by Alleen Betzenhauser (chapter 3). The argument for a rapid transformation of the social and physical landscape, the so-called Big Bang, importantly, is examined over a large number of sites (n = 273), and not just at a single center or small locality (i.e., a center and a few outlying sites). The adoption of new forms of domestic architecture and site plans, as well as a standardized, tribute-based material assemblage, with strong religious underpinnings, served to signify broad-based acceptance of what was occurring at the most fundamental levels of everyday life (see also Emerson 1997; Pauketat and Emerson 1997; Pauketat 2013; Pauketat and Alt 2003, 2016a, 2016b). Nodal households marked new forms of organization, integrating local communities and highlighting the role of horizontal organization, or heterarchy, operating within more traditionally conceived vertical hierarchies (Betzenhauser 2006, 2011; Emerson 1997). This chapter reminds us that urbanization and complex polity formation involve impacts not just at centers but over much larger rural hinterlands; similar landscape-based analyses should be routinely adopted in other parts of the region.

The nature of Cahokian contact in the Illinois River Valley is explored by Gregory Wilson, Colleen M. Delaney, and Phillip G. Millhouse (chapter 4) as part of an examination of the process by which Cahokian influence or, in effect, Mississippianization occurred in the upper Midwest. They offer a compelling argument on how to differentiate between assemblages created by direct population movement as opposed to a local adoption or emulation of material culture using ceramics assemblages associated with the processing, cooking, and serving of foods; fortunately, these are among the most-common and best-preserved artifacts found on most sites of the period. It is the overall organization of technology that must be examined, they argue, on the assumption that food preparation and serving is a conservative aspect of life that will not quickly change. The analysis also assumes that artifacts made locally in foreign styles can be differentiated from those made elsewhere, something that can be resolved through sourcing studies, an area of research that is expanding rapidly, given recent technological advances. Pottery, Wilson et al. demonstrate, can simultaneously tell us about many things, including chronology, function, domestic foodways, daily practice, and identity. In the absence of human remains that can used to demonstrate biological affiliation or area of origin, ceramic analyses like those reported here should be conducted wherever cultural contact is indicated, in the Mississippian world and beyond.

Using isotope analyses to infer population movements is another aspect of recent work yielding important results, as Robert Cook's analysis of Fort Ancient culture demonstrates (chapter 5). The results, although somewhat ambiguous as to the places of origin for some individuals, can usually differentiate people who originated locally from those who came from elsewhere. These analyses also highlighted the importance of directly dating the human remains, in this case using AMS, in interpreting the isotope results, particularly regarding diet, since burial assemblages sometimes contained people of varying time periods. Direct dating was essential, for example, to determine whether an absence of evidence for maize consumption reflected a burial from a period when maize wasn't present, or a special diet when it was prevalent. Likewise, the isotope results were important in showing whether individuals could have come from the same area as exotic artifacts interred with them; one individual with a possible Ramey knife of Cahokian origin was found to have spent his life in the local middle Ohio River area. Cook's study shows how multiple lines of evidence from archaeological and bioanthropological analyses can be used to indicate population movement, both related to Mississippian beginning and in later times. Indeed, the analyses suggested the possibility that some later Fort Ancient peoples may have come from the so-called Vacant Quarter area of the lower Midwest and Midsouth, providing clues about where the once-resident peoples may have gone. Cook concludes by offering a scenario that is becoming evident in many areas: what we think of as Fort Ancient was created by the interaction between Mississippian and local peoples, different in character from what came before, but a largely local product nonetheless. Except in rare cases where population movement and replacement occurred, Mississippianization in areas where outside contact is indicated, this and other chapters in this volume indicate, appears to have been a process involving small numbers of people moving into new areas and exerting unusual cultural influence on those local peoples; impacts likely occurred on the source areas as well, as people went back and forth. Great differences are evident in Mississippian cultures over the region, of course, and how Mississippianization occurred and what is even meant by the concept warrants examination on a case-by-case basis.

Amanda Regnier's work (chapter 6) on Caddo emergence, examined using data from the Bud Wright and other sites in Oklahoma, makes use of ceramics to help untangle relationships between earlier Coles Creek and Fourche Maline and subsequent Caddo and Plaquemine traditions in the general region. The emergence of centers in the Caddo area, Regnier states, appears to be slightly earlier and largely independent of developments to the north and east, in areas where Mississippian cultures were present. I would argue that while the Caddoan ritual landscape and material culture certainly had distinctive aspects, such as in shaft tombs, patterns of mound construction, and ritual and exotic artifacts, so too did many other societies in what has come to be known as the Mississippian world. Mississippian culture was highly variable across the Southeast; even communities within the American Bottom varied in layout and associated material culture, making it difficult to unequivocally identify sites of the culture (e.g., Emerson 2002; Milner 1998). As Regnier and several authors herein also note, mound construction in many areas was far more elaborate and ritually charged than we have traditionally assumed. The mounds themselves also saw different uses in different areas, highlighting the variability present during the era of Mississippian origins and, indeed, throughout the period these monuments were built and used. Research on variability in the construction and engineering practices associated with monumental architecture has been occurring in recent years across eastern North America at sites of all periods, with particularly comprehensive analyses conducted at sites like Feltus, Monks Mound, Poverty Point, and Shiloh (e.g., Anderson et al. 2013; Kassabaum et al. 2014; Sherwood and Kidder 2011). Regnier's work exemplifies a trend evident in many of the chapters in this volume, that Mississippian, or in this case Caddo, monumentality was as much about religious and ceremonial practice as about the political and administrative considerations that dominated earlier arguments about Mississippian complexity.

King, Thornock, and Stephenson's examination of the Hollywood site and the emergence of Mississippian culture in the central Savannah River valley (chapter 8), like Boudreaux's work at Town Creek (chapter 7), shows how reanalyses of material excavated long ago—in this case during the explorations of the Mound Division of the Bureau of Ethnology in the 1880s and early 1890s (King and Stephenson 2012)—can yield critically important information about site history and content. Since the results of early excavations were rarely thoroughly reported, the analyses and detailed descriptions and illustrations of the materials at Hollywood are especially significant in an era when archaeological assemblages are being repatriated and in some cases reburied with no provision for further documentation. King et al.'s work shows that there is always much more that can be learned, and a far better understanding of local developments to be obtained, even in areas of the Mississippian Southeast where extensive work has occurred and been synthesized at length (e.g., Anderson 1994). As in the lower Chattahoochee (Blitz and Lorenz 2002, 2006), and at Ocmulgee (Bigman 2012), King et al. have shown that initial Mississippian developments in the central Savannah River included the direct in-migration of people from areas well to the west. How these outsiders interacted with local populations is a subject for research comparable to that now being explored in many parts of the region and is here examined in terms of the variability in the material culture in its placement and associations in the mound at Hollywood. Widespread population movement, and not cultural isolation and stasis, is now accepted as occurring throughout prehistory in the southeast (Anderson and Sassaman 2012; Kidder and Sassaman 2009; Sassaman 2010). Mississippianization, however, was not instantaneous across the region. The emergence of recognizably Mississippian cultures in the central Savannah River does not occur until around AD 1200 to 1250, for example, highlighting the time-transgressive nature of Mississippian beginnings across the region; a late appearance in eastern Georgia and the Carolinas has long been argued by local researchers (e.g., Anderson 1999:225–226; Boudreaux 2007a, 2007b, 2011; Ferguson 1971; Pauketat 2007). While massive population aggregations and monumentality were occurring in the central Mississippi Valley in the eleventh century at places like Cahokia, very different events were occurring in other parts of the region.

Mississippian beginnings in the North Carolina Piedmont are examined by Tony Boudreaux (chapter 7), whose research focuses on the Town Creek site, which is unusual in the Mississippian world in that the site plan was derived from near-total excavation instead of from remote sensing. Boudreaux and his colleagues are working with legacy as well as new data from Town Creek and surrounding sites in nearby areas of Piedmont North Carolina. As with Ocmulgee, the work at Town Creek shows how major excavation projects, in this case conducted over many decades, can provide materials and research questions for generations of scholars. Well-curated assemblages and records can lead to continuing important discoveries and interpretations, as we saw at Hollywood, even when the sites have been previously extensively reported, as is the case with Town Creek (e.g., Boudreaux 2007; Coe 1995). The increasingly precise dating of Town Creek documented by Boudreaux, with complicated stamping not appearing until ca. AD 1200, reinforces ideas and observations like those by King et al. (chapter 8) and others about the late beginnings for Mississippian in the South Appalachian area. Care must of course be taken to avoid equating presumed Mississippian *material culture* (i.e., house forms, stone tools, or ceramic types) with what is occurring during the Mississippian *time period*, ca. AD 1000–1500, the span widely accepted across the region (Anderson and Sassaman 2012:5, 152).

Boudreaux's research shows how artifact analyses conducted over large areas and directed to things as seemingly prosaic as sequence development and dating can play a critically important role in interpreting developments. The recognition of a widespread Late Woodland/Early Mississippian period simple stamped horizon over large portions of the South Appalachian area (Anderson 1985; Anderson et al. 1982, Elliott and Wynn 1991; Pluckhahn 1997; Riggs et al. 2015), a finish formerly thought to commonly occur much earlier in time, during the Early and Middle Woodland periods, helped demonstrate that local populations, instead of being absent or largely replaced by outsiders, played a major role in what was occurring in the Carolinas and Georgia during the early Mississippian period. As one of the first to argue for a Late Woodland simple stamped horizon in this part of the region more than 30 years ago (e.g., Anderson 1985), I am gratified to realize that this pattern is becoming increasingly well documented, as seen at the Teal phase sites near Town Creek (Oliver 1992; Boudreaux, this volume) at Ocmulgee (Bigman 2012), and most recently by Brett Riggs and colleagues (2015) at the Ashe Ferry site along the Catawba River in northern South Carolina. Riggs, interestingly enough, was a crew member on the 1979 project at Mattassee Lake, where simple stamped materials were found and dated to the AD 800–1200 time range. During the work at Mattassee Lake, it took us quite some time to accept what the site stratigraphy and later the radiocarbon dates were telling us about the late occurrence for these wares, given their long placement much earlier in the Woodland period (Anderson 1985:42–44; Anderson and Schuldenrein 1983:99; Anderson et al. 1982:308). Until misconceptions about the age and dating of these common pottery finishes could be overcome, received wisdom dating as far back as Great Depression era survey and excavation projects (as documented in Keel 1976:228; Wauchope 1966; Williams 1994:135), our understanding of site occupational histories across the region were confused and often seriously in error.

Boudreaux's analyses, with those of other contributors, also highlight the fact that initial Mississippian communities differed appreciably from one another. A fairly common pattern, however, were multiple clusters of houses, sometimes associated with mounds and plazas, suggesting the formation and operation of kin groups. At Town Creek, unlike at many other early sites, extensive mortuary data are available to suggest that these clusters do indeed conform to kin groupings (Boudreaux 2010, this volume). The Town Creek site plan, like that of most or probably all Mississippian communities, is thus a sociogram, indicating kinship and status relations between groups, as has also been proposed at Moundville, Ocmulgee, and Washausen (Barrier 2014; Bigman 2012; Knight 1998; Wilson et al., this volume). Exploring the life histories of individual households, neighborhoods, or household-mound-plaza clusters is now routinely conducted at many Mississippian sites (e.g., Barrier 2014; Bigman 2012; Kelly 1990; Morse and Morse 1990; Wilson 2008).

Du Vernay and White (chapter 9) provide a data-rich and thoroughly referenced summary of Fort Walton beginnings; such overviews require great effort but are critically important, serving as fundamental baseline statements of what we know, think we know, and want to know (see also Marrinan and White 2007; White et al. 2012). Problem-oriented subregional summaries have been produced by Mississippian researchers in many parts of the region in recent years, but many more are still needed and, indeed, new ones should be produced in each area every generation or so. The authors, like many others in the volume, argue that local Fort Walton Mississippian emerged through processes of interaction and hybridity (Alt 2006; Bhabha 1990), in reaction to an influx of people and practices from other Mississippianized areas in the region into the lower Chattahoochee River (Blitz and Lorenz 2002, 2006). Part of this process included continuity or reconnection with earlier sites for occupation or use for burial, as was observed in several other parts of the region, including in the Illinois River and Fort Ancient areas (Wilson et al., this volume; Cook, this volume). The absence of any significant evidence for maize agriculture at early Fort Walton in the southern reaches of the Apalachicola–lower Chattahoochee River valley is interesting, given its presence further upriver. The development of complex social formations in the absence of agriculture in the late prehistoric era appears to have extended well beyond the Coles Creek or south Florida regions in the lower Southeast (e.g. Fritz and Kidder 1993; VanDerwarker et al., this volume); abundant aquatic and other wild resources locally are assumed by the authors to have precluded the need for maize agriculture. Fort Walton may have been a source of marine shell and *Ilex* for societies further inland; interaction between Mississippian societies likely was not just one-way and, given the desirability of what was being moved, be it material or spiritual in nature, may have persisted for generations or centuries (e.g., Brown et al. 1990; Marrinan and White 2007).

Paleoethnobotanical evidence from a wide range of Mississippian societies across the region is examined by Amber VanDerwarker, Dana Bardolph, and C. Margaret Scarry, with a particular emphasis on the role of plant foods, including maize agriculture, in their beginnings (chapter 2). Few regional synthetic analyses of paleosubsistence data exist for any period, making this chapter, with its attendant summaries of trends in numerous significant research localities, an invaluable reference. As with other aspects of Mississippian beginnings examined in this volume, the authors demonstrate that great variability in subsistence practices occurred, and that the development of intensive agricultural food production and complex social organization were not invariably linked (see also Scarry 1993). However, their analysis also indicates that surplus generation and the mobilization of large quantities of either wild or domesticated foods were critical to the development of strongly hierarchical (i.e., more complex) social formations. Surplus generation through intensified maize production, additionally, appears to have spread along with other aspects of Mississippian culture, although it was clearly present earlier in some localities. Becoming Mississippian, at least in some areas, thus involved becoming intensive agriculturalists, which in turn likely influenced behavior patterns across whole communities and by age and gender.

Conclusions

The nature of Mississippian beginnings is becoming better understood, but there is clearly much that remains to be learned, at both the site and locality levels, and about the relations between societies over the larger region. We cannot view Mississippian communities as static or monolithic entities but instead must view them as changing, highly diverse and sometimes rapidly changing communities, kin groups, and social arenas, whose elements must be examined as closely as possible, in microhistorical reconstruction. As Pauketat (2001:87) has argued, "answers to ultimate 'why' questions will be found only through the cumulative, painstaking, data-rich, multi-scalar studies of proximate causation." This is increasingly being done at the site level, where we have seen that individual communities are highly varied in form and history, as are the Mississippian societies of which they are a part. This is a major change from earlier perspectives couched in neoevolutionary frameworks emphasizing broad similarities, and large-scale processes. We now use multiple feature and artifact categories to examine changes occurring within Early Mississippian times, and hence the practices and processes by which local identities were formed. The use of varied remote sensing procedures has revolutionized our approaches to site exploration, obviating the need, at least in cases where the sites are not threatened with destruction, for the large-scale excavations that were our traditional and indeed once our only means of revealing site plans. However, the archaeological record in eastern North America is finite and threatened in many areas, meaning there will always be a need for exploratory and large-scale fieldwork, primary site and assemblage documentation, and sequence development in exploring Mississippian beginnings and change over time. Vast excavations result in massive assemblages, of course, and require responsible follow-through in analysis, reporting, and curation by the archaeologists and institutions involved in the work. Fortunately, basic reporting is mandated by the environmental legislation that has resulted in so much archaeological fieldwork in recent decades, although there will also be a need for continual investigation of these assemblages, informed by new methods and theoretical approaches. Both new fieldwork and examination of older assemblages will continue to be necessary if our understanding of Mississippian beginnings is to grow.

There are many tools that we can use and are using. The increasing use of AMS dating, with its 15-to-25-year standard deviations common in the Mississippian era, is forcing us to reevaluate our chronological reconstructions and cultural sequences. Indeed, AMS dating on annual plants should be the preferred approach to absolute dating, barring the presence of wood amenable to dendrochronological dating, work that has been done in eastern Tennessee in recent years with remarkable success (Koerner et al. 2009). Remote sensing, of course, can and should guide where fieldwork can be expended efficiently, as research at many sites has shown. Moundville, Ocmulgee, and Shiloh, for example, were more complex and interesting much earlier in the Mississippian period than we have traditionally assumed, given the recent recognition of structures under later plaza fills (Bigman 2012; Davis et al. 2015; Lydick et al. 2013).

The archaeology of mound building and not merely of mound contents and associated structures and burials, we have seen, is coming to be a major area of research. Determining how often and how quickly and carefully mounds were built, and how the people came together to participate in these ceremonial constructions (i.e., scheduling, and how they fed, housed, worked, and entertained), is being explored by increasing numbers of scholars (e.g., Blitz and Livingood 2004; Hally 1993, 1996; Kassabaum et al. 2014; Pauketat et al. 2002; Sherwood and Kidder 2011). Complexly layered mound strata reflecting multiple filling episodes can be built quickly, with the time involved perhaps best determined by looking for erosional and patching episodes, given that the work on individual stages likely occurred over a period of days or weeks rather than the years or decades that often occurred between major stages (Anderson 2012; Anderson et al. 2013; Blitz and Livingood 2004; Hally 1993, 1996; Kidder 2012:466; Sherwood and Kidder 2011).

Mound and plaza complexes, structures and compounds, major posts, and earthworks and causeways, while common in the Mississippian period, are architectural features having great antiquity in eastern North America, dating back thousands of years (e.g., Anderson 2012; Anderson and Sassaman 2012; Kassabaum and Nelson 2016; Kidder and Sassaman 2009; Sassaman 2010;

Saunders et al. 1997). Both entire site as well as individual structure layouts sometimes referenced important astronomical alignments and, hence, cosmological and religious themes (Pauketat 2013; Romain 2000). While astronomical alignments have long been proposed with regard to Mississippian sites like Cahokia (e.g., Krupp 1983:29–32; O'Brien and McHugh 1988; Wittry 1964, 1980, 1996), alignments of mounds and other landscape features are now being made with solstices and lunar standstills with a high degree of confidence (Aveni 2003:170–171; Pauketat 2013; Pauketat and Alt 2015a, 2015b). Cahokia's big idea, Pauketat and his colleagues argue, may well have been tied to the moon, the most dramatic regularly appearing object in a night sky seen by peoples lacking electric lights and the distraction of television. But this implies much more than a basic knowledge of astronomy. To recognize an 18.6-year cycle in the places on the horizon where the maximum northern and southern rising or setting of the sun or moon occurred would have required observations by generations of observers. Recognition and marking of astronomical alignments likely has great time depth in the East. They are inferred for the Toltec site/Plum Bayou culture of Eastern Arkansas, a possible source population or area for these activities in the Cahokia area (Sherrod and Rolingson 1987; Pauketat et al. 2012; Pauketat and Alt 2015a, 2015b). Earlier Hopewellian astronomical alignments are known (Hively and Horn 2006, 2010; Lynott 2014:153–154; Romain 2000), and the care with which Middle Archaic mounds were laid out suggests this information may have been known millennia earlier (Clark 2004; Clark et al. 2010). As John Clark (2004:210) noted a few years ago, commenting on regularities in the layout of Louisiana's Mid-Holocene mounds, our emphases on Mesoamerican astronomy, calendrics, and monumentality may be misplaced, and "maybe we are looking in the wrong place for early astronomy in the Americas." The fact that alignments are observed at small as well as large sites, and in the orientation of structures as well as in the placement of mounds, suggests such information had great time depth and was widely shared (Pauketat 2013; Pauketat and Alt 2015a, 2015b). Just as remote sensing should be a default option in the advance of any excavation wherever possible, consideration of astronomical alignments should also be a routine part of our work at sites of all time periods. The linkage of politics, spatial organization, and cosmology and religion, recent work in the Eastern Woodlands demonstrates, cannot be disentangled, and was as important in the past as it is at present.

Likewise, interactions between and changes within Mississippian societies are increasingly being explored in terms of the movements and practices of people, and not merely the occurrence of objects over the landscape. The formation of the Cahokian polity, for example, appears to have involved the movement of large numbers of people from many parts of the region to and from the American Bottom, either relocating permanently or visiting temporarily (see also Alt 2006, 2010; Emerson et al. 2016; Pauketat 2007, 2009; Skousen and Butler 2012). Such population movements were rarely one-way, furthermore, with return migration by subsets of the relocating population, by which wealth and knowledge were transferred back to homelands, an argument discussed in some detail by Anthony (1990:904). Given evidence for cosmologically based legitimization strategies by Cahokian elites, that is, the use of astronomical knowledge about solar and lunar cycles to demonstrate their closeness with powerful supernatural forces (e.g., Pauketat 2013; Pauketat and Alt 2015a, 2015b), such back-and-forth movement was likely frequent, and some of these people were pilgrims rather than migrants. That is, some people would have visited the Cahokian heartland, perhaps for major feasts and festivals, and then returned home rather than settling permanently, although the latter also appears to have happened, given evidence for Yankeetown material culture at the Knoebel community in the uplands east of the American Bottom (Alt 2002, 2006, 2010; Pauketat and Alt 2015a). Similar arguments about the role of pilgrimages in the prehistoric Eastern Woodlands have been applied to the Late Archaic Poverty Point site as well as to numerous Middle Woodland Hopewellian centers, indicating such practices have a long history and, if not common save in times when great things were happening or great monuments being erected, was also not unknown (Anderson 2015:233–236; Carr 2005:54; Spivey et al. 2015). How pilgrims and proselytizers operated during the Mississippian era (e.g., Skousen and Butler 2012), and indeed over all periods, will undoubtedly be a subject for much future research. How people could have traveled long distances over the landscape, especially during periods of intense or increased warfare, like portions of the Mississippian period, will also need to be examined; symbols of neutrality such as the calumet and associated ceremonies facilitated movement in the early historic era, and comparable artifacts and practices likely have great antiquity in the region (e.g., Carr 2005; Drooker 2004; Dye 2009; Hall 1997; Rafferty and Mann 2004; Steinmetz 1984).

Our ideas and understanding of Mississippian beginnings have thus changed markedly in recent years, as exemplified by the chapters herein, and a wealth of associated research. In 1997 I examined the role of Cahokia in the development of Mississippian culture in various parts of the eastern Woodlands. While previous researchers had tended to underestimate its influence, a new school led by scholars like Pauketat and Emerson were arguing exactly the opposite, that Cahokia was the likely source of Mississippian. For reasons detailed in that paper, I agreed with them, noting that:

Cahokia was extremely complex, had established far-reaching exchange contacts, and had an elaborate religious and ceremonial infrastructure in place at a very early time level when compared with developments in other parts of the Mississippian world. [Cahokia . . .] vastly exceeded anything seen before or since elsewhere in the region. This society was an order of magnitude larger in scale than the incipient hierarchies seen to the south in the Coles Creek area during the earlier Late Woodland era and was far beyond the simple chiefdoms reported from elsewhere in the Southeast at this time. A marked increase in the occurrence of extralocal raw materials characterizes the Lohmann phase (A.D. 1050–1100), indicating Cahokian contacts were far-reaching at an early time level. . . . In a very real sense, much of what we think of as Mississippian across the region appears to be the idea of Cahokia writ large. (Anderson 1997:261, 263)

If I had to rewrite these thoughts, I might conclude by saying that Mississippian was the "idea of Cahokia writ variably" across the region, reflecting our new thinking on such concepts as hybridity, cosmology, and coalescence in the Mississippian and Contact periods (e.g., Alt 2006; Beck 2013; Pauketat 2013). Because at that time there was little evidence in the lower Southeast for two-way interaction with the American Bottom beyond the occurrence of a few unusual artifacts, typically at major centers, I further argued that Cahokia directed most of its efforts at direct colonization or domination to the north, into the upper Midwest, with minimal direct population movement to the south. We now know that people were moving widely over the landscape, and back and forth as well, perhaps not always or even often as colonizers or conquerors, or pilgrims and proselytizers, but still bringing about profound changes in many local societies. While accepting the possibility that much of what we think of as Mississippian may have originated at Cahokia, how these events were perceived, received, and transformed elsewhere, and at Cahokia itself, is what is important. The exploration of Mississippian beginnings shows that continuing fruitful results can come from long-term research by scholars working together on common problems.

Acknowledgments

Greg Wilson deserves great thanks for his patience and advice in putting this manuscript together. The participants of the original SEAC session where the papers that made up this volume were first presented also deserve thanks for their advice and observations then and down through the years. Finally, I would be remiss if I did not acknowledge the advice and mentorship about Mississippian archaeology from, in chronological order, Leland Ferguson, Dan and Phyllis Morse, David Hally, James B. Griffin, Henry T. Wright, Richard I. Ford, John Kelly, Paul D. Welch, and Tim Pauketat and Susan Alt, and many younger colleagues whose work over the past decade has been so inspiring. Tim Pauketat offered detailed comments on this manuscript, as did two anonymous reviewers, and I thank them, and the volume editor; this chapter is much improved for their efforts. A model for producing outstanding Mississippian research seen in action in many parts of the Southeast in recent years is to (1) throw bright and energetic graduate students or CRM teams into the field and at data, under the direction of dedicated mentors; (2) stir by mandating periodic summary reports at professional conferences where they can interact with their colleagues and peers; and (3) watch how much exciting information develops as the papers, theses, dissertations, and books are published. The process continues recursively as these students move into permanent positions and mentor new generations.

References Cited

Alt, Susan M.
   2002   The Knoebel Site: Tradition and Change in the Cahokian Suburbs. Unpublished master's thesis, Department of Anthropology, University of Illinois, Urbana-Champaign.
   2006   The Power of Diversity: The Roles of Migration and Hybridity in Culture Change. In *Leadership and Polity in Mississippian Society*, edited by Brian M. Butler and Paul D. Welch, pp. 289–308. Center for Archaeological Investigations, Occasional Paper 33. Southern Illinois University, Carbondale.
   2010   Complexity in Action(s): Retelling the Cahokia Story. In *Ancient Complexities: New Perspectives in Pre-Columbian North America*, edited by Susan Alt, pp. 119–137. Foundations of Archaeological Inquiry Series. University of Utah Press, Salt Lake City.

Alt, Susan M., Jeffery D. Kruchten, and Timothy R. Pauketat
   2010   The Construction and Use of Cahokia's Grand Plaza. *Journal of Field Archaeology* 35(2):131–146.

Ambrose, Stanley H., Jane Buikstra, and Harold W. Krueger
   2003   Status and Gender Differences in Diet at Mound 72, Cahokia, Revealed by Isotopic Analysis of Bone. *Journal of Anthropological Archaeology* 22:217–226.

Anderson, David G.
   1985   Middle Woodland Societies on the Lower South Atlantic Slope: A View from Georgia and South Carolina. *Early Georgia* 13:29–66.
   1994   *The Savannah River Chiefdoms: Political Change in the Late Prehistoric Southeast*. University of Alabama Press, Tuscaloosa.
   1995   Paleoindian Interaction Networks in the Eastern Woodlands. In *Native American Interaction: Multiscalar Analyses and Interpretations in the Eastern Woodlands*, edited

by Michael S. Nassaney and Kenneth E. Sassaman, pp. 1–26. University of Tennessee Press, Knoxville.

1997   The Role of Cahokia in the Evolution of Mississippian Society. In *Cahokia: Domination and Ideology in the Mississippian World*, edited by Timothy R. Pauketat and Thomas E. Emerson, pp. 248–268. University of Nebraska Press, Lincoln.

1999   Examining Chiefdoms in the Southeast: An Application of Multiscalar Analysis. In *Great Towns and Regional Polities in the Prehistoric American Southwest and Southeast*, edited by Jill E. Neitzel, pp. 215–241. Amerind Foundation New World Study Series 3. University of New Mexico Press, Albuquerque.

2001   Climate and Culture Change in Prehistoric and Early Historic Eastern North America. *Archaeology of Eastern North America* 29:143–186.

2012   Monumentality in Eastern North America during the Mississippian Period. In *Early New World Monumentality*, edited by Richard L. Burger and Robert M. Rosenswig, pp. 78–108. University of Florida Press, Gainesville.

2015   Event and Structure: Culture Change and Continuity in the Ancient Southeast. In *The Archaeology of Events: Cultural Change and Continuity in the Pre-Columbian Southeast*, edited by Zackary I. Gilmore and Jason M. O'Donoughue, pp. 223–242. University of Alabama Press, Tuscaloosa.

Anderson, David G., and Kenneth E. Sassaman

2012   *Recent Developments in Southeastern Archaeology: From Colonization to Complexity*. Society for American Archaeology Press, Washington, D.C.

Anderson, David G., and Joseph Schuldenrein

1983   Mississippian Settlement in the Southern Piedmont: Evidence from the Rucker's Bottom Site, Elbert County, Georgia. *Southeastern Archaeology* 2(2):98–117.

Anderson, David G., Charles E. Cantley, and A. Lee Novick

1982   *The Mattassee Lake Sites: Archaeological Investigations along the Lower Santee River in the Coastal Plain of South Carolina*. National Park Service, Interagency Archaeological Services–Atlanta, Special Publication 1.

Anderson, David G., John E. Cornelison Jr., and Sarah C. Sherwood

2013   *Archeological Investigations at Shiloh Indian Mounds National Historic Landmark, 40HR7, 1999–2004*. Southeast Archeological Center, National Park Service, Tallahassee.

Anderson, David G., Ashley M. Smallwood, and D. Shane Miller

2015   Pleistocene Human Settlement in the Southeastern United States: Current Evidence and Future Directions. *Paleoamerica* 1(1):7–51.

Anthony, David W.

1990   Migration in Archaeology: The Baby and the Bathwater. *American Anthropologist* 92:895–914.

Aveni, Anthony F.

2003   Archaeoastronomy in the Ancient Americas. *Journal of Archaeological Research* 11:149–191.

Baires, Sarah

2014a   Cahokia's Origins: Religions, Complexity, and Ridge-Top Mortuaries in the Mississippi River Valley. Unpublished Ph.D. dissertation, Department of Anthropology, University of Illinois, Urbana.

2014b   Cahokia's Rattlesnake Causeway. *Midcontinental Journal of Archaeology* 39(2):145–162.

Baires, Sarah E., Melissa R. Baltus, and Meghan E. Buchanan
   2015   Correlation Does Not Equal Causation: Questioning the Great Cahokia Flood. *Proceedings of the National Academy of Sciences of the United States of America* 112. http://www.pnas.org/content/112/29/E3753.full.pdf. Accessed 19 August 2016.

Barrier, Casey
   2014   *The Mississippian Transition at the Washausen Site: Demography and Community at a Tenth–Eleventh Century A.D. Mound Town in the American Bottom, Illinois.* Ph.D. dissertation, Department of Anthropology, University of Michigan, Ann Arbor.

Beck, Robin
   2013   *Chiefdoms, Collapse, and Coalescence in the Early American South.* Cambridge University Press, Cambridge.

Beck, Robin A. Jr., Douglas J. Bolender, James A. Brown, and Timothy K. Earle
   2007   Eventful Archaeology: The Place of Space in Structural Transformation. *Current Anthropology* 48:833–860.

Benson, Larry V., Timothy R. Pauketat, and Edward R. Cook
   2009   Cahokia's Boom and Bust in the Context of Climate Change. *American Antiquity* 74:467–483.

Betzenhauser, Alleen
   2006   Greater Cahokian Farmsteads: A Quantitative and Qualitative Analysis of Diversity. Unpublished master's paper, Department of Anthropology, University of Illinois, Urbana.
   2011   Creating the Cahokian Community: The Power of Place in Early Mississippian Sociopolitical Dynamics. Unpublished Ph.D. dissertation, Department of Anthropology, University of Illinois, Urbana.

Bhabha, Homi K.
   1990   The Third Space. In *Identity, Community Culture, Difference*, edited by Jonathan Rutherford, pp. 207–221. Lawrence and Wishart, London.

Bigman, Daniel P.
   2012   An Early Mississippian Settlement History of Ocmulgee. Unpublished Ph.D. dissertation, Department of Anthropology, University of Georgia, Athens.

Bigman, Daniel P., Adam King, and Chester P. Walker
   2011   Recent Geophysical Investigations and New Interpretations of Etowah's Palisade. *Southeastern Archaeology* 30:20–37.

Blitz, John H.
   1999   Mississippian Chiefdoms and the Fission-Fusion Process. *American Antiquity* 64:577–592.

Blitz, John H., and Patrick Livingood
   2004   Sociopolitical Implications of Mississippian Mound Volume. *American Antiquity* 69:291–301.

Blitz, John H., and Karl G. Lorenz
   2002   The Early Mississippian Frontier in the Lower Chattahoochee–Apalachicola River Valley. *Southeastern Archaeology* 21(2):117–135.
   2006   *The Chattahoochee Chiefdoms.* University of Alabama Press, Tuscaloosa.

Boudreaux, Edmond A. III
   2007a *The Archaeology of Town Creek.* University of Alabama Press, Tuscaloosa.

2007b A Mississippian Ceramic Chronology for the Town Creek Region. *North Carolina Archaeology* 56:1–57.
2010 Mound Construction and Change in the Mississippian Community at Town Creek. In *Mississippian Mortuary Practices: Beyond Hierarchy and the Representationist Perspective*, edited by Robert C. Mainfort Jr. and Lynne P. Sullivan, pp. 195–233. University Press of Florida, Gainesville.
2011 The Current State of Town Creek Research: What Have We Learned after the First 75 Years? In *The Archaeology of North Carolina: Three Archaeological Symposia*, edited by Charles R. Ewen, Thomas R. Whyte, and R. P. Stephen Davis Jr. Publication Number 30. North Carolina Archaeological Council, Raleigh.

Brown, James A., R. A. Kerber, and Howard D. Winters
1990 Trade and the Evolution of Exchange Relations at the Beginning of the Mississippian Period. In *The Mississippian Emergence*, edited by Bruce D. Smith, pp. 251–280. Smithsonian Institution Press, Washington, D.C.

Butler, Brian M., R. Berle Clay, Michael L. Hargrave, Staffan D. Peterson, John E. Schwegman, John A. Schwegman, Paul D. Welch
2011 A New Look at Kincaid: Magnetic Survey of a Large Mississippian Town. *Southeastern Archaeology* 30(1):20–37.

Carr, Christopher
2005 Historical Insights into the Direction and Limitations of Recent Research on Hopewell. In *Gathering Hopewell: Society, Ritual, and Ritual Interaction*, edited by Christopher Carr and D. Troy Case, pp. 51–70. Kluwer Academic/Plenum, New York.

Clark, John E.
2004 Surrounding the Sacred: Geometry and Design of Early Mound Groups as Meaning and Function. In *Signs of Power: The Rise of Cultural Complexity in the Southeast*, edited by Jon L. Gibson and Philip J. Carr, pp. 162–213. University of Alabama Press, Tuscaloosa.

Clark, John E., Jon L. Gibson, and James Ziedler
2010 First Towns in the Americas: Searching for Agriculture, Population Growth, and Other Enabling Conditions. In *Becoming Villagers: Comparing Early Village Societies*, edited by Matthew S. Bandy and Jake R. Fox, pp. 205–245. University of Arizona Press, Tucson.

Cobb, Charles R.
2003 Mississippian Chiefdoms: How Complex? *Annual Review of Anthropology* 32:63–84.

Coe, Joffre L.
1995 *Town Creek Indian Mound: A Native American Legacy.* University of North Carolina Press, Chapel Hill.

Cook, Robert A., and T. Douglas Price
2015 Maize, Mounds, and the Movement of People: Isotope Analysis of a Mississippian/Fort Ancient Region. *Journal of Archaeological Science* 61:112–128.

Crown, Patricia L., Thomas E. Emerson, Jiyan Gu, W. Jeffrey Hurst, Timothy R. Pauketat, and Timothy Ward
2012 Ritual Black Drink Consumption at Cahokia. *Proceedings of the National Academy of Sciences* 109(25):13944–13949.

Dalan, Rinita A.
1997 The Construction of Mississippian Cahokia. In *Cahokia: Domination and Ideology in*

the Mississippian World, edited by Timothy R. Pauketat and Thomas E. Emerson, pp. 89–102. University of Nebraska Press, Lincoln.

Dalan, Rinita A., George R. Holley, William I. Woods, Harold W. Watters Jr., and John A. Koepke
    2003   *Envisioning Cahokia: A Landscape Perspective*. Northern Illinois University Press, DeKalb.

Davis, Jera R., Chester A. Walker, and John H. Blitz
    2015   Remote Sensing as Community Settlement Analysis at Moundville. *American Antiquity* 80(1):161–169.

Diaz-Granados, Carol, James R. Duncan, and F. Kent Reilly III
    2015   *Picture Cave: Unraveling the Mysteries of the Mississippian Cosmos*. University of Texas Press, Austin.

Drooker, Penelope B.
    2004   Pipes, Leadership, and Interregional Interaction in Protohistoric Midwestern and Northeastern North America. In *Smoking and Culture: The Archaeology of Tobacco Pipes in Eastern North America*, edited by Sean Rafferty and Rob Mann, pp. 73–124. University of Tennessee Press, Knoxville.

Dye, David
    2009   *War Paths, Peace Paths: An Archaeology of Cooperation and Conflict in Native Eastern North America*. AltaMira Press, Lanham.

Elliott, Daniel T., and Jack T. Wynn
    1991   The Vining Revival: A Late Simple Stamped Phase in the Central Georgia Piedmont. *Early Georgia* 19:1–18.

Emerson, Thomas E.
    1997   *Cahokia and the Archaeology of Power*. University of Alabama Press, Tuscaloosa.
    2002   An Introduction to Cahokia 2002: Diversity, Complexity, and History. *Midcontinental Journal of Archaeology* 27:127–148.
    2003   Materializing Cahokian Shamans. *Southeastern Archaeology* 22:135–154.

Emerson, Thomas E., and Kristin M. Hedman
    2016   The Dangers of Diversity: The Consolidation and Dissolution of Cahokia, Native North America's First Urban Polity. In *Beyond Collapse: Archaeological Perspectives on Resilience, Revitalization, and Transformation in Complex Societies*, edited by Ronald K. Faulseit, pp. 147–175. Center for Archaeological Investigations, Occasional Paper No. 42. Southern Illinois University Press, Carbondale.

Emerson, Thomas E., Kristin M. Hedman, Eve Hargrave, D. Cobb, and A. Thompson.
    2016   Paradigms Lost: Reconfiguring Cahokia's Mound 72 Beaded Burial. *American Antiquity* 81(3):405–425.

Emerson, Thomas E., Randall E. Hughes, Mary R. Hynes, and Sarah U. Wisseman
    2003   The Sourcing and Interpretation of Cahokia-Style Figurines in the Trans-Mississippi South and Southeast. *American Antiquity* 68:287–313.

Ferguson, Leland G.
    1971   South Appalachian Mississippian. Unpublished Ph.D. dissertation, Department of Anthropology, University of North Carolina, Chapel Hill.

Ford, James A., and Gordon R. Willey
    1941   An Interpretation of the Prehistory of the Eastern United States. *American Anthropologist* 43:325–363.

Fortier, Andrew C., and Dale L. McElrath
  2002 Deconstructing the Emergent Mississippian Concept: The Case for the Terminal Late Woodland in the American Bottom. *Midcontinental Journal of Archaeology* 27:171–215.
Fritz, Gayle J., and Tristram R. Kidder
  1993 Recent Investigations into Prehistoric Agriculture in the Lower Mississippi Valley. *Southeastern Archaeology* 12:1–14.
Gilmore, Zackary I.
  2016 *Gathering at Silver Glen: Community and History in Late Archaic Florida*. University Press of Florida, Gainesville.
Gilmore, Zackary I., and Jason M. O'Donoughue (editors)
  2015 *The Archaeology of Events: Cultural Change and Continuity in the Pre-Columbian Southeast*. University of Alabama Press, Tuscaloosa.
Griffin, James B.
  1946 Culture Change and Continuity in Eastern United States Archaeology. In *Man in Northeastern North America*, edited by Frederick Johnson, pp. 37–95. Papers of the Robert S. Peabody Foundation for Archaeology. Andover.
  1961 Some Correlations of Climatic and Cultural Change in Eastern North American Prehistory. *Annals of the New York Academy of Sciences* 95:710–717.
  1967 Eastern North American Archaeology: A Summary. *Science* 156:175–191.
Hall, Robert
  1997 *An Archaeology of the Soul: North American Indian Belief and Ritual*. University of Illinois Press, Urbana.
Hally, David J.
  1993 The Territorial Size of Mississippian Chiefdoms. In *Archaeology of Eastern North America: Papers in Honor of Stephen Williams*, edited by James B. Stoltman, pp. 143–168. Archaeological Report No. 25. Mississippi Department of Archives and History, Jackson.
  1996 Platform-Mound Construction and the Political Stability of Mississippian Chiefdoms. In *Political Structure and Change in the Prehistoric Southeastern United States*, edited by John F. Scarry, pp. 92–127. University Press of Florida, Gainesville.
Hively, Ray, and Robert Horn
  2006 A Statistical Study of Lunar Alignments at the Newark Earthworks. *Midcontinental Journal of Archaeology* 31(2):281–322.
  2010 Hopewell Cosmography at Newark and Chillicothe, Ohio. In *Hopewell Settlement Patterns, Subsistence, and Symbolic Landscapes*, edited by A. Martin Byers and DeeAnne Wymer, pp. 126–164. University Press of Florida, Gainesville.
Holley, George R., Rinita A. Dalan, and Phillip A. Smith
  1993 Investigations in the Cahokia Site Grand Plaza. *American Antiquity* 58:306–319.
Kassabaum, Megan C., and Erin Stevens Nelson
  2016 Standing Posts and Special Substances: Gathering and Ritual Deposition at Feltus (22Je500), Jefferson County, Mississippi. *Southeastern Archaeology* 35(2):134–154.
Kassabaum, Megan C., Edward R. Henry, Vincas P. Steponaitis, and John W. O'Hear
  2014 Between Surface and Summit: The Process of Mound Construction at Feltus. *Archaeological Prospection* 14:27–37.
Keel, Bennie C.
  1976 *Cherokee Archaeology: A Study of the Appalachian Summit*. University of Tennessee Press, Knoxville.

Kelly, John E.
    1987   Emergent Mississippian and the Transition from Late Woodland to Mississippian: The American Bottom Case for a New Concept. In *The Emergent Mississippian, Proceedings of the Sixth Mid-South Archaeological Conference, June 6–9, 1985*, edited by Richard A. Marshall, pp. 87–101. Cobb Institute of Archaeology, Mississippi State University, State College.
    1990   The Emergence of Mississippian Culture in the American Bottom. In *The Mississippian 'Emergence*, edited by Bruce D. Smith, pp. 113–152. Smithsonian Institution Press, Washington, D.C.

Kidder, Tristram R.
    2012   Poverty Point. In *The Oxford Handbook of North American Archaeology*, edited by Timothy R. Pauketat, pp. 460–470. Oxford University Press, Oxford.

Kidder, Tristram R., and Kenneth E. Sassaman
    2009   The View from the Southeast. In *Archaic Societies: Diversity and Complexity across the Midcontinent*, edited by Thomas E. Emerson, Dana L. McElrath, and Andrew C. Fortier, pp. 667–694. State University of New York Press, Albany.

King, Adam
    2006   Whither SECC? In *Southeastern Ceremonial Complex: Chronology, Content, Context*, edited by Adam King, pp. 251–258. University of Alabama Press, Tuscaloosa.

King, Adam, and Keith Stephenson
    2012   Archival Research of the Hollywood Mound Site. *Early Georgia* 40(1):87–101.

King, Adam, Chester P. Walker, F. Kent Reilly III, Robert V. Sharp, and Duncan P. McKinnon
    2011   Remote Sensing from Etowah's Mound A: Architecture and the Re-creation of Mississippian Tradition. *American Antiquity* 76:355–371.

Knight, Vernon James Jr.
    1998   Moundville as a Diagrammatic Ceremonial Center. In *Archaeology of the Moundville Chiefdom*, edited by Vernon J. Knight Jr. and Vincas P. Steponaitis, pp. 44–62. Smithsonian Institution Press, Washington, D.C.
    2006   Farewell to the Southeastern Ceremonial Complex. *Southeastern Archaeology* 25(1):1–5.
    2010   *Mound Excavations at Moundville: Architecture, Elites and Social Order.* University of Alabama Press, Tuscaloosa.
    2012   *Iconographic Method in New World Prehistory.* Cambridge University Press, Cambridge.

Koerner, Shannon D., Henri Grissino-Mayer, Lynne P. Sullivan, and Georgina G. Deweese
    2009   Dendroarchaeological Approach to Mississippian Cultural Occupational History in Eastern Tennessee, USA. *Tree-Ring Research* 65:81–90.

Krupp, Edwin C.
    1983   *Echoes of the Ancient Skies: The Astronomy of Lost Civilizations.* Harper and Row, New York.

Lankford, George E., F. Kent Reilly III, and James Garber (editors)
    2011   *Visualizing the Sacred: Cosmic Visions, Regionalism, and the Art of the Mississippian World.* University of Texas Press, Austin.

Lewis, R. Barry, and Charles Stout
    1998   *Mississippian Towns and Sacred Spaces: Searching for an Architectural Grammar.* University of Alabama Press, Tuscaloosa.

Lydick, Christopher M., David G. Anderson, and John E. Cornelison Jr.
  2013 Integrated Remote Sensing Surveys. In *Archeological Investigations at Shiloh Indian Mounds National Historic Landmark, 40HR7, 1999-2004*, edited by David G. Anderson, John E. Cornelison Jr., and Sarah C. Sherwood, pp. 196–288. Southeast Archeological Center, National Park Service, Tallahassee, Florida.

Lynott, Mark J.
  2014 *Hopewell Ceremonial Landscapes of Ohio: More than Mounds and Geometric Earthworks*. Oxbow Books, Oxford.

Marrinan, Rochelle A., and Nancy Marie White
  2007 Modeling Fort Walton Culture in Northwest Florida. *Southeastern Archaeology* 26: 292–318.

Meeks, Scott C., and David G. Anderson
  2013 Drought, Subsistence Stress, and Population Dynamics Assessing Mississippian Abandonment of the Vacant Quarter. In *Soils, Climate, and Society: Archaeological Investigations in Ancient America*, edited by John D. Wingard and Sue Eileen Hayes, pp. 61–83. University of Colorado Press, Boulder.

Milner, George R.
  1998 *The Cahokia Chiefdom: The Archaeology of a Mississippian Society*. Smithsonian Institution Press, Washington, D.C.

Morse, Dan F. Jr., and Phyllis A. Morse
  1990 The Zebree Site: An Emerged Early Mississippian Expression in Northeast Arkansas. In *The Mississippian Emergence*, edited by Bruce D. Smith, pp. 51–66. Smithsonian Institution Press, Washington, D.C.

Munoz, Samuel E., Kristine E. Gruley, David A. Fike, Sissel Schroeder, and John W. Williams
  2015 Reply to Baires et al.: Shifts in Mississippi River Flood Regime Remain a Contributing Factor to Cahokia's Emergence and Decline. *Proceedings of the National Academy of Sciences of the United States of America*. 112. http://www.ncbi.nlm.nih.gov/pmc/articles/PMC4517204/ Accessed 19 August 2016.

Munoz, Samuel E., Kristine E. Gruley, Ashtin Massie, David A. Fike, Sissel Schroeder, and John W. Williams
  2015 Cahokia's Emergence and Decline Coincided with Shifts of Flood Frequency on the Mississippi River. *Proceedings of the National Academy of Sciences of the United States of America* 112:6319–6324.

O'Brien, Patricia J., and William P. McHugh
  1988 Mississippian Solstice Shrines and a Cahokian Calendar: An Hypothesis Based on Ethnohistory and Archaeology. *North American Archaeologist* 8:227–247.

Oliver, Billy L.
  1992 Settlements of the Pee Dee Culture. Unpublished Ph.D. dissertation, Department of Anthropology, University of North Carolina, Chapel Hill.

Pauketat, Timothy R.
  1994 *The Ascent of Chiefs: Cahokia and Mississippian Politics in Native North America*. University of Alabama Press, Tuscaloosa.
  1997 Cahokian Political Economy. In *Cahokia: Domination and Ideology in the Mississippian World*, edited by Timothy R. Pauketat and Thomas E. Emerson, pp. 30–51. University of Nebraska Press, Lincoln.

2001   Practice and History in Archaeology: An Emerging Paradigm. *Anthropological Theory* 1:73–98.
2003   Resettled Farmers and the Making of a Mississippian Polity. *American Antiquity* 68(1):39–66.
2007   *Chiefdoms and Other Archaeological Delusions.* AltaMira, Walnut Creek.
2009   *Cahokia: Ancient America's Great City on the Mississippi.* Viking-Penguin, New York.
2010   Of Leaders and Legacies in Native North America. In *The Evolution of Leadership and Complexity*, edited by John Kantner, Kevin Vaughn, and John Eerkins, pp. 169–192. School for Advanced Research Press, Santa Fe.
2013   *An Archaeology of the Cosmos: Rethinking Agency and Religion in Ancient America.* Routledge, New York.

Pauketat, Timothy R., and Susan Alt
2003   Agency in a Postmold? Physicality and the Archaeology of Culture-Making. *Journal of Archaeological Method and Theory* 12(3):213–236.
2015a   The Elements of Cahokian Shrine Complexes and the Basis of Mississippian Religion. In *Religion and Politics in the Ancient Americas*, edited by Sarah Barber and Arthur. Joyce. University of Colorado Press, Boulder.
2015b   Religious Innovation at the Emerald Acropolis: Something New under the Moon. In *Religion and Innovation: Antagonists or Partners?*, edited by Donald A. Yerxa. Bloomsbury Academic Press, London.

Pauketat, Timothy R., Susan M. Alt, and Jeffery D. Krutchen
2015   City of Earth and Wood: Cahokia and Its Material-Historical Implications. In *A World of Cities*, edited by Norman Yoffee, pp. 437–454. Cambridge University Press, New York.

Pauketat, Timothy R., Arleen Betzenhauser, and William Romain
2012   Redesigned Communities of the Early Mississippian World: From Toltec and Washausen to Obion and Cahokia. Paper presented at the 69th Annual Meeting of the Southeastern Archaeological Conference, Baton Rouge.

Pauketat, Timothy R., Robert Boszhardt, and Danielle Benden
2015   Trempealeau Entanglements: An Ancient Colony's Cause and Effects. *American Antiquity* 80:260–289.

Pauketat, Timothy R., and Thomas E. Emerson
1997   *Cahokia: Domination and Ideology in the Mississippian World.* University of Nebraska Press, Lincoln.

Pauketat, Timothy R., Andrew C. Fortier, Susan M. Alt, and Thomas E. Emerson
2013   A Mississippian Conflagration at the East St. Louis Civic-Ceremonial Precinct in Illinois and Its Political-Historical Implications. *Journal of Field Archaeology* 38(3):210–226.

Pauketat, Timothy R., Lucretia Kelly, Gail Fritz, Neal Lopinot, Scott Elias, and Eve Hargrave
2002   The Residues of Feasting and Public Ritual at Early Cahokia. *American Antiquity* 67(2):257–279.

Pluckhahn, Thomas J.
1997   Rethinking Early Mississippian Chronology and Cultural Contact in Central Georgia: The View from Tarver (9J06). *Early Georgia* 25:21–54.

Pursell, Corin C.
2004   Geographic Distribution and Symbolism of Colored Mound Architecture in the Mis-

sissippian Southeast. Unpublished master's thesis, Department of Anthropology, Southern Illinois University Press, Carbondale.

2013   Colored Monuments and Sensory Theater among the Mississippians. In *Making Senses of the Past: Toward a Sensory Archaeology*, edited by Jo Day, pp. 69–89. Center for Archaeological Investigations, Occasional Paper No. 40. Southern Illinois University Press, Carbondale.

Rafferty, Sean, and Rob Mann

2004   *Smoking and Culture: The Archaeology of Tobacco Pipes in Eastern North America*. University of Tennessee Press, Knoxville.

Rasmussen, Morten, Martin Sikora, Anders Albrechtsen, Thorfinn Sand Korneliussen, J. Víctor Moreno-Mayar, G. David Poznik, Christoph P. E. Zollikofer, Marcia S. Ponce de León, Morten E. Allentoft, Ida Moltke, Hákon Jónsson, Cristina Valdiosera, Ripan S. Malhi, Ludovic Orlando, Carlos D. Bustamante, Thomas W. Stafford Jr., David J. Meltzer, Rasmus Nielsen, and Eske Willerslev

2015   The Ancestry and Affiliations of Kennewick Man. *Nature* 523:455–458.

Reilly, F. Kent III, and James F. Garber (editors)

2007   *Ancient Objects and Sacred Realms: Interpretations of Mississippian Iconography*. University of Texas Press, Austin.

Riggs, Brett H., R. P. Stephen Davis, and Mary E. Fitts

2015   *Archaeology at Ashe Ferry: Late Woodland and Middle Mississippian Period Occupations in the Lower Catawba River Valley, York County, South Carolina*. Research Report 36. Research Laboratories of Archaeology, University of North Carolina, Chapel Hill.

Romain, William F.

2000   *Mysteries of the Hopewell: Astronomers, Geometers, and Magicians of the Eastern Woodlands*. University of Akron Press, Akron.

Sassaman, Kenneth E.

1995   The Cultural Diversity of Interactions among Mid-Holocene Societies of the American Southeast. In *Native American Interaction: Multiscalar Analyses and Interpretations in the Eastern Woodlands*, edited by Michael S. Nassaney and Kenneth E. Sassaman, pp. 174–204. University of Tennessee Press, Knoxville.

2001   Hunter-Gatherers and Traditions of Resistance. In *The Archaeology of Traditions: Agency and History before and after Columbus*, edited by Timothy R. Pauketat, pp. 218–236. University Press of Florida, Gainesville.

2010   *The Eastern Archaic, Historicized*. AltaMira Press, Lanham.

Sassaman, Kenneth E.

2012   Futurologists Look Back. *Archaeologies* 8:250–268.

Sassaman, Kenneth E.

2016   A Constellation of Practice in the Experience of Sea-Level Rise. In *Knowledge in Motion: Constellations of Learning across Time and Place*, edited by Andrew P. Roddick and Ann B. Stahl, pp. 271–298. University of Arizona Press, Tucson.

Saunders, Joe W., Rolfe D. Mandel, Roger T. Saucier, E. Thurman Allen, C. T. Hallmark, Jay K. Johnson, H. Edwin Jackson, Charles M. Allen, Gary L. Stringer, Douglas S. Frink, James K. Feathers, Stephen Williams, Kristen J. Gremillion, Malcolm F. Vidrine, and Reca Jones

1997   A Mound Complex in Louisiana at 5400–5000 Years before the Present. *Science* 277:1796–1799.

Scarry, C. Margaret
  1993 Variability in Mississippian Crop Production Strategies. In *Foraging and Farming in the Eastern Woodlands*, edited by C. Margaret Scarry, pp. 78–90. University Press of Florida, Gainesville.

Schilling, Timothy
  2010 An Archaeological Model of the Construction of Monks Mound and Implications for the Development of Cahokian Society (800–1400 A.D.). Unpublished Ph.D. dissertation, Department of Anthropology, Washington University in St. Louis, St. Louis.
  2012 Building Monks Mound, Cahokia, Illinois, A.D. 800–1400. *Journal of Field Archaeology* 37:302–313.
  2013 The Chronology of Monks Mound. *Southeastern Archaeology* 32(1):14–28.

Sherrod, P. Clay, and Martha Ann Rolingson
  1987 *Surveyors of the Ancient Mississippi Valley: Modules and Alignments in Prehistoric Mound Sites.* Arkansas Archeological Survey, Research Series 1. Fayetteville.

Sherwood, Sarah C., and Tristram R. Kidder
  2011 The DaVinci's of Dirt: Geoarchaeological Perspectives on Native American Mound Building in the Mississippi River Basin. *Journal of Anthropological Archaeology* 30:69–87.

Simek, Jan F., Alan Cressler, Nicholas P. Hermann, and Sarah Sherwood
  2013 Sacred Landscapes of the Southeastern USA: Prehistoric Rock and Cave Art in Tennessee. *Antiquity* 87:430–446.

Skousen, Jacob B., and Amanda J. Butler
  2012 Pilgrims and Proselytizers: The Movers and Shakers of Mississippian Beginnings. Paper presented at the 69th Annual Southeastern Archaeological Conference, Baton Rouge.

Slater, Philip A., Kristin M. Hedman, and Thomas E. Emerson
  2014 Immigrants at the Mississippian Polity of Cahokia: Strontium Isotope Evidence for Population Movement. *Journal of Archaeological Science* 44:117–127.

Smith, Bruce D. (editor)
  1978 *Mississippian Settlement Patterns.* Academic Press, New York.
  1984 Mississippian Expansion: Tracing the Historical Development of an Explanatory Model. *Southeastern Archaeology* 3(1):13–32.
  1990 *The Mississippian Emergence.* Smithsonian Institution Press, Washington, D.C.

Spivey, S. Margaret, Tristram R. Kidder, Anthony L. Ortman, and Lee J. Arco
  2015 Pilgrimage to Poverty Point. In *The Archaeology of Events: Cultural Change and Continuity in the Pre-Columbian Southeast*, edited by Zackary I. Gilmore and Jason M. O'Donoughue, pp. 141–159. University of Alabama Press, Tuscaloosa.

Steinmetz, Paul B.
  1984 The Sacred Pipe in American Indian Religions. *American Indian Culture and Research Journal* 8(3):27–80.

Sullivan, Lynne P., Thomas M. N. Lewis, and Madeline K. Lewis
  1995 *The Prehistory of the Chickamauga Basin in Tennessee.* 2 vols. University of Tennessee Press, Knoxville.

Sullivan, Lynne P., Bobby R. Braly, Michaelyn S. Harle, and Shannon D. Koerner
  2011 Remembering New Deal Archaeology in the Southeast: A Legacy in Museum Collec-

tions. In *Museums and Memory*, edited by Margaret W. Huber, pp. 64–107. Newfound Press, University of Tennessee Libraries, Knoxville.

Thompson, Andrew R., Kristin M. Hedman, and Philip A. Slater
2015 New Dental and Isotope Evidence of Biological Distance and Place of Origin for Mass Burial Groups and Cahokia's Mound 72. *American Journal of Physical Anthropology* 158:341–357.

Townsend, Richard F., and Robert V. Sharp
2004 *Hero, Hawk and Open Hand: American Indian Art of the Ancient Midwest and South.* Art Institute of Chicago and Yale University Press, New Haven.

Walthall, John, Kenneth Farnsworth, and Thomas E. Emerson
1997 Constructing (on) the Past. *Common Ground* 2:26–33.

Wauchope, Robert
1966 *Archaeological Survey of Northern Georgia.* Memoir 21. Society for American Archaeology, Salt Lake City.

Webb, Paul
2002 *Cultural and Historic Resource Investigation of the Ravensford Land Exchange Tract, Great Smoky Mountains National Park, Swain County, North Carolina.* TRC-Garrow, Chapel Hill.

Welch, Paul D.
2006 *Archaeology at Shiloh Indian Mounds, 1899–1999.* University of Alabama Press, Tuscaloosa.

White, Nancy Marie, Jeffrey Du Vernay, and Amber Yuellig
2012 Fort Walton Culture in the Apalachicola Valley, Northwest Florida. In *Late Prehistoric Florida: Archaeology at the Edge of the Mississippian World*, edited by Keith Ashley and Nancy White, pp. 231–274. University Press of Florida, Gainesville.

Willey, Gordon R.
1953 A Pattern of Diffusion-Acculturation. *Southwestern Journal of Anthropology* 9:369–383.

Williams, Mark
1994 The Origins of the Macon Plateau Site. In *Ocmulgee Archaeology, 1936–1986*, edited by David J. Hally, pp. 130–137. University of Georgia Press, Athens.

Wilson, Gregory D.
2008 *The Archaeology of Everyday Life at Early Moundville.* University of Alabama Press, Tuscaloosa.

Wittry, Warren L.
1964 The American Woodhenge. *Cranbrook Institute of Science News Letter* 33(9):49–55.
1980 Cahokia Woodhenge Update. *Archaeoastronomy* 3:12–14.
1996 Discovering and Interpreting the American Woodhenge. *Wisconsin Archaeologist* 77(3/4):26–35.

Contributors

David G. Anderson is professor in the Department of Anthropology at the University of Tennessee, Knoxville. He has written over 50 books and monographs and over 150 papers encompassing Paleoindian through recent historic assemblages, including work at the Zebree, Rucker's Bottom, and Shiloh Mississippian period sites.

Dana N. Bardolph is a Ph.D. candidate in the Department of Anthropology at the University of California, Santa Barbara. Her research interests include culture contact, gender and identity studies, and foodways in the Mississippian Southeast and the pre-Columbian Andes. She approaches these issues primarily through the lens of paleoethnobotany, but she also considers ceramic assemblages and pit feature data to assess how cooking practices, agricultural production, and the spatial dimensions of foodways shape identity construction and social life. In addition to her archaeological research, she has published on discipline sociopolitics, including gender equity issues in archaeology.

Alleen Betzenhauser is senior research archaeologist at the American Bottom Field Station of the Illinois State Archaeological Survey–Prairie Research Institute. She earned her M.A. and Ph.D. in Anthropology from the University of Illinois Urbana-Champaign. Her research interests include the Terminal Late Woodland–Mississippian transition in the American Bottom, ceramic analysis, and the relationships between spatiality and community formation and dissolution.

Edmond A. Boudreaux III is associate professor in the Department of Sociology and Anthropology and director of the Center for Archaeological Research at the University of Mississippi. His research has focused on various Late Prehistoric through Contact period Native American communities across the southeastern United States. Recent publications include "Community and Ritual within the Mississippian Center at Town Creek" in *American Antiquity* and a monograph entitled *Archaeological Investigations at Jackson Landing (22Ha515): An Early Late Woodland Mound and Earthwork Site in Coastal Mississippi*.

Robert A. Cook is associate professor in the Department of Anthropology at Ohio State University. His research interests are primarily focused on cultural evolution in relation to mortuary patterns, migration, and interregional interaction. His specific methodological interests include the integration of biological and archaeological data sets focused on questions of diet, relatedness, identity, and cultural affiliation studies and multivariate field methods, including geophysical prospecting. His regional focus has included fieldwork in the midwestern and southwestern United States and Mesoamerica.

Colleen M. Delaney is professor in the Department of Anthropology at California State University, Channel Islands. Most of Delaney's research and fieldwork focuses on the U.S. Midwest and California. Topically, her interests center on sociocultural and interregional interaction and exchange in Illinois during prehistory, the emergence of sociopolitically complex societies, and social identity in situations of culture contact. Her current research examines changing land use and cultural interaction among different populations in Ventura County, California, over the last 500 years.

Jeffrey P. Du Vernay is research assistant professor at the University of South Florida's Center for Virtualization and Applied Spatial Technologies (CVAST). He specializes in 3-D technology applications for archaeological research and the archaeology of Florida and the southeastern United States.

Adam King is research associate professor for the South Carolina Institute of Archaeology and Anthropology and Special Projects Archaeologist for the Savannah River Archaeological Research Program. Using archaeological excavation coupled with remote sensing and the study of ancient imagery, he researches the way Mississippian societies came into being and changed during their individual histories.

Phillip G. Millhouse is the principal investigator at Red Gates Archaeology LLC, Stoughton, Wisconsin. His primary interests include archaeological site preservation and community outreach, culture contact, cultural landscapes, midwestern archaeology, and history of the Upper Mississippi Valley lead mining frontier.

Amanda Regnier is director of the Oklahoma Archaeological Survey at the University of Oklahoma, Norman. Her research focuses on the prehistoric Caddo and historic post-removal Native American archaeology in eastern Oklahoma and Spanish contact and protohistoric archaeology in Alabama.

C. Margaret Scarry is professor of anthropology and director of the Research Laboratories of Archaeology at the University of North Carolina at Chapel Hill. She is an authority on the precolonial and colonial use of plants in the American South and has published extensively on Moundville and related areas. Her publications include *Foraging and Farming in the Eastern Woodlands, Case Studies in Environmental Archaeology* (with E. J. Reitz and S. J. Scudder) and *Rethinking Moundville and Its Hinterland* (with Vin Steponaitis).

Keith Stephenson is research archaeologist with the Savannah River Archaeological Research Program of the South Carolina Institute of Archaeology and Anthropology, University of South Carolina. His research interests focus on the socio-political organization of South Appalachian Woodland and Mississippian societies of the interior Coastal Plain with a theoretical emphasis on class relations and labor history.

Lynne P. Sullivan is adjunct professor of anthropology and emerita curator of Archaeology at the McClung Museum of Natural History and Culture at the University of Tennessee. Her primary research is the Mississippian period in the Upper Tennessee Valley, an area on which she has published extensively. Her publications include *The Prehistory of the Chickamauga Basin in Tennessee* (editor and compiler), *Mississippian Mortuary Practices* (with R. C. Mainfort Jr.), *Archaeology of the Appalachian Highlands* (with S. C. Prezzano), and numerous articles and book chapters on gender roles in Mississippian societies.

Christopher L. Thornock is an archaeologist and the Acting Heritage Program manager with the U.S. Forest Service at Land between the Lakes National Recreation Area, and a former research archaeologist with the Savannah River Archaeological Research Program. His research focuses on the organization of space across the Mississippian landscape and how it influences, and is influenced by, the ideologies and iconography recognized in Mississippian cultures.

Amber M. VanDerwarker is professor in the Department of Anthropology at the University of California, Santa Barbara. Her research encompasses a variety of methods, regions, and issues that revolve around the relationship between humans and food in the New World. Some themes of her research encompass the development of socio-political complexity, agricultural intensification, social identity and feasting, gender, the effects of warfare on the food quest, and exploratory data analysis.

Nancy Marie White is professor of anthropology and registered professional archaeologist at the University of South Florida in Tampa, specializing in the prehistoric and early historic archaeology of the Southeast.

Gregory D. Wilson is associate professor in the Department of Anthropology at the University of California, Santa Barbara. His research is concerned with issues of social inequality, identity politics, and violence in pre-Columbian North and South America. His perspective is informed by contemporary theoretical research on human agency, practice, and political economy. He investigates these issues through a household and community-centered archaeology with an emphasis on the methodologically rigorous analysis of large and diverse data sets.

Index

A. C. Mackin site, 180, 192
acorns, 46–48, 50
Adena, 143
agency, 12, 13, 72, 141, 234
aggrandizement, 8, 30, 54, 56
aggrandizers, 6, 8
agriculture, 15, 39, 40, 56, 132, 134, 137, 139, 148, 220, 222, 224, 238, 272, 281, 282, 284, 294, 296, 304. *See also* cultivation
amaranth, domesticated, 45, 46
American Bottom, 1, 9, 12–14, 33, 34, 37–44, 46, 47, 48, 52, 54, 55, 71–76, 78, 79, 82, 85–88, 99, 100, 109, 110, 114, 116–119, 190, 195, 197, 235, 251, 299, 301, 308, 309. *See also* Cahokia
American Southwest, 33
Angel site, 146, 154, 156, 157, 158, 164, 167. *See also* Ohio River Valley
Apalachicola–lower Chattahoochee River valley, 2, 10, 15, 260, 261, 262, 265, 270, 279, 282, 284, 304
Apple River Valley, 2, 14, 97–100, 105, 106, 109, 112, 113
architecture: ceremonial, 41, 99, 104; domestic, 6, 9, 77, 84, 104, 165, 182, 210, 212–214, 216, 222, 225, 299; flexed pole, 37, 183, 210, 224; single post, 80, 82, 104, 107; wall trench, 80, 81, 104, 105, 118, 148
Ashe Ferry site, 206, 208, 303. *See also* Catawba River Valley
Audrey site, 42, 102, 103, 108, 110, 113, 114, 119. *See also* Lower Illinois River Valley
authority, chiefly, 6, 37, 135, 158, 160, 163, 195, 196, 218
Averbuch site, 156–158. *See also* Nashville Basin
Averett, groups, 10
Aztalan site, 99

Battle Mound site, 197. *See also* Red River Valley
Bauer Branch phase, 104, 110. *See also* Central Illinois River Valley

Baupläne, 141, 164
Bayesian analysis, 207, 212, 216
beads, shell, 49, 108, 134, 151, 194, 242
beans, domesticated, 36, 45
Beaverdam phase, 214, 248. *See also* Savannah River Valley
Bentsen-Clark site, 180, 187–189, 192, 194, 195. *See also* Red River Valley
Bhabha, Homi, 11
Big Sandy site, 51. *See also* Black Warrior River Valley
biodistance analysis, 99, 100, 132, 141, 154, 156–158, 160, 162, 166
biomechanical skeletal markers, 35
bird man, 166
Black Drink, 114, 295. *See also* Ilex vomitoria
Black Warrior River Valley, 13, 49, 50. *See also* Moundville
Bottle Creek site, 49, 50, 51, 283
Braden, 246, 251
Brasstown River Valley, 51–53, 215
Bud Wright site, 179, 183–185, 187–189, 198, 300. *See also* Red River Valley
building, 9, 31, 41, 56, 82, 99, 102, 104, 105, 183, 192, 198, 210, 212, 213, 216–220, 252. *See also* architecture
bundle, 15, 213, 241, 243, 244, 250–253
Busycon, 160, 272

Caddo, 2, 14, 32, 83, 178–198
Cahokia, 1, 2, 6, 8–10, 13–17, 30, 31, 37, 39, 40, 41, 44, 54–56, 71–80, 83, 85–88, 97–100, 104, 108–119, 132, 142, 144, 154, 156, 164, 167, 181, 190, 195, 235, 294–300, 302, 307, 308, 309. *See also* American Bottom
captives, 167
Cartersville phase, 52. *See also* Brasstown River Valley
Catawba River Valley, 206, 303

Cayson site, 264, 265, 275, 276, 280–283, 285. *See also* Apalachicola–lower Chattahoochee River valley
celts, 85, 193, 194, 197, 239, 242, 243, 248–251, 272
cemeteries, 102, 103, 182, 183, 197, 219, 222, 268, 271, 272
Central Illinois River Valley, 10, 31, 41–46, 53–57, 98–100, 103–105, 108–119
Central Mississippi Valley, 5, 9, 13, 31, 44, 45, 46, 208, 250, 251, 296, 302
Charles Towne Landing site, 210, 213
Chattahoochee Landing site, 264, 265, 267, 268, 275–279, 285. *See also* Apalachicola–lower Chattahoochee River valley
Chattahoochee River Valley, 2, 10, 15, 260, 261, 262, 265, 270, 274, 275, 279, 282, 284, 304
chenopod, 39, 43, 48, 52. *See also* goosefoot
chief, 5, 6, 16, 37, 47, 194, 196, 284
chiefdom, 6, 7, 14, 16, 72, 137, 195, 196, 234, 282, 294, 297, 309
Chipola Cutoff site, 268. *See also* Apalachicola–lower Chattahoochee River valley
chunky stone, 151
Clark, Jeffrey, 98
Clear Lake site, 104. *See also* Central Illinois River Valley
Clement site, 180, 184, 185, 186, 187, 188, 189, 196. *See also* Red River Valley
climate, 134, 146, 293, 295, 296
coalescence, 265, 298, 309
Coastal Plain, 178, 184, 204, 236, 237, 255, 325
Cole, Fay-Cooper, 4
Coles Creek, 14, 47, 48, 49, 142, 181, 182, 183, 184, 185, 186, 187, 188, 190, 193, 195, 300, 304, 309
colonialism, 11
commensal events, 11, 31, 32, 46, 55, 111, 116. *See also* feast / feasting, ceremonial
community: formation, 14, 32, 50, 75, 85, 86, 223; organization, 49, 165, 205, 216, 220
competitive feasting, 30. *See also* commensal events
complexity, sociopolitical, 30, 31, 36, 42, 49, 53, 55, 56, 57, 73, 99, 111, 139, 301
conflict, 9, 141, 203, 221, 248, 285. *See also* warfare
copper, 41, 159, 193, 194, 195, 219, 239, 242, 243, 244, 245, 246, 248, 249, 250, 251, 253, 272, 279, 286
Corbin-Tucker site, 264, 266, 267, 270, 271, 272. *See also* Apalachicola–lower Chattahoochee River valley
corn, 35, 194, 212, 220, 221, 222, 224, 238, 255. *See also* maize
cosmogram, 194
crafts, crafting, 6, 8, 31, 40, 41, 51, 99, 219
Crenshaw site, 190. *See also* Red River Valley
cultivation, 5, 13, 29–33, 35, 365–40, 42, 43, 45–48, 50, 52, 55, 56, 82, 255, 282. *See also* agriculture
culture contact, 5, 9–12, 44, 54, 56, 98–100, 118, 119
Culture History, 5, 130, 137, 262
Cumberland River Valley, 32, 154, 156, 167
Curlee site, 265, 270, 271, 282. *See also* Apalachicola–lower Chattahoochee River valley

Dallas phase, 11, 214, 215
Dan Holdeman site, 180. *See also* Red River Valley
Dickson Mounds Mortuary site, 43, 104. *See also* Central Illinois River Valley
diffusion, 5, 137, 148, 297. *See also* migration
Divers site, 80, 82. *See also* American Bottom

eastern Tennessee, 1, 166, 250, 251, 306
East St. Louis site, 78, 79, 117, 298. *See also* American Bottom
effigy, 82, 106, 134, 135, 162, 194, 248, 249, 251, 262, 269
elites, 6, 7, 8, 16, 30, 40, 72, 85, 196, 260, 285, 308. *See also* aggrandizers
Emerald Mounds site, 9, 117. *See also* American Bottom
entanglement, 2, 4, 9, 10, 12, 14, 15, 16, 100, 165, 234, 236, 274, 294, 297
ethnicity, 4, 74, 86, 107, 223, 237
Etowah, phase, 52
Etowah, polity, 9, 30
Etowah, site, 16, 31
Etowah River Valley, 51
Eveland phase, 104, 105. *See also* Central Illinois River Valley
Eveland site, 104, 105, 108, 110, 113, 114, 119. *See also* Central Illinois River Valley
Ewell III site, 33
exchange, 2, 5, 29, 33, 49, 72, 78, 86, 100, 111, 117, 130, 178, 295, 309. *See also* trade

Fandel site, 104. *See also* Central Illinois River Valley

farming, 29, 35, 36, 45, 209, 220, 238, 282, 283, 286. *See also* agriculture; cultivation
Fasken site, 180, 192. *See also* Red River Valley
feasts/feasting, ceremonial, 8, 13, 30, 31, 40, 46, 51, 53, 55, 73, 75, 79, 82, 84, 107, 111, 198, 308. *See also* commensal events
Feltus site, 48, 301
Fisher Mound site, 118. *See also* western Wisconsin
foodways, 31, 53, 85, 98, 111, 114, 116, 118, 299
Fort Ancient, 131–168
Fort Walton, 1, 10, 15, 32, 50, 260–286, 304
Fourche Maline, 181–183, 187, 190, 198, 300
Fred Edwards site, 108. *See also* western Wisconsin
functionalism, 8

Gahagan site, 190, 193–195. *See also* Red River Valley
Garren site, 105. *See also* Central Illinois River Valley
gender, 7, 33, 54, 305
George C. Davis site, 190, 192–196, 198. *See also* Red River Valley
goosefoot, 39. *See also* chenopod
Grossman site, 80. *See also* American Bottom
Guard site, 135, 148, 150, 151, 152, 154, 156–158, 165. *See also* Fort Ancient

Haag site, 143, 148. *See also* Fort Ancient
Halliday site, 111, 112. *See also* American Bottom
Hartley Fort site, 108. *See also* northeast Iowa
hickory nuts, 47, 48, 50, 152
hierarchy, 8, 30, 37, 43, 51–54, 56, 142. *See also* complexity, sociopolitical
hinterland, 13, 14, 44, 49, 51, 97, 99, 100, 109, 110, 114, 116, 118, 119, 195, 299
Hiwassee Island site, 11, 154, 156, 157, 158, 165, 166, 167, 215, 295. *See also* eastern Tennessee
Hog Pen site, 51. *See also* Black Warrior River Valley
Hohokam, 98
Holder, Preston, 16
Holding site, 33, 38. *See also* American Bottom
Hollywood phase, 237, 238, 239, 242, 248, 249, 251, 253, 255, 256. *See also* Savannah River Valley
Hollywood site, 2, 234, 236, 239, 240, 241, 243, 244, 245, 246, 247, 249, 250, 251, 252, 253, 254, 255, 256. *See also* Savannah River Valley
hominy, 35, 40, 50

Hopewell, 143, 160, 307, 308
house, 9, 87, 107, 108, 132, 144, 149, 150, 151, 152, 153, 156, 187, 188, 191, 192, 198, 210–213, 216, 217, 220–225, 247, 262, 264, 295, 302, 303
household, 6, 36, 44, 74, 79, 82, 85, 99, 111, 144, 165, 196, 205, 210, 213, 220–223, 299, 303
hybrid, hybridity, 5, 11, 12, 16, 106, 108–110, 149, 150, 166, 274, 297, 304, 309

Icehouse Bottom site, 33, 39
Identity, 4, 9, 14, 71, 73, 75, 85, 98, 99, 100, 118, 120, 154, 221, 222, 223, 236, 272, 274, 286, 295, 298
ideology, 74, 132, 178, 190, 195, 206, 208, 220, 255
Ilex vomitoria, 114, 295. *See also* Black Drink
intensification, agricultural, 2, 14, 29–37, 39, 40, 43, 44, 46–56, 220–222, 224, 260, 283, 285

Jernigan II site, 33
Jersey Bluff phase, 101, 102. *See also* Lower Illinois River Valley
John Chapman site, 106–108, 110, 113. *See also* Apple River Valley

Kincaid site, 164, 167, 295
kinship, 31, 51, 74, 303
Knoebel site, 111, 112, 308. *See also* American Bottom
knotweed, erect, 39, 43, 52

labor, 6, 30, 31, 33, 40, 87, 222, 223, 234, 285, 295
Lake George site, 48. *See also* Yazoo Basin
Lamb site, 105, 108, 110, 113, 114, 119. *See also* Central Illinois River Valley
Late Woodland period, 2, 14, 34, 35, 37, 38, 41–45, 47, 49–52, 54, 56, 71, 72, 75–84, 86, 101, 104, 106, 109–111, 114, 117, 118, 138, 142, 143, 148, 151, 158, 159, 166, 167, 178–183, 188, 203, 206, 208, 215, 237, 252, 260, 261, 262, 265, 268–271, 275, 278–280, 282, 284–286, 303, 309
Lawton, phase, 237, 238
Lawton, site, 255
leadership, 7–9, 30, 51, 134, 138, 148, 165, 216, 217, 284
Leak phase, 205, 206. *See also* North Carolina Piedmont
Leak site, 210, 213. *See also* North Carolina Piedmont
Lindeman phase, 81, 82
lineages: maize, kinship, 34, 119, 163

little barley, 39, 43
Little Ice Age, 146
Lohmann phase, 37, 39, 40, 78–84, 104, 109, 111, 114, 117, 118, 309. *See also* Cahokia
Lohmann site, 111, 117. *See also* American Bottom
long-nosed god maskettes, 195
Lower Illinois River Valley, 41, 98–102, 109, 119
Lower Mississippi Valley, 13, 14, 31, 39, 47–49, 56, 57, 83, 181, 250
Lundy site, 106, 108, 110, 113. *See also* Apple River Valley

Macon Plateau, 295. *See also* Ocmulgee site
Madisonville site, 135, 140, 146, 148, 154, 156, 157. *See also* Fort Ancient
Mahaffey site, 179, 182, 188, 189. *See also* Red River Valley
maize, 2, 5, 13, 14, 15, 29–57, 79, 82, 83, 107, 132, 139, 140, 148, 150–154, 158, 159, 164, 178, 197, 260, 262, 265, 272, 281–283, 285, 294, 296, 300, 304, 305
Maples Mills phase, 104. *See also* Central Illinois River Valley
marine shell, 49, 132, 178, 194, 304
Mason's Plantation site, 238, 255. *See also* Savannah River Valley
maygrass, 39, 43, 52
McCurtain phase, 183, 185. *See also* Red River Valley
memory, social, 142, 143, 163
Mesoamerica, 7, 142, 307
mica, 240, 243, 247
Middle Woodland, 33, 38, 52, 134, 142, 159, 163, 166, 262, 265, 268, 270, 278–281, 303, 308
Midwestern Taxonomic System, 130
migration, 2, 5, 10, 98–100, 106, 111, 116–118, 130, 137, 141, 150, 159, 164, 167, 168, 204, 294, 297, 302, 308. *See also* diffusion
Mill Creek hoes, 83, 85
Miller's Farm site, 111. *See also* American Bottom
Mills site, 106, 108. *See also* Apple River Valley
Mississippi River Valley, 13, 49, 251, 298
Missouri River Valley, 45
Monks Mound, 294, 298, 301. *See also* Cahokia
monumentality, 142, 294, 301, 302, 307
monuments, construction of, 74, 142, 143, 281, 301, 308
Morrison site, 78. *See also* American Bottom
mortuary, 6, 8, 15, 16, 41, 84, 98, 102–104, 141, 142, 143, 144, 158, 165, 178, 184, 190, 191, 193–196, 198, 205, 213, 216, 223, 234, 236, 248, 249, 252–256, 275, 303. *See also* cemeteries
Moss Cemetery site, 102. *See also* Lower Illinois River Valley
Mossville phase, 104, 109, 110. *See also* Central Illinois River Valley
Mossville Village site, 118. *See also* Central Illinois River Valley
mound, construction of, 8, 13, 15, 29, 47, 48, 50, 52, 56, 78, 99, 118, 142, 185, 187, 192, 193, 195, 197, 198, 262, 274, 275, 277–279, 281, 284, 285, 296, 301, 306
Mound 72, 40, 84. *See also* Cahokia
Mounds Plantation site, 190, 193, 195. *See also* Red River Valley
Moundville, 6, 9, 16, 30, 31, 49, 50, 51, 54–56, 215, 295, 296, 303, 306
Moundville I phase, 49, 50, 51. *See also* Black Warrior River Valley
Moundville II phase, 50. *See also* Black Warrior River Valley
Mouse Creek site, 214, 215

Nashville Basin, 250
Natchez Bluffs, 47, 48
nodal site, 41, 79, 80, 81, 83, 85, 86, 111, 299
North Carolina Piedmont, 2, 14, 203–208, 210, 213, 220–224, 302
northeast Iowa, 108
nut mast, 34, 38, 46. *See also* acorns; hickory nuts

Ocmulgee site, 295, 301, 302, 303, 306. *See also* Macon Plateau
Ohio River Valley, 130, 146, 148, 300
Old Rambo site, 268. *See also* Apalachicola–lower Chattahoochee River valley
Oliver site, 51. *See also* Black Warrior River Valley
Omussee Creek mound site, 268, 275. *See also* Apalachicola–lower Chattahoochee River valley
Oneota, 10, 11
Ouachita River Valley, 47

palisade, 4, 44, 103, 108, 119, 210, 221, 225. *See also* conflict; warfare
Patrick phase, 82

Payne site, 206, 207, 208, 209. *See also* North Carolina Piedmont
Pee Dee culture, 14, 15, 248
Pee Dee River Valley, 208
phytoliths, maize, 33, 34
Pierce site, 264–268, 275–280, 284, 285. *See also* Apalachicola–lower Chattahoochee River valley
pilgrimage, pilgrims, 2, 9, 98, 100, 117, 118, 297, 308, 309
pipe, 13, 83, 134, 135, 183, 194, 195, 219, 239, 241–243, 248–251
Plaquemine, 47, 49, 300
plaza, 4, 9, 35, 50, 73, 74, 80, 83, 102, 106, 108, 111, 143, 216–220, 222, 225, 279, 295, 296, 303, 306
Plum Bayou phase, culture, 1, 307
political economy, 5–8, 205, 216
population pressure, 30, 44, 49
porotic hyperostosis, 48
pottery: check stamped, 241, 248, 249, 262, 266, 268–274, 278, 279, 280, 281, 284; complicated stamped, 206, 208, 220, 223, 237, 238, 248, 249; Ramey Incised, 41, 99, 108, 116, 117; fineware, 114, 118, 119, 179, 181, 182, 184, 185, 187–189, 193, 198; Powell Plain, 99, 109; Yankeetown, 83, 308
Poverty Point site, 301, 308
Powell Canal site, 1
power, 6, 8, 14, 31, 32, 49, 71, 72, 75, 79, 82, 85, 165, 196, 284, 308
Prather site, 146
prestige goods, 6, 298
Processual Archaeology, 5, 7, 130, 132, 133, 134, 135, 138, 141, 144, 159, 160, 163, 168
Pueblo, 32, 98. *See also* American Southwest
Pulcher site, 78, 79. *See also* American Bottom

radiocarbon dating, 1, 45, 57, 137, 148, 149, 151, 152, 158, 188, 194, 205–208, 212, 216, 218, 224, 238, 248, 249, 262, 264, 270, 273, 278, 280, 281, 286, 294, 303. *See also* Bayesian analysis
raiding, 221
Range site, 78, 80, 81, 82. *See also* American Bottom
ranking, social, 5, 41, 47, 52, 55, 195, 255, 256
Ray site, 180, 182, 183, 188, 198. *See also* Red River Valley
Red Lake site, 238, 255. *See also* Savannah River Valley

Red River Valley, 47, 178, 179, 181, 183, 184, 189, 190, 191, 194–198
Red Wing Area, 99
religion, 8, 9, 37, 196, 293, 294, 296–298, 307
Rembert phase, 215, 248
remote sensing, 108, 294, 295, 302, 305–307
Rench site, 57, 104, 108, 109, 112, 114, 118. *See also* Central Illinois River Valley
risk, reduction, strategies of, management, 34, 46, 146, 213, 221
ritual, economy, 7, 8, 55
ritual, specialists, 37
Roitsch/Sam Kaufman site, 180, 187, 188. *See also* Red River Valley
Rood phase, 10, 15, 260, 269, 272–275, 286. *See also* Chattahoochee River Valley

Sanders phase, 185, 192. *See also* Red River Valley
Savannah I phase, 237, 238. *See also* Savannah River Valley
Savannah River Valley, 15, 234–239, 247, 249, 252, 254, 255, 256
Schild Cemetery site, 103. *See also* Lower Illinois River Valley
sedentism, 72, 224
shaft tombs, 187, 193, 194, 197, 301
Shiloh site, 294, 295, 296, 301, 306
Silver Bluff phase, 237. *See also* Savannah River Valley
Sleepy Hollow phase, 237, 238. *See also* Savannah River Valley
Smith, Bruce D., 1, 2, 5, 17, 46
Southeastern Ceremonial Complex (SECC), 16, 197, 238, 239, 246, 285, 298
South Fort site, 148. *See also* Fort Ancient
Spring Lake site, 238. *See also* Savannah River Valley
squash, mixta, 36, 45
St. Louis site, 78, 79, 117, 298, 255. *See also* American Bottom
stable isotopes, 141, 154, 155, 158, 159, 160, 166
Stallings site, 180, 187, 188. *See also* Red River Valley
starchy seeds, seed masses of, 30, 38, 39, 40, 42, 43, 45, 46, 48, 52, 53, 55, 181
State Line site, 148, 150, 151, 154, 156, 159, 166. *See also* Fort Ancient

status, 14, 31, 32, 33, 35, 40, 48, 54, 74, 75, 84, 87, 158, 160, 163, 165, 197, 216, 218, 219, 221, 252, 275, 295, 303. *See also* elites; hierarchy
Stirling phase, 109, 110, 111, 113–116. *See also* Cahokia
stone box graves, 143, 159, 160
storage, 34, 36, 79, 80, 83, 105, 108, 111, 114
strontium, 154, 155, 158, 159, 160, 166. *See also* stable isotopes
sub-Mound 51, 40. *See also* Cahokia
sumpweed, 45
sunflower, 45
Sunstroke site, 262, 264, 266, 267. *See also* Apalachicola–lower Chattahoochee River valley
Sun Watch site, 158. *See also* Fort Ancient
surplus, agricultural, 30, 31, 40, 51, 53–57, 83, 305
Swift Creek, 262, 279
Sycamore site, 262, 264, 265, 282. *See also* Apalachicola–lower Chattahoochee River valley

tableau, 194, 252
Teal phase, 205, 206, 303. *See also* Town Creek phase
Teal site, 205, 207, 208, 209, 213, 216, 224. *See also* North Carolina Piedmont
Tensas Basin, 47
Terminal Late Woodland period, 14, 37, 38, 41, 43, 49, 72, 75, 76, 78–84, 86, 101, 106, 111, 117
Toltec Mounds site, 1, 46, 307
Town Creek phase, 206, 208, 214. *See also* Town Creek site
Town Creek site, 15, 205, 207, 209–225, 301–303. *See also* North Carolina Piedmont
trade, 71, 72, 297, 298
tradition, 2, 4, 8–11, 14, 15, 17, 29, 31, 32, 35, 47, 54, 57, 82, 85, 86, 97, 98, 108–110, 117, 119, 139, 144, 148, 156, 159, 166, 178–181, 188–190, 197, 198, 203, 208, 234, 236–238, 242, 254–256, 261, 270, 272–275, 281, 283–287, 297, 299, 300

Trempealeau site, 99, 118. *See also* western Wisconsin
tributary economy, 6, 30
tribute, 55, 78, 83

Underwater Indian Mound site, 268. *See also* Apalachicola–lower Chattahoochee River valley

Vacant Quarter, 300
village, 4, 9, 35, 36, 37, 38, 41, 42, 44–46, 49, 71, 73, 77–83, 85, 86, 88, 100, 102–104, 106, 108, 111, 118, 132, 133, 134, 135, 137–145, 148, 151, 152, 158, 160, 163, 164, 165, 167, 196, 264, 267, 268, 271–273, 278, 279, 280, 282, 286
violence, 72, 221. *See also* conflict; warfare

warfare, 5, 221, 285, 294, 308
Waring, Antonia, 16
Washausen site, 295, 303. *See also* American Bottom
Weeden Island, 15, 261, 262, 265, 266, 268, 271, 272, 273, 274, 279–282. *See also* Apalachicola–lower Chattahoochee River valley
western Wisconsin, 74, 99, 105, 108, 118
West Jefferson phase, 49, 50. *See also* Black Warrior River Valley
Whiteside site, 42, 102, 103. *See also* Lower Illinois River Valley
Wilbanks phase, 249
Woodstock, phase, 51
Woodstock, site, 52, 53
WPA, 180, 181, 184, 185, 186, 187

Yazoo Basin, 47, 48
Yon site, 265, 266, 267, 273, 274, 275, 282, 283. *See also* Apalachicola–lower Chattahoochee River valley

Zebree Site, 1. *See also* Central Mississippi Valley

Ripley P. Bullen Series
Florida Museum of Natural History

Tacachale: Essays on the Indians of Florida and Southeastern Georgia during the Historic Period, edited by Jerald T. Milanich and Samuel Proctor (1978)

Aboriginal Subsistence Technology on the Southeastern Coastal Plain during the Late Prehistoric Period, by Lewis H. Larson (1980)

Cemochechobee: Archaeology of a Mississippian Ceremonial Center on the Chattahoochee River, by Frank T. Schnell, Vernon J. Knight Jr., and Gail S. Schnell (1981)

Fort Center: An Archaeological Site in the Lake Okeechobee Basin, by William H. Sears, with contributions by Elsie O'R. Sears and Karl T. Steinen (1982)

Perspectives on Gulf Coast Prehistory, edited by Dave D. Davis (1984)

Archaeology of Aboriginal Culture Change in the Interior Southeast: Depopulation during the Early Historic Period, by Marvin T. Smith (1987)

Apalachee: The Land between the Rivers, by John H. Hann (1988)

Key Marco's Buried Treasure: Archaeology and Adventure in the Nineteenth Century, by Marion Spjut Gilliland (1989)

First Encounters: Spanish Explorations in the Caribbean and the United States, 1492–1570, edited by Jerald T. Milanich and Susan Milbrath (1989)

Missions to the Calusa, edited and translated by John H. Hann, with an introduction by William H. Marquardt (1991)

Excavations on the Franciscan Frontier: Archaeology at the Fig Springs Mission, by Brent Richards Weisman (1992)

The People Who Discovered Columbus: The Prehistory of the Bahamas, by William F. Keegan (1992)

Hernando de Soto and the Indians of Florida, by Jerald T. Milanich and Charles Hudson (1993)

Foraging and Farming in the Eastern Woodlands, edited by C. Margaret Scarry (1993)

Puerto Real: The Archaeology of a Sixteenth-Century Spanish Town in Hispaniola, edited by Kathleen Deagan (1995)

Political Structure and Change in the Prehistoric Southeastern United States, edited by John F. Scarry (1996)

Bioarchaeology of Native American Adaptation in the Spanish Borderlands, edited by Brenda J. Baker and Lisa Kealhofer (1996)

A History of the Timucua Indians and Missions, by John H. Hann (1996)

Archaeology of the Mid-Holocene Southeast, edited by Kenneth E. Sassaman and David G. Anderson (1996)

The Indigenous People of the Caribbean, edited by Samuel M. Wilson (1997; first paperback edition, 1999)

Hernando de Soto among the Apalachee: The Archaeology of the First Winter Encampment, by Charles R. Ewen and John H. Hann (1998)

The Timucuan Chiefdoms of Spanish Florida, by John E. Worth: vol. 1, *Assimilation*; vol. 2, *Resistance and Destruction* (1998)
Ancient Earthen Enclosures of the Eastern Woodlands, edited by Robert C. Mainfort Jr. and Lynne P. Sullivan (1998)
An Environmental History of Northeast Florida, by James J. Miller (1998)
Precolumbian Architecture in Eastern North America, by William N. Morgan (1999)
Archaeology of Colonial Pensacola, edited by Judith A. Bense (1999)
Grit-Tempered: Early Women Archaeologists in the Southeastern United States, edited by Nancy Marie White, Lynne P. Sullivan, and Rochelle A. Marrinan (1999; first paperback edition, 2000)
Coosa: The Rise and Fall of a Southeastern Mississippian Chiefdom, by Marvin T. Smith (2000)
Religion, Power, and Politics in Colonial St. Augustine, by Robert L. Kapitzke (2001)
Bioarchaeology of Spanish Florida: The Impact of Colonialism, edited by Clark Spencer Larsen (2001)
Archaeological Studies of Gender in the Southeastern United States, edited by Jane M. Eastman and Christopher B. Rodning (2001)
The Archaeology of Traditions: Agency and History Before and After Columbus, edited by Timothy R. Pauketat (2001)
Foraging, Farming, and Coastal Biocultural Adaptation in Late Prehistoric North Carolina, by Dale L. Hutchinson (2002)
Windover: Multidisciplinary Investigations of an Early Archaic Florida Cemetery, edited by Glen H. Doran (2002)
Archaeology of the Everglades, by John W. Griffin (2002; first paperback edition, 2017)
Pioneer in Space and Time: John Mann Goggin and the Development of Florida Archaeology, by Brent Richards Weisman (2002)
Indians of Central and South Florida, 1513–1763, by John H. Hann (2003)
Presidio Santa María de Galve: A Struggle for Survival in Colonial Spanish Pensacola, edited by Judith A. Bense (2003)
Bioarchaeology of the Florida Gulf Coast: Adaptation, Conflict, and Change, by Dale L. Hutchinson (2004; first paperback edition, 2020)
The Myth of Syphilis: The Natural History of Treponematosis in North America, edited by Mary Lucas Powell and Della Collins Cook (2005)
The Florida Journals of Frank Hamilton Cushing, edited by Phyllis E. Kolianos and Brent R. Weisman (2005)
The Lost Florida Manuscript of Frank Hamilton Cushing, edited by Phyllis E. Kolianos and Brent R. Weisman (2005)
The Native American World Beyond Apalachee: West Florida and the Chattahoochee Valley, by John H. Hann (2006)
Tatham Mound and the Bioarchaeology of European Contact: Disease and Depopulation in Central Gulf Coast Florida, by Dale L. Hutchinson (2006)
Taíno Indian Myth and Practice: The Arrival of the Stranger King, by William F. Keegan (2007)
An Archaeology of Black Markets: Local Ceramics and Economies in Eighteenth-Century Jamaica, by Mark W. Hauser (2008; first paperback edition, 2013)

Mississippian Mortuary Practices: Beyond Hierarchy and the Representationist Perspective, edited by Lynne P. Sullivan and Robert C. Mainfort Jr. (2010; first paperback edition, 2012)

Bioarchaeology of Ethnogenesis in the Colonial Southeast, by Christopher M. Stojanowski (2010; first paperback edition, 2013)

French Colonial Archaeology in the Southeast and Caribbean, edited by Kenneth G. Kelly and Meredith D. Hardy (2011; first paperback edition, 2015)

Late Prehistoric Florida: Archaeology at the Edge of the Mississippian World, edited by Keith Ashley and Nancy Marie White (2012; first paperback edition, 2015)

Early and Middle Woodland Landscapes of the Southeast, edited by Alice P. Wright and Edward R. Henry (2013; first paperback edition, 2019)

Trends and Traditions in Southeastern Zooarchaeology, edited by Tanya M. Peres (2014)

New Histories of Pre-Columbian Florida, edited by Neill J. Wallis and Asa R. Randall (2014; first paperback edition, 2016)

Discovering Florida: First-Contact Narratives from Spanish Expeditions along the Lower Gulf Coast, edited and translated by John E. Worth (2014; first paperback edition, 2016)

Constructing Histories: Archaic Freshwater Shell Mounds and Social Landscapes of the St. Johns River, Florida, by Asa R. Randall (2015)

Archaeology of Early Colonial Interaction at El Chorro de Maíta, Cuba, by Roberto Valcárcel Rojas (2016)

Fort San Juan and the Limits of Empire: Colonialism and Household Practice at the Berry Site, edited by Robin A. Beck, Christopher B. Rodning, and David G. Moore (2016)

Rethinking Moundville and Its Hinterland, edited by Vincas P. Steponaitis and C. Margaret Scarry (2016; first paperback edition, 2019)

Handbook of Ceramic Animal Symbols in the Ancient Lesser Antilles, by Lawrence Waldron (2016)

Paleoindian Societies of the Coastal Southeast, by James S. Dunbar (2016; first paperback edition, 2019)

Gathering at Silver Glen: Community and History in Late Archaic Florida, by Zackary I. Gilmore (2016)

Cuban Archaeology in the Caribbean, edited by Ivan Roksandic (2016)

Archaeologies of Slavery and Freedom in the Caribbean: Exploring the Spaces in Between, edited by Lynsey A. Bates, John M. Chenoweth, and James A. Delle (2016; first paperback edition, 2018)

Setting the Table: Ceramics, Dining, and Cultural Exchange in Andalucía and La Florida, by Kathryn L. Ness (2017)

Simplicity, Equality, and Slavery: An Archaeology of Quakerism in the British Virgin Islands, 1740–1780, by John M. Chenoweth (2017)

Fit for War: Sustenance and Order in the Mid-Eighteenth-Century Catawba Nation, by Mary Elizabeth Fitts (2017)

Water from Stone: Archaeology and Conservation at Florida's Springs, by Jason O'Donoughue (2017)

Mississippian Beginnings, edited by Gregory D. Wilson (2017; first paperback edition, 2019)

Honoring Ancestors in Sacred Space: The Archaeology of an Eighteenth-Century African-Bahamian Cemetery, by Grace Turner (2017)

Investigating the Ordinary: Everyday Matters in Southeast Archaeology, edited by Sarah E. Price and Philip J. Carr (2018)

Harney Flats: A Florida Paleoindian Site, by I. Randolph Daniel Jr. and Michael Wisenbaker (2017)

Early Human Life on the Southeastern Coastal Plain, edited by Albert C. Goodyear and Christopher R. Moore (2018)

New Histories of Village Life at Crystal River, by Thomas J. Pluckhahn and Victor D. Thompson (2018)

The Archaeology of Villages in Eastern North America, edited by Jennifer Birch and Victor D. Thompson (2018)

The Cumberland River Archaic of Middle Tennessee, edited by Tanya Peres and Aaron Deter-Wolf (2019)

Pre-Columbian Art of the Caribbean, by Lawrence Waldron (2019)

Iconography and Wetsite Archaeology of Florida's Watery Realms, edited by Ryan Wheeler and Joanna Ostapkowicz (2019)

New Directions in the Search for the First Floridians, edited by David K. Thulman and Ervan G. Garrison (2019)

Cahokia in Context: Hegemony and Diaspora, edited by Charles H. McNutt and Ryan M. Parish (2019)

Archaeology of Domestic Landscapes of the Enslaved in the Caribbean, edited by James A. Delle and Elizabeth C. Clay (2019)

Contact, Colonialism, and Native Communities in the Southeastern United States, edited by Edmond A. Boudreaux III, Maureen Meyers, and Jay K. Johnson (2020)

Bears: Archaeological and Ethnohistorical Perspectives in Native Eastern North America, edited by Heather A. Lapham and Gregory A. Waselkov (2020)

An Archaeology and History of a Caribbean Sugar Plantation on Antigua, edited by Georgia L. Fox (2020)

www.ingramcontent.com/pod-product-compliance
Lightning Source LLC
Chambersburg PA
CBHW071658170426
43195CB00039B/2226